TWO VIEWS ON
WOMEN IN MINISTRY

Books in the Counterpoints Series

Church Life

Exploring Theology

REVISED EDITION

TWO VIEWS ON WOMEN IN MINISTRY

- Linda L. Belleville
- Craig L. Blomberg
- Craig S. Keener
- Thomas R. Schreiner

- **Stanley N. Gundry** *series editor*
- **James R. Beck** *general editor*

GRAND RAPIDS, MICHIGAN 49530 USA

$\mathcal{Z}$ONDERVAN™

Two Views on Women in Ministry—Revised Edition
Copyright © 2001, 2005 by James R. Beck

Requests for information should be addressed to:

Zondervan, *Grand Rapids, Michigan 49530*

Library of Congress Cataloging-in-Publication Data

Two views on women in ministry / Linda L. Belleville . . . [et al.] ; general editor,
James R. Beck.—2nd ed.
    p. cm.— (Counterpoints)
    Includes bibliographical references and index.
    ISBN–10: 0-310-25437-X (softcover)
    ISBN–13: 978-0-310-25437-9
    1. Women clergy. I. Belleville, Linda L. II. Beck, James R. III. Series:
Counterpoints (Grand Rapids, Mich.)
    BV676.T96 2005
    262'.14'082—dc22   2005008670

Printed in the United States of America

---

05 06 07 08 09 10 /❖ DCI/ 10 9 8 7 6 5 4 3 2 1

CONTENTS

ABBREVIATIONS

Bible Texts, Versions, Etc.

ASV	American Standard Version
AT	Author Translation
BBE	The Bible in Basic English
Bishop	The Bishop's Bible
BJ	La Bible de Jèrusalem (French version of the Jerusalem Bible)
CEV	Contemporary English Version
Copt.	Coptic
CSB	Christian Standard Bible
Darby	*The Darby Translation*
DV	Douay Version (also called Douay-Rheims Bible)
ESV	English Standard Version
Geneva	Geneva Bible
Great	Great Bible
GWT	God's Word Translation
JB	Jerusalem Bible
KJV	King James Version
Luther	The Luther Bible
LXX	Septuagint (the Greek OT)
MT	Masoretic Text of the OT
NAB	New American Bible
NASB	New American Standard Bible
NCV	New Century Version
NEB	New English Bible
NET	New English Translation
NIV	New International Version
NJB	New Jerusalem Bible
NKJV	New King James Version
NLT	New Living Translation
NRSV	New Revised Standard Version

NT	New Testament
OT	Old Testament
Phillips	*New Testament in Modern English,* J. B. Phillips
REB	Revised English Bible
Reina-Valera	Reina-Valera Bible
Revised NAB	Revised New American Bible
Rheims	Rheims New Testament (NT of DV)
RSV	Revised Standard Version
RVR	Reina Valera Revisada
Syr.	Syriac
TEV	Today's English Version
TNIV	Today's New International Version
Tyndale	Tyndale New Testament
UBS	United Bible Societies
Vulg.	Vulgate
Webster	Webster's Bible
Weymouth	*Weymouth's New Testament in Modern Speech*

Old Testament, New Testament, Apocrypha

Gen.	Genesis	Eccl.	Ecclesiastes
Exod.	Exodus	Song	Song of Songs
Lev.	Leviticus	Isa.	Isaiah
Num.	Numbers	Jer.	Jeremiah
Deut.	Deuteronomy	Lam.	Lamentations
Josh.	Joshua	Ezek.	Ezekiel
Judg.	Judges	Dan.	Daniel
Ruth	Ruth	Hos.	Hosea
1–2 Sam.	1–2 Samuel	Joel	Joel
1–2 Kgs.	1–2 Kings	Amos	Amos
1–2 Chr.	1–2 Chronicles	Obad.	Obadiah
Ezra	Ezra	Jonah	Jonah
Neh.	Nehemiah	Mic.	Micah
Esth.	Esther	Nah.	Nahum
Job	Job	Hab.	Habakkuk
Ps./Pss.	Psalm/Psalms	Zeph.	Zephaniah
Prov.	Proverbs	Hag.	Haggai

Zech.	Zechariah	1–2 Tim.	1–2 Timothy
Mal.	Malachi	Titus	Titus
Matt.	Matthew	Phlm.	Philemon
Mark	Mark	Heb.	Hebrews
Luke	Luke	Jas.	James
John	John	1–2 Pet.	1–2 Peter
Acts	Acts	1–2–3 John	1–2–3 John
Rom.	Romans	Jude	Jude
1–2 Cor.	1–2 Corinthians	Rev.	Revelation
Gal.	Galatians	Add. Esth.	Additions to
Eph.	Ephesians		Esther
Phil.	Philippians	1 Macc.	1 Maccabees
Col.	Colossians	Sir.	Sirach/
1–2 Thess.	1–2 Thessalonians		Ecclesiasticus

Other Ancient Texts

Aeth.	*Aethiopica* (Heliodorus)
Ag. Ap.	*Against Apion* (Josephus)
Bibl. hist.	*Bibliotheca historica* (Diodorus Siculus)
Bride	*Advice to the Bride and Groom* (Plutarch)
Cic.	*Cicero* (Plutarch)
Cyr.	*Cyropaedia* (Xenophon)
Did.	*Didache*
Epist.	*Epistulae* (Jerome)
Facta	*Facta et dicta memorabilia* (Valerius Maximus)
Fam.	*Epistulae ad familares* (Cicero)
Flight	*On Flight and Finding* (Philo)
Herm. Sim.	*Shepherd of Hermas, Similitudes*
Herm. Vis.	*Shepherd of Hermas, Visions*
Hist.	*Historicus* (Polybius)
Hist. eccl.	*History of the Church* (Eusebius)
Hist. Rome	*The History of Rome* (Livy)
Hom. 1 Tim.	*Homilies on 1 Timothy* (John Chrysostom)
Hom. Rom.	*Homilies on Romans* (John Chrysostom)
Hypoth.	*Hypothetica* (Philo)
J.W.	*Jewish War* (Josephus)

L.A.E.	Life of Adam and Eve
Mor.	Moralia (Plutarch)
Onir.	Onirocritica (Artemidorus)
Paed.	Paedagogus (Clement of Alexandria)
Phil.	To the Philippians (Polycarp)
Pss. Sol.	Psalms of Solomon
QG	Questions and Answers on Genesis 1,2,3,4 (Philo)
Rhet.	Volumina rhetorica (Philodemus)
4Q502	Ritual of Marriage (texts from Qumran)
Strom.	Stromata (Clement of Alexandria)

Journals, Periodicals, Reference Works, Series

AB	Anchor Bible
AnBib	Analecta biblica
BA	Biblical Archaeologist
BAGD	Bauer, Arndt, Gingrich, and Danker (2d ed.). Greek-English Lexicon of the New Testament and Other Early Christian Literature
BBR	Bulletin for Biblical Research
BDAG	Bauer, Danker, Arndt, and Gingrich (3d ed.). Greek-English Lexicon of the New Testament and Other Early Christian Literature
BDB	Brown, Driver, and Briggs. A Hebrew and English Lexicon of the Old Testament
BDF	Blass, Debrunner, and Funk. A Greek Grammar of the New Testament and Other Early Christian Literature
BECNT	Baker Exegetical Commentary on the New Testament
BGU	Aegyptische Urkunden aus den Königlichen Staatlichen Museen zu Berlin, Griechische Urkunden
BibInt	Biblical Interpretation
BJS	Brown Judaic Studies
BR	Biblical Research
BSac	Bibliotheca sacra
BST	The Bible Speaks Today
BT	The Bible Translator

BTB	*Biblical Theology Bulletin*
BZNW	Beihefte zur Zeitschrift für die neutestamentliche Wissenschaft
CBMW	The Council on Biblical Manhood and Womanhood
CBQ	*Catholic Biblical Quarterly*
CBTJ	*Calvary Baptist Theological Journal*
Chm	*Churchman*
ChrHist	*Christian History*
ChrT	*Christianity Today*
CII	*Corpus inscriptionum iudaicarum*
CTJ	*Calvin Theological Journal*
CTR	*Criswell Theological Review*
EBC	Expositor's Bible Commentary
ECC	Eerdmans Critical Commentary
ETS	Evangelical Theological Society
EvQ	*Evangelical Quarterly*
ExpTim	*Expository Times*
FaithMiss	*Faith and Mission*
Fd Xanthos	Fouilles de Xanthos
GRBS	*Greek, Roman, and Byzantine Studies*
HALOT	Koehler, Baumgartner, and Stamm. *The Hebrew and Aramaic Lexicon of the Old Testament*
HNTC	Harper's New Testament Commentaries
ICC	International Critical Commentary
IGR	*Inscriptiones Graecae ad Res Romanas pertinentes*
Int	*Interpretation*
InscrMagn.	*Die Inschriften von Magnesia am Meander*
IVPNTC	IVP New Testament Commentary
JBL	*Journal of Biblical Literature*
JBMW	*Journal for Biblical Manhood and Womanhood*
JETS	*Journal of the Evangelical Theological Society*
JGRChJ	*Journal of Greco-Roman Christianity and Judaism*
JSNT	*Journal for the Study of the New Testament*
JSNTSup	JSNT Supplement Series
JSOT	*Journal for the Study of the Old Testament*
JSOTSup	JSOT Supplement Series
JTS	*Journal of Theological Studies*

L&N	Louw and Nida. *Greek-English Lexicon of the New Testament: Based on Semantic Domains*
LCL	Loeb Classical Library
LSAM	Lois sacrées de l'Asie mineure
LSCG Suppl.	Lois of the sacrées cités grecques, supplement
LSJ	Liddell, Scott, and Jones. *A Greek-English Lexicon*
LuthThJ	*Lutheran Theological Journal*
MM	Moulton and Milligan. *The Vocabulary of the Greek Testament*
NAC	New American Commentary
NIBC	New International Biblical Commentary
NICNT	*New International Commentary on the New Testament*
NICOT	*New International Commentary on the Old Testament*
NIDOTTE	*New International Dictionary of Old Testament Theology and Exegesis*
NIGTC	New International Greek Testament Commentary
NIVAC	NIV Application Commentary
NovT	*Novum Testamentum*
NTC	New Testament Commentary (Baker)
NTS	*New Testament Studies*
PG	Patrologia graeca
PGL	*Patristic Greek Lexicon*
PHI	*Packard Humanities Institute*
PL	Patrologia latina
PNTC	Pillar New Testament Commentary
Presb	*Presbyterion*
RAT	*Revue Africaine de Theologie*
RBibLit	*Review of Biblical Literature*
RefJ	*Reformed Journal*
ResQ	*Restoration Quarterly*
SBJT	*Southern Baptist Journal of Theology*
SBLDS	Society of Biblical Literature Dissertation Series
SBLSP	*Society of Biblical Literature Seminar Papers*

SEG	Supplementum epigraphicum graecum
SNTSMS	Society for New Testament Studies Monograph Series
SP	Sacra Pagina
TDNT	Kittel and Friedrich. *Theological Dictionary of the New Testament*
TDOT	Botterweck and Ringgren. *Theological Dictionary of the Old Testament*
ThEv	*Theologia Evangelica*
ThTo	*Theology Today*
TJ	*Trinity Journal*
TLG	*Thesaurus linguae graecae*
TLNT	*Theological Lexicon of the New Testament*
TNTC	Tyndale New Testament Commentaries
TOTC	Tyndale Old Testament Commentaries
TS	*Theological Studies*
TSFBul	*Theological Students Fellowship Bulletin*
TWOT	*Theological Wordbook of the Old Testament*
TynBul	*Tyndale Bulletin*
WBC	Word Biblical Commentary
WisconsinLuthQ	*Wisconsin Lutheran Quarterly*
WMANT	Wissenschaftliche Monographien zum Alten und Neuen Testament
WTJ	*Westminster Theological Journal*
WUNT	Wissenschaftliche Untersuchungen zum Neuen Testament
YCS	*Yale Classical Studies*
ZNW	*Zeitschrift für die neutestamentliche Wissenschaft und die Kunde der älterern Kirche*

General

AD	*anno Domini* (in the year of [our] Lord)
BC	before Christ
ca.	*circa* (around, about, approximately)
cf.	*confer*, compare
ch(s).	chapter(s)
diss.	dissertation
ed(s).	editor(s), edited by

e.g.	*exempli gratia*, for example
esp.	especially
frg.	fragment
ibid.	*ibidem*, in the same place
i.e.	*id est*, that is
Lat.	Latin
lit.	literally
n.	note
p(p).	page(s)
par.	parallel (indicates textual parallels)
s.v.	*sub verbo*, under the word
trans.	translator, translated by
v(v).	verse(s)

INTRODUCTION

James R. Beck

The four contributors to this volume recently gathered for lunch at the Atlanta Hilton. Together with a representative from our publisher and me, we enjoyed renewing our friendships and planning this revision of the first edition of *Two Views on Women in Ministry* (2001). Normally one would assume that the production of a volume dealing with a controversial topic would require the editor to serve as a referee among the various contributors, all of whom hold strong views on divergent sides of the topic. The assumption doesn't hold true for this project. The six of us are friends. We enjoy one another's company and strongly respect the scholarship of each member of this team. Our hope is that our camaraderie can serve as a model for other scholars working in this difficult area of gender and ministry.

One of the more important accomplishments of this working lunch—a lunch that would hardly qualify as a "power" lunch—was the crafting of a statement to which all the contributors and the editor could agree: *We believe one can build a credible case within the bounds of orthodoxy and a commitment to inerrancy for either one of the two major views we address in this volume, although all of us view our own positions on the matter as stronger and more compelling.* The implications of this simple statement of concord are enormous and merit close attention by all students of the issue of women in ministry.

The three broad reasons for producing the first edition of this book remain true for this second edition. First, evangelicals have not yet settled the exegetical and theological issues involved in deciding if churches should place some limits or no limits on the ministry of women in the church. The exegetical issues are complex, and even the most enthusiastic of promoters for one side or the other cannot justifiably claim that the opposing view is beyond the limits of orthodoxy. Nor can one assert that a particular view is the only one reflecting a belief in biblical inerrancy.

Second, the need for a more irenic spirit among proponents on both sides of this debate is as strong as ever. Too often more heat than light emerges when people get together to debate about women in ministry. The church cannot afford to waste precious energy and time on advocacy reflecting excess and overkill. The enemies who truly threaten the integrity of the church are outside its walls, not inside its walls. We need to demonstrate a Christ-honoring irenic spirit when we work on this issue. As a concerned editor, I challenged each contributor to demonstrate this irenicism in their responses to each other's essays. I am happy to inform you that they all succeeded admirably in accomplishing this assignment.

Third, the fruit of relevant scholarship continues to appear in journals in remarkable volume. Each of the essays in this second edition reflects new literature that has emerged since 2001. New findings will occasionally weaken an existing argument; sometimes new evidence will bolster an otherwise sagging set of data. More exciting, advancing scholarship can sometimes set forth an entirely new line of reasoning that can help one side or the other better explain its case. On the whole, we must all stay abreast of cutting-edge scholarship if we are going to participate in this debate effectively.

Readers will notice several changes from the first edition of this book. Dr. Blomberg has moved from serving as a coeditor of the first edition to the role of a contributor of one of the four main essays in this book. He reworked and greatly expanded his appendix essay in the first volume to provide us with the essay that appears here. Also, we have asked each contributor to respond to the other three essays in this edition. None of the contributors saw any of the other essays until each had completed his or her own chapter. I have arranged the essays in this second edition alphabetically by the contributor's last name. The order of the three responses to each essay begins and ends with responses from contributors who hold the opposite view, sandwiching a response from the contributor who argues the same position in this volume. The essays and the responses to them vary somewhat in length. However, the total number of pages devoted to an examination of each of the two views discussed in this volume is almost exactly the same.

The four contributors to this volume are evangelical NT scholars who hold seminary faculty positions. Their material gives broad coverage to the relevant issues, although one could also have selected four evangelical theologians or four evangelical OT scholars to argue the case from the perspective of their respective disciplines. However, since so many of the disputed texts, terms, and theological issues are centered in the books of the NT, it makes good sense to engage NT scholars as resource persons in this discussion.

In the spirit of full disclosure, readers should know that the editor is an egalitarian by conviction. But I have striven hard to oversee this project with evenhanded fairness. I trust that readers will not find evidence to the contrary in the following pages. Happy reading.

Chapter One

WOMEN IN MINISTRY: AN EGALITARIAN PERSPECTIVE

Linda L. Belleville

WOMEN IN MINISTRY:
AN EGALITARIAN PERSPECTIVE
Linda L. Belleville

One of the continuing hotbeds of debate in evangelical circles today is the nature and scope of leadership roles open to women in the church. Can a woman preach God's word? Can she serve communion, baptize, or lead in worship? Can she marry and bury? Can she serve as the lead or solo pastor? Can she teach an adult Bible class? Can she serve as a bishop, elder, or deacon? Can she put "Reverend" or "Doctor" before her name?

These are the questions with which numerous churches in the last fifty years have struggled and over which some have divided. In large part this has been due to the absence of any middle ground. The issues and terms have been defined so as to force a choice either wholly for or wholly against women in leadership. The interpretive approach of traditionalists, in particular, has been notably selective. The focus has been on one or two highly debated passages (first and foremost, 1 Tim. 2:11–15), with little acknowledgment of the roles of women in Scripture as a whole.[1]

What about today? Has any middle ground been reached? What currently separates the traditionalist and egalitarian? As recently as two decades ago the polarity was vast. It was not uncommon to hear evangelicals talking about a woman's flawed,

---

[1]E.g., the role of women in the church is reduced to an analysis of 1 Timothy 2:9–15 in *Women in the Church: A Fresh Analysis of 1 Timothy 2:9–15*, eds. Andreas J. Köstenberger, Thomas R. Schreiner, and H. Scott Baldwin (Grand Rapids: Baker), 1995.

self-deceived nature or her secondary creation in God's image, which ruled out any leadership role for her in the church.[2] Now there are very few who would go this far,[3] and most who thought this way in the past have changed their minds.[4]

What accounts for the change? It is not that a biblical consensus has emerged, for traditionalists still claim that theirs is the "Christ-honoring, Bible-believing perspective" and that the egalitarian's perspective is the "liberal, culturally acceptable view."[5] The primary impetus is actually social in nature. The feminist movement and economic pressures have catapulted women into the workplace, where they have shown themselves to be equally talented, wise, and levelheaded—so that whereas twenty-five years ago only young adult males were challenged with the slogan "Uncle Sam wants you," today women and men alike are encouraged to "be all that you can be."

To a great extent evangelicals have followed suit. There is now general agreement that women possess exactly the same spiritual gifts men do and are to be encouraged to develop and exercise these gifts to their fullest potential. In effect, women are urged to "be all that they can be spiritually." A case in point is a

---

[2]See, e.g., Douglas Moo, "1 Timothy 2:11–15: Meaning and Significance," *TJ* 2 (1981): 175.

[3]See, however, Robert Culver, "A Traditionalist Position: Let Your Women Keep Silence," in *Women in Ministry: Four Views*, ed. Bonnidell Clouse and Robert G. Clouse (Downers Grove, Ill.: InterVarsity, 1989), 36; more recently, Bruce Ware ("Male and Female Complementarity and the Image of God," *JBMW* 7 [2002], 20) argues that men bear God's image directly and women only derivatively; hence the priority of male over female. Evangelical scholarship (with rare exception) has come to see that female self-deception and a derivative divine image conflict with scriptural teaching elsewhere. If women were so inclined, Paul would have forbidden women from teaching per se. But he does not do so; indeed, he does just the opposite. For instance, he instructs older women to teach and train the younger women (Titus 2:3–4). Also, while Paul does assert that all human beings without exception sin, at no time does he suggest that women are more susceptible to sin's deceiving activity than men (e.g., Rom. 3:9–20). In fact, it was two *men* (not women) Paul expelled from the Ephesian church for false teaching that stemmed from personal deception (1 Tim. 1:19–20).

[4]Compare Moo in "1 Timothy 2:11–15," 175, and ten years later in "What Does It Mean Not to Teach or Have Authority over Men? 1 Timothy 2," in *Recovering Biblical Manhood and Womanhood: A Response to Evangelical Feminism*, ed. John Piper and Wayne Grudem (Wheaton, Ill.: Crossway, 1991), 189–90.

[5]Berta Delgado, "Baptists take stand on role of women," *Dallas Morning News*, Nov. 10, 1999, 1.

recent catalog statement from one of America's largest and most conservative evangelical seminaries: "As members of the faculty of Trinity Evangelical Divinity School, and leaders in the church of our Lord, we recognize that God has given his gifts to both men and women in the body of Christ," and "It is our goal that each woman be encouraged and receive the training she needs to be fully prepared for future ministry."[6]

So the issue that divides traditionalists (now self-identified as "complementarians") and egalitarians today is not that of women in ministry per se (i.e., women exercising their spiritual gifts). It is rather *women in leadership*, for while a consensus has emerged regarding women and spiritual gifting, a great divide has emerged on the issue of women in leadership—especially women leading men.

What accounts for the great divide? The patriarchal structures that were in place in the American workplace thirty years ago have been replaced by an ethic of gender equality—in theory, if not always in practice. Here, however, evangelicals have not generally followed suit. While mainline denominations have embraced gender equality, evangelical churches by and large have not. It is the rare evangelical church that has a woman in its pulpit on Sunday morning, a woman as lead pastor, a female chairperson or chief elder of its council, or a female teacher of its adult Bible classes. It is also the uncommon evangelical denomination that ordains women, installs women in key administrative positions, or appoints women to governing boards.

The reason for this state of affairs is not hard to pinpoint: the relationship of male and female continues to be perceived in hierarchical ways. God created men to lead; God created women to follow.[7] It is this that fundamentally differentiates a traditionalist from an egalitarian today.

This distinction has become highly politicized. Councils are formed, supporters are sought, newsletters are generated,

---

[6]Trinity Evangelical Divinity School Catalog (2003/2004), "Statement on Gender References in Speech and Writing"; and "Women's Programs" (Dean of Students), pp. 46, 51. These statements were removed subsequent to the writing of this essay.

[7]See, e.g., John Piper, "A Vision of Biblical Complementarity: Manhood and Womanhood Defined According to the Bible," in *Recovering Biblical Manhood and Womanhood*, 35–36.

speaker bureaus are created, business meetings are held, and funds are solicited. For example, the Council on Biblical Manhood and Womanhood (CBMW) was formed and the Danvers Statement formulated in 1987 in reaction to the egalitarian view espoused by participants at the "Evangelical Colloquium on Women and the Bible" held on October 9–11, 1984, in Oak Brook, Illinois.[8] Moreover, there is little room for dialogue on the issue. Only the publications that fully follow the party line are referenced.[9] Bible translations are judged by the presence or absence of gender-inclusive language.[10] Books are either wholly in or wholly out.[11] And organizations, denominations, and churches are either entirely affirmed (e.g., Southern Baptist Convention, Presbyterian Church in America, Bethlehem Baptist Church) or completely rejected (e.g., InterVarsity Christian Fellowship (IVCF), Fuller Seminary, Presbyterian Church [U.S.A.], United Methodist Church, Willow Creek Community Church).[12]

Invariably the debate between egalitarians and traditionalists comes down to four basic questions:

Does the Bible teach a hierarchical structuring of male and female relationships?

Do we find women in leadership positions in the Bible?

Do women in the Bible assume the same leadership roles as men?

Does the Bible limit women from filling certain leadership roles?

---

[8]See Alvera Mickelsen, ed., *Women, the Bible and Authority* (Downers Grove, Ill.: InterVarsity Press, 1986), 4.

[9]See, e.g., "CBMW Books and Resources," *CBMW News* 1 (Nov. 1995): 15 (renamed *Journal for Biblical Manhood and Womanhood* (*JBMW*) with the March 1998 issue).

[10]See, e.g., *CBMW News* 2 (June 1997): 1–13; "A List of Translation Inaccuracies Primarily (but Not Exclusively) Related to Gender Language in the TNIV" (online at www.cbmw.org/resources/tniv/inaccuracies.pdf, 2003; Wayne Grudem, "Cultural Pressures on Language Are Not Always Neutral" (online at www.cbmw.org/tniv/cultural_pressures.php, 2003).

[11]E.g., *Women in Ministry: Four Views* is labeled as feminist for the "clear editorial sympathies of the editors" (*CBMW News* 1 [Nov. 1995]: 12).

[12]Nearly half of a 1997 *CBMW News* issue was devoted to the "ironic" and "tragic" egalitarian position at Willow Creek ("Willow Creek enforces egalitarianism," *CBMW News* 2 [Dec. 1997]: 1, 3–6).

THE MALE-FEMALE RELATIONSHIP IN GENESIS 1–3

Gender Creation: Genesis 1–2

The creation narratives are the starting point for discussion, for it is here that a foundational understanding of male and female first appears. Although traditionalists claim that male leadership is intrinsic to God's creation of male and female, support is hard to come by from the creation accounts themselves. To be sure, there *is* distinction. God created two sexually distinct beings ("male and female he created them" [Gen. 1:27]).[13] And this distinction was a deliberate, calculated act on God's part ("Let us make ..." [v. 26]). For what purpose, though? The propagation of the human race is decidedly one reason ("Be fruitful and increase in number" [v. 28]). Yet, fruitfulness is not the primary, long-term reason for sexual diversity. Its absence from NT discussions of human sexuality make this plain. Instead, what the NT writers affirm as God's essential purpose is that "they [male + female; the two] will become one flesh" (2:24; see Matt. 19:5–6; Mark 10:7–8; Eph. 5:31). Western mind-set has the tendency to understand "one flesh" solely in terms of sexual intimacy. But the Hebrew concept has more to do with that which is "mortal" or "human" (cf. "flesh and blood"). A "one flesh" union, then, has to do with the joining of one human being with another. As Jesus states, "They are no longer two, but one" (Matt. 19:6). In fact, for Paul the oneness of male and female is a type of the union between Christ and the church (Eph. 5:32).[14]

So there is distinction. But the primary thrust of Genesis 1–2 is the sameness of male and female. Both are formed from the ʾădāmâ ("earth," "reddish-brown soil"), and so both are appropriately named ʾādām ("he called them ʾādām" [5:2]). Both are created in God's image ("in the image of God he created them" [1:27]). Although there is a great deal of theological speculation about what creation in God's image means, Genesis 1 unmistakably affirms that male and female equally share it. After all, this is what the first male recognized when he exclaimed, "This is now bone of

---

13The English translation unless otherwise indicated is Today's New International Version (TNIV).

14For further discussion, see John Oswalt, "*bāśār*," *TWOT*, ed. R. L. Harris, G. L. Archer, and B. K. Waltke (Chicago: Moody Press, 1980), 1:136; Claus Westermann, *Genesis 1–11* (Minneapolis: Augsburg, 1981), 233.

my bones and flesh of my flesh," and then called the female "woman" (*ʾiššâ*), for she was "taken out of man" (*mēʾîš*; 2:23).

There is also sameness of function. Both male and female are commanded to exercise dominion over the earth—to "rule over" all of it (1:26, 28) and to "subdue" it (v. 28). The language is significant. The Hebrew term *rādâ* ("rule") is used twenty-two times in the OT of human dominion (e.g., Ps. 110:2; Isa. 14:2, 6). The Hebrew word *kābaš* ("subdue") occurs fifteen times in the OT, in each instance with the meaning "to bring into submission by brute force" (e.g., 2 Chr. 28:10; Neh. 5:5; Jer. 34:11, 16).[15] No separate spheres of rule are specified (e.g., private versus public). There is not even a division of labor (e.g., domestic versus nondomestic).

Although male and female can decide on practical grounds how to divide the labor, the assumption of the creation accounts is that both have what it takes to rule and subdue the entirety of what God has created. This stems from their creation in God's image. The sequence of ideas in Genesis 1 shows it is God's image that enables male and female to rule and subdue. "Let us make the *ʾādām* in our image" comes first; "let them have dominion over all the earth" comes second (vv. 26–30).

There is also sameness of family function. Both male and female are given joint responsibility in the bearing and rearing of children. The idea that it is the woman's job to produce and raise the children and the man's job to work the land is simply not found in the creation accounts. *Both* are called to be fruitful. And *both* are called to enjoy the produce of the land. The pronouns are plural throughout: "God ... said to *them*, 'Be fruitful and increase in number.... I give *you* [plural] every seed-bearing plant on the face of the whole earth and every tree that has fruit with seed in it. They will be *yours* [plural] for food'" (vv. 28–29, emphasis added).

There is likewise sameness in God's sight. Both male and female are created as spiritual equals. Both are blessed by God (v. 28). Both relate directly to God ("The LORD God called to the man.... The LORD God said to the woman" [3:9, 13]). And both are held personally accountable by God ("To the woman he said.... To Adam [the man] he said..." [vv. 16–19]).

The portrayal in Genesis 1–2 of male and female as personal, social, and spiritual equals is compelling. Where then is the gen-

---

[15]See Oswalt, "*kābaš*," *TWOT*, 1:430.

der hierarchy of the traditionalist? Four things are typically pointed to. The first is 2:18–20, where the female is created as a "help" for the male: "It is not good for the man to be alone. I will make a help [*ʿēzer*] corresponding to him [*kĕnegdô*]" (v. 18 AT). Traditionalists typically translate the Hebrew term *ʿēzer* as "helper" (NIV, TNIV, NASB, NKJV, RSV, NJB, ESV) and argue that implicit in the term is the notion of subordination. To be a helper is to offer "submissive assistance"; the one who receives help (it is claimed) has a certain authority over the one who gives help.[16]

Many have pointed to the fatal flaw in this line of thinking. All of the other occurrences of *ʿēzer* in the OT have to do with the assistance that one of strength offers to one in need (i.e., help from God, the king, an ally, or an army). There is no exception.[17] More, fifteen of the nineteen references speak of the help that God alone can provide (Exod. 18:4; Deut. 33:7, 26, 29; Pss. 20:2; 33:20; 70:5; 115:9–11 [3x]; 121:1–2 [2x]; 124:8; 146:5; Hos. 13:9). Psalm 121:1–2 is representative: "I lift up my eyes to the mountains—where does my *help* come from? My *help* comes from the LORD, the Maker of heaven and earth" (emphasis added). Help given to one in need fits Genesis 2:18–20 quite well. The male's situation was that of being "alone," and God's evaluation was that it was "not good." The woman was hence created to relieve the man's aloneness through *strong partnership*.

Some traditionalists counter with the argument that, in offering help, God becomes the human's subordinate or servant.[18] Divine accommodation, maybe; but divine subordination, hardly. And what about the other uses of *ʿēzer*? Judah's allies would hardly have thought of themselves as Judah's subordinates. Nor would Judah under the circumstances have viewed itself as "in

---

[16]See Bruce Ware, "Summaries of the Egalitarian and Complementarian Positions on the Role of Women in the Home and in Christian Ministry" (2004), 4; online at www.cbmw.org/resources/articles/positionsummaries.pdf. Compare Raymond C. Ortlund Jr., Male-Female Equality and Male Headship," in *Recovering Biblical Manhood and Womanhood*, 104.

[17]The CBMW appeals to the context of Gen. 2:18. "The context makes it very unlikely," they argue, "that *helper* should be read on the analogy of God's help because in verses 19–20, Adam is caused to seek his 'helper' first among the animals"; online at www.cbmw.org/questions/45.php. However, what is overlooked is the fact that the animals' *priority* in creation does not qualify as an *ʿēzer*. It is the woman's qualitative distinction from the animals and her sameness with the man that qualify her as an *ʿēzer kĕnegdô* (a "help corresponding to him").

[18]See Ortlund, "Male-Female Equality," 104.

charge." When Jerusalem was besieged by the Babylonians and Egypt came to the city's "help," it was as one with superior strength (Isa. 30:5). And when Judah sought again the "help" of allies, they hardly came to Judah's aid in a subordinate capacity (Ezek. 12:14 KJV).

Neither is there any warrant here for female superiority. The woman was created as a help "in correspondence to" (kĕnegdô) the man. This, once again, is the language of sameness, not superiority. The "she" is the personal counterpart in every way to the "he." Therefore, "partner" (REB, NAB, NRSV, CEV)—and not "helper"—accurately captures the sense of the Hebrew term ʿēzer.

A second traditionalist indicator of gender hierarchy is the fact that the male names the female. "She shall be called 'woman,'" the male said, "for she was taken out of man" (Gen. 2:23). It is argued that by naming the female, the male exercises his rightful authority over her and demonstrates his created role as leader of the relationship.[19] Yet, right before this, the male states, "This is now bone of my bones and flesh of my flesh"—hardly something someone would say about a subordinate (although some traditionalists resort to the language of "paradox").[20]

But perhaps with the recognition of sameness came the attempt to put the female in her place. This assumes, however, that there is power in naming. Traditionalists frequently say this, but biblical scholarship has shown otherwise.[21] Naming in antiquity was a way of memorializing an event or capturing a distinctive attribute; it was not an act of control or power. For instance, Isaac names the well he had dug "Esek" ("Dispute") because he and the herdsmen of Gerar had argued about who owned it (26:20; cf. vv. 21–22). Hagar names a well "Beer Lahai Roi" ("well of the Living One who sees me") to commemorate the place where God spoke to her in the desert (16:13–14). The son of Hagar is named "Ishmael" ("God hears") as a reminder of God's intervention on Hagar's behalf (16:11).[22] Even after the fall, the man gives his wife the name "Eve" (ḥawwâ, or "living") not as an

---

[19]Ibid., 102–3.

[20]Ibid., 99–100.

[21]See Anthony Thiselton, "The Supposed Power of Words in the Biblical Writings," JTS 25 (1974): 283–99; George Ramsey, "Is Name-Giving an Act of Domination in Genesis 2:23 and Elsewhere?" CBQ 50 (1988): 33.

[22]See Linda Belleville, Women Leaders and the Church: 3 Crucial Questions (Grand Rapids: Baker, 2000), 102–3.

attempt to reassert his control but in recognition that through childbearing (or *the* childbearing [3:15, cf. 1 Tim. 2:15]) "she would become the mother of all the *living*" (Gen. 3:20, emphasis added).[23]

What about the naming of the animals? Isn't this the male exercising his God-given role as leader? Yes, the man names the animals, yet not as an exercise of male initiative but as a process of discernment. The text is quite clear. Naming was the means by which the man sought to discern an associate from among the animals. It is worth noting that the Hebrew of Genesis 2:20 states the man found no counterpart (*kĕnegdô*) to relieve his aloneness, not that he found no subordinate to follow his lead or helper to accept his direction. Here finally was "bone of [his] bones and flesh of [his] flesh." Simply put, "wo-man" is the language of sameness, and the male's naming is the recognition of this fact (i.e., the naming describes, not prescribes).

A third traditionalist indicator of gender hierarchy is the name *ʾādām* in Genesis 1:26–27. One traditionalist even states that it "whispers male headship."[24] This is a rather puzzling claim, for the lexica agree that *ʾādām* is not a term that denotes gender.[25] In Genesis, it is connected with *ʾădāmâ* ("earthen," "reddish-brown soil") and is properly translated with a generic term like "human" or "humankind." When gender comes into play in the creation narratives, the Hebrew terms *zākār* ("male") and *nĕqēbâ* ("female") are used—as in the last part of 1:27: "male and female he created them." That *ʾādām* is a gender-inclusive term is clear from the repeated reference to *ʾādām* as "they" and "them" (vv. 26, 27; 5:1–2). God named the created male and female *ʾādām* (5:2)—a point conveniently passed over by some traditionalists. The Septuagint's consistent choice of the generic term *anthrōpos* ("person," "human") to translate *ʾādām* points to this very thing.

---

[23]CBMW continues to ignore the function of naming in antiquity. Indeed, they now emphasize that Adam named his wife not once but twice, thereby signifying "in an OT cultural context, Adam's right of authority over the one whom he named" (Ware, "Egalitarian and Complementarian Positions," 6).

[24]Ortlund, "Male-Female Equality," 98.

[25]See, e.g., "*ʾādām*" in BDB, *HALOT*, and *TDOT* Hebrew lexica. Compare "*ʾādām*," in *NIDOTTE*, ed. W. A. VanGemeren (Grand Rapids: Zondervan, 1997), 1:264.

A fourth (and often claimed "definitive") traditionalist indicator of gender hierarchy is the fact that the male was created before the female (2:7–23). Surely, isn't the male's temporal priority God's way of saying the man must take the lead? "First is best and second is less" is certainly the way Americans are educated to think. But is this what God intended? Jesus' teaching that many who are first will be last, and the last first, should caution against this line of thinking (Mark 10:31 par.). The account in Genesis 2 certainly attaches no significance to the order of *male—then female*; the creation of the animals prior to the male obviously has none.

What Genesis 1–2 does emphasize is the human completeness that occurs after the creation of woman. The male alone is "not good"; male + female is "very good" (2:18; 1:31). If there is any subordination in the creation accounts, it is not that of the female to the male but that of both the female and male to God. It is God who commands, and it is the male and the female who are expected to obey (2:16–17; 3:2–3, 11).

The dangers of a traditionalist line of thinking become especially apparent in looking at a number of biblical "firsts." If "first" in the divine plan designates the "leader," then the followers of John the Baptist (the Mandaeans) were right in elevating John over Jesus; Mary (and not Peter) should have been the leader of the apostles, since Jesus appeared "first" to her (Mark 16:9); and "the dead in Christ" should be the leaders of Christ's future kingdom, since they are to be raised "first" when Christ returns, and only "after that" the living (1 Thess. 4:16–17).

Traditionalists typically appeal to Paul's use of "Adam was formed first, then Eve" in 1 Timothy 2:13 as the definitive biblical support that God intended the male to lead. Yet, the notion of hierarchy simply does not appear in Paul's language of "first." To read it this way is to import an idea alien to Paul's thinking. And once it is translated as such, it is difficult not to be predisposed to a Western way of thinking. Indeed, Paul uses *prōton . . . epeita* in this very way just ten verses later. Deacons, he states, must be tested "first" (*prōton*), and "then" (*eita*) let them serve (3:10). Moreover, "first-then" (*prōton . . . epeita*), meaning "leader-follower," doesn't fit NT usage, for "first . . . then" elsewhere merely defines a sequence of events in time or thought (e.g., Mark 4:28; 1 Cor. 15:46; 1 Thess. 4:16–17; 1 Tim. 3:10; Jas. 3:17; Heb. 7:2).

Gender Dysfunction: Genesis 3:16

Some have recognized the futility of squeezing hierarchy out of the creation accounts and have turned instead to Genesis 3:16b: "Your desire will be for your husband, and he will rule over you." If hierarchy is not there before the fall, it is certainly there afterward (so it is argued). The idea of "male rule" plays such a prominent role in evangelical thinking and this verse is so often treated as a factual statement about the way God intends things to be between a man and a woman that a brief consideration is in order.

The first thing to note is that male rule finds no explicit place in the Bible's theology at all. Adam's sin is noted (Rom. 5:12–19; 1 Cor. 15:20–22), as is Eve's deception (2 Cor. 11:3; 1 Tim. 2:14). But the man's rule over the woman is not cited even once (not even for the husband-wife relationship). The simple fact is that male rule does not reappear in the OT. The woman is nowhere commanded to obey the man (not even her husband), and the man is nowhere commanded to rule the woman (not even his wife). On the other hand, the fact that male rule is part of the fallen condition does indicate something of the direction to which human nature will incline, given any encouragement.

Some discount this and say male rule is implicit in the apostle Paul's use of *kephalē* (commonly translated "head") to define the husband-wife relationship ("the husband is *kephalē* of the wife as Christ is *kephalē* of the church" [Eph. 5:23]). But too often what is *implicit* is simply a matter of imposing twenty-first-century understandings on the biblical texts. What is *explicit* is that the man is the woman's *source*—she who was created *out of him* and so *of [his] flesh and of [his] bones* (Gen. 2:23; cf. "for desire is the *source* [*kephalē*] of every kind of sin" (*epithymia gar estin kephalē pasēs hamartias* [L.A.E. 19.12]). "Source" language is what Paul uses to describe the *theological* relationship both between Christ and his bride, the church (Eph. 4:15–16; Col. 2:19, "from"), and between a man and woman (1 Cor. 11:8, "from"; Eph. 5:30, "of his flesh, and of his bones" KJV).[26]

The CBMW objects that gender hierarchy and not mutuality is what one finds in today's society: "Relationships within

---

[26]See DV, Reina-Valera, Luther, KJV, NKJV. Although "of his flesh and of his bones" is lacking in the earliest Alexandrian texts, its antiquity is attested by its presence in the Old Latin, the Vulgate, and the second-century church father Irenaeus.

authority structures surround us. We live and work in them every day."[27] And so, they conclude, it must also be there in the Bible. This, however, ignores the fact that Christianity is essentially countercultural. Jesus himself points to the existing social hierarchy of his day with the caveat "Not so with you [believers]" (Matt. 20:26). And it makes moot the Council's contention that, because we lack an extrabiblical Hellenistic example of one person as the *source* of another person, *kephalē* can't have this meaning.[28] The creation of the woman out of the man is distinctively Judeo-Christian; gender hierarchy is not. The husband and wife ("two") becoming *one* is distinctively Judeo-Christian; the rule of one over the other is not. Paul recognizes the theological distinctiveness of Christ/the husband as *kephalē* of the church/the wife in Ephesians 5:21–33 by calling it "a profound mystery"—a clear indication something countercultural and nonhierarchical is in view.

The second thing to notice is that what the rest of Scripture lifts up as normative is not Genesis 3:16 but 1:27 and 2:23–24. Male-female relationships are to be lived out, not in light of the fall, but of God's intent to create two sexually distinct beings in partnership. This is clear from Jesus' corrective that God from the beginning had made them male *and female* (Greek emphasis [Matt. 19:4; Mark 10:6]). Jesus also makes it clear that the marriage relationship is a functional "oneness," not a hierarchical "two-ness." In God's sight, "they are no longer two, but one" (Matt. 19:6; Mark 10:8).

The third thing to observe is the nature of the woman's disobedience. Some traditionalists are quick to state that Eve disobeyed in taking the lead and then forcing the male's hand.[29] This is simply not the case. Nowhere is it stated (or implied) that

---

[27]Ware, "Egalitarian and Complementarian Positions," 9.

[28]Wayne Grudem (*"Kephalē Revisited," ChrT* 46 [June 2003]): 12) thinks that *kephalē* here bears the sense *beginning,* or *first in a series* (e.g., *A* is the beginning of the alphabet) and not *beginning,* or *source.* He is certainly correct that this is a common meaning of *kephalē.* The difficulty here, though, is that "desire as the *first of a series* of every kind of sin" does not really fit, while "desire as the *source, origin,* or *root* of every kind of sin" does. A close parallel to *epithymia gar estin kephalē pasēs hamartias* is 1 Timothy 6:10: *rhiza gar pantōn tōn kakōn estin hē philargyria* ("For the love of money is a *root* of all kinds of evil").

[29]See Ortlund, "Male-Female Equality," 109; Ware, "Egalitarian and Complementarian Positions," 6.

the female's desire was to take the lead. On the contrary, the text *explicitly* states that her desire in eating was to be wise like God ("when you eat of it your eyes will be opened, and you will be like God, knowing good and evil"); the male followed suit undoubtedly because of a similar desire (Gen. 3:5). A divine command had been given ("you must not eat from the tree of the knowledge of good and evil" [2:17]). Disobedience on the part of both the man and the woman followed (3:6). And there was a price to pay for both as a result of their desire for knowledge (vv. 14–19).

The fourth thing to see is the consequence of this act of disobedience. Two statements are made in Genesis 3:16—the first about the woman's marital desires: "Your desire will be for your husband." Some take this to be a punishment or even a curse.[30] Yet God's intent that the two become one flesh surely indicates that a desire for intimacy was a key element of the pre-fall relationship (2:24). Part of the difficulty is that the Hebrew term *těšûqâ* ("desire," "yearning") is found only two other times in the OT, and neither is an exact parallel. In Genesis 4:7 God says to Cain that sin is like a crouching beast *hungering* for him; Song of Songs 7:10 speaks of the bridegroom's *desire* for his beloved. Traditionalists commonly argue that the woman's desire is to dominate her husband. This, however, imports an idea that is alien to the context. Gender intimacy, not rule, is what links all three OT uses of the Hebrew term *těšûqâ* (the lion's desire is to eat, not rule, Cain). Even more, a yearning for personal intimacy is what makes sense in the context. Since the immediately preceding clause has to do with childbearing ("with pain you will give birth to children"), it is most natural to think in these terms.

What about the second part of 3:16: "and he will rule over you"? What does the male's post-disobedience role entail? Some traditionalists think "rule over" is the husband's requiring the wife's obedience to his decision making. Headship (so it goes) is God's way of keeping the post-fall woman faithful and submissive.[31] Indeed, the CBMW sees "rule over" as a relationally redemptive statement.[32] But this interjects an idea that has little

---

[30]For "curse," see Ware, "Egalitarian and Complementarian Positions," 6.

[31]See, e.g., Ortlund, "Male-Female Equality," 107; Susan Foh, "A Male Leadership View," in *Women in Ministry: Four Views*, 75–76.

[32]Man's ruling over woman forecasts a "restored role differentiation through redemption in Christ" (Ware, "Egalitarian and Complementarian Positions," 5).

connection with the immediate context. It also makes 3:16 prescriptive, and there is nothing prescriptive about the text. Roles are prescribed in 1:28 ("God blessed them and said to them, 'Be fruitful and increase in number.... Rule over the fish ...'"). The facts regarding sin's impact are what one finds in Genesis 3—and these facts do not include role distinctions.

Other traditionalists think "to rule" is to *dominate* the wife. The male will get her submission by brute force. This does not fit, however, with the meaning of the Hebrew term for "rule." *Māšal* is the standard term for "rule" or "reign" (occurring some eighty times in the OT). It is not inherently negative (contrary to the CBMW);[33] so we are not talking about a word that refers to brute force—as the word *kābas* ("to subdue") in 1:28 does. This speaks against 3:16's having to do with the corruption of a benevolent rule given to the male at creation. If this were the case, then the term "rule" would be modified by an adjective like "harsh" or "domineering." And all we have is the word "rule." A better fit with the context is that the male's rule takes the form of sexual demands.[34] This provides a good link with what precedes ("childbirth," "yearning for her husband"). The translation would then be, "Your desire will be for your husband, and he will rule over that desire."

Overlooked but equally possible is to read the pronoun *hûʾ* as a neuter "it" rather than a masculine "he." The wife's desire will be for her husband, and *it* will dominate her. This nicely fits the context. It is also quite close to the wording of 4:7: "Sin's desiring is for you [*tĕšûqātō*, same noun], but you can still master [*timšāl*, same verb] *it*."[35] The sense would then be that increased pain in childbearing is offset by a desire for personal intimacy. But beware that it does not gain the upper hand.

The context of Genesis 3 is human disobedience and its impact, so it is difficult not to see the male's (or desire's) domination as something different from the divine intent of Genesis 1–2. The divine intent was that of a partnership—a co-dominion

---

[33]The man's "ruling over woman ... can be either rightfully-corrective or wrongfully-abusive" (Ware, "Egalitarian and Complementarian Positions," 5).

[34]See, e.g., Gordon Wenham, *Genesis 1–15* (WBC 1; Waco, Tex.: Word, 1987), 81.

[35]CBMW imports "to rule over" into Genesis 4:7 (Ware, "Egalitarian and Complementarian Positions," 6). The Hebrew *wĕʾēleykā tĕšûqātō* is literally "and for you is its [sin's] yearning" and not "sin desires to rule over you."

over the earth and a co-responsibility to bear and raise children. Dominion of one over the other was not the intent. This is gender dysfunction, not gender normalcy. It is also a gender dysfunction that entered the picture through human choice, not divine mandate. Instead of partnership in tackling the temptation to disobey God, the woman acted unilaterally; instead of ownership when confronted by God, the man deflected blame onto the woman. Genesis 3:16b is thus a recapping of the relational dysfunction that transpired much earlier in the narrative. It is a sad state of affairs, indeed, when one must seek biblical warrant for gender hierarchy in a male-female relational dysfunction that resulted from disobeying God.

WOMEN IN LEADERSHIP: GIFTING FOR MINISTRY

If to be egalitarian is to believe in the mutual gifting of women and men, the biblical support is easy to come by. One can hardly move from one NT chapter to the next without the matter-of-fact mention of a woman prophet, teacher, evangelist, and the like. The stage is already set in Judaism for a good range of female ministry roles. Israel from the start had its female prophets, judges, counselors, and worship leaders. Some, in fact, were multi-gifted women. Moses' sister Miriam possessed instrumental, hymnic, and prophetic gifts that served Israel well during the wilderness years (Exod. 15:20; Mic. 6:4). Deborah was named a "prophet" (Judg. 4:4), a judge (vv. 4–5), and a "mother in Israel" (5:7).[36]

The foremost ministry role was that of *prophet*. Women functioned as prophets during every epoch of Israel's history. Besides Miriam and Deborah, there was the prophetess God instructed Isaiah to marry (Isa. 8:3); the prophetess Huldah (2 Kgs. 22:14), who was active during the time of Jeremiah (Jer.

---

[36]"Mother" and "father" were titles given to benefactors and synagogue officers of some stature in the Jewish community. See, e.g., *CII* 694 (third century): "I Claudius Tiberius Plycharmos ... father of the synagogue at Stobi ... erected the buildings for the holy place ... with my own means without in the least touching the sacred [funds]." An early second-century inscription from Italy ranks "father of the synagogue" before *gerousiarch* (a high-ranking official of the local Jewish ruling council). For further inscriptions and discussion, see Bernadette J. Brooten, *Women Leaders in the Ancient Synagogue: Inscriptional Evidence and Background Issues* (BJS 36; Chico, Calif.: Scholars Press, 1982), 83–90.

1:2), Zephaniah (Zeph. 1:1), Nahum (Nah. 3:8–10), and Habakkuk (Hab. 1:6); and prophetesses during exilic (Ezek. 13:17–24) and postexilic (Neh. 6:14) times. Like their male counterparts, both faithful and unfaithful ones could be found.

A ministry that was almost exclusively female was that of *mourning*. David in his lament for Saul calls on the daughters of Israel to weep for the king (2 Sam. 1:24). The prophet Jeremiah refers to professional female lamenters, who were paid to mourn at funerals and other sorrowful occasions (Jer. 9:17–18). The prophet Ezekiel speaks of the lament the daughters of the nations will chant for Egypt (Ezek. 32:16).

One of the more intriguing OT ministry references is to the women who served at the entrance to the tabernacle (Exod. 38:8; 1 Sam. 2:22), for the Hebrew word translated "served" (*ṣābā'*) is used elsewhere in the OT of the work of the Levites in the tabernacle (Num. 4:23, "serve"; 8:24, "take part") and of Israel's warriors (Num. 31:7, "fought"; 31:42, "fighting"). While certainty is impossible, it is quite plausible to suppose that these women guarded the entrance to the tabernacle. Indeed, when Jesus was brought before Annas for questioning (the patriarch of the high priestly family), the guard on duty was a woman (*thyrōros* [John 18:16]). Cultural counterparts can be easily found. One first-century letter, for instance, mentions "Thenapunchis, a door-keeper [*pros tēi tērēsei thyrōron*] of Euhemeria in the division of Themistes" (*BGU* 4.1061.10).

The number and range of female ministry roles took a leap forward in the early church. Paul's greetings to the Roman church reflect this. No less than one out of every three individuals greeted is a woman. It is the same with the rest of the NT record. Women are singled out in the early church as apostles (Rom. 16:7), prophets (Acts 21:9; 1 Cor. 11:5), evangelists (Phil. 4:2–3), patrons (Rom. 16:2), teachers (Acts 18:24–26; Titus 2:3–5), deacons (Rom. 16:1; 1 Tim. 3:11), prayer leaders (1 Cor. 11:5), overseers of house churches (Acts 12:12; 16:14–15; Col. 4:15), prayer warriors (1 Tim. 5:5), and those who were known for their mercy and hospitality (5:10).

What accounts for this leap? In large part, it is because corporate worship and service were based on the Spirit's gifting each and every member of the local church for "the work of the ministry" (*eis ergon diakonias*, not the TNIV "works of service" [Eph. 4:12; cf. 1 Cor. 12:11]). The nature of early Christian worship is succinctly spelled out in 1 Corinthians 14:26: "When you come together," Paul states, "each of you has a hymn, or a word of instruction [*didachēn*], a revelation, a tongue or an interpretation. Everything must be done so that the church may be built up." The gender-inclusive character of Paul's statement is not to be overlooked, nor is the public and verbal nature of this gifting. It was assumed both women and men were actively involved in worship in didactic and public ways.

One of the ministries for which women in the church became renowned was that of *patronage*. To use Paul's language, "if [your gift] is giving, then give generously" (Rom. 12:8). It has long been noted that women alone are mentioned as the source of financial support for both Jesus and the Twelve. The gospel writer Luke recounts that a group of women traveled from place to place with Jesus and the Twelve and "were helping to support them out of their own means" (Luke 8:1–3). The imperfect tenses show this was an ongoing activity and not a mere excursion or two. These women "*continuously* followed him [*ēkolouthoun autō*] and *repeatedly* ministered to him [*kai diēkonoun autō*]" (Mark 15:41 AT, emphasis added; cf. Luke 8:3).

While this fit with the increased mobility of women at that time in the Roman Empire, within Jewish society it was quite striking. Yet it rarely gets noted by traditionalists. Attention is alternatively directed to the fact that none of the Twelve were women. But the truly amazing detail is that Jesus welcomed women into his itinerant group and allowed them to make the same radical commitment in following him that the Twelve did. That two are identified as married women is especially striking (Joanna, the wife of Herod's steward, and Salome, the wife of Zebedee [Luke 8:1–3; Mark 15:40–41]).[37]

Women are also singled out as patrons of house churches. Two women were sufficiently well-off to own their own homes, which they in turn offered as meeting places for local believers: Mary in Jerusalem (Acts 12:12) and Nympha in Laodicea (Col. 4:15). A third woman, Lydia—a businesswoman from Thyatira, opened her home in Philippi to Paul and his converts as a base of operations (Acts 16:15). Offering one's home as a meeting place involved more than cleaning the house and making the

---

[37]For discussion, see Richard Bauckham, *Gospel Women: Studies of the Named Women in the Gospels* (Grand Rapids: Eerdmans, 2002).

coffee. Homeowners in Greco-Roman times were in charge of all groups that met under their roof. This was essential, since they were legally responsible for the group's behavior (see, e.g., Jason's responsibility to post bond [Acts 17:7])—not unlike the fiduciary responsibilities of the chairperson of a board today.[38]

Women in the early church assumed other patronage roles as well. Paul refers to Phoebe in Romans 16:1–2 as a *prostatis* of many, including himself. Translations are wide-ranging in their rendering of this Greek word. They include "succourer" (KJV), "helper" (ASV, RSV, NIV, NASB, NLT, NKJV), "of great assistance" (Phillips), "a help to many" (NAB), "a good friend" (TEV, NEB, REB), "has looked after" (JB), and "a respected leader" (CEV). Sociologists, however, have shown that a *prostatis* was a "benefactor" (CSB, TNIV, NRSV, Revised NAB) or "patron" (ESV). Benefactors in the first century did more than write checks to cover expenses. They welcomed clients to their house, rendered assistance as called for, and offered legal aid as needed.[39]

Women were also recognized for their *apostolic labors*. Junia, for instance, is commended as a woman whom Paul considered "outstanding among the apostles" (Rom. 16:7). Some traditionalists translate the Greek text as "esteemed by the apostles," but this introduces an idea totally foreign to Paul's thinking. Paul would surely have said "us apostles" (1 Cor. 4:9; cf. Gal. 1:17; 1 Thess 2:6), as he does elsewhere, not "the apostles" (thereby excluding himself). This translation also overlooks the surrounding context, which points to a role distinctly comparable to Paul's. Junia was Paul's co-patriot and co-prisoner—not to mention the fact that she was "in Christ" before Paul. Perhaps she was among "all the apostles" (1 Cor. 15:7) or one of the five hundred to whom Christ appeared (15:6 [pre-Pauline tradition]). Priscilla and Aquila are also spoken of in ways that suggest apostolic activity. Their joint tentmaking operation with Paul in Corinth (Acts 18:1–3) and risking their necks for him to the benefit of "all the churches of the Gentiles" (Rom. 16:3–4) are easily understood in this fashion.

---

[38]For discussion, see Wayne Meeks, *The First Urban Christians* (New Haven, Conn.: Yale Univ. Press, 1983), 76.

[39]Jason, for instance, posted bond to ensure the good behavior of his client Paul (Acts 17:5–9), and the Philippian church sent Paul money as the need arose (Phil. 4:10–19; cf. 1 Cor. 9:15–18 and 1 Thess. 2:9). For a concise treatment of Greco-Roman patronage, see Everett Ferguson, *Backgrounds of Early Christianity* (Grand Rapids: Eerdmans, 1987), 45.

The presence of female apostles is noteworthy. Apostleship stands at the head of two NT lists of spiritual gifts ("[Christ] ... gave some to be apostles" [Eph. 4:11 NIV]; cf. 1 Cor 12:28) and, along with prophet, is viewed as foundational to the establishment and growth of the church (Eph. 2:20). The latter reference points to the function of an apostle in the early church as the equivalent of today's church planter. This is clear from the immediate context where the Pauline term appears. Barnabas, Silas, Timothy, and Titus, for example, are named apostles in texts that stress their role as coworkers in church planting (1 Cor. 9:5–6; 2 Cor. 8:16–21; 1 Thess. 2:7–9 [cf. 1:1]).

Some traditionalists question the female gender of the Greek name *Iounian* in Romans 16:7. Yet there is no reason to read *Iounian* in any way but feminine. Both older versions and translations (Vulg., Syr., Copt., Wycliffe, Tyndale, Great, Geneva, Bishop, KJV, Rheims, Webster, Reina-Valera, Weymouth, BBE) and more recent revisions and translations (NRSV, REB, Revised NAB, NKJV, NCV, NLT, GWT, NET, ESV, CSB, TNIV) render *Iounian* as the feminine Junia. And rightly so. The masculine name Junias simply does not occur in any inscription, on any tombstone, in any letterhead or letter, or in any literary work contemporary with NT writings. In fact, "Junias" does not exist in any extant Greek or Latin document of the Greco-Roman period. On the other hand, the feminine "Junia" is quite common and well attested in both Greek and Latin inscriptions. Over 250 examples to date have been documented in Rome alone.[40]

---

[40]See Bernadette J. Brooten, "'Junia ... Outstanding among the Apostles' (Romans 16:7)," in *Women Priests*, ed. Leonard Swidler and Arlene Swidler (New York: Paulist, 1977), 141–43; Peter Lampe, "Iunia/Iunias: Sklavenherkunft im Kreise der vorpaulinischen Apostel (Rom. 16:7), *ZNW* 76 (1985): 132; Lampe, "Die stadtrömischen Christen in den ersten beiden Jahrhunderten," WUNT 2.18 (Tübingen: Mohr, 1987): 156–64; and Richard S. Cervin, "A Note Regarding the Name 'Junia(s)' in Romans 16:7," *NTS* 40 (1994): 464–70. John Piper and Wayne Grudem (*Recovering Biblical Manhood and Womanhood*, 79–81) claim that the name "Junia" was rare. The difficulty, however, is that they limited their search to a *literary* Greek database where only the names of the famous appear—such as Brutus's sister Junia. And, even so, they found only three of the actual seven present in the database. Daniel Wallace's footnote on Romans 16:7 in the NET repeats the inaccuracy: "The feminine name *Junia* ... is quite rare in Greek (apparently only three instances of it occur in Greek literature outside Rom 16.7, according to the data in the *TLG*)." And compare the more recent CBMW's "Question 38" in "Fifty Crucial Questions" (2003); online at www.cbmw.org/questions/38.php. The Council also failed to do a search

Add to this the fact that none of the early versions of the Greek NT considered *Iounian* as anything but feminine. For example, the Vulgate (the standard Latin translation of the Western church) has "Junia ... well-known among the apostles." Plus, the only variation in the ancient manuscripts is also feminine ("Julia"). The fact is that no translation or commentary prior to the Middle Ages understood *Iounian* as other than feminine. Indeed, there is an unbroken tradition in the "Who's Who" lists from Origen in the third century through Peter Lombard in the twelfth century that not only recognized a female apostle but lauded her as "notable among the apostles." John Chrysostom (fourth-century bishop of Constantinople) said: "How great is the devotion of this woman [Junia] that she should be even counted worthy of the appellation of apostle" (*Hom. Rom.* 31 [on Romans 16:7]).[41]

Patristic evidence for a feminine *Junia* has long been available. Yet translations from the mid-1940s to the mid-1970s consistently rendered *Iounian* in Romans 16:7 as a masculine (e.g., RSV, Phillips, RVR, NEB, NASB, JB, TEV, NEB, NIV).[42] The reason is clear. The presumption was that the term "apostle" could not be used of a woman, hence the Greek must be construed as

---

of the standard patristic reference sources J. P. Migne's *Patrologia Graeca* and *Patrologia Latina*, which yield six Greek fathers and fourteen Latin fathers. The latter are particularly significant, since the name *Junia* is the feminine form of the Latin *Junius*—a prestigious clan of the day. It was the custom of freedmen and freedwomen to adopt the *nomen gentilicium* of their patron, which explains the 250 or more *Junia* in and around Rome.

[41]Piper and Grudem claim to have found a masculine *Junias* in Origen and Epiphanius (*Index discipulorum* 24.125.18–19). But they overlook the fact that the masculine in Origen (the other two references are feminine) is actually the error of Rufinus's Latin translation of Romans. Now we have a complete critical edition, which shows that *Junias* is a variant in two of three twelfth-century manuscripts that belong to a single subgroup, while earlier manuscripts have *Junia* (Caroline P. Hammond Bammel, *Der Römerbriefkommentar des Origenes: Kritische Ausgabe der Übersetzung Rufins* (3 vols.; *Vetus Latina, Aus der Geschichte der lateinischen Bibel* 16, 33, 34; Freiburg: Herder, 1990, 1997, 1998). Also, numerous inaccuracies (including a masculine Priscas) have caused patristic scholars to question the authorial attribution of *Index discipulorum*, especially since it was only first attributed to Epiphanius in the ninth century.

[42]German translations from Luther forward, Dutch translations, and French translations were also masculine, while Italian and Spanish translations (until recently) were feminine. Yet, there is no linguistic basis for the masculine. Early Germanic and French versions were dependent on the Byzantine text type, which has a feminine accent. So the source of the masculine *Junias* may well reflect Luther's personal disposition against an apostolic attribution.

masculine (*Junias*). Indeed, the rationale given by majority opinion in the most recent edition of Bruce Metzger's *Textual Commentary on the Greek New Testament* is the unlikelihood a woman would be among those styled "apostles."[43] This presumption is reflected in the change in 1927 of the feminine acute accent to the masculine circumflex accent in both critical Greek NT editions (Nestle-Aland and United Bible Societies).[44]

The masculine *Junias* is sometimes justified as the contracted nickname of *Iounianus* (*Junianus*). Yet, it is Greek nicknames, and not Latin ones, that were abbreviations of longer names (e.g., *Zenas* for *Zenadoros* [Titus 3.13]; *Epaphras* for *Epaphroditos* [Col. 1.7]). Latin nicknames were typically formed by lengthening the name, not shortening it—hence *Priscilla* for *Prisca* (Acts 18:2, 18, 26; cf. Rom. 16:3, 1 Cor. 16:19, 2 Tim. 4:19)[45] And when there was a final *i* in the stem of the shortened name, it was omitted in the transcribing. So the shortened form of *Iounianos* (if it existed) would be *Iounas*, not *Iounias*.[46] The inaccuracy is perpetuated by users of Thayer's Greek lexicon even to date. Because it was the standard lexicon until the mid-1950s, its influence has been profound.

More recently, the NET and the ESV concede the feminine *Junia* but change the attribution from the long-standing "of note *among* the apostles" to "well known *to* the apostles." The justification for this change is the contention that all biblical and extra-biblical parallels to Romans 16:7 are *exclusive* ("esteemed *by* the apostles," "well known *to* the apostles") rather than *inclusive* ("honored *as one of* the apostles," "notable *among* the apostles"). Yet, when looked at more closely, the burden of proof is wholly lacking.[47] First, the standard Greek lexica uniformly treat *episēmos*

---

[43]See Bruce Metzger, *A Textual Commentary on the Greek New Testament*, 2nd ed. (Stuttgart: United Bible Societies, 1994), 475.

[44]The German Bible Society's sixth printing (2001) of the United Bible Societies' fourth revised edition happily has corrected the mistake and omits the masculine circumflex in both the text and the apparatus.

[45]See John Thorley, "Junia, A Woman Apostle," *NovT* 38 (1996): 24–26.

[46]Ibid., 25. See also P. Chantraine, *La formation des noms en grec ancien* (Paris: Champion, 1933), 31–32. Bauckham (*Gospel Women*, 168, n. 253) rightly notes that the nonexistence of a contracted form is hardly surprising, since *Iounianos* itself is rare (found only once).

[47]For discussion, see L. L. Belleville, "Iounian ... ἐπίσημοι ἐν τοις ἀποστόλοις: A Re-examination of Romans 16:7 in Light of Primary Source Materials," *NTS* (forthcoming).

as a compound of *epi* ("upon") and *sēma* ("mark"), yielding the literal sense of "having a mark, inscription" and "bearing the marks of," and the metaphorical sense of "remarkable," "notable." Junia then is a distinguished, or remarkable *member of* (and not simply *known to*) the apostles (LSJ, s.v.).[48]

Second, the standard grammars don't sustain such a rendering.[49] The preposition *en* plus the dative plural with rare exception is *inclusive* "in"/"among" and not *exclusive* "to" (as claimed by Burer and Wallace).[50] The following are representative:

- "But you, Bethlehem, in the land of Judah, are by no means least *among the rulers of Judah* [*en tois hēgemosin Iouda*]" (Matt. 2:6).
- "There were no needy persons *among them* [*en autois*]" (Acts 4:34).
- "To the elders *among you* [*en hymin*], I appeal as a fellow elder" (1 Pet. 5:1).

Third, Burer and Wallace assume a conclusion not found in the evidence. Despite their assertions to the contrary, they fail to offer one clear Hellenistic Greek example of an "exclusive" sense of *episēmos en* and a plural noun to mean "well known to." The authors themselves admit this early on, but then go on to conclude otherwise.[51] More, in this pool (despite

---

[48]See LSJ, MM, *PGL*, L&N. Michael Burer and Daniel Wallace ("Was Junia Really an Apostle? A Re-examination of Rom 16.7," *NTS* 47 [2001]: 76–91) appeal to Louw and Nida's lexicon as supporting "well known to." However, the entry at 28.31 reads "pertaining to being well known or outstanding either because of positive or negative characteristics—'outstanding,' 'famous,' 'notorious,' 'infamous.'" Indeed, Louw and Nida render Romans 16:7 as "they are outstanding *among* the apostles."

[49]E.g., Nigel Turner (*Syntax*, vol. 3, in *A Grammar of New Testament Greek*, ed. Moulton, Howard, and Turner [Edinburgh: T&T Clark, 1963], 261) states that "in" or "among" for *en* plus the plural dative is the primary meaning in the Greek of the NT period; see, e.g., 2 Thess. 1:4: "Therefore, *among God's churches* we boast about your perseverance and faith" (emphasis added).

[50]For a list of NT examples of an adjective followed by *en* plus the personal plural dative as "inclusive," see A. T. Robertson, *A Grammar of the Greek New Testament in the Light of Historical Research* (Nashville: Broadman, 1934), 587.

[51]See Burer and Wallace, "Was Junia an Apostle?" 86–87; compare 87 and 90, "every instance." Burer and Wallace do in fact concede, somewhat grudgingly, that the one certain instance (Lucian, *On Salaried Posts*, 28) actually supports the traditional view of Romans 16:7.

claims to the contrary), the parallels to *episēmos en* plus the dative plural bear the inclusive meaning "a notable member of the larger group" and not exclusive "well known to."

- "So then you shall observe this with all good cheer as a *notable* day [*episēmon hēmeran*] *among* your commemorative festivals [*en tais epōnymois hymōn heotrais*]" (Add. Esth. 16.22 [8.22], first century).
- "[—] ... president of the Lycians, general and admiral of the nation, *prominent among* Rome's allies [*en tais hyper Rōmaiōn symmachiais episēmon genomenon*], secretary of the Lycian nation, illustrious and great" (Fd Xanthos VII Asia Minor, 76-1-12).
- "While Laban ... had a flock devoid of all distinctive marks, ... Jacob ... had a flock whose appearance was *distinctive* and varied *in the whole universe* [*episēmon ... en men tois holois to eidos*]" (Philo, *Flight*, 9–10, first century).
- "So the men of power sent ambassadors; some to Florus ... and others to Agrippa, *eminent among* whom were [*en hois ēsan episēmoi*] Saul, Antipas, and Costobarus" (Josephus, *J.W.* 2.418, first century).
- "So you must raise your thirsty voice like a stranded frog, taking pains to be *conspicuous among* those who praise [the mistress's page; *episēmos ese en tois epainousi*]" (Lucian, *On Salaried Posts in Great Houses*, 28.4, second century).
- "We had quite a crowd with us on our way down; *most distinguished among whom* were [*en autois de episēmoi*] our rich countryman Ismenodorus" (Lucian, *Dialogues of the Dead*, 438, second century).
- " ... the fame which is given by the multitude and to be *the conspicuous one in a crowd* [*to episēmon einai en plēthesi*]" (Lucian, *Harmonides*, 1.17, second century).

Another gift that women consistently possessed and exercised throughout the history of God's people was that of *prophecy*. As already noted, there are numerous examples of women prophets, stretching back to Mosaic times. Anna continues this tradition in the NT period. Luke calls her a "prophet," for she "spoke about the child to all who were looking forward to the redemption of Jerusalem" (Luke 2:36, 38). Philip, one of the leaders of the Hellenistic wing of the Jerusalem church, had four daughters who were prophets (Acts 21:9; Eusebius, *Hist.*

eccl., 3.31).[52] Women in the church at Corinth exercised the gift of prophecy in public worship (1 Cor. 11:5), and their contributions were affirmed ("I praise you for remembering me in everything and for holding to the traditions just as I passed them on to you" [v. 2]).[53]

Paul exhorted the Corinthian believers to "eagerly desire spiritual gifts, especially the gift of prophecy" (14:1). A look at the prophet's role in the early church shows why this was so. Although prophecy is sometimes assumed to be predictive in nature (e.g., Acts 21:10–11), the primary task of the NT prophet was comparable to the forthtelling role of the OT prophet in reminding God's people of their covenant obligations. Done in the context of public worship ("when you come together" [1 Cor. 14:26]), prophecy served to convict of sin (v. 24), to instruct (v. 19 [*katēchēsō*]), to exhort (v. 31), to encourage (Acts 15:32), and to guide in the decision-making process (13:3–4; 16:6). Just how consequential it was can be gauged from the fact that prophecy alone calls for examination of falseness or truthfulness by those with the gift of discernment (1 Cor. 14:29–30; 1 Thess. 5:20–21). Also, the prophets, along with the apostles, are viewed as foundational in the establishment and growth of the church (Eph. 2:20).

Another gift women exercised in NT times was that of *teaching*. Priscilla, for example, instructed Apollos "in the way of the Lord" (Acts 18:25). The older women in the church at Crete were expected to teach the younger women (Titus 2:3–5). Teaching was also a part of what a prophet did. "You can all prophesy in turn," Paul says to the Corinthians, "so that everyone may be instructed and encouraged" (1 Cor. 14:31 [*manthanōsin ... parakalōntai*]; cf. v. 19, "instruct" [*katēcheō*]). Instruction, therefore, was most definitely part of the prophetic role.

The gifting of women as teachers in the early church was quite countercultural. Both women learners and teachers were comparatively rare. In Greek society, the education of women beyond the elementary grades was not thought to be all that

---

[52]Proclus (third-century leader of the Phrygian Montanists) places the prophetic ministry of Philip's daughters in Hierapolis, Asia.

[53]Another female prophet during NT times was a Philadelphian woman named Ammia (Eusebius, *Hist. eccl.* 5.17.2–4). Second-century Montanists Priscilla and Maximilla used women like Ammia and Philip's daughters to legitimize their own prophetic office (Ibid., 5.17.4).

practical or necessary. The education of Roman women began to be taken more seriously in the centuries before Christ. But even so, there were still relatively few women teachers in the public arena during NT times (still playing catch-up, so to speak). Within Judaism especially, women learners and teachers were a rarity—which makes Jesus' instruction of Mary and the inclusion of female disciples particularly noteworthy (Luke 10:38–42). It also explains Jesus' exclusion of women among the Twelve. While male and female patronage was known and accepted in Jewish circles, women teachers and preachers were not. Traditionalists argue this is the definitive reason for excluding women from leading men. What they overlook, however, is that Jesus did not exclude women for *theological* reasons; indeed, he challenged male privilege at every opportunity and attributed it to hard hearts (e.g., Matt. 19:1–12; Mark 10:1–12).

Furthermore, while Jesus did not have a woman among his immediate Twelve, it was commonly assumed by the church fathers from Origen in the third century to Herveus Burgidolensis in the twelfth century that Jesus did include women among the group of seventy-two who were commissioned and sent out.[54] He was simply a realist in terms of the amount of change Palestinian culture could accommodate at that point in time. Diaspora Judaism was quite a bit more open. Female synagogue rulers were found in Asia Minor, Greece, and Crete.[55] And seven tomb inscriptions in which women bear the title "elder" have been identified to date in Crete, Malta, Thrace,

---

[54]See Origen (PG 14.1279–80, 1289–90); Rabanus Maurus (PL 111–12); Haymo of Faversham (PL 117.505); Hatto of Vercelli (PL 134.282A–B); Bruno of Querfurt (PL 153.119–20); Herveus Burgidolensis (PL 181).

[55]See, e.g., "Rufina, a Jewess, *synagogue ruler*, built this tomb for her freed slaves and the slaves raised in her household. No one else has a right to bury anyone here" (second century, Smyrna, Asia Minor [*CII* 741; *IGR* IV.1452]). Compare Peristeria of Thebes in Thessaly (a city in Greece [*CII* 696b]), Theopempte of Myndos in Asia Minor (a short distance from Ephesus [*CII* 756]), and Sophia of Gortyn in south-central Crete (*CII* 731C). See Hannah Safrai, "Women and the Ancient Synagogue," in *Daughters of the King*, ed. Susan Grossmann (New York: Simon and Schuster, 1974), 41; Shaye J. D. Cohen, "The Women in the Synagogues of Antiquity," *Conservative Judaism* 34 (1980): 25; Brooten, *Women Leaders*, 137–38; Randall Chestnutt, "Jewish Women in the Greco-Roman Era," in *Essays on Women in Earliest Christianity*, vol. 1, ed. Carroll Osborne (Joplin, Mo.: College Press, 1993), 124; Dorothy Irvin, "The Ministry of Women in the Early Church," *Duke Divinity School Review* (1980): 76–86; Belleville, *Women Leaders and the Church*, 21–31.

North Africa, and Italy.[56] The outpouring of the Spirit at Pentecost, empowering male and female alike, took it the next step (Acts 2:17–18).[57]

The role of female teachers increased during the post-apostolic period. Women were especially at the forefront in exposing and condemning heretics. Perhaps the best known was Marcella, who was praised by Jerome for her ability to confront heretical error.[58]

What about *evangelistic ministries*? Here too women were actively engaged. This was especially the case in the Roman church. Paul commends Priscilla as a "co-worker" (Rom. 16:3) and singles out Tryphena, Tryphosa, and Persis as those who "work hard in the Lord" (v. 12). This is missionary language. Paul uses exactly the same language in regard to his own and other male colleagues' missionary labors. The men are fellow prisoners (v. 7; Col. 4:10), coworkers (Rom. 16:3, 9, 21; 1 Cor. 3:9; 16:16–17; 2 Cor. 8:23; Phil. 2:25; 4:3; Col. 4:11; 1 Thess. 3:2; Phlm. 1, 24), and hard workers (1 Cor. 4:12; 16:16; 1 Thess. 5:12) who "risked their lives" for Paul (Rom. 16:4) and "contended at [his] side in the cause of the gospel" (Phil. 4:3). The women are equally "co-workers" (Rom. 16:3–4; Phil. 4:3) and hard workers (Rom. 16:6, 12) who "risked their lives" for Paul (Rom. 16:4) and "contended at [his] side in the cause of the gospel" (Phil. 4:3). Paul's joint imprisonment with Junia and Andronicus indicates they too were engaged in some sort of evangelistic activity (Rom. 16:7; cf. Acts 16:19–24; 2 Cor. 11:23).

Syntyche and Euodia were active female evangelists. Paul says they "contended at [his] side in the cause of the gospel"

---

[56]See, e.g., "The tomb of the blessed Mazauzala, *elder*. She lived [. . .] years. Rest. God is with the holy and the righteous ones." (SEG 27 [1977] no. 1201). Compare "Tomb of Faustina the *elder*. Shalom" (*CII* 597); "Sophia of Gortyn, *elder* and head of the synagogue of Kisamos" (*CII* 731c); "Tomb of Rebeka, the *elder*, who has fallen asleep" (*CII* 692); "Tomb of Beronikene, *elder* and daughter of Ioses" (*CII* 581); "Tomb of Mannine, *elder*, daughter of Longinus, father, granddaughter of Faustinus, father, 38 years" (*CII* 590; SEG 27 [1977] no. 1201); "Here lies Sara Ura, *elder* [perhaps "aged woman"]" (*CII* 400); "[. . .] gerousiarch, lover of the commandments, and Eulogia, the *elder*, his wife (Antonio Ferrua, "*Le catacombe di Malta*," *La Civiltà Cattolica* [1949]: 505–15).

[57]See Belleville, *Women Leaders and the Church*, 58–59, 95–96.

[58]Jerome, *Epist.* 127.2–7. For further discussion, see Walter Liefeld's article "Women and Evangelism in the Early Church" (*Missiology* 15 [1987]: 297).

(Phil. 4:2–3). Some traditionalists say Paul is merely acknowledging their financial support or their hospitality. The language indicates otherwise. The term Paul uses to describe their role is a strong one. *Synathleō* ("to contend with") describes the athlete who strains every muscle to achieve victory in the games.[59]

Female apostles, prophets, teachers, and evangelists can be grouped under the rubric of "ministry of the word" (*tē diakonia tou logou* [Acts 6:2]). Another grouping of gifts can be broadly classified as "ministry of serving" (literally, "to wait on tables" [*diakonein trapezais*], Acts 6:2). This also fits the distinction between ministries of "speaking" and "serving" found in 1 Peter 4:11.

Those engaged in service ministries primarily attended to the physical needs of the local body of believers (e.g., Acts 6:1–6; 11:27–30, Rom. 12:7).[60] The title "deacon" was the early church's recognition of the leadership such believers provided. In the church at Philippi, for instance, one of two identified leadership positions was that of deacon (Phil. 1:1).

Women are readily labeled "deacons" in the NT. Phoebe, for example, is applauded by Paul as a deacon.[61] That Paul is using *diakonos* of an official capacity is clear from the technical language of commendation and the church specification: "I commend to you our sister Phoebe, a deacon of the church in Cenchreae" (Rom. 16:1). The list of qualifications for women deacons in 1 Timothy 3 makes it plain this was not an isolated case: "In the same way, [male] deacons are to be worthy of respect, sincere [i.e., 'not double-tongued'], not indulging in much wine, and not pursuing dishonest gain. . . . In the same way, the women [who are deacons] are to be worthy of respect, not malicious talkers but temperate and trustworthy in everything" (vv. 8, 11).[62]

---

[59]See LSJ, s.v.

[60]Although the term *diakonos* is not used in Acts 6:1–6, the activity of caring for those with material needs is certainly present.

[61]Cf. 1 Cor. 16:15–18; 2 Cor. 8:18–24; Phil. 2:19–30. See Linda Belleville, "A Letter of Apologetic Self-Commendation: 2 Cor. 1:8–7:16," *NovT* 31 (1989): 142–64.

[62]Some translate *gynaikas* in 1 Timothy 3:11 as "their wives." This is highly unlikely for several reasons. First, the grammar does not support it. If Paul were turning to the wives of deacons, he would have written "*their* women likewise" (*gynaikas tas autōn hosautōs*) or included some other indication of marital status. Also, there are no parallel requirements for the wives of overseers in the immediately preceding verses. Why would Paul highlight the wives of one group of leaders and

The post-apostolic church not only recognized the role of women deacons but continued the tradition with enthusiasm. Pliny (governor of Bithynia in the early years of the second century) tried to obtain information by torturing two female deacons (*Letters* 10.96.8). In the third, fourth, and fifth centuries, virtually every Eastern father and church document mentions women deacons with approval.[63] The *Didascalia Apostolorum* 16 (a third-century book of church order) spells out their duties. The *Apostolic Constitutions* (a fourth-century work about pastoral and liturgical practice) spells out their duties (3.15) and includes an ordination prayer for them (8.20), and canon 15 of the Council of Chalcedon (fifth century) details the ordination process for women deacons and places them in the ranks of the clergy: "A woman shall not receive the laying on of hands as a deaconess under forty years of age, and then only after searching examination. And if, after she has had hands laid on her and has continued for a time to minister, she shall despise the grace of God and give herself in marriage, she shall be anathematized as well as the man united to her."[64] We also possess fourth- through sixth-century AD inscriptions that name women deacons from a range of geographical locations. Two are from Jerusalem; two from Italy and Dalmatia; one from the island of Melos; one from Athens; and ten from the Asian provinces of Phrygia, Cilicia, Caria, and Nevinne.

The practicality of female deacons is not to be overlooked. Women could gain entry into places that were taboo for men and perform activities that would be thought inappropriate for a male minister.[65] The duties of female deacons in the post-apostolic

---

ignore the wives of another? More, to read "likewise their wives are to be ..." is to assume that all deacons' wives possessed the requisite gifting and leadership skills. This plainly contradicts Pauline teaching elsewhere (e.g., 1 Cor. 12:11). For further discussion, see Belleville, *Women Leaders and the Church*, 60–64.

[63]Women were also ordained to the diaconate in Italy and Gaul, but their numbers did not match those in the Eastern churches. For discussion, see P. Hünermann, "Conclusions Regarding the Female Deaconate," *TS* 36 (1975): 329.

[64]See also R. Gryson, *The Ministry of Women in the Early Church* (Collegeville, Minn.: Liturgical Press, 1976), 90–91; D. R. MacDonald, "Virgins, Widows, and Paul in Second Century Asia Minor" (*SBLSP* 16; Atlanta: Scholars Press, 1979), 181, n. 11.

[65]Women in the early centuries were able to take advantage of their social mobility to visit friends and set up networks for evangelism. See Wendy Cotter, "Women's Authority Roles in Paul's Churches: Countercultural or Conventional," *NovT* 36 (1994): 369.

period were quite varied. They taught children and youth, evangelized unbelieving women, discipled new believers, visited the sick, cared for the ailing, administered Communion to shut-ins, and disbursed funds to the needy. In the worship service, they served as doorkeepers, assisted with the baptism of women, and administered Communion as the occasion arose.[66]

Another group of women singled out for their distinctive service to the church were the *widows*:

> Let a widow be enrolled if she is not less than sixty years of age, having been the wife of one husband; and she must be well attested for her good deeds, as one who has brought up children, shown hospitality, washed the feet of the saints, relieved the afflicted, and devoted herself to doing good in every way.
>
> 1 Timothy 5:9–10 RSV

There is every reason to think Paul is describing a ministerial role. To start with, he lists requirements that parallel the qualifications for an elder, overseer (or bishop), and deacon. The widow must have been the wife of one husband (cf. 1 Tim. 3:2, 12; Titus 1:6), raised children (cf. 1 Tim. 3:2, 12; Titus 1:6), be known for her good deeds (cf. Titus 1:8), and have a reputation for hospitality (cf. 1 Tim. 3:2; Titus 1:8). Also, these widows are designated by the technical term for the official "enrollment" of a recognized group (*katalegesthō* [1 Tim. 5:9]; see ASV, NAB, ESV, RSV, JB, NJB, REB; versus NIV, NASB, NRSV, NLT, TNIV "put on the list").[67] More, Paul instructs that these widows be financially compensated for their time (v. 3, *timaō* "to reward" or "to pay";[68] cf. v. 17); and he speaks of a broken pledge, suggesting these women took a vow of widowhood in which they pledged full-time service to Christ (vv. 11–12).

The corrective nature of Paul's instruction in 1 Timothy 5 indicates that a widows' ministry had been in place for some time. The length of Paul's corrective reveals that the ministry had gotten off track (perhaps because of an unexpected growth in the number of widows in Ephesus) and was in need of clear protocols.

Paul's list of qualifications provides insight into the nature and scope of ministering widows. Among the good deeds listed

---

[66]See *Didascalia Apostolorum* 3.
[67]See LSJ, s.v.
[68]See LSJ, s.v.

are showing hospitality, washing the feet of the saints, and relieving the afflicted (v. 10). Hospitality was something the church became known for early on—especially since there was little by way of decent accommodations for the average traveler. Foot washing was a common courtesy extended to guests attending a meal in one's home. The order of hospitality followed by foot washing suggests that one piece of the widow's job description included providing food and lodging for Christians on the road. "Relieving the afflicted" can be more literally translated "helping those persecuted for their faith" (*thlibō* = "to press," "to oppress").[69] The form this help took is difficult to determine. It could have involved visiting and caring for those in prison, providing shelter for those fleeing persecution, or meeting the basic needs of those who had lost family and jobs because of their commitment to Christ.[70]

The widow's job description may also have included caring for orphans, which would explain the parenting requirement. House-to-house visitation is suggested by Paul's criticism that younger widows (with too much time on their hands) were "going about from house to house . . . , saying things they ought not to" (v. 13). "Saying things they ought not to" points to a teaching role—perhaps along the lines of what is found in Titus 2:3–4. Some traditionalists think Paul is targeting female busybodies in 1 Timothy 5:13. The typical Greek idioms are, however, missing. "To mind one's own affairs" (*prassein ta idia*; cf. 1 Thess. 4:11), "to meddle in the affairs of others" (*periergazesthai* [2 Thess 3:11]), or similar phraseology is what one would have expected, if mere nosiness were the problem.

Ministering widows flourished in the post-apostolic period. The nature of their ministry was decidedly pastoral. Their duties included praying for the church, teaching the basics of the faith, showing hospitality, caring for the sick, fasting, prophesying, and caring for the needs of destitute widows and orphans.[71] Pseudo-Ignatius greets "the order of widows [*to tagma tōn chemrōn*]. May they give me joy [*hōn kai onaimēn*]" (*Philippians* 15). Polycarp called them "God's altar" (*Phil.* 4:3); Clement of Alexandria ranked them after elders, bishops, and deacons

---

[69]See LSJ, s.v.; BDAG, s.v.

[70]See Belleville, *Women Leaders and the Church*, 65–67.

[71]For discussion, see Bonnie Thurston, *The Widows: A Women's Ministry in the Early Church* (Minneapolis: Fortress, 1989), 54.

(*Paed.* 3.12.97; *Homily* 9.36.2), and Augustine says they are "dedicated to be hand-maids of Christ by a holy vow" (*Letter* 211.14). A rite of ordination for widows is found in the *Apostolic Tradition of Hippolytus* (appendix 6).[72]

The early church was not unique in recognizing the ministry potential of its seniors. Older women (and men) took up leadership roles in the Essene communities: "The woman [shall raise her voice and say] the thanksgivings ... and she shall stand in the council of the elder men and women" (4Q502 [frg. 24]).[73]

WOMEN LEADERS IN THE BIBLE

Women Leaders in Old Testament Times

It is clear that historically women have been gifted for ministry. Gifting, however, does not necessarily make a leader. While women appear in a variety of ministry roles in the Bible, the key questions are whether these roles warrant the label of *leadership*—especially leadership over men—and whether the community of faith affirms women in these roles. The answer on both accounts is a decided *yes*.

As early as Mosaic times, women were affirmed as leaders of God's people. Miriam, for instance, was sent by the Lord (along with her two brothers) to "lead" (MT *heʿĕlitîkā*; LXX *anēgagon*) Israel during the wilderness years (Mic. 6:4). She was held in such high regard as a leader that Israel would not travel until she was back at the helm (Num. 12:1–16). Micah 6:4 is particularly important because it shows that Miriam's role was traditionally and historically understood as a leadership one by the community of faith centuries later.

---

[72]The genuine canons of Hippolytus were preserved in Arabic, Ethiopic, Coptic, and Latin versions and translated into French by M. L. McClure and into English by L. Duchesne in a volume titled Apostolic Tradition of Hippolytus, in *Christian Worship: Its Origin and Evolution* (New York: E. & J. B. Young, 1903), 531. For the order of widows in the early and late councils, see the canons of Basil #24 (fourth century) and canon #40 of the Quinisext Council (seventh century).

[73]The church's philanthropic work on behalf of widows was a natural outgrowth of Judaism. One of the ministries of the local synagogue was meeting the basic needs of the sojourner and the poor in their midst. The latter group would have included widows. See Bruce Winter, "Providentia for the Widows of 1 Timothy 5:3–16" (*TynBul* 39 [1988]: 31–32, 87).

Deborah's role during the pre-monarchical period is described in leadership language. According to Judges 4:4–5, she held court in the hill country of Ephraim between Ramah and Bethel, and men and women alike came to her to have their disputes settled. Her stature as a judge was high and her leadership exemplary. She adjudicated intertribal quarrels and local disputes that proved too difficult for the tribal judges (Deut. 17:8). Her ability to command was also a matter of record. When the tribes of Israel were incapable of unifying against their northern Canaanite oppressors, Deborah not only united them but also led them on to victory (Judg. 4:5–24). Her military standing is shown by the position of her name in the historical records ahead of Barak, Israel's military commander (5:1). In her honor, the community of faith named the site of her ministry *mer děbôrâ* ("Palm of Deborah" [4:5]).

Huldah provided similar leadership during the time of the divided monarchy. Although there were other prestigious prophets around (e.g., Jeremiah, Zephaniah, Nahum, and Habakkuk), it was Huldah's counsel concerning the Book of the Law that King Josiah sought out (2 Kgs. 22:11–14). The large, prominent delegation sent to her (the high priest, the father of a later Babylonian gubernatorial appointee, the son of a prophet, the secretary of state, and the king's officer) says something about Huldah's professional stature. Their confidence was well placed, for it was Huldah's counsel that inspired the well-known religious reforms of the seventh century BC and helped elevate all the true prophets to their rightful place in Judah's religious community (2 Chron. 34:14–33).

During the postexilic period, the female prophet Noadiah was one of the Jewish prophets hired by Sanballat to thwart Nehemiah's efforts to rebuild the temple walls (Neh. 6). The fact that Noadiah is only one of two prophets mentioned by name in Nehemiah 6 is indicative of her stature as a leader at that time—albeit not an exemplary one, but then neither was her male contemporary Shemaiah (vv. 10–13).

Women in the ancient Near East provided political leadership. Some were heads of state. Athaliah, for example, "ruled the land" of Israel from 842 to 836 BC (2 Kgs. 11:3), and Salome Alexandra, honored queen of the Hasmonean dynasty, reigned from 76 to 67 BC. The queens of Egypt and Ethiopia had a long history as reigning monarchs. Two of the best known are Cleopatra, the effective ruler in Egypt from 51 to 31 BC, and Candace, the queen of Ethiopia in the first century AD (see Acts 8:27).[74] Other women were advisers to heads of state. For example, Joab, David's military commander, sent a female adviser from Tekoa to persuade David to forgive his son Absalom's act of violence against his stepbrother and so pave the way for reconciliation (2 Sam. 14). It was also the expert advice of a woman who saved her city, Abel Beth Maakah, from destruction at the hand of David's troops (ch. 20). These things would not have happened had there not been women of significant standing and authority on local and national levels.

Politically astute women are likewise easy to identify. The appeal of Zelophehad's daughters for a woman's right to inherit matched the best legal argumentation of the day (Num. 36:1–13). Bathsheba's efforts to gain the kingship for Solomon showed fine diplomacy. Jezebel, daughter of the priest-king of Tyre and Sidon and wife of Israel's reigning king (Ahab), was infamous for her political maneuverings. There was also no lack of female political prowess. The queen of Sheba's savvy as a negotiator was legendary (1 Kgs. 10:1–10; 2 Chr. 9:1–9), and Queen Esther's word commanded instant obedience (Esth. 4:15–17; 9:29–32).

It is common for traditionalists to refer to such women as "exceptions." When God could not find a willing man to lead (so the argument goes), he resorted to using women. It is true there were far fewer women leaders than their male counterparts—but not because of any intrinsic inferiority, basic incompetence, or gender unsuitability. There is no hint in the Bible that female leadership is wrong. The reality was that domestic chores (especially the bearing and raising of children) left women little time to pursue public roles. Those involved in the public arena were generally upper-class women able to delegate their domestic tasks to other women in the household.[75] The only exception was the Levitical priesthood, where purity laws precluded Jewish women from serving in certain ceremonial roles due to uncleanness related to childbirth and menstruation. Men too were excluded but for different reasons (e.g., not being a Levite, sexual uncleanness, or

---

[74]"Candace"; "Cleopatra," in *Encyclopaedia Britannica* CD-ROM (2001). The CBMW disallows Athaliah on the basis of her being "a wicked usurper of the throne" (Ware, "Egalitarian and Complementarian Positions," 3). This overlooks the fact that not a few of Israel's and Judah's kings are described in the same way. Usurper or not, she was still head of state.

[75]See Belleville, *Women Leaders and the Church*, 94–95.

physical defect). Other roles, however, show men and women serving side by side. Both helped build and furnish the tabernacle (Exod. 35:22–26); both played musical instruments in public processions (Ps. 68:25–26); both danced and sang at communal and national festivals (Judg. 21:19–23); both chanted at victory celebrations (1 Sam. 18:7); and both sang in the temple choir (2 Chr. 35:25; Ezra 2:65; Neh. 7:67).

Women Leaders in New Testament Times

There was also no lack of women leaders in the early church. This is not surprising, given the many women who responded to the gospel message. Luke records that Mary the mother of Jesus and "the women" were among the 120 empowered by the Holy Spirit for witness in Jerusalem, Judea and Samaria, and beyond (Acts 1:7–8, 14–15; 2:1–4). This empowerment fulfilled what was spoken by the prophet Joel: "In the last days, God says, I will pour out my Spirit on all people. Your sons *and daughters* will prophesy.... Even on my servants, both men *and women*, I will pour out my Spirit in those days" (Acts 2:17–18; citing Joel 2:28 [emphasis added]).

Male leaders may have been more numerous, but virtually every leadership role that names a man also names a woman. In fact, there are more women named as leaders in the NT than men. Phoebe is a "deacon" and a "benefactor" (Rom. 16:1–2). Mary, Lydia, and Nympha are overseers of house churches (Acts 12:12; 16:15; Col. 4:15). Euodia and Syntyche are among "the overseers and deacons" at Philippi (Phil. 1:1; cf. 4:2–3). The only role lacking specific female names is "elder"—but then male names are lacking as well.

Female church leaders are partly a carryover from the involvement of women in the top leadership positions in the cults. For example, women served continuously as high priests of the imperial cult in Asia from the first century AD until the middle of the third century. Since there was only one high priest in any single city at one time, the consistent naming of women in this leadership role is especially significant.[76] Women also served

---

[76]Inscriptions dating from the first century until the middle of the third century place these women in Ephesus, Cyzicus, Thyatira, Aphrodisias, Magnesia, and elsewhere. See R. A. Kearsley, "Asiarchs, Archiereis, and the Archiereiai of Asia," *GRBS* 27 [1986]: 183–92.

as civil servants and public officers in such positions as magistrate and comptroller (*IGR* III 800–902 [first century]).

Some traditionalists contend that female high priestesses were young girls who did not serve in and of their own right—a position (so it is argued) analogous to the private priestesses of Hellenistic queens (i.e., not a public role serving both genders).[77] The evidence, however, does not bear this out. The majority of women who served as high priests were hardly young girls. The prestigious Delphic priestess, for instance, had to be at least fifty years of age, was drawn from a breadth of social classes, and served as oracles for the male god Apollo. Vestal virgins were the lone exception—and theirs was a prominent, public role and not a private, domestic position.[78]

Others maintain that priestesses did not hold positions in and of their own right. The title was merely honorific—riding on the coattails of a husband, brother, or other male relative. Epigraphical evidence indicates otherwise. Juliane, for example, served as high priestess of the imperial cult long before her husband did. And many inscriptions naming women as high priestesses do not name a father or husband. More, the position of high priestess was hardly nominal. Priests and priestesses were responsible for the sanctuary's maintenance, its rituals and ceremonies, and the protection of its treasures and gifts. Liturgical functions included ritual sacrifice, pronouncing the prayer or invocation, and presiding at the festivals of the deity. So, when a husband, son, or other relative was named, it was done so because there was prestige attached to being a relative of a high priestess.[79] This is not unlike the husband of Proverbs 31, who increased in stature because of the standing of his wife ("takes his seat among the elders" [v. 23]).

A recent study claims the imperial high priestess was a post-NT development. The evidence, however, points to something much earlier.[80] For instance, while Paul was planting the

---

[77]See, e.g., Steven M. Baugh, "A Foreign World: Ephesus in the First Century," in *Women in the Church: A Fresh Analysis*, 43–44.

[78]See Belleville, *Women Leaders and the Church*, 31–38; Riet Van Bremen, "Women and Wealth," in *Images of Women in Antiquity*, ed. A. Cameron and A. Kuhrt (Detroit: Wayne State Univ. Press, 1987), 231–41.

[79]See Kearsley's carefully documented study, "Archiereiai of Asia," 183–92.

[80]See Baugh, "Foreign World," 42–45. The primary difficulty with Baugh's study is that it confined itself to Ephesian inscriptions and data and so wasn't broad-based

Ephesian church, Juliane served as high priestess of the imperial cult in Magnesia, a city fifteen miles southeast of Ephesus (*InscrMagn.* 158). Also, because religion and government were inseparable, to lead in one arena was often to lead in the other. Mendora, for example, served at one time or another during the first century as magistrate, priestess, and comptroller (*dekaprotos*) of Sillyon, a town in Pisidia, Asia (*IGR* III 800–902).

For women in the early church, a lot had to do with location. The more Romanized the area, the more visible the leadership of women.[81] Since Paul's missionary efforts focused on the major urban areas of the Roman Empire, it is not at all unexpected that most of the women named as leaders in the NT surface in the Pauline churches.[82] Virtually all of the churches Paul planted were in heavily Romanized cities, where the population was a mix of Latin- and Greek-speaking people. Thessalonica, Corinth, and Ephesus, for instance, were provincial capitals. Philippi was a leading city in the province of Macedonia. Cenchreae housed a Roman naval station. Rome was the hub of the empire. So it should come as no surprise that many of the leaders Paul greets in the Roman church are women (Rom. 16).

Early Church Leadership Roles

Patron of a House Church

Most of the ministry roles in the early church had a leadership dimension to them. The *patron* of a house church was no exception. As noted earlier, the homeowner in Greco-Roman times was in charge of any group that met in his or her domicile and was legally responsible for the group's activities. Moreover, households in the first century included not only the immediate family and relatives but also slaves, freedmen and freedwomen, hired workers, and even tenants and partners in a trade or craft. This meant the female head of the house had to have good

---

enough to accurately reflect the religious and civic roles of first-century women in either Asia or in the Greco-Roman empire as a whole. To ignore the oriental cults (especially Isis) and their impact on women's roles is particularly egregious. See the detailed discussion and presentation of the evidence in Belleville, *Women Leaders and the Church,* 31–38.

[81]See Meeks, *The First Urban Christians,* 23–25.
[82]See Belleville, *Women Leaders and the Church,* 49–50.

administrative and management skills. For this reason, Paul places great emphasis on a person's track record as a family leader, as it is a definite indicator of church leadership potential (1 Tim. 3:4–5; 5:14). In fact, the term used for the female head of the household (*oikodespotein* ["household master," or "lord"], 5:14) is much stronger than that used for the male (*prostēnai* ["to lead, guard, protect"], 3:5; see LSJ, s.v.).

Prophet

Prophet was also a recognized leadership role. Prophesying was not an impromptu, uncontrollable movement of the Spirit (as some have argued). Luke makes this plain when he identifies the leadership of the church in Antioch as "prophets and teachers" (Acts 13:1–3). More, Paul teaches that prophecy was subject to the control of the prophet (1 Cor. 14:29–33).

Some traditionalists claim prophecy was a less "authoritative" activity (to use their language) than other forms of ministry (such as teaching, discernment of spirits, pastoring, or administrating) and so women were able to prophesy in the early church. Yet the biblical evidence indicates otherwise. Prophecy was exercised in the context of public, not private, worship ("when you [both men and women] come together," 14:26). And the prophet's job description included such corporate leadership activities as conviction of sin (v. 24), instruction (*katēcheō*, v. 19), exhortation (v. 31), and guidance (Acts 13:3–4; 16:6). In point of fact, it was to "God's holy apostles and prophets" that "the mystery of Christ ... has now been revealed by the Spirit" (Eph. 3:4–5). In a very real sense, therefore, the NT prophet carried on the "Thus saith the Lord" task of the OT prophet. This is why Paul can call their utterances "revelation" (*apokalyphthē*, 1 Cor. 14:29–30) and why the fourth-century church historian Eusebius ranked Philip's four daughters "among the first stage in the apostolic succession" (*Hist. eccl.* 3.37.1).

Some traditionalists argue that first-century female prophets were subject to the male leadership of the church. Yet Paul treats the prophetic activity of women as identical to the prophetic activity of men: "Every man who prays or prophesies ... every woman who prays or prophesies" (11:4–5). Plus, he states that prophecy is subject to the control of the individual prophet—and not to some outside source (14:32).

Other traditionalists claim that the NT prophet differed from the OT prophet in that the word of the latter was wholly authoritative and that of the former was not. The fact that the NT prophet had to be evaluated (14:29) indicates (so they say) that his or her word was merely a Spirit-prompted utterance with no guarantee of divine authority in its details.[83] To say this, however, is to overlook the equal (if not stricter) testing of the OT prophet. The word of an OT prophet was not true if it did not come to pass (Deut. 18:21–22), conflicted with God's covenant with Israel (13:1–5), did not encourage obedience and moral living (Mic. 3:11), or was a message of peace and prosperity (Jer. 28:8–9). The testing of Hananiah in Jeremiah 28 is a classic example of the evaluative process in OT times.

Teacher

The question of whether there were women in the early church who publicly taught men is the primary point of contention between traditionalists and egalitarians. This is because traditionalists identify public teaching with authoritative, official activity.

In Paul's time, there definitely were *women teachers*. Priscilla instructed Apollos "in the way of the Lord" (Acts 18:25); the female prophets at Corinth instructed the congregation (cf. 1 Cor. 11:5 and 14:19); and the older women in the Cretan church taught the younger women (Titus 2:3–5). The leadership component of the NT teacher is unmistakable. The gift of teaching comes after apostleship and prophecy in one spiritual gift list (1 Cor. 12:28), is inseparably linked with the gift of pastoring (lit., "shepherding") in another ("pastor-teacher" [Eph. 4:11]),[84] and is part of the job description of a prophet in still another ("to instruct" [katēcheō], 1 Cor. 14:19).

So how does one avoid the conclusion that women instructed men? Some traditionalists do so by distinguishing

---

[83]See D. A. Carson, "'Silent in the Churches': On the Role of Women in 1 Corinthians 14:33b–36," in *Recovering Biblical Manhood and Womanhood*, 153.

[84]In the NT, pastoring is inseparable from teaching. This is clear from Ephesians 4:11, where the two nouns *poimenas* and *didaskalous* have a single article and are connected by *kai*. This arrangement of the grammatical pieces serves to conceptually unite the two ideas and should be translated "pastor-teachers." For discussion, see Maximilian Zerwick, *Biblical Greek* (Rome: Pontifical Biblical Institute, 1963), #184.

between public and private, authoritative and nonauthoritative, and formal and informal types of instruction—female teaching being of the latter sorts. Priscilla's instruction of Apollos was private, teaching was only incidental to the prophetic role at Corinth (and hence nonauthoritative), and the instruction provided by the older women at Crete was informal (so the argument goes). Such distinctions, however, are decidedly modern ones. The NT knows no such distinctions. Teaching was an integral part of every facet of church life. Everyone in the congregation was expected to be able to teach (Col. 3:16; cf. Heb. 5:12). Also, to make such distinctions is to lose the essentially charismatic nature of the NT teaching role. When the Corinthian church gathered for worship, it was taken for granted that both men and women would verbally instruct in one way or another ("a hymn, or a word of instruction, a revelation, a tongue or an interpretation" [1 Cor. 14:26]).

Some traditionalists make a distinction between the Greek *didaskō* (which, it is argued, denotes authoritative, official teaching) and other Greek terms for instruction (e.g., *katēcheō, ektithemai*). One difficulty, though, is that once again the NT itself draws no such distinctions. At Corinth, both men and women are instructed to bring, literally, a "teaching" [*didachēn*]) to the worship gathering (1 Cor. 14:26). The congregation at Colossae is called to "teach" (*didaskontes*) one another (Col. 3:16). Timothy is instructed to devote himself to "teaching" (*didaskalia*) the church at Ephesus (1 Tim. 4:13). Antioch chose its missionaries from among the ranks of prophets and "teachers" (*didaskaloi* [Acts 13:1]). The older women at Crete are told to "teach well" (*kalodidaskalous*) the younger women (Titus 2:3). And an overseer was expected to be "able to teach" (*didaktikon* [1 Tim. 3:2]).

It is true that Priscilla is said to have "explained" (*exethento*), not "taught" (*edidaxe*), the way of God to Apollos (Acts 18:26). But this is the same term Luke uses for Paul's preaching to Jews in Rome ("he explained" [*exetitheto*], Acts 28:23). It is also true that the term for prophetic instruction in 1 Corinthians 14:19 is not *didaskō*. But *katēcheō* and *didaskō* are virtual synonyms in the NT. Paul, for example, can speak of being "instructed" (*katēchoumenos*) by the law (Rom. 2:18) and command the Galatian believers to share all good things with their "instructor" (*ho katēchoumenos* [Gal. 6:6]). Luke uses *katēcheō* and *didaskō* interchangeably in Acts 18:25. Apollos had been "instructed" (*katēchēmenos*) in the way of the Lord and in turn "taught" (*edidasken*) about Jesus. So to draw a distinction between different Greek terms for instruction at this stage in the church's development is exegetically wrongheaded.

Deacons and Overseers

Were there any female overseers or deacons in the early church? Euodia and Syntyche are described in language that places them squarely in the ranks of one of these two positions in the Philippian church ("to all God's holy people in Christ Jesus at Philippi, together with the overseers and deacons" [Phil. 1:1]). Otherwise, Paul would have no need to make a public appeal to a third party to help these women work out their differences ("I plead with Euodia and I plead with Syntyche to be of the same mind in the Lord. Yes, and I ask you, my true companion, help these women" [4:2–3]). To begin with, it is very rare for Paul to name names in his letters. To do so here is indicative of the stature of these two women in the community of faith. Paul speaks early on in the letter about the disunity of the Philippian congregation (2:1–18). For him to go on and specifically urge Euodia and Syntyche (whom he names as "co-workers" and partners "in the cause of the gospel" [4:3]) to be "of the same mind in the Lord" (v. 2) indicates that their role was so distinctly a leadership one that their disagreement put the unity of the church in jeopardy.

In similar fashion, Paul explicitly salutes Phoebe as a deacon of the church in Cenchreae: "I commend to you our sister Phoebe, a deacon [*diakonon*] of the church in Cenchreae" (Rom. 16:1). Yet one wouldn't know it from some translations. The KJV, NKJV, ASV, NASB, TEV, ESV, CSB, and NIV translate *diakonon* as "servant." But this misses the official character of Paul's statement. Phoebe is the person Paul chose to deliver his letter to the Roman church. This is why Paul commands the Roman church to "receive her in the Lord" and "give her any help she may need" (v. 2). Acceptance into a Christian community in Paul's day required the presentation of credentials. One of the letter carrier's responsibilities was to read the letter to the congregation and to answer questions afterward. The carrier's credentials were therefore vitally important, spelling the difference between the person's acceptance and rejection. Paul quite consistently commends other colleagues (e.g., 2 Cor. 8:16–24; Eph. 6:21–22; Phil. 2:25–30; Col. 4:7–9). But it was especially important in Phoebe's case, because Paul himself had never visited Rome.

"Servant," then, would hardly suffice.[85] "Co-worker" (2 Cor. 8:23; Phil. 2:25), "faithful servant" (Eph. 6:21), and "faithful minister" (Col. 4:7) might do for familiar leaders like Tychicus, Titus, and Epaphroditus. But "a deacon of the church in Cenchreae" (NLT, NRSV, TNIV) would have been essential for a virtual unknown like Phoebe (cf. NEB, "who holds office in"; CEV, "a leader in"; NJB and RSV, "deaconess").

Some traditionalists protest that the Greek term *diakonos* is masculine. But this overlooks the fact that there was simply no feminine form in use at this time—*diakonissa* ("deaconess") is postapostolic). Nor was it needed, for the masculine singular in Greek often did double duty. This was especially the case with nouns that designated a particular leadership role such as apostle (*apostolos*), prophet (*prophētēs*), or evangelist (*euangelistēs*). Context made the gender clear.[86]

This was certainly the way the church fathers understood it. Origen (third century) states that "this text [Rom. 16:1] teaches with the authority of the apostle that even women are instituted deacons in the church" (*Epistle to the Romans* 10.17). John Chrysostom (fourth century) observes that Paul "added her rank by calling her a deacon [*diakonon*]" (*Hom. Rom.* 30 [on Rom. 16:1]).

The Ephesian church also had female deacons: "In the same way, the women [who are deacons] are to be worthy of respect,

---

[85]The REB's "minister" for *diakonon* also falls short. "Minister" was not the officially recognized position it is today. Another unlikely translation is "deaconess" (NASB, RSV, JB, NJB, Phillips), for the feminine term *diakonissa* was not in use until the Nicene Council in AD 325 (canon 19). For further discussion, see A. A. Swidler, "Women Deacons: Some Historical Highlights," in *A New Phoebe: Perspectives on Roman Catholic Women and the Permanent Diaconate*, ed. V. Ratigan and A. Swidler (Kansas City, Mo.: Sheed & Ward, 1990), 81; V. V. FitzGerald, "The Characteristics and Nature of the Order of the Deaconess," in *Women and the Priesthood*, ed. Thomas Hopko (Crestwood, N.Y.: St. Vladimir's Seminary Press, 1983), 78.

[86]The leadership list in Ephesians 4:11 (NIV) is a good example of the gender inclusivity of the Greek masculine. "[Christ] . . . gave some to be apostles [*tous apostolous*], some to be prophets [*tous prophētas*], some to be evangelists [*tous euangelistas*], and some to be pastors and teachers [*tous poimenas kai didaskalous*]." Women are named in each of these roles (e.g., Junia [Rom. 16:7]; Philip's daughters [Acts 21:9]; Syntyche and Euodia [Phil. 4:2]; and elderly widows at Ephesus [1 Tim. 5:9–10]).

not malicious talkers but temperate and trustworthy in everything" (1 Tim. 3:11). That Paul is speaking of women in a recognized leadership role is apparent not only from the listing of credentials but also from the fact that these credentials are exact duplicates of those listed for male deacons in verses 8–10. Also, the Greek word order of verses 8 and 11 is identical: "[Male] deacons likewise must be worthy of respect, not double-tongued, not given to much wine [*diakonous hosautōs semnous, mē dilogous, mē oinō*].... Female [deacons] likewise must be worthy of respect, not slanderers, temperate [*gynaikas hosautōs semnas, mē diabolous, nēphalious*]" (AT).

The post-apostolic writers understood Paul to be speaking of women deacons. Clement of Alexandria (second century) says, "We know what the honorable Paul in one of his letters to Timothy prescribed regarding women deacons" (*Strom.* 3.6.53). And John Chrysostom (fourth century) talks of women who held the rank of deacon in the apostolic church (*Hom. 1 Tim.* 11 [on 1 Tim. 3:11]).

What about female elders? There are good reasons for thinking that Paul is talking about just such a leadership role in 1 Timothy 5:9–10. First, Paul limits the role to women over the age of sixty (v. 9), which fits the primary meaning of the Greek *presbyteros* as "elderly." This is a carryover from Judaism, where the elders of the town (a civic role) were those considered wise by virtue of their age.[87] Second, he lists requirements that parallel the qualifications for elders found elsewhere in his writings. The widow must have been the wife of one husband (cf. Titus 1:6), have raised children (cf. v. 6), be well known for her good deeds (cf. v. 8), and have a reputation for offering hospitality (cf. v. 8). Third, like an elder, she is to be remunerated for her ministry (*timaō* = "to reward," "to pay" [1 Tim. 5:3];[88] cf. v. 17).

Traditionalists typically argue that there are certain leadership qualifications that exclude women. "Able to teach" (1 Tim. 3:2) is only problematic for those who would say that women in the early church were forbidden from teaching men.

---

[87]The primary function of Jewish elders was that of community leaders. They held no official status in the local synagogue. This is quite different from Christian elders, who seem to have had official standing in the early church. See Emil Schürer, *The History of the Jewish People in the Age of Jesus Christ*, rev. ed. (Edinburgh: T&T Clark, 1979), 3:87–107.

[88]See LSJ, s.v., and BAGD, s.v.

"The husband of one wife" (KJV, NKJV, NJB, RSV, NASB, British NIV, ESV) as a qualification for overseers (v. 2), deacons (v. 12), and elders (Titus 1:6) needs a closer look. Would Paul include such a qualification if he envisioned women serving in these capacities? The point is a good one. But a knowledge of the mores of a Greek city like Ephesus sheds important light. Greek married women simply were not prone to multiple marriages or illicit unions, while Greek men were. In fact, extramarital affairs were par for the Greek male but not tolerated for Greek women (because of the concern for legitimate sons). Also, the divorce rate among Greek men rivaled ours today.[89]

So the fact that Paul includes this qualification for male deacons (1 Tim. 3:12) and omits it for female deacons (v. 11) is exactly what one would expect. Anything else would be surprising—unless, of course, Paul had the widow in view. A widow back then was inclined to remarry—as Paul himself acknowledged (1 Cor. 7:8–9). Therefore Paul includes "the wife of one husband" for them (1 Tim. 5:9). It was the widow who was content to remain a widow that would serve the church with the kind of single-minded devotion effective ministry in the first century AD required (1 Cor. 7:32–35).

Beyond "the husband of one wife," there are no qualifications that are male-specific. Elderly widows and female deacons are called to exhibit the same character and lifestyle qualities as their male counterparts (1 Tim. 3:8–9, 11). Some qualities, in fact, are more suitable to women than to men. For instance, hospitality would be more natural for Greco-Roman women. The ability to care for one's household (as indicative of the ability to care for the church) would also be a good fit. In fact (as noted earlier), the term used for the leadership role of the woman of the household (oikodespotein, "to be household master" [5:14] is much stronger than that used of the man (prostēnai, "to lead, guide, care for" [3:5]).

So if no first-century leadership activities were distinctively male in character, why the impasse about women in leadership? And if there are no qualifications that would prohibit women

---

[89]For further discussion, see J. Neuffer, "First-Century Cultural Backgrounds in the Greco-Roman Empire," in Symposium on the Role of Women in the Church, ed. J. Neuffer (Plainfield, N.J.: General Council of the Seventh-Day Adventist Church, 1984), 69.

from serving as leaders, why do some persist in excluding them today?

WOMEN AND AUTHORITY

The issue for many traditionalists is not whether the Spirit gifts women in the same way he gifts men but whether a particular activity is authoritative or not. If it is, then women are excluded. To publicly teach is to exercise authority; to publicly preach is to exercise authority; to corporately lead is to exercise authority (whether one names the leader "elder," "deacon," "bishop," "pastor," "chairperson," or "president"). Therefore, women cannot publicly teach, preach, or lead in any way. Why? Because God created the male alone to lead, and to lead is to exercise authority. To be male, then, is to possess and exercise authority, and to be female is not to possess and exercise authority.

But is this truly the case from a biblical perspective? It is one thing to hold a conviction; it is another to find biblical support for it. Quite frankly, one is hard-pressed to find a biblical link between local church leadership and "authority" (exousia).[90] The NT writers simply do not make this connection. In fact, no leadership position or activity in the NT is linked with authority—with one exception. In 1 Corinthians 11:10, Paul states that a female's head covering is her "authority" (exousia) to pray and prophesy in corporate worship.

Since the Greek exousia appears frequently in the NT (some one hundred times), the absence of a link with local church leadership is quite significant. Traditionalists make the connection between local church leadership and authority, but the closest we come to it in the NT is Titus 2:15. This is where Paul tells Titus to

---

[90]Some traditionalists associate the Greek prohistēmi with "exercise of rule" or "authority" and cite 1 Thess. 5:12; 1 Tim. 3:4–5; 5:17 as examples. However, there is no lexical basis for this association. Louw and Nida list as meanings: (1) guide, (2) be active in helping, and (3) strive to. Compare BAGD and LSJ, s.v. The Greek term literally means "to stand before," or "to lead," and is used in contexts where the main idea is to shepherd or care for God's people (i.e., a pastoral association). In Rom. 12:8, e.g., prohistēmi is grouped with the spiritual gifts of offering practical assistance to those in need ("give generously," "show mercy"). Also, in 1 Tim. 3:4–5, to prohistamenon the church is to "care for" (epimelēsetai) it. This fits with the role of a prostatis ("benefactor," "protector") in the culture of the day. See LSJ, s.v.

"rebuke" the Cretan congregation "with all authority." Even so, Titus's prerogative is not *exousia* ("authority") but *epitagē* ("command" [see LSJ, s.v.]). More, Titus possessed this prerogative solely as Paul's deputy and not as a local church leader. Plus, because the Greek term *pas* ("all") lacks the article, the emphasis is on "each and every kind." So a better translation would be "rebuke with every form of command at your disposal."

A look at the relevant NT texts shows it is the church that possesses authority and not particular individuals (or positions, for that matter). It is to the church that Jesus gives the "keys of the kingdom" and the authority to "bind" (i.e., enforce) and "loose" (i.e., waive [Matt. 16:19]). It then becomes the church's responsibility to test and weigh prophetic utterances (1 Cor. 14:29; 1 Thess. 5:19–22), to choose missionaries (Acts 13:1–3) and church delegates (15:22–23; 20:4–5), to discipline (Matt. 18:18; 1 Cor. 5:4–5), and to reinstate (2 Cor. 2:7–8; cf. Matt. 18:10–14). The church's authority comes from the power of the Lord Jesus present with believers gathered in his name (Matt. 18:20; 1 Cor. 5:4) and from corporate possession of "the mind of Christ" (2:16).[91]

Churches can, to be sure, choose individuals to represent their interests and to work on their behalf (e.g., Acts 6:1–7; 13:1–3; 15:2–3; 20:1–6). But in no way do these individuals exercise authority over the congregation. They are, rather, empowered to minister to the congregation and to equip the people for ministry. As Paul states, "[Christ] . . . gave some to be apostles, some to be prophets, some to be evangelists, and some to be pastors and teachers [*tous de poimenas kai didaskalous*], *to prepare God's people* [NIV] for the work of the ministry [*eis ergon diakonias*]" (KJV; Eph. 4:11–12, emphasis added).

The most frequent NT use of *exousia* is with reference to secular rulers. Both Paul and Peter call congregations to submit to the political powers in authority over them ("rulers and authorities" [*archais exousiais*], Titus 3:1; "supreme" [*hyperechonti*], 1 Pet. 2:13–17). Paul tells the Roman church, "Everyone must submit himself to the governing authorities [*exousiais hyperechousais*]. . . . For rulers hold no terror for those who do right, but for those who do wrong" (Rom. 13:1, 3 NIV). Even here, though, authority is

[91]See Linda Belleville, "Authority," in *Dictionary of Paul and His Letters*, eds. G. Hawthorne, R. Martin, and D. Reid (Downers Grove, Ill.: InterVarsity, 1993), 54–59.

divinely delegated. The authorities that exist have been established by God ("for there is no authority [*exousia*] except that which God has established" [Rom. 13:1]; cf. John 19:11 ["given to you from above"]).

What about the twelve apostles? Didn't Jesus invest them with the authority? All three gospel writers do record that the Twelve were sent out by Jesus with authority. But interestingly enough, it was an "authority (*exousian*) to drive out evil spirits and to heal every disease and sickness" (Matt. 10:1; cf. Mark 3:14–15, 6:7; Luke 9:1; 10:19) and not to preach and teach. The Twelve were sent out "to preach" the good news (Mark 3:14; cf. Matt. 10:7; Luke 9:2)—but authority is not mentioned in connection with this activity. Yet it is all too common today to say that preaching is an authoritative activity.

What about the apostle Paul? Certainly he laid claim to apostleship and hence to authority, didn't he? He did indeed. Yet Paul rarely claims or makes reference to his apostolic authority. There are only two places where he does so—both of them in 2 Corinthians: "the authority [*exousian*] the Lord gave us for building you [the church] up rather than tearing you down" (10:8; see 13:10). Also, while Paul does not hesitate to command when necessary (e.g., 2 Thess. 3:6), his usual modus operandi is to "urge" (*parakaleō*) and not to "command" (*parangellō*). More, although Paul does refer to his apostleship at the start of nine letters (Romans, 1–2 Corinthians, Galatians, Ephesians, Colossians, 1–2 Timothy, Titus), he also declares himself to be "a servant [slave] of Christ Jesus" at the beginning of three (Romans, Philippians, and Titus ["prisoner of Christ Jesus," in Philemon). Two letters, in fact, combine "Paul, a servant" with "an apostle" (Rom. 1:1, Titus 1:1)—which would suggest that "apostle" and "servant" (not "apostle" and "ruler") are two sides of the same coin.

Why is there so little mention of Paul's authority? The explanation is easy to come by. Paul (along with other NT writers) simply refused to buy into the top-down leadership style of the day as an effective and appropriate one for the church. Paul told the Corinthian church (2 Cor. 1:24) that his aim was not to "lord it over" (*kyrieuomen*) their faith but to "work with [them]" (*synergoi esmen*). Peter similarly exhorted the leaders of the Asian churches to be "shepherds of God's flock ... not lording it over [*katakyrieuontes*] those entrusted to you, but being examples to the flock" (1 Pet. 5:2–3).

In this respect, Paul and the other apostles are merely being obedient to the teaching of Jesus. For when James and John came to Jesus asking for positions of power in his future kingdom, Jesus reminded his disciples that Roman leaders "lord it over" (*katakurieuousin*) and "exercise authority over" (*katexousiazousin*) them. But it was not to be so with them (Matt. 20:25–26). Traditionalists would claim Jesus was warning against a misuse or abuse of power, but neither the Greek terms nor the context suggests this. A negative sense is not inherent in either term. Both merely denote the possession and exercise of authority (*katakurieuō* = "to gain or exercise dominion over or against someone"; *katexousiazō* = "the exercise of rule or authority").[92] Indeed, the Greek term *katakurieuō* is the one used for the "dominion" over the earth that God gives to human beings (Gen. 1:28; 9:1; Sir. 17:4), the king of Israel (Ps. 72:8), and the Messiah (Ps. 110:2).

But doesn't Paul himself call for submission to local church leadership? And doesn't submission assume the exercise of authority? There are indeed two NT passages that call for congregational submission. In Paul's first letter to the Corinthians, the congregation is called on to "submit" (*hypotassēsthe*) to "such as these" (i.e., the household of Stephanas [16:16]). In the letter to the Hebrews, the readers are instructed to "remember" (*mnēmoneuete*), "follow" (*peithesthe*), and "yield to" (*hypeikete*) their "leaders" (*hēgoumenoi* [13:7, 17 AT]).[93]

What is sometimes overlooked, however, is the reason for the submission. In neither instance is the submission based on the possession of authority or the holding of an office. It is, rather, the appropriate response to the exercise of pastoral care. The "such as these" to whom the Corinthians were to submit were "everyone who joins in the work and labors at it" (1 Cor. 16:16). And the leaders to whom the "Hebrews" were to submit were those who "keep watch over" them (*agrypnousin* [Heb. 13:17]).[94] This is undoubtedly why the NT writers do not use the Greek verb *hypakouō* ("to obey") but instead use words that denote a voluntary deferring to another's wishes (e.g., 1 Cor.

---

[92]See LSJ, s.v.; L&N 37.48–49.

[93]*Hypeikō* is found only here in the NT. The verb means "to yield, give way, submit." In Homer's *Iliad* 16.305, e.g., it refers to making room for another person by yielding one's seat. See LSJ, s.v. "Obey" is therefore not an accurate translation.

[94]*Agrypneō* means "to watch over, stay alert," implying continuous and wakeful concern. See L&N, s.v.

16:16, *hypotassēsthe* = a voluntary act [middle voice] of deferring to the wishes of an equal; Heb. 13:17, *peithesthe* = "to follow," and *hypeikete* = "to give way to").[95] The distinction is an important one. Obedience can be willingly or unwillingly given. It can also be something demanded of someone in a lesser position (e.g., one's boss). Submission, on the other hand, is the voluntary act of a free agent.

Does this speak to the issue of the *ordination* of women? Unfortunately, it does not. Both the term and the concept are lacking in the NT—with respect to both men and women. The idea of commissioning (i.e., to set apart, dedicate) for a particular ministry is more what we find (generally through the laying on of hands). For example, the church at Antioch commissioned Saul and Barnabas as missionaries (Acts 13:1–3), elders were commissioned at Ephesus (1 Tim. 5:22), Timothy was commissioned as an evangelist (1 Tim. 4:14; 2 Tim. 1:6), and Paul was commissioned as an apostle to the Gentiles (Acts 9:17–19; 22:12–16). But this is a far cry from how churches use "ordain" today. In my denomination, for example, ordination authorizes a person to "preach the Word, administer the sacraments, and bear rule in the church."[96]

WOMEN LEADERS AND BIBLICAL LIMITS

If biblical authority resides in the church and not the leader, and if women are commended in the NT as church leaders, on what basis do traditionalists exclude women from leadership? The CBMW lists five primary NT passages: Matthew 10:1–4; 1 Corinthians 14:33–35; 1 Timothy 2:12; 1 Timothy 3:1–7; and Titus 1:5–9.[97]

Matthew 10:1–4 is the passage where Jesus calls his twelve disciples to him and gives them authority to drive out evil spirits and to heal every disease and sickness. How exactly one gets from driving out evil spirits and healing diseases to the exclusion of women from leadership roles is far from clear. If these twelve men had been given authority to preach or teach, one

---

[95]See LSJ, s.v.; *TLNT* 3:424.

[96]The Evangelical Covenant Church, *The Covenant Book of Worship* (Chicago: Covenant Press, 1981), 298.

[97]See *CBMW News* 1 (Nov. 1995), 1.

could see the Council's logic (although not necessarily agree with it). But Jesus' disciples are not given this kind of authority. So the ambiguity remains.

Traditionalists typically argue that the very fact Jesus was male and the Twelve Jesus chose to be with him were males legislates male leadership for the church.[98] Although a common way of thinking today, once again it is not particularly logical. For Jesus did not merely choose twelve men but twelve *Jewish* men, and he himself was not merely a male but a *Jewish* one. Yet no one argues that Jewish leadership is thereby legislated.

There is also the biblical symbolism of twelve Jewish males to represent the twelve tribes to consider. The twelve tribes of Israel will be judged by the Twelve (Matt. 19:28; Luke 22:30). The new Jerusalem will have twelve gates, twelve angels, and twelve foundations on which were the names of the Twelve (Rev. 21:12, 14). Following traditionalist logic, future judgment of the non-Israelite would then be in the hands of the male leadership of the church. But it is not. Male leaders will not serve as judges in the future; nor, for that matter, will female leaders. "Do you not know," Paul says, "that the Lord's people will judge the world ... [and] will judge angels?" (1 Cor. 6:2–3). But then this is what we saw in the previous section. The church possesses authority; church leaders do not—be they male or female.

The CBMW similarly points to the qualifications for overseers and elders in 1 Timothy 3:1–7 and Titus 1:5–9 as being gender exclusive. But again, it is difficult to see how they exclude women. "Husband of one wife" has already been dealt with (p. 63). "Able to teach"(1 Tim. 3:2) and able to "refute those who oppose [sound doctrine]" (Titus 1:9) are hardly gender-exclusive activities. The post-apostolic church esteemed a number of women who were gifted in doing just that (e.g., Marcella; see Jerome, *Epist.* 127).

To be honest, only three NT passages are worthy of consideration: 1 Corinthians 14:34–35, where women are commanded to be silent in the church; 1 Timothy 2:11–15, where women (according to the TNIV) are not permitted to teach or to

---

[98]See, e.g., James I. Packer, "Let's Stop Making Women Presbyters," *ChrT* 35 (Feb. 11, 1991): 20; James A. Borland, "Women in the Life and Teachings of Jesus," in *Recovering Biblical Manhood and Womanhood*, 120; Ware, "Egalitarian and Complementarian Positions," 8.

have authority over a man; and 1 Corinthians 11:2–16, where the male and female relationship is defined in terms of *kephalē* (commonly translated "head"). Of these three, 1 Timothy 2:11–15 is the one on which traditionalists normally fix their attention. For instance, a 1995 traditionalist book offers the promising title *Women in the Church* but has as its subtitle *A Fresh Analysis of 1 Timothy 2:9–15*.[99] Have we really come to the point where 1 Timothy 2:9–15 is the lone biblical text that defines and informs this issue? Or is it that this text is all traditionalists have as a biblical basis for male leadership?

First Corinthians 14:34–35

First Corinthians 14:34–35 certainly deserves attention, for it commands the silence of women in the churches:

> [34]Women should remain silent in the churches. They are not allowed to speak, but must be in submission, as the law says. [35]If they want to inquire about something, they should ask their own husbands at home; for it is disgraceful for a woman to speak in the church.

The text is cited in full because traditionalists often stop at the end of verse 34 and miss the important qualifiers that follow. The entirety of chapter 14 must also be looked at, otherwise Paul ends up flatly contradicting what he says earlier in the letter. According to 1 Corinthians 11:2–5, women were anything but silent, and Paul commended them for it: "I praise you for remembering me in everything and for holding to the traditions just as I passed them on to you. . . . Every woman who prays or prophesies . . ." (vv. 2, 5).

Some traditionalists dismiss the prophetic activity of women in 1 Corinthians 11. Paul (in their opinion) was only speaking hypothetically, the setting was not a formal one (and hence the prophecy wasn't authoritative),[100] and prophetic activity was vertical (i.e., talking to and for God) as opposed to horizontal (i.e., exercising authority over another person).

Yet there is nothing at all hypothetical about the grammar, for Paul puts everything in the indicative (the mood of fact) and

---

[99]See n. 1, p. 21.

[100]F. W. Grosheide (*The First Epistle to the Corinthians* [Grand Rapids: Eerdmans, 1953], 341–43) states that "women are allowed to prophesy but not when the congregation officially meets."

not in the subjunctive (the mood of possibility). Also, the setting is most assuredly formal (i.e., public, corporate worship). "We have no other practice—nor do the churches of God" (v. 16) indicates as much. Plus, there is nothing particularly vertical about prophetic activity. Prophecy, by definition, is a spiritual gift intended to build up the church (14:4, 26); it is exercised when believers "come together as a church" (11:18; 14:26). Tongue speaking (without interpretation) may be vertical: "For those who speak in a tongue," Paul states, "do not speak to other people but to God. . . . But those who prophesy speak to people . . ." (14:2–3). So the burden of the interpreter lies in explaining what Paul means (and does not mean) by "women should remain silent in the churches" (vv. 34–35).

Several things are clear from the context. First, the setting is public worship. "So if the whole church comes together" is the context for Paul's instruction (v. 23; cf. v. 26 and 11:17–18; 12:7). Second, the command for silence is not absolute. "When you come together," Paul states, "each of you has a hymn, or a word of instruction, a revelation, a tongue or an interpretation" (14:26a; cf. 1:5). Had Paul intended to limit public involvement to men, he surely would have said so here. Instead he emphasizes that women and men alike are to contribute for the upbuilding of the church (14:26b).

Third, Paul's comments are corrective (versus informational) in nature. The topic is the orderly speaking of participants during worship, and the problem is the current disorderly state of affairs. Paul begins and ends this block with a command that everything be done in a fitting and orderly way (vv. 26, 40), "for God is not a God of disorder but of peace" (v. 33). At the top of his agenda is the orderly contribution of verbal gifts (hymns, teachings, revelations, tongues, interpretations, v. 26). Two or three at the most can speak—and then only one at a time. If the speaking is in tongues, there must be someone to interpret. If there is no interpreter, the speaker must speak only to themselves and God (vv. 26–28). If the speaker is a prophet, "the others" should weigh carefully what is said,[101] and if a prophetic revelation comes to someone who is sitting down, the first speaker must yield the floor to that person (vv. 29–31).

---

[101]It is not clear who "the others" are. They could be other prophets (v. 29), the rest of the congregation, or those with the gift of discernment. The latter two options

Paul concludes with a word of rebuke addressed to the entire congregation. The pronouns are plural: "Did the word of God originate with *you*? Or are *you* the only people it has reached?" (v. 36, emphasis added). Paul clearly foresees that some at Corinth will reject his correction because they think they are spiritually superior. *Ei tis dokei* is a condition of fact: *If (as is the case) any think they are prophets or otherwise gifted by the Spirit . . . "* (v. 37, emphasis added). Thus, he challenges the so-called spiritual elite to use their gifting to affirm that what he has been saying about orderly worship is really "the Lord's command" (v. 37).

So what kind of disorderly speaking were the Corinthian women engaging in? Scholars tend to lean toward one of three interpretations. Some think in terms of a form of inspired speech; Paul is restraining women from mimicking the ecstatic frenzy of certain pagan cults.[102] Or he is silencing women who speak in tongues without interpretation ("If there is no interpreter, the speaker should keep quiet in the church; let them speak to themselves and to God" [v. 28]).[103] Or yet again, he is prohibiting women from taking part in evaluating prophetic speech ("Two or three prophets should speak, and the others should weigh carefully what is said" [v. 29]). Traditionalists tend to gravitate toward the last of these, for to evaluate the prophecies of men (so it is argued) would be for the woman to usurp the man's created role as leader.[104]

---

find support elsewhere in Paul's writings. In 1 Thessalonians, he urges the congregation to test prophecies, with the intent of proving their genuineness (5:21). And he pairs the gift of discernment with the gift of prophecy in 1 Cor. 12:10. Based on the context, the last option is the likeliest. It is Paul's expectation that speaking in tongues will be followed by interpretation (14:27–28), so it makes sense to think that prophecy would in turn be subjected to the scrutiny of those gifted to determine whether the speaking is truly from God.

[102]See, e.g., Richard and Catherine Kroeger, "Pandemonium and Silence at Corinth," in *Women and the Ministries of Christ*, ed. R. Hestenes and L. Curley (Pasadena, Calif.: Fuller Theol. Seminary, 1979), 49–55; Kroeger and Kroeger, "Strange Tongues or Plain Talk," *Daughters of Sarah* 12 (1986): 10–13.

[103]See, e.g., Joseph Dillow, *Speaking in Tongues: Seven Crucial Questions* (Grand Rapids: Zondervan, 1975), 170.

[104]See, e.g., James Hurley, "Did Paul Require Veils or the Silence of Women? A Consideration of 1 Corinthians 11:2–16 and 1 Corinthians 14:33b–36," *WTJ* 35 (1973): 190–220; E. Earle Ellis, "The Silenced Wives of Corinth (1 Cor. 14:34–5)," in *New Testament Textual Criticism*, ed. E. J. Epp and Gordon Fee (Oxford: Clarendon, 1981), 216–18; Wayne Grudem, *The Gift of Prophecy in 1 Corinthians* (Lanham, Md.: University Press of America, 1982), 249–55; Carson, "Silent in the Churches," 52.

Others opt for some form of disruptive speech. The Corinthian women were publicly contradicting or embarrassing their husbands by questioning a particular prophecy or tongue.[105] Or, women were chattering during worship and so disturbing those around them.[106] Or yet again, women were flaunting the social conventions of the day by assuming the role of a teacher.

One rather recent interpretation is that verses 34–35 are the traditionalist position of certain members of the Corinthian congregation, which Paul cites ("Women should remain silent in the churches") and then responds to in verse 36 ("What! Did the word of God originate with you [Corinthians], or are you the only ones it has reached?" [RSV]).[107]

Which is the correct interpretation? A closer look at verses 34–35 helps to narrow the options. It is clear Paul is addressing married women. The women creating the disturbance are those who could "ask their own husbands at home" (v. 35). Some claim that "women should remain silent" includes all women (married

---

[105]See, e.g., W. F. Orr and J. A. Walther, *1 Corinthians* (AB; Garden City, N.Y.: Doubleday, 1976), 312–13; C. K. Barrett, *A Commentary on the First Epistle to the Corinthians*, 2d ed. (HNTC; New York: Harper & Row, 1971; repr. Peabody, Mass.: Hendrickson, 1987), 332; cf. L. Ann Jervis, "1 Corinthians 14:34–35: A Reconsideration of Paul's Limitation of the Free Speech of Some Corinthian Women," *JSNT* 58 (1995): 60–73.

[106]See, e.g., G. Engel, "Let the Woman Learn in Silence. II," *ExpTim* 16 (1904–05): 189–90; Scott Bartchy, "Power, Submission, and Sexual Identity Among the Early Christians," in *Essays on New Testament Christianity*, ed. C. Wetzel (Cincinnati, Ohio: Standard, 1978), 68–70.

[107]See, e.g., Neal Flanagan and Edwina Snyder, "Did Paul Put Down Women in 1 Cor. 14:34–36?" *BTB* 11 (1981): 1–12; Chris Ukachukwu Manus, "The Subordination of Women in the Church: 1 Cor. 14:33b–36 Reconsidered," *RAT* 8 (1984): 183–95; David Odell-Scott, "Let the Women Speak in Church: An Egalitarian Interpretation of 1 Cor 14:33b–36," *BTB* 13 (1983): 90–93; Odell-Scott, "In Defense of an Egalitarian Interpretation of 1 Cor 14:34–36: A Reply to Murphy-O'Connor's Critique," *BTB* 17 (1987): 100–103; Gilbert Bilezikian, *Beyond Sex Roles*, rev. ed. (Grand Rapids: Baker, 1985), 151–52; Linda McKinnish Bridges, "Silencing the Corinthian Men, Not the Women," in *The New Has Come*, ed. A. T. Neil and V. G. Neely (Washington, D.C.: Southern Baptist Alliance, 1989); Charles Talbert, "Biblical Criticism's Role: The Pauline View of Women as a Case in Point," in *Unfettered Word*, ed. R. B. James (Waco, Tex.: Word, 1987), 62–71. Verse 36 begins with the particle *ē* (translated "What!" in the KJV and RSV), which (it is argued) Paul uses to reject or refute what has come before (see Daniel Arichea, "The Silence of Women in the Church: Theology and Translation in 1 Cor. 14:33b–36," *BT* 46 [1995]: 101–12). One difficulty is that there is no indication verses 34–35 are a quotation (like one finds elsewhere in 1 Corinthians [6:12, 13; 7:1b; 8:1b; 10:23]). Also, while the particle *ē* can express disapproval, it is a double *ē ē* that functions in this way and not the single *ē* found in 11:36. See LSJ, s.v.

or otherwise).[108] This is not technically correct. The Greek *gynē* could mean either "wife" or "woman." Only the context determines which is correct; and here the context explicitly states that these women are married ("If they want" = the women of v. 34).

It is further clear that Paul was targeting married women as a subset of the Corinthian women as a whole. A quick look at 1 Corinthians 7 shows that the women of the church included married (vv. 2–5), widows (vv. 8–9), divorcees (vv. 11, 15–16), the engaged (v. 36), and the never-married (vv. 27–28). It is also plain that the desire of these married women was to learn: "If they want to *learn* something [*mathein thelousin*] ..." (14:35 NKJV). This rules out tongues, prophecy, and the like. Paul is not addressing women who are exercising their spiritual gifts by contributing a teaching, a revelation, a tongue, or other Spirit-inspired gift to the worship experience (14:26). Nor is he speaking to women who are exercising their gift of discernment in evaluating the truthfulness of the prophetic word (v. 30). These are, rather, married women in the congregation who are asking questions because they want to learn ("they should ask ... " [v. 35]). Their fault was not in the asking per se but in the corporate disorder their asking produced.

It is likewise manifest that the questions of these women were directed at men other than their husbands, for Paul instructs them to ask "their own men" (*tous idious andras*). While today we might look askance at someone interrupting the preacher at a confusing spot in the sermon, at Corinth it would have involved interrupting a teaching, revelation, tongue, and the like (v. 26). This would have been considered shameful behavior in Greco-Roman society. The idea of women blurting out questions wasn't tolerated during pagan worship. The native cults were strictly regulated, and such activity would most certainly have been frowned on. Even in the oriental cults, matters of worship were in the hands of the professional clergy (i.e., priests and priestesses) and not the laity.[109]

Why would married women be the ones asking the questions? Wouldn't all women want to learn? The key is in grasping the educational limits of married women. Formal instruction stopped for most girls at the marriageable age of fourteen (Greek) or sixteen to eighteen (Roman). Greek boys, by contrast, contin-

---

[108]See, e.g., Carson, "Silent in the Churches," 147, 151.

[109]For further discussion, see Belleville, *Women Leaders and the Church*, 32.

ued their education well into their twenties and did not typically
marry until their thirties. A good liberal arts education was seen
as crucial for the development of boys into responsible male citizens. Thus, the men brought a maturity to the marriage relationship the women did not have, and they were in a position to
"rule," while women were not. Lower-class women, in particular, would not have been in a position to pursue a career path
involving formal instruction ("not many of you were wise by
human standards" [1:26]). Add to this the all-consuming task of
raising children and running a household, and we have a group
who, tasting freedom in Christ to expand their minds, grabbed
at the opportunity—albeit in a less than suitable fashion.[110]

The fact that Paul concludes this section (14:26–40) with a
congregational rebuke regarding orderliness indicates the
Corinthian leaders were encouraging a disorderly exercise of
gifts and the questions that came in their wake. The solution is
not to fixate on one aspect of Paul's corrective ("Women should
remain silent in the churches") and ignore the rest ("If they [the
married women] want to inquire about something, let them ask
their own husbands at home). While the Corinthian women in
their eagerness to learn may have been at fault back then, it
could easily be a different group today.

This is as far as a plain reading of the text goes. There are
several other aspects, however, that beg for clarification. First,
with what does "as in all the congregations of the Lord's people"
go (v. 33b)? If it goes with what follows, then Paul is saying that
the silence of women in the church is a matter of universal practice: "As in all the congregations of the Lord's people, women
should remain silent in the churches." If it goes with what precedes, then Paul is stating that orderly worship is a matter of universal practice: "God is not a God of disorder but of peace, as in
all the congregations of the Lord's people." Readers of the NIV
will not know this is an issue, for the NIV starts Paul's correction
with "As in all the congregations of the saints" (v. 33b) and does
not even provide a footnote indicating a genuine ambiguity.[111]

---

[110]D. A. Carson calls this "unbearably sexist" ("Silent in the Churches," 147),
but it is only so if judged by modern educational standards. It is crucial to read the
text in light of first-century Greco-Roman culture and not twenty-first century Western culture. For more on cultural background, see Belleville, *Women Leaders and the
Church*, 31–32.

[111]Both are equally Paul's practice. See, e.g., Eph. 5:1 NIV: "Be imitators of God,
therefore, *as dearly loved children*," and Eph. 5:8 AT: "*As children of light*, so walk." Yet,

Second, Paul does not specify to what or to whom these inquisitive women should "be in submission" (v. 34). And he states that women are to submit "as *the law* says," but he does not spell out whether this is Mosaic law, church law, or the laws of the land. Paul's brief remarks undoubtedly made sense to the Corinthians (as part of his continuing instruction). But to a modern ear listening to half of a conversation carried on almost two millennia ago, the best that can be done is to hazard an educated guess or to graciously admit ignorance.[112]

The problem is that traditionalists have difficulty admitting ignorance or even ambiguity. They tend to treat these matters as plain and factual. All too often it is simply assumed Paul is commanding women to submit to their husbands in keeping with

---

Paul's other appeals to universal practice appear only as a concluding point. "Timothy," Paul writes, "will remind you of my way of life in Christ Jesus, *as I teach everywhere in every church*" (1 Cor. 4:17 AT). "Each should retain the place in life that the Lord assigned . . . *and so I command in all the churches*" (7:17 AT). "If anyone wants to be contentious about this, *we have no other practice—nor do the churches of God*" (11:16 NIV). "For God is not a God of disorder but of peace—*as in all the congregations of the Lord's people*" fits this pattern exactly (14:33b). Also, to start a new paragraph at verse 33b would produce an awkward redundancy: "As *in all the churches* of the saints, let the women *in the churches* be silent." Why repeat "in the churches" twice in one sentence? Plus, "Let the women . . ." is a typical Pauline start to a new paragraph (e.g., Eph. 5:22; Col. 3:18 AT). Thus, it is wrongheaded for traditionalists to treat as a given the start of a paragraph at verse 33b and thus assume the universality of Paul's injunction in verse 34. See, e.g., D. A. Carson's statement ("Silent in the Churches," 147) that "Paul's rule [of silence] operates in all the churches."

[112]The sudden spotlight on married women, the awkward change of subject ("When you [plural] gather" [vv. 26–33] . . . "Let them [women] be silent" [vv. 34–35] . . . "Or did the word of God originate with you [plural]" [vv. 36–40]), and the seeming contradiction between verse 34 and 11:5 were difficult for copyists in the early centuries. This is obvious from the different places these verses appear in the text tradition. In some early manuscripts and versions, verses 34–35 follow verse 40 (D F G Itala, a Vulgate manuscript); in other early manuscripts and versions, verses 34–35 come after verse 33 (p^{46} ℵ A B Ψ K L Itala, Vulgate, Syriac, Coptic, and others). Also there is a bar-umlaut sign in codex Vaticanus indicating awareness of a textual problem, and p^{46} ℵ A D and 33 have a breaking mark at the beginning of verse 34 and at the end of verse 35. Codex Fuldensis (sixth-century manuscript of the Vulgate) has a scribal sign directing the reader to skip verses 34–35 and go to the text of verses 36–40 in the margin. (It does not move verses 34–35 to the end of the chapter, as Carson asserts ["Silent in the Churches," 141].) See Metzger, *Textual Commentary*, 499–500. The paragraphing of the UBS and Nestle-Aland editions at verse 33b and then again at verse 37 is therefore highly misleading. For a detailed treatment, see Philip B. Payne, "Fuldensis, Sigla for Variants in Vaticanus, and 1 Cor 14.34–5," *NTS* 41 (1995): 240–62; Payne, "Ms. 88 as Evidence for a Test without 1 Cor 14.34–5," *NTS* 44 (1998): 152–58.

the so-called "law" of Genesis 3:16—"and [your husband] will rule over you." Yet this is a most improbable (if not impossible) interpretation. For one thing, neither Genesis 3:16 nor any other OT text commands women to submit to their husbands. Would Paul take an OT text (Gen. 3:16) that is descriptive of a post-fall, dysfunctional marital relationship and cite it as prescriptive for the husband-wife Christian relationship? He does not do so elsewhere; why would he do so here? In fact, when the topic of marital relations surfaces in Paul, he cites Genesis 2:24 as prescriptive (Eph. 5:31–32)—and not 3:16.[113]

Actually, the immediate context offers the better clues. In 1 Corinthians 14:32 Paul states that the spirits of the prophets are submissive to the prophets. So when another prophet receives a revelation, the first prophet is to sit down and *be silent*. Those who speak in tongues are also commanded to *be silent*, if there is no one to interpret. If one follows Paul's thinking carefully, "submission" and "silence" are two sides of the same coin. To be silent is to be submissive—and to be submissive (in the context of worship) is to be silent. Control of the tongue is most likely what Paul is talking about. The speaker (be they tongue speaker, prophet, or inquirer) must "bite his or her tongue" for the sake of orderly worship.[114]

"As the law says" could then easily be understood as Roman law. Official religion of the Roman variety was closely supervised. The women who participated were carefully organized and their activities strictly regulated. The unrestrained activity and inclusive nature of oriental cults (such as the popular cult of Isis) made them immediately suspect, if for no other reason than the fear that such uninhibited behavior would adversely affect the family unit and erupt in antisocial behavior.[115]

The text tradition and versional evidence have led some scholars to conclude (with understandable justification) that verses 34–35 are not original to 1 Corinthians. See, e.g., Gordon Fee, *The First Epistle to the Corinthians* (NICNT; Grand Rapids: Eerdmans, 1987), 699–705; Jacobus Petzer, "Reconsidering the silent women of Corinth—a note on 1 Corinthians 14:34–35," *ThEv* 26 (1993): 132–38; Payne, "Fuldensis and 1 Cor 14.34–5," 240–62; Peter Lockwood, "Does 1 Corinthians 14:34–35 Exclude Women from the Pastoral Office?" *LuthThJ* 30 (1996): 30–37; Payne, "Ms. 88," 152–58.

[113]D. A. Carson ("Silent in the Churches," 152) believes Paul is citing Genesis 2:24. Yet to forsake existing loyalties, cleave to one's spouse, and become "one flesh" is the language of mutuality, not hierarchy.

[114]Other suggestions include submission to (1) the elders of the church, (2) those who evaluate prophecies, and (3) one's own spirit.

[115]See Belleville, *Women Leaders and the Church*, 36–38.

While we must leave room for some uncertainty, enough is clear about 1 Corinthians 14:34–35 to form an intelligent reconstruction: Married women, in exercising their newly acquired freedom to learn alongside the men, were disturbing the orderly flow of things by asking questions during the worship service. Paul instructs them to ask these questions of their own husbands at home (v. 35) so that worship can progress in an orderly fashion ("Everything should be done in a fitting and orderly way," v. 40). Eugene Peterson's *The Message* captures the sense with his paraphrase: "Wives must not disrupt worship, talking when they should be listening, asking questions that could more appropriately be asked of their husbands at home."

Sometimes in the heat of debate several aspects of 1 Corinthians 14 are overlooked. It is important to notice that Paul affirms the right of women to learn and be instructed. This, in and of itself, is a progressive, not a restrictive, attitude. He also affirms the right of women to ask questions. He does not question the what (women asking questions) but the how/where (during the worship service). Then too, it was not merely inquiring women who were silenced but also long-winded prophets (vv. 29–30) and unintelligible speakers (vv. 27–28). Paul's target was anyone and anything that would compromise the internal edification and external witness of the church (vv. 12, 23, 32, 40).

First Timothy 2:11–15

First Timothy 2:11–15 deals with teaching roles in a seemingly prohibitive fashion. In language somewhat similar to 1 Corinthians 14:34–35, Paul states:

> [11]A woman should learn in quietness and full submission. [12]I do not permit a woman to teach or to have authority over a man; she must be silent. [13]For Adam was formed first, then Eve. [14]And Adam was not the one deceived; it was the woman who was deceived and became a sinner. [15]But women will be saved through childbearing—if they continue in faith, love and holiness with propriety. (NIV)

The first step in getting a handle on these verses is to be clear about the letter as a whole. Why was Paul writing? It certainly was not to provide routine instruction. His stance throughout was a *corrective* one. Paul was reacting to a situation that had gotten out of hand. False teachers needed silencing (1:3–7, 18–20; 4:1–8; 5:20–22; 6:3–10, 20–21). Certain widows were going from house to house, speaking things they ought not (5:13); others had turned away from the faith altogether to follow Satan (v. 15). Certain elders needed public rebuking on account of their continuing sin ("those elders who are sinning you are to reprove before everyone, so that the others may take warning" [v. 20]);[116] others had been expelled (1:20). The men of the congregation had become angry and quarrelsome (2:8); the women were dressing inappropriately (v. 9) and learning in a disruptive manner (vv. 11–12). The congregation had turned to malicious talk, malevolent suspicions, and perpetual friction (6:4–5). Some members of the church had wandered from the faith altogether (vv. 20–21). Overall, it was an alarming scenario.

Congregational contention is likewise the keynote of chapter 2. A command for peace (as opposed to disputing) is found four times in the space of fifteen verses. Prayers for secular governing authorities are urged, "that we may live peaceful and quiet lives" (v. 2). The men of the church are enjoined to lift up hands in prayer that are free from "anger or disputing" (v. 8). The women are commanded to behave "with propriety" (vv. 9, 15), to "be quiet" (v. 12), and to learn in a peaceful (not quarrelsome) fashion (v. 11). That this contention is tied to the false teaching and divisive influence in the previous chapter (1:3–7, 18–20) is clear from the opening "I urge, then [*oun*], first of all . . ." (2:1). The subsequent "therefore [*oun*] I want . . ." does the same (v. 8).

Who were these women? Some interpret *anēr* and *gynē* in verses 11–15 as "husband" and "wife." This is reflected in the NRSV's footnote (also TNIV) at verse 12: "I permit no wife to teach or to have authority over her husband; she is to keep silent." Yet "husband" and "wife" do not fit the broader context of congregational worship. "Therefore I want the men everywhere to pray [*boulomai proseuchesthai tous andras*] . . ." (v. 8) and

---

[116]The NIV's translation of 1 Timothy 5:20 ("those who sin are to be rebuked publicly, so that the others may take warning") is misleading. The tense and mood are present indicative. So Paul is not treating a hypothetical possibility ("Should any sin, they are to be rebuked publicly") but a present reality ("Those who continue in sin, rebuke in the presence of all" NASB). The TNIV is closer to the mark: "Those elders who are sinning you are to reprove before everyone."

"Likewise, I want women . . ." (vv. 9–10 NASB) simply cannot be limited to husbands and wives. Nor can the verses that follow be read in this way. There is no indication whatsoever that Paul is shifting at verse 11 from women in general to married women in specific. True, Paul does refer to Adam and Eve in verses 13–14; but it is to Adam and Eve as the prototypical male and female, not as a married couple.

What were these women doing? One pointer is Paul's command that women learn "quietly" (*en hēsychia*, v.11) and behave "quietly" (*einai en hēsychia*, v.12; Phillips, NEB, REB, NLT, NASB, ESV). This suggests that women were disrupting worship. The men were too; they were praying in an angry and contentious way (v. 8). Since Paul targets women who teach men (v. 12) and uses the example of Adam and Eve as a corrective, it would be a fair assumption that there was a battle of the sexes going on in the congregation.

Traditionalists commonly translate the Greek *hēsychia* as "silent" and understand Paul to be prohibiting women from all forms of public speaking. In public (it is argued) women are to learn "in silence" and "be silent" (vv. 11–12; KJV, NKJV, RSV, NSRV, TEV, CEV, NIV, JB; cf. "keep quiet" TEV). This is problematic on a number of grounds. For one, it makes no sense in an instructional context. Silence is not compatible with the Socratic dialogical approach to learning in Paul's day. Also, Paul does not use the Greek term in this way elsewhere. When he has absence of speech in mind, the word he chooses is *sigaō* (Rom. 16:25; 1 Cor. 14:28, 30, 34). When he has quiet behavior in view, he uses *hēsychia* and its cognate forms (1 Thess. 4:11; 2 Thess. 3:12; 1 Tim. 2:2). In fact, the adjective *hēsychion* appears nine verses earlier with this very sense: "I urge . . . that petitions, prayers, intercession and thanksgiving be made . . . for kings and all those in authority, that we may live peaceful and quiet lives in all godliness and holiness" (1 Tim. 2:1–2).[117]

Women are encouraged to learn not merely "quietly" but also in "full submission" (v. 11). In full submission to whom or what is the question. Traditionalists usually take submission to husbands as a given. But on what grounds? "Let a woman learn

---

[117]This is also the case for the rest of the NT. See *sigaō* in Luke 9:36; 18:39; 20:26; Acts 12:17; 15:12–13 and *sigē* (noun) in Acts 21:40 and Rev. 8:1. For *hēsychia* (and related forms) as "calm" or "restful," see Luke 23:56; Acts 11:18; 21:14; 1 Thess. 4:11; 2 Thess. 3:12; 1 Pet. 3:4. For the sense "not speak," see Luke 14:4 and, perhaps, Acts 22:2.

..." does not suggest anything of the sort. In a learning context, it is logical to think in terms either of submission to teachers or of self-control (e.g., 1 Cor. 14:32). Submission to a teacher well suits a learning context, but so does self-control. A calm, submissive spirit was a necessary prerequisite for learning back then.[118]

What about the teaching prohibition in verse 12? There are several aspects that make the plain sense difficult to determine. One problematic feature is Paul's choice of verb form. Paul's command in verse 11 sets the reader up to expect an imperative in verse 12—especially since verse 12 is set in contrast with verse 11. The initial *de* ("but") makes this quite clear: "Let a woman learn in a quiet and submissive fashion, but *do not* let her teach ..." is what we expect. Instead, we have the indicative: "Let a woman learn ... , but *I do not* permit her to teach ..." (AT). Some have suggested that the present indicative is used because it allows Paul to give a temporary restriction: "I am not permitting [at this time]" (JB). This has some merit. "Do not let a woman teach ..." would certainly communicate a universal norm. If this wasn't Paul's intent, then a shift from a command (*manthanetō*) to a present state of affairs (*epitrepō*) would make sense.

The exact wording of Paul's restriction needs to be carefully examined. What kind of teaching is Paul prohibiting here? Traditionalists are quick to assume a teaching office or other position of authority. But teaching in the NT period was an activity, not an office (Matt. 28:19–20), and it was a gift, not a position of authority (Rom. 12:7; 1 Cor. 12:28; 14:26; Eph. 4:11). It was something every believer was called to do, not merely church leaders (Col. 3:16; Heb. 5:12).

There is also the assumption that authority resides in the act of teaching (or in the person who teaches). In point of fact, it resides in the deposit of truth ("the truths of the faith" [1 Tim. 3:9; 4:6], "the faith" [4:1; 5:8; 6:10, 12, 21], "what has been entrusted" [6:20])—that which Jesus passed on to his disciples and they in turn passed on to their disciples [2 Tim. 2:2]). The Greek term for "authority" (*exousia*) is simply not used of either local church leadership or the activity of teaching (see above). Teaching is subject to evaluation, just like any other ministry role. This is why Paul instructed Timothy to "reprove before

---

[118]For further discussion, see Kevin Giles, "Response," in *The Bible and Women's Ministry: An Australian Dialogue*, ed. A. Nichols (Canberra: Acorn Press, 1990), 73.

everyone" (1 Tim. 5:20) anyone who departed from "the sound instruction of our Lord Jesus Christ" (6:3).

Traditionalists counter with the claim that teaching in 1 Timothy takes on the more official sense of "doctrine"—and teaching doctrine is something women can't do. Yet "doctrine" as a system of thought is foreign to 1 Timothy. Traditions, yes; doctrines, no. While Paul urged Timothy to "command and teach these things" (4:11), these "things" are not doctrines. They included matters like avoiding godless myths and old wives' tales (4:7), godly training (vv. 7–8), God as the Savior of all (vv. 9–10), and slaves treating masters with full respect (6:1–2). The flaw therefore lies in translating the Greek *hygiainousē didaskalia* as "sound doctrine" instead of "sound [good] teaching" (1:10; 4:6; cf. 6:1, 3; 2 Tim. 4:3; Titus 1:9; 2:1).

Without a doubt, the most difficult phrase in 1 Timothy 2:12 to unpack is *oude authentein andros*—variously translated "nor to dominate a man" or "nor to exercise authority over a man." To unpack its meaning two questions must be answered. First, what is the sense of *authentein*? Does it mean "to exercise authority" (i.e., to carry out one's official duties)? Or is its sense "to dominate," "to get one's way," as a growing number of NT scholars are saying? A second, equally important question is the function of the "neither . . . nor" (*ouk . . . oude*) construction. In general, it serves to define a single, coherent idea. But defining the exact coherent idea in the case of this verse needs careful attention.

It cannot be stressed enough that in *authentein* Paul picked a term used nowhere else in the NT and only twice in the entire Greek Bible. More, in the Greek OT (LXX), its usage does not easily fit our passage. In the Wisdom of Solomon 12:6, it is used of the act of "murder": "Those [the Canaanites] who lived long ago in your holy land, you hated for their detestable practices . . . parents who murder [*authentas*] helpless lives" (NRSV). In 3 Maccabees 2:28–29, it means place of "origin": "All Jews [in Alexandria] shall be subjected to a registration . . . in accordance with their [Egyptian] *origin* [*authentian*] of record."[119]

---

[119]R. H. Charles's edition of the Pseudepigrapha (*The Apocrypha and the Pseudepigrapha of the Old Testament*, 2 vols. [London: Oxford, 1913]) has "they shall also be registered according to their former *restricted status*." But this does not fit the lexical range of possibilities for *authentia*.

These two uses in the Greek Bible should give us pause in opting for the translation "to exercise or to have authority over." If Paul had wanted to speak of an ordinary exercise of authority, he could have picked any number of words. For instance, within the semantic domain of "to exercise authority," Louw and Nida's lexicon has twelve entries, and of "to rule," "to govern," forty-seven.[120] Yet Paul picked none of these. Why not? A logical reason is that *authentein* carried a needed nuance that was particularly suited to the Ephesian situation.

What is this nuance, though? The semantic range of *authentein* includes not only *murderer* but also *sponsor*, *perpetrator*, *originator*, and *mastermind* of a crime or act of violence. For instance, the Jewish historian Josephus speaks of the "author" (*authentēn*) of a poisonous drink (*J.W.* 1.582; 2.240). Diodorus of Sicily talks of the "sponsors" (*authentas*) of daring plans, the "perpetrators" (*authentais*) of a sacrilege, and the "mastermind" (*authentas*) of a crime (*Bibl. hist.* 17.5.4.5., first century BC). But there is nothing that comes close to the NIV's "have authority over" or the ESV's "exercise authority over." "Master" can be found, but it is in the sense of the "mastermind" of a crime rather than one who exercises authority over another. For example, in the first and second centuries BC, historians used it of those who masterminded and carried out such exploits as the massacre of the Thracians at Maronea (Polybius, *Hist.* 22.14.2.3, second century BC) and the robbing of the sacred shrine at Delphi (Diodorus, *Bibl. hist.* 17.5.4.5).

Verb forms contemporary with or prior to Paul (including the verbal noun [infinitive] and verbal adjective [participle]) are rare to nonexistent in Greek literary and nonliterary materials. There are a mere handful of uses of *authenteō* in the Greek databases (*TLG*; *PHI*); but they do shed some light on the verbal noun *authentein* in 1 Timothy 2:12.

In his explanatory remarks—or *scholia*—on a passage from Aeschylus's tragedy *Eumenides*, the commentator uses this Greek term in its typical sense of the perpetrator of a murder: "[Orestes's] hands *were dripping* blood ..." (42). Comment: "This is the murderer, who has just now *committed an act of violence* [*authentēkota*]." The first-century BC grammarian Aristonicus uses this term of the *author* or *originator* (*ho authentōn*) "who would speak for

---

[120]L&N 37.35–47; 48–95. *Authentein* is noticeably absent from either of these domains.

Odysseus, who relates the things which had been spoken by Achilles" (*On the Signs of the Iliad* 9.694).

In a 27/26 BC letter, the term is used of *having one's way* in a dispute about what to pay the ferryman for shipping a load of cattle: "And I had my way with him [*authentēkotos pros auton*], and he agreed to provide Calatytis the boatman with the full fare within the hour" (BGU IV 1208).[121]

Philodemus, the first-century BC Greek poet and Epicurean philosopher from Gadara, Syria, employs this term to describe *dominating* public figures: "Rhetors harm a great number of people in many ways—those 'shot through with dreadful desires'; [rhetors] fight every chance they get with prominent people— 'with *powerful* lords' [*syn authent[ou]sin anaxin*].... Philosophers, on the other hand, gain the favor of public figures ... not having them as enemies but friends ... on account of their endearing qualities" (*Rhet.* II, 133. Fragmenta Libri [V] frg. IV line 14).[122]

Late first- / early second-century astrological poets use the term to denote *dominating* planets. Dorotheus states that "if Jupiter aspects the Moon from trine, ... it makes [the natives] leaders or chiefs, some of civilians and others of soldiers, especially if the Moon is increasing; but if the Moon decreases, it does not make them *dominant* [*authentas*] but subservient [*hyperetoumenous*]" (*Carmen Astrologicum*, 346). Along similar lines, the second-century mathematician Ptolemy states, "Therefore, if Saturn alone takes planetary control of the soul and *dominates* [*authentēsas*] Mercury and the moon [who govern the soul] [and]

---

[121]Evangelical scholarship has been erroneously dependent for its understanding of *authentein* on George Knight III's 1984 study ("*Authenteō* in Reference to Women in 1 Timothy 2:12," *NTS* 30 [1984]: 143–57) and his translation of *authentēkotos pros auton* as "I exercised authority over him." Yet this hardly fits the mundane details of the text (i.e., payment of a boat fare). Nor can *pros auton* be understood as "*over* him." The preposition plus the accusative does not bear this sense in Greek. "To/toward," "against," and "with" (and less frequently "at," "for," "with reference to," "on," and "on account of") are the range of possible meanings. See LSJ 1497 [C. *with the accusative*]. Here it likely means something like "I had my way *with* him, or perhaps "I took a firm stand *with* him."

[122]See Philodemus, "The Rhetorica of Philodemus," trans. Harry Hubbell (Transactions of the Connecticut Academy of Arts and Sciences [1920], 23:306). Knight's analysis is flawed. He states that "the key term is *authent[ou]sin*" and claims that the rendition offered by Hubbell is "they [orators] are men who incur the enmity of those in authority." But Hubbell actually renders *authent[ou]sin* rightly as an adjective meaning "powerful" and modifying the noun "lords."

if Saturn has a dignified position toward both the solar system and its angles, then [Saturn] makes [them] lovers of the body ... *dictatorial, ready to punish.* ... But Saturn allied with Jupiter ... makes his subjects good, respectful to elders, sedate, noble-minded" (*Tetrabiblos* III. 13 [#157]).[123]

Ancient Greek grammarians and lexicographers give the meaning "to dominate," "to hold sway," and find its origin in first-century popular ("vulgar" versus literary) usage. That is why the second-century lexicographer Moeris states that the Attic *autodikein* ("to have independent jurisdiction," "self-determination") is to be preferred to the Hellenistic (or Koine) *authentēs*.[124] Modern lexicographers agree. Those who have studied the Hellenistic letters argue that *authenteō* originated in the popular Greek vocabulary as a synonym for "to dominate someone" (*kratein tinos*).[125] Biblical lexicographers Louw and Nida put *authenteō* into the semantic domain "to control, restrain, domineer," and define the verb as "to control in a domineering manner": "I do not allow women ... to dominate men" (1 Tim. 2:12).[126] Other meanings do not appear until well into the third and fourth centuries AD.[127]

---

[123]Although Dorotheus and Ptolemy postdate Paul, they nonetheless provide an important witness to the continuing use of *authenteō* to mean "to hold sway over," "to dominate," and to the developing meaning of "leader," "chief," in the post-apostolic period.

[124]See Moeris, *Attic Lexicon*, ed. J. Pierson (Leyden, 1759), 58. Compare fourteenth-century Atticist Thomas Magister (*Grammar* 18.8), who urges his pupils to use *autodikein* because *authentein* is vulgar.

[125]See, e.g., Theodor Nageli, "*Authenteō*," in *Der Wörtschatz des Apostles Paulus* (Göttingen: Vandenhoeck & Ruprecht, 1905), 49–50; compare MM, "*Authenteō*," and Liddell, Scott, and Jonès, *Greek-English Lexicon*, "*Authenteō*," to have full power over"; online at www.perseus.tufts.edu/cgi-bin/ptext?doc=Perseus%3Atext%3A1999.04.0057%3Aentry%3D%2317366.

[126]Louw and Nida also note that "to control in a domineering manner" is often expressed idiomatically as "to shout orders at," "to act like a chief toward," or "to bark at." The use of the verb in 1 Tim. 2:12 comes quite naturally out of the word "master," or "autocrat"; cf. BDAG, which defines *authentēs* as "to assume a stance of independent authority, give orders to, dictate to," s.v.

[127]The noun *authentēs* used of an "owner" or "master" appears a bit earlier. See, e.g., *Shepherd of Hermas* 9.5.6: "Let us go to the tower, for the *owner* of the tower is coming to inspect it." For the second-century dating of the *Hermas* 5.82, see Michael Holmes, *Apostolic Fathers*, 2d ed. (Grand Rapids: Baker, 1992), 331. There is a disputed reading of *authentēs* in Euripides' *Suppliant Women* (442). Arthur Way (*Euripides: Suppliants* [Cambridge, Mass.: Harvard Univ. Press, 1971], 534) emends the text to read *euthyntes* ("when people *pilot* the land") instead of *authentēs*. David

So there is no first-century warrant for translating *authentein* as "to exercise or have authority over" and for understanding Paul in 1 Timothy 2:12 to be speaking of the carrying out of one's official duties. Rather the sense in everyday usage is "to dominate," "to get one's way." The NIV's "to have authority over," therefore, must be understood in the sense of holding sway or having dominance over another. This is supported by the grammar of the verse. If Paul had a routine exercise of authority in view, he would have put it first, followed by teaching as a specific example. Instead he starts with teaching, followed by *authentein* as a specific example. Given this word order, *authentein*—meaning "to dominate or to gain the upper hand"—provides the best fit in the context.

Early Latin versions share a similar opinion (emphasis added):

- Old Latin (second–fourth century AD): "I permit not a woman to teach, neither to *dominate* a man [*neque dominari viro*]."
- Vulgate (fourth–fifth century AD): "I permit not a woman to teach, neither to *domineer over* a man [*neque dominari in virum*]."

In fact, there is a basically unbroken tradition, stemming from the oldest version and running down to the twenty-first century, that translates *authentein* as "to dominate" and not "to exercise authority over":[128]

Kovacs (*Euripides: Suppliant Women, Electra, Heracles* [Cambridge, Mass.: Harvard Univ. Press, 1998], 57) deletes lines 442–55 as not original. Thus Carroll Osburn erroneously cites this text as "establishing a fifth-century B.C. usage of the term *authentēs*, meaning 'to exercise authority,'" and mistakenly faults Catherine Clark Kroeger for not dealing with it (Carroll Osburn, "*Authentēs* [1 Timothy 2:12]," *ResQ* [1982]: 2, n. 5).

[128]A wide range of moderns follow the same tradition: *Louis Segond Version* (French, 1910): "I do not permit the woman to teach, neither to take authority over [*prendre autorite sur*] the man." *Goodspeed* (1923): "I do not allow women to teach or to domineer over men." *La Sainte* (French, 1938): "I do not permit the woman to teach, neither to take authority over [*prendre de l'autorité sur*] the man." NEB (1961): " I do not permit a woman to be a teacher, nor must woman domineer over man." BJ (French, 1973): "I do not permit the woman to teach, neither to lay down the law for [*faire la loi a*] the man." REB (1989): "I do not permit women to teach or dictate to the men." *The Message*: "I don't let women take over and tell the men what to do." *The New Translation* (1990): "I do not permit a woman to teach or *dominate* men." CEV (1991): "They should . . . not be allowed to teach or to tell men what to do."

There are two notable exceptions: (1) Martin Luther (1522): "Einem Weibe aber gestatte ich nicht, daß sie lehre, auch nicht, daß sie des Mannes Herr sei." Luther, in

- Geneva (1560 edition): "I permit not a woman to teache, neither to vsurpe authoritie ouer the man."
- Casiodoro de Reina (1560–61): "I do not permit the woman to teach, neither to take authority over the man [*ni tomar autoridad sobre el hombre*]."
- Bishop (1589): "I suffer not a woman to teache, neither to vsurpe auctoritie ouer ye man."
- KJV (1611): "I suffer not a woman to teach, nor to usurp authority over the man."

English translations from the 1940s to the early 1980s tend to obscure this. A hierarchical, noninclusive understanding of leadership is partly to blame. Women aren't supposed to be leaders, so the language of leadership, where women are involved, tends to be manipulated. First Timothy 2:12 is one of the primary places where this sort of bias surfaces. Post–World War II translations routinely render the clause as "I do not permit a woman to teach or to have [exercise, assume] authority over a man" (e.g., RSV, NRSV, NAB, Revised NAB, TEV, NASB, JB, NJB, NCV, GWT, NLT, CSB, ESV, NIV, TNIV)—although some, such as the BBE, qualify it with "In my [Paul's] opinion."

Post-NT, the noun *authentēs* does not appear in Christian literature until the mid- to late-second century AD (Irenaeus, Clement of Alexandria, and the Shepherd of Hermas)—far too late to provide a linguistic context for Paul. The verb does not occur until well into the third century AD (Hippolytus). The predominant usage is still "murderer" (Clement), but one also finds divine "authority" (Irenaeus, Clement, Origen) and "master" (Hermas). The rest (the vast majority) are uses of the adjective ("authentic," "genuine") so common in Greek papyri and inscriptions in the AD period (Pseudo-Clement, Clement of Alexandria, Origen).

But where do we go from here? The correlative construction "neither ... nor" (*ouk ... oude*) is what links the infinitives "to teach" and "to dominate." So it is important to establish the nature

---

turn, influenced William Tyndale (1525–26): "I suffer not a woman to teach, neither to have authority over the man." (2) DV (1582): "But to teach I permit not vnto a woman, nor to haue dominion ouer the man" The DV, in turn, influenced the ASV ("nor to have dominion over a man") and subsequent revisions of Reina's *La Santa Biblia*. See, e.g., the 1602 Valera revision: "*ni ejercer domino sobre* [neither to exercise dominion over]."

of this linkage. In biblical Greek (and Hebrew), "neither ... nor" is a poetic device that normally sets in parallel two or more natural groupings of words, phrases, or clauses (e.g., "will neither slumber nor sleep" [Ps. 121:4]). "Neither ... nor" constructions in the NT serve to pair or group synonyms (e.g., "neither despised nor scorned" [Gal. 4:14 AT]), closely related ideas (e.g., "neither of the night nor of the dark" [1 Thess. 5:5 AT]), or antonyms (e.g., "neither Jew nor Gentile, neither slave nor free" [Gal. 3:28]). They also function to move from the general to the particular (e.g., "wisdom neither of this age nor of the rulers of this age" [1 Cor. 2:6 AT]), to define a natural progression of related ideas (e.g., "they neither sow nor reap nor gather into barns" [Matt. 6:26 AT]), or to define a related purpose or a goal (e.g., "where thieves neither break in nor steal [i.e., break in to steal]" [6:20 AT]).[129]

Of the options listed above, it is plain that "teach" and "dominate" are not synonyms, closely related ideas, or antonyms. If *authentein* did mean "to exercise authority," we might have a movement from general to particular. But the word order would need to be "neither to exercise authority [general] nor to teach [particular]." They do not form a natural progression of related ideas either ("first teach, then dominate"). On the other hand, to define a purpose or goal actually provides quite a good fit: "I do not permit a woman to teach in order to gain mastery over a man," or "I do not permit a woman to teach with a view to dominating a man."[130] It also results in a good point of

---

[129]Other examples (all AT) include (1) *Synonyms*: "neither labors nor spins" (Matt. 6:28); "neither quarreled nor cried out" (Matt. 12:19); "neither abandoned nor given up" (Acts 2:27); "neither leave nor forsake" (Heb. 13:5); "neither run in vain nor labor in vain" (Phil. 2:16). (2) *Closely related ideas*: "neither the desire nor the effort" (Rom. 9:16); "neither the sun nor the moon" (Rev. 21:23). (3) *Antonyms*: "neither a good tree ... nor a bad tree" (Matt. 7:18); "neither the one who did harm nor the one who was harmed" (2 Cor. 7:12). (4) *General to particular*: "you know neither the day nor the hour" (Matt. 25:13); "I neither consulted with flesh and blood nor went up to Jerusalem" (Gal. 1:16–17). (5) *Natural progression of closely related ideas*: "born neither of blood, nor of the human will, nor of the will of man" (John 1:13); "neither the Christ, nor Elijah, nor the Prophet" (John 1:25); "neither from man nor through man" (Gal. 1:1). (6) *Goal or purpose*: "neither hears nor understands [i.e., hears with the intent to understand]" (Matt. 13:13); "neither dwells in temples made with human hands nor is served by human hands [i.e., dwells with a view to being served]" (Acts 17:24). See Belleville, *Women Leaders and the Church*, 176–77.

[130]Along somewhat similar lines, Donald Kushke ("An Exegetical Brief on 1 Timothy 2:12," *WisconsinLuthQ* 88 [1991]: 64) suggests that *oude* introduces an explanation: "to teach in an authoritative fashion."

contrast with the second part of 1 Timothy 2:12: "I do not permit a woman to teach a man in a dominating way but to have a quiet demeanor" (lit., "to be in calmness").[131]

Paul would then be prohibiting teaching that tries to get the upper hand (not teaching per se). A reasonable reconstruction would be as follows: The women at Ephesus (perhaps encouraged by false teachers) were trying to gain an advantage over the men in the congregation by teaching in a dictatorial fashion. The men in response became angry and disputed what the women were doing. This interpretation fits the broader context of 1 Timothy 2:8–15, where Paul aims to correct inappropriate behavior on the part of both men and women (vv. 8, 11). It also fits the grammatical flow of verses 11–12: "Let a woman learn in a quiet and submissive fashion. I do not, however, permit her to teach with the intent to dominate a man. She must be gentle in her demeanor."

Why were the Ephesian women acting this way? One explanation is that they were influenced by the cult of Artemis, where the female was exalted and considered superior to the male. The importance of this cult to the citizens of Ephesus in Paul's day is evident from Luke's record of their two-hour chant—"Great is Artemis of the Ephesians" (Acts 19:28, 34). One reason is the legend that Iphigenia, the daughter of Agamemnon, landed with the image of Artemis when she fled from the Tauroi (Pausanias, *Guide to Greece* 1.33.1), and the renown of the Amazons, who traditionally dedicated the image.[132] Another reason is Artemis's genealogy. Artemis (and brother Apollo), it was believed, was the child of Zeus and Leto (Lat. *Latona*); she spurned the male gods and sought the company of a human consort named Leimon. This is played out at the feast of the Lord of Streets, when the priestess of Artemis pursues a man,

---

[131]Philip Payne highlighted the importance of the "neither ... nor" construction in a paper presented at an ETS annual meeting ("*Oude* in 1 Timothy 2:12," [Nov. 21, 1986]). His own position is that "neither ... nor" in this verse joins two closely associated couplets (e.g., "hit-and-run"—"teach-and-domineer").

[132]See Pausanias, *Guide to Greece* 4.31.8; 8.53.3. Artemis is sometimes misrepresented as the goddess of the hunt. She became known as a huntress in tracking down Oeneus son of Porthaon, king of Calydon, because in sacrificing the firstfruits of the annual crops of the country to all the gods, Artemis alone was forgotten. It is told that in her wrath she sent a boar of extraordinary size and strength, which prevented the land from being sown and destroyed the cattle and the people that fell in with it. See Pseudo-Apollodorus, *Library* 1.67; Pausanias, *Guide to Greece* 7.18.10.

pretending she is Artemis herself pursuing Leimon. This made Artemis and all her female adherents superior to men.[133]

An Artemis influence would certainly explain Paul's correctives in verses 13–14. While some may have believed that Artemis appeared first and then her male consort, the true story was just the opposite. For Adam was formed first, then Eve (v. 13).[134] And Eve was deceived to boot (v. 14)—hardly a basis on which to claim superiority. It would also explain Paul's statement (v. 15) that "women will be kept safe through childbirth" (BBE, *Darby*, NASB, NIV [1973, 1978 editions]); for Artemis was the protector of women. Women turned to her for safe travel through the childbearing process (Pausanias, *Guide to Greece* 10.38.12).[135] Pseudo-Apollodorus records that immediately after

---

[133]For further details, see Sharon H. Gritz, *Paul, Women Teachers, and the Mother Goddess at Ephesus: A Study of 1 Timothy 2:9–15 in Light of the Religious and Cultural Milieu of the First Century* (Lanham, Md.: University Press of America, 1991), 31–41; "Artemis," *Encyclopaedia Brittanica Online* at www.eb.com. "Of the daughters of Coeus, Asteria in the likeness of a quail flung herself into the sea in order to escape the amorous advances of Zeus, and a city was formerly called after her Asteria, but afterwards it was named Delos. But Latona for her intrigue with Zeus was hunted by Hera over the whole earth, till she came to Delos and brought forth first Artemis, by the help of whose midwifery she afterwards gave birth to Apollo" (Pseudo-Apollodorus, *Library* 1.27).

[134]Traditionalists typically interpret *gar* at the start of verse 13 as causal rather than explanatory, and so they see it as introducing a "creation order" dictum: Women (so it goes) must not teach men because men according to the order of creation were intended to lead; and Eve's proneness to deception while taking the lead demonstrates this. This reading of the text is problematic for a number of reasons. First, there is nothing in the context to support it. In fact, verse 15 is against it: "Women must not teach men because Eve was deceived, but she will be saved through childbearing" is nonsense. Second, although some are quick to assume a creation-fall ordering in verses 13–14, virtually all stop short of including "women will be saved [or kept safe] through childbearing" (v. 15). To do so, though, is to lack hermeneutical integrity. Either all three statements are normative or all three are not.

[135]As the mother-goddess, Artemis was the mother of life, the nourisher of all creatures, and the power of fertility in nature. Maidens turned to her as the protector of their virginity, barren women sought her aid, and women in labor turned to her for help. See Gritz, *Mother Goddess at Ephesus*, 31–41; "Artemis," *Encyclopaedia Brittanica Online*. S. M. Baugh ("A Foreign World," 28–33) takes issue with the premise that Artemis worship was a fusion of a fertility cult of the mother-goddess of Asia Minor and the Greek virgin goddess of the hunt. The fourth-century BC "Rituals for Brides and Pregnant Women in the Worship of Artemis" (*LSCG Suppl.* 15) and other literary sources support the fusion. See Gritz, *Mother Goddess at Ephesus*, 31–41; F. Sokolowski, *Lois sacreaes de l'Asie Mineure* (Paris, 1955).

her birth Artemis helped her younger twin brother Apollo to be born into the world (*Library*, 1.26; cf. Servius, *In Vergili carmina commentarii* 3.73; Vatican mythographers). For this reason, the maiden-goddess Artemis was invoked by women during labor.

Traditionalists claim that by naming Adam as "first" in the process of creation, Paul is saying something about male leadership ("For Adam was formed first, then Eve" [v. 13]). Yet "first ... then" (*prōtos ... eita*) language in Paul (and, for that matter, in the NT) does nothing more than define a sequence of events or ideas (e.g., Mark 4:28; 1 Cor. 15:46; 1 Thess. 4:16–17; Jas. 3:17). In fact, ten verses later Paul uses it in this very way. "Let them also be tested first [*prōton*]," he states, "then [*eita*] let them serve as deacons" (1 Tim. 3:10 ESV).

And what about Eve's seniority in transgression? Isn't Paul using Eve as an example of what can go wrong when women usurp the male's created leadership role ("And Adam was not the one deceived; it was the woman who was deceived and became a sinner," 2:14)?[136] Traditionalists say this, but without scriptural support, for Eve was not deceived by the serpent into taking the lead in the male-female relationship. She was deceived into disobeying a command of God (not to eat the fruit from the tree of the knowledge of good and evil). She listened to the voice of false teaching and was deceived by it. Paul's warning to the Corinthian congregation confirms this: "I am afraid that just as Eve was deceived by the serpent's cunning, your minds may somehow be led astray from your sincere and pure devotion to Christ" (2 Cor. 11:3).

The language of deception calls to mind the activities of the false teachers at Ephesus. If the Ephesian women were being encouraged to assume the role of teacher over men as the superior sex, this would go a long way toward explaining 1 Timothy 2:13–14. The relationship between the sexes was not intended to be one of female domination and male subordination; but neither was it intended to be one of male domination and female subordination. Such thinking is native to a fallen creation order (Gen. 3:16).

---

[136]See, e.g., Michael Stitzinger, "Cultural Confusion and the Role of Women in the Church: A Study of 1 Timothy 2:8–14," *CBTJ* 4 (1988): 34; James Hurley, *Man and Woman in Biblical Perspective* (Grand Rapids: Zondervan, 1981), 216.

We must not lose track, however, of Paul's flow of thought in these verses. Paul affirms a woman's right to learn and to be instructed. "Let a woman learn" is the way the passage begins. *How* they are to learn is the issue at hand, not their right to do so. It is reasonable, then, to think that how they learned and how they taught were the actual issues behind Paul's statements in verses 11–12.

THE RELATIONSHIP OF MALE AND FEMALE

What the foregoing demonstrates is that what fundamentally separates traditionalists and egalitarians is a different understanding of the created order of male and female. While 1 Timothy 2:11–15 (with rare exception) is the starting point for traditionalists, the reason for this is easily missed. It is not a belief that women are not to teach, for Paul himself instructed the older women in the Cretan congregation to (literally) "teach well" (*kalodidaskalous*) the younger women (Titus 2:3–5); nor is it a belief that women are not to teach publicly—although this is a common traditionalist conclusion. It is rather a belief that women are not to *lead* men— not in the family, not in the workplace, not in the community, and not in the church. For instance, a woman who is asked by a male passerby for directions must provide them in such a way that the man's leadership is not compromised.[137] To do otherwise (so it is argued) is to reverse God's created order and to blur the basic distinction between male and female: Men are created to lead; women are created to submit.

Gender hierarchy is what is behind the egalitarian challenge that appeared in the March 1998 newsletter of the CBMW.[138] Wayne Grudem challenged egalitarians either to answer six questions or to admit once and for all that an egalitarian (i.e., an equal and mutual) relationship of male and female is not a biblical one. The first five challenges were to produce one extrabiblical text where:

- the Greek *kephalē* is used of one person being the "source" of another (versus "person in authority over" [Eph. 5:22–33]);

---

[137]See Piper, "Vision of Biblical Complementarity," 50–51.
[138]Wayne Grudem, "An open letter to egalitarians," *JBMW* 3 (March 1998): 1, 3–4.

- the Greek *hypotassō* is used of mutual (versus one-directional) submission (Eph. 5:21);
- the Greek particle *ē* introduces a negative response ("What!") to the previously stated position of the reader (versus "or" [1 Cor. 14:36]);
- the Greek verb *authenteō* bears the sense "to domineer," or "to usurp authority" (versus "to exercise authority over" [1 Tim. 2:12]);
- the verbs in the Greek construction "neither" + [verb 1] + nor + [verb 2] can be antonyms (versus synonymous or parallel ideas [1 Tim. 2:12]).

The sixth challenge was to show that women teaching false doctrine at Ephesus was the problem Paul addressed in 1 Timothy.

One difficulty with such challenges is that egalitarians can produce a similar list of questions that pose an equal challenge. Egalitarians, for example, can challenge traditionalists to produce one first-century extrabiblical text where:

- the Greek reciprocal pronoun *allēlous* means "submit *some to others*" (versus *"one to another"* as claimed in Eph. 5:21);
- the apostle *Iounian* is a masculine *Junias* versus feminine *Junia* (as claimed in Rom. 16:7);
- the Greek word *authentein* is used of the routine exercise of the authority of one person (or group) over another (as claimed in 1 Tim. 2:12).

If examples are not forthcoming, then traditionalists must admit a hierarchical relationship of male and female is not the divine standard.

Another difficulty is how the questions are framed. The CBMW's challenge does not recognize two key facts. First, Christianity is by nature countercultural. Just because mutual submission was not the Greco-Roman way (and so not found in extrabiblical first-century texts) does not mean it was not the Christian way (and so found in the biblical texts).[139] In fact, the standard lexica state as much: "To spontaneously position oneself as a servant toward one's neighbor in the hierarchy of love ... is

---

[139]Every Greek lexicon I consulted states that Ephesians 5:21 has no secular parallel. See, e.g., BAGD, s.v.; *TLNT* 3:424–26. Even the NT concept of submission has no secular parallel.

absolutely new."[140] Second, the CBMW's challenge ignores two basic principles in interpreting biblical texts: (1) Context determines meaning, and (2) Scripture interprets Scripture. If these two principles are applied to their six questions, then answers are easy to come by.

Mutual Submission

Even a cursory look at Paul's writings shows that mutual submission is basic to his understanding of how believers are to relate to one another (over against Greco-Roman hierarchy). "Not looking to your own interests," Paul states, "but each of you to the interests of the others" (Phil. 2:4). The addition of the reciprocal pronoun *allēlois* ("to one another") to Paul's command for submission (lit., "submit yourselves" [*hypotassomenoi*]) in Ephesians 5:21 makes this absolutely clear. *Allēlois* simply cannot bear any other lexical meaning but a reciprocal one (see LSJ, s.v.).[141]

Also, the grammar and syntax of Ephesians 5:18–21 demand the idea of mutual submission. The main verb (and therefore the main command) is in verse 18: "Do not get drunk on wine. . . . Instead, be filled with the Spirit." What follows in verses 19–21 (all participles) are examples of Spirit-filled congregational life and worship, namely, "speaking to one another with psalms . . . , sing[ing] and mak[ing] music . . . to the Lord, always giving thanks to God . . . , submit[ting] to one another." It is hence wrong for Dr. Grudem to translate *hypotassomenoi* as a passive verb ("to be subject to"). It is the last of a series of participles that spell out the "how" of Paul's command (i.e., "Be filled with the Spirit [*by*] addressing . . . , singing . . . , giving thanks . . . , submitting to one another" ESV [emphasis added]). More, the first and fourth participles are modified by pronouns that are reciprocal in meaning ("speaking psalms . . . to each other [*lalountes heautois*]) . . . , submitting to one another"

---

[140]*TLNT* 3:426.

[141]Grudem's claim that *allēlous* [sic] in Ephesians 5:21 takes the common meaning "some to others" (as opposed to "each to the other," "mutually" [BAGD, s.v.]) does not have a lexical basis ("An open letter," 3; "The Myth of Mutual Submission," *CBMW News* 1 [1996]: 3). "Some to others" does not fit Galatians 6:2 ("Carry each other's burdens"), 1 Corinthians 11:33 ("When you gather to eat, you should all eat together"), or Revelation 6:4 ("To make people [on earth] slay each other"), as the CBMW would claim.

[*hypotassomenoi allēlois*])—making clear the specified activities are two- (versus one-) directional.[142]

To interpret verse 21 (as Grudem) "Be subject some to others in authority" smacks of an act of desperation to avoid the conclusion that the wife's submission immediately following in verses 22–24 is one example of mutuality and the husband's love in verses 25–33 another example. Because verse 22 lacks a verb (the text merely reads: "Wives to your husbands"), the preceding participle and reciprocal pronoun ("submitting one to the other" [v. 21]) must therefore be supplied. Translations such as the NIV that begin a new paragraph at verse 22 destroy the essential connection with what precedes.

The Greek Particle *Ē*

The CBMW's third challenge is rather puzzling. There are few evangelicals who argue that the Greek particle *ē* in 1 Corinthians 14:36 is Paul's signal that he is responding to the Corinthian position ("Let the women in the churches be silent" [v. 34 AT]). The simple fact is that, while *ē* can denote an exclamation expressing disapproval, the standard Greek-English lexicon of Hellenistic Greek lists only two instances, and in both cases there is a double *ē ē* ("Hey, hey!" as in, *ē ē siōpa* ["Hey, hey! Be quiet!"], Aristophanes, *Nubes* 105) and not the single *ē* we have in 1 Corinthians 14:36 (which is surely why the revisions of the KJV [i.e., NKJV] and the RSV [i.e., NRSV] drop the "What").[143]

Authenteō

The CBMW's challenge to produce extrabiblical texts where the Greek *authentein* bears the sense "to domineer" is easily met. In fact, all known extrabiblical instances of *authentein* (rare though they be) prior to the second century AD without exception have to do with power or domination.[144]

---

[142]*Heautōn* functions as a reciprocal pronoun in Ephesians 5:19. It is used this way already in classical times. *Allēlōn* and *heautōn* often appear alongside one another (e.g., Luke 23:12; 1 Cor 6:7; Col. 3:13, 16). See BDF #287.

[143]See LSJ, s.v.

[144]Compare Leland Wilshire, "1 Timothy 2:12 Revisited: A Reply to Paul W. Barnett and Timothy J. Harris," *EvQ* 65 (1993): 46–47.

1. *Scholia Graeca* in Aeschylus, *Eumenides* 42a (first century BC): "[Orestes's] hands were dripping blood; he held a sword just drawn [from avenging the death of his father by killing his mother." *Were dripping* is explained as, "The murderer, who has just now *committed an act of violence [authentēkota]*."

2. BGU 1208 (first century BC): "I had my way with him [*kamou authentēkotos pros auton*], and he agreed to provide Calatytis the boatman with the full fare within the hour." In a letter to his brother regarding the family business, Tryphon recounts the resolution of a dispute between himself and another individual regarding the amount to be paid the ferryman for shipping a load of cattle. "I exercised authority over him" hardly fits the mundane details of the text. Nor can the preposition *pros* be construed as "over." It must mean something like "I had my way with him"—or perhaps "I took a firm stand [*fest auftreten*, to stand firm]."[145]

3. Philodemus, *Rhetorica* II Fragmenta Libri [V] frg. IV line 14 (first century BC). This text is too fragmented to be certain about the exact wording. What we have is: *hoi rhētores . . . pros tous epiphanestatous hekastote diamachontai kai "syn authent[ ]sin an[ ]."* The editor's guess is *authent[ou]sin an[axin]*. The text would then read, "Rhetors . . . fight every chance they get with prominent people—'*with powerful lords.*' Philosophers, on the other hand, "gain the favor of public figures . . . not having them as enemies but friends . . . on account of their endearing qualities."

4. Artistonicus, *On the Signs of the Iliad* 9.694 (1st century BC). Commenting on this sentence from Homer's *Iliad* 9.693–4 ("So [Odysseus] spoke and [King Agamemnon and his people] all became hushed in silence, marveling at his words; for so masterfully did he address their gathering"), Aristonicus states, "This line, which appears in other places, does not fit well here; for it usually is spoken, where *the author [ho authenten]* of the message delivered something striking. But now, however,

---

[145]For this reading, see Friedrich Preisigke, "*Authenteō*," in *Wörterbuch der griechischen Papyrusurkunden*.

he [the author] would speak for Odysseus, who relates the things which had been spoken by Achilles."

5. Ptolemy, *Tetrabiblos* III. 13 [#157] (second century AD): This astronomical text "briefly considers in due order the particular traits resulting from the very nature of the planets, in this kind of domination [*tēn toiautēn kyrian*].... Therefore, if Saturn alone *takes* planetary *control* [*ten oikodespotian*] of the soul and *dominates* [*authentēs*] Mercury and the moon [who govern the soul] [and] if Saturn has a dignified position toward both the solar system and *its angles* [*ta kentra*],[146] then [Saturn] makes [them] lovers of the body ... dictatorial, ready to punish.... But Saturn allied with Jupiter ... makes his subjects good, respectful to elders, sedate, noble-minded."

"Committed an act of violence," "had my way with," "author," and "dominates"—what warrant, then, do traditionalists have in persisting to translate *authentein* as "to exercise authority" and to understand Paul in 1 Timothy 2:12 to be speaking of the carrying out of one's official duties? What makes the situation even more problematic is that the scholarship of traditionalists has not always been done with care. Most have merely quoted the flaws of George W. Knight's study of *authenteō* and have ignored subsequent scholarly corrections. More, subsequent traditionalists claim to do "fresh studies" but in fact do not translate and analyze.[147] Otherwise they would have observed such mistakes as Knight's mistranslation of Philodemus's *diamachontai kai syn authentousin anaxin* as "men who incur the enmity of those in authority" instead of "rhetors who fight with powerful lords."

"Neither ... Nor" Constructions

Current traditionalist scholarship is also flawed in its understanding of the Greek correlative *ou(k) ... oude* ("neither ... nor").

---

[146]George Knight ("*Authenteō* in Reference to Women," 145) misreads (or perhaps mistypes) translator F. E. Robbins's (LCL edition) "angles" as "angels." H. Scott Baldwin, one of the editors of *Women in the Church: A Fresh Analysis of 1 Timothy 2:9–15*, once again cites Knight's inaccuracy rather than doing a "fresh analysis," as the book's subtitle claims (see his "Appendix 2: *Authenteō* in Ancient Greek Literature," in *Women in the Church: A Fresh Analysis*, 275).

[147]See, e.g., *Women in the Church: A Fresh Analysis*.

In English, "neither" and "nor" are coordinating conjunctions that connect sentence elements of equal grammatical rank.[148] In biblical Greek, however, "neither . . . nor" connects similar or related ideas, like "[the LORD] who watches over Israel will neither slumber nor sleep" in Psalm 121:4.[149] What we are dealing with is a poetic device. And so to do a study of the Greek construction "neither" + [verb 1] + "nor" + [verb 2] is to ignore both the literary form and the nature of Greek correlatives.[150] Moreover, the most recent traditionalist study of syntactical parallels to 1 Timothy 2:12 looks only for correlated verbs (see n. 150). But verse 12 correlates infinitives (i.e., verbal nouns), not verbs. The infinitive may have tense and voice like a verb, but it functions predominantly as a noun or adjective.[151] The verb in verse 12 is actually "I permit." "To teach" modifies the noun "woman" and answers the question "What?"[152] It would be logical, then, to look for correlated nouns or adjectives. But since the Greek correlative pairs ideas, the grammatical form is really unimportant.

Does the Greek correlative pair opposites? Of course it does. "Neither Jew nor Gentile [ouk ... oude], neither slave nor free [ouk ... oude]" in Galatians 3:28 is a perfect example. Does the Greek correlative pair particular and general ideas (such as "neither to teach nor to exercise authority over")? No, it does not. It pairs general and particular ideas, as in 1 Corinthians 2:6 (AT): "wisdom neither of this age nor of the rulers of this age."[153] So, if Paul had the exercise of authority in mind, he would have put it first, followed by teaching as a specific example (i.e., "I permit a woman neither to exercise authority over nor to teach a man").

---

[148]See M. D. Shertzer, *The Elements of Grammar* (New York: Macmillan, 1986), 45–46.

[149]See BDF #445.

[150]As, e.g., Andreas J. Köstenberger does in "A Complex Sentence Structure in 1 Timothy 2:12," in *Women in the Church: A Fresh Analysis*, 81–103.

[151]Nigel Turner (*Syntax*, vol. 3, in *Grammar of New Testament Greek*, 134) classifies infinitives as "noun forms."

[152]See, e.g., James A. Brooks and Carlton L. Winbery, *Syntax of New Testament Greek* (Lanham, Md.: University Press of America, 1979), esp. "The Infinitive as a Modifier of Substantives," 141–42). Köstenberger ("Complex Sentence Structure," 81–103) does not seem to recognize that the infinitive is a verbal noun.

[153]Compare "you know *neither* the day *nor* the hour" (Matt. 25:13 NRSV); "*neither* did I consult with flesh and blood *nor* did I go up to Jerusalem to meet with those who were apostles before me" (Gal. 1:16–17 AT, emphasis added).

False Teaching and the Women of Ephesus

Dr. Grudem claims there are no explicit examples of female false teachers in 1 Timothy, and he is correct. The cumulative picture of the activities of women in 1 Timothy may well imply the existence of female false teachers, but there is no explicit reference to such. Yet this overlooks the standard interpretive principle of considering the historical situation: What prompted Paul to write this letter? Was false teaching the primary problem? Of course it was. Why else would Paul begin by instructing Timothy to "stay there in Ephesus so that you may command certain persons not to teach false doctrines any longer" (1:3). In fact false teaching consumes 35 percent of Paul's explicit attention.

Women also receive a great deal of attention in 1 Timothy. In fact, there is no other NT letter in which women figure so prominently. Paul deals with how women who pray in public are to attire themselves (2:9–11), behavior befitting women in the worship service (vv. 12–15), qualifications for women deacons (3:11), appropriate pastoral behavior toward older and younger women (5:2), the credentials of widows in ministry (vv. 9–10), and correction of younger widows (vv. 11–15). All told, 20 percent of the letter focuses on women.

Were any of the impacted leaders women? "Going about from house to house . . . , saying things they ought not to" (v. 13), having "turned away to follow Satan" (v. 15), and "always learning but never able to come to a knowledge of the truth" (2 Tim. 3:7) certainly suggest they were. At a minimum, Paul's language points to some sort of proselytizing activity (similar to Jehovah's Witnesses today).

It would therefore be very foolish (not to mention misleading) not to read 1 Timothy 2 against the backdrop of false teaching. In fact, "[the false teachers] forbid people to marry" (4:3) alone explains Paul's otherwise obscure comment that "women will be saved [or kept safe] through childbearing" (2:15) and his seemingly inconsistent command that younger widows marry and raise a family (5:14; against his advice in 1 Cor. 7).

Kephalē

The real bone of contention between traditionalists and egalitarians is the meaning of *kephalē*. For this goes to the heart of the male-female relationship. What does Paul mean when he speaks of the man as *kephalē* of the woman? Extrabiblical meanings of "source" and "leader" exist, but both, quite frankly, are rare. In a Jewish work contemporary with Paul's writings, Eve speaks of "desire" as "the source [*kephalē*] of every kind of sin" (*L.A.E.* 19), and the first-century Greek historian and moralist Plutarch recounts Catiline's plan to become the "leader" (*kephalē*) of the Roman Republic (*Cic.* 14.5). For the most part, however, biblical and extrabiblical nonliteral uses of *kephalē* have to do with the idea of "chief" or "prominent"—like the top of a mountain (e.g., Gen. 8:5), the foremost position in a column or formation (e.g., Job 1:17), the capstone of a building (e.g., Ps. 117:22), or the end of a pole (e.g., 2 Chr. 5:9). What this means is that the uses of *kephalē* in Paul (the only biblical writer to use this language) must be decided on a case-by-case basis.

Does Paul use *kephalē* to mean "source"? He most certainly does. Paul's four references to Christ as *kephalē* of his church without a doubt mean "source." Paul's language is thoroughly biological. The church is a living organism that draws its existence and nourishment from Christ as *kephalē*. Christ is *kephalē* and "savior" of the church, "his body" (Eph. 4:16; 5:22–23; Col. 1:18; 2:19);[154] he is its "beginning" and "firstborn" (Col. 1:18). "From him" (*ex hou*) the church is supported, held together, and grows (Eph. 4:16; Col. 2:19). As *kephalē* of the church, Christ "feeds and cares" for it as people do for "their own bodies" (Eph. 5:29).

Biology shapes Paul's usage in each instance, but theology is ultimately what explains it. *Kephalē* as "source" goes back to the creation of male and female. It derives from the theological notion of the first man as the "source" (*kephalē*) of the first woman. So it would be wholly inappropriate to seek parallels in Greco-Roman literature (as egalitarians are challenged to do). "We [the church]," Paul states, "are members of his [Christ's] body, [that is,] of his flesh, and of his bones" (Eph. 5:30 KJV).[155]

---

[154]In Ephesians 5:22–23, the lack of articles with *kephalē* and *sōtēr* is significant. If the text read "the Head" and "the Savior" of the church, we might think in terms of a CEO. However, the absence of articles means these two nouns describe rather than define (i.e., point not to a specific person or thing but rather to its nature or quality; so not "the Savior" (a title) but "savior," "deliverer," "preserver"). For discussion, see Zerwick, *Biblical Greek*, #171–73.

[155]Ephesians 5:30 in the Western and Byzantine families of manuscripts and versions and in church fathers from the second century on reads, "For we are members of his body, of his flesh and of his bones."

The allusion to Genesis 2:21–23 and the creation of the woman from the rib of the man is unmistakable. And so is the notion of source. The church is the Eve of the second Adam, "bone of [his] bones and flesh of [his] flesh" (Gen. 2:24). How this comes to be Paul rightly calls a "profound mystery" (Eph. 5:32).

Traditionalists would argue that Paul is speaking of the church's submission to Christ as CEO. But this certainly would not constitute a profound mystery at all. This is simply the way of the Greco-Roman world—as Jesus reminded his disciples on more than one occasion (e.g., Matt. 20:25–26). It is the church as Christ's flesh and bone that is the mystery—as early church tradition echoes.[156] This is not to say that Christ is not Lord of the church. That he is. The fact that Paul greets all his churches with the "grace of our Lord Jesus Christ" drives this home as a point of first importance. But that lordship is what Paul means by the term *kephalē* is contextually unsupportable. While our twenty-first-century thinking may lead us in this direction, the theology of Ephesians 5:23–33 does not.

It is important to not miss the real crux of the matter. What these six questions boil down to is a patriarchal view of society. The male was created as the "ruler" (*kephalē*) who "exercises authority over" (*authentein*) a woman. The woman was created to "submit" (*hypotassesthai*) to the male's authority. Women, therefore, are to be "silent" in the church; they are not permitted to lead men (like the women in Ephesus were trying to do). An egalitarian view, by contrast, is theological. It sees the male as the "source" (*kephalē*) of the female, whom God created "from him" to be his "partner." The divinely ordained relationship of male and female is therefore a mutually submissive one (*hypotassesthai*). Neither the male nor the female is to lead in a "domineering" (*authentein*) fashion (like the women in Ephesus were trying to do).

CONCLUSION

In rethinking the issue of women in ministry, several things come to the fore in light of recent societal trends. The battle of the sexes has not improved. Edith Bunker's "Yes, dear" has given way to a parity of insult between feminists and traditionalists that is reflected in the many guy-bashing and gal-bashing

---

[156]See previous note.

websites. The feminist solution to male domination is a rewriting of history that inverts the hierarchy rather than equalizes the power; the traditionalist solution (particularly in the CBMW) has been to radicalize the hierarchy. Women are not merely functionally subordinate to men but ontologically so—bearing the image of God derivatively rather than principally and essentially.[157]

In so doing, traditionalists fail to observe the psychological and sociological impact in evangelical circles. A rhetoric of gender hierarchy has contributed to (1) an increase of failed marriages, (2) an intensification of gender conflict, and (3) a worsening of the lines of communication. Hierarchy does not work because male domination does not address the foundational human core issues of identity, dignity, and significance that can only be realized in a two-directional relationship. Relationships are hard work, requiring a context of mutual consent (1 Cor. 7:5), interdependence (11:11), and mutual submission (Eph. 5:21; 1 Pet. 3:1) to grow and thrive. This applies not only to the marriage relationship but to all male-female relationships in society, the workplace, and the church. Hierarchy is a unilateral relationship—or perhaps more accurately, a nonrelational one. God created human relationships—including male and female—to be bilateral; male and female were created for mutuality and partnership.

Recent statements and publications of the CBMW cut to the core of human sexuality and further undermine gender reconciliation. A paper by David L. Talley ("Gender and Sanctification: From Creation to Transformation [Gen. 1–3 and Eph. 5]") at the 2004 Evangelical Theological Society annual meeting claims that egalitarian marriages can have no joy. Another paper by David W. Jones argues that the egalitarian thinking of organizations such as Christians for Biblical Equality (CBE) leads by necessity to lesbianism.[158] Although Jones recognizes that the CBE statement of faith unequivocally affirms "the family, celibate singleness, and faithful heterosexual marriage as the patterns God designed for us," he iterates the belief that evangelical

---

[157]E.g., Bruce Ware ("Male Priority in Man and Woman") argues that men bear God's image directly and women only derivatively; hence the priority of male over female (see n. 3).

[158]See David W. Jones, "Egalitarianism and Homosexuality: Connected or Autonomous Ideologies," *JBMW* 8 (Fall 2003): 5.

feminism ultimately leads to the embrace of homosexuality. Perhaps the fault lies in equating egalitarianism and feminism. They are not at all the same. Feminists tend to minimize (if not eliminate) sexual distinction and devalue heterosexism, whereas egalitarians not only affirm distinction but see it as basic to God's created design and essential for the kind of partnership God intended. Indeed, to be made male and female is to be created in God's image (Gen. 1:27). Male and female in relationship as "two become one" is a divine creation ("what God has joined together" [Matt. 19:6]) and a profound mystery that mirrors the one-spirit relationship between Christ and the church (Eph. 5:31–32). It is indeed traditionalists and feminists that represent the extremes in the gender discussion. The one subordinates the genders; the other collapses them. Egalitarians, on the other hand, see male and female as equal yet complementary, "bone of bones and flesh of flesh," who, when in a relationship of mutual submission, function as equal to the task of co-dominion over creation and coworkers in the church.

Although the topic of this volume is *women in ministry*, the fundamental issue is that of women leading men and the extent to which they can do so. That women in antiquity did so has been amply demonstrated. That we move in biblical times from perhaps the exceptional in someone such as Deborah to the usual in Paul's day is amply shown in the Roman church, where women and men are affirmed in equal roles and mutual partnerships—Phoebe, deacon of the church in Cenchreae; Syntyche and Euodia, leaders in the church in Philippi; and Nympha, overseer of a house church in Colossae, show that women were fully invested in roles many would deny to them today.

A RESPONSE TO LINDA BELLEVILLE

Thomas R. Schreiner

Linda Belleville is well known for her scholarship and provides a fine defense of the egalitarian view from the Scriptures, and I agree with many of her arguments in the essay. She rightly claims that women played a vital role in ministry in both the OT and the NT. Linda gives compelling arguments for women serving as deacons, prophets, and patrons. She cogently defends the near consensus view that Junia in Romans 16:7 was a woman. Further, she raises some serious objections to the view of Michael Burer and Daniel Wallace that Junia and Andronicus are designated as "well known to the apostles," compiling evidence supporting the rendering "well known among the apostles." It should be noted, however, that the word "apostles" here probably refers to "church planters" or "missionaries" and so does not place Junia and Andronicus at the same level as the Twelve or Paul.

Given the space constraints of my response, I must now emphasize some disagreements with Linda. I shall begin with her analysis of Genesis 1–3. Linda thinks the language of Adam's being created first simply designates sequence and nothing more. No one argues that order *always* signifies dominion. The basic rule of Bible study applies here, which says that each text must be interpreted in context. What is clear is that in both 1 Timothy 2:11–13 and 1 Corinthians 11:3–9, Adam's priority in creation signifies a role differentiation between men and women. Many egalitarian interpreters of Genesis proclaim that the order of creation says nothing about role differences, but such an interpretation slights the importance of reading the

Scriptures canonically, for Paul clearly understands the order of creation to signify a difference in function.

Linda also rejects the idea that the naming of the woman suggests male headship, suggesting it is only an act of memorializing or recognition that is in view. The significance of naming must also be discerned in context. In Genesis, the naming of the animals is linked with the dominion of Adam over all of creation (1:26, 28; 2:15). Therefore, we are justified in detecting a notion of male headship in the naming of the woman.

Linda thinks that the word "head" (*kephalē*) means "source," not "authority" in Ephesians 5 (though she maintains it refers to the one who has prominence or "pride of place" in 1 Corinthians 11). Even if the word means "source" in a few texts (a conclusion Wayne Grudem seriously contests in his careful study of the term), the conclusions drawn by Linda still do not follow. If women are instructed to adorn themselves in a certain way because men function as their head (1 Cor. 11:2–16), then, even if the word "head" means "source" or "prominence," a role differentiation between men and women is established. Linda is also unconvincing in her explanation of "head" in Ephesians 5:21–33. She alleges there is no contextual support in this passage for the notion that "head" means "authority." But notice Paul's argument in verses 22–23. Wives are to submit to husbands because the latter function as the head. So, even if the word "head" means "source" here (which is doubtful in this context), wives are to submit to their source. The primary role of leadership (yes, loving and servant leadership!) for the husband is clearly taught here, just as the church is to submit to the lordship of Christ.

Linda presents a number of unpersuasive arguments supporting women in leadership. She apparently thinks that because the church met in a woman's house, the woman in question functioned as a leader. She lists Mary, the mother of Mark, whose house was used by the early church (Acts 12:12) in support of her view. Functioning as a patron does not necessarily indicate one served as a leader, for the leaders named in the Jerusalem church are the apostles and the elders, not Mary. To claim that women patrons functioned as leaders is an argument from silence, and it is unclear that anything else in the NT suggests such a conclusion.

Linda is also unhelpful in the conclusions she draws from women teaching. She rules out any idea that some teaching is informal and private over against teaching that is formal and public. By doing so, she can lift up Priscilla as a teacher because she instructed Apollos (Acts 18:24–26). Linda falls into a logical error in her presentation. She rightly says everyone in the NT was expected to teach at some level (Col. 3:16), but it does not follow that everyone exercised a public ministry as a teacher. There is a difference between the instruction and mutual teaching all believers participate in and public formal teaching. The Pastoral Epistles focus on the latter (e.g., 1 Tim. 2:7; 4:6, 13, 16; 5:17; 6:2; 2 Tim. 2:2; 3:10; 4:2; Titus 1:9; 2:1). Linda misconstrues the biblical evidence by lumping together verses such as Colossians 3:16 with texts like 1 Timothy 2:11–15. Denying women the role of regular public teaching does not rule out the mutual teaching from the Scriptures enjoined in Colossians 3:16. On the one hand, complementarians must not fall into the error of failing to listen to wise words from women nurtured in the Scriptures. On the other hand, we should not conclude there is no distinction between the mutual instruction among all believers and a more formal teaching position.

Linda argues that women functioned as elders, seeing an example in 1 Timothy 5:9–10. Her argument fails to convince. First, the passage is not about elders serving as leaders but about supporting widows in financial need (vv. 3–16). Second, those who are over sixty years old are to be helped because they need financial assistance in their old age, not because this is the age at which one could begin to serve as a leader. One wonders about the energy level of elders if they have to be over sixty! Third, if Linda is right, then only widows could serve as elders; thus any older married woman would be excluded. Finally, verse 16 clarifies that the issue addressed is widows needing financial help.

Linda also argues that the church possesses authority, not individuals. Her thesis is artificial and divides what should be kept together. Ultimate authority does not reside in individuals but in the gospel. Still, Linda's attempt to say that the authority of the Twelve did not include their preaching (Matt. 10:1–8) wrongly separates their authority to heal from their authority to preach. She is certainly correct in saying that submission to leaders is voluntary in Hebrews 13:17, but she does not see that the leaders still possess authority. They are not to coerce submission, but the position of elder does involve leadership (1 Tim. 3:4–5; 5:17; Titus 1:9). Jesus modeled servant leadership (and so should church leaders today), but he was still a leader.

Linda says that in 1 Timothy 2:12 the infinitive *authentein* has a negative meaning, so that it should be rendered with a word like "dominate." In her own study of the term *authentein*, Linda does not distinguish carefully enough between verbal and nominal forms. The recent studies of H. Scott Baldwin and Al Wolters show the term signifies a positive use of authority.[1] It is certainly possible in particular contexts that the term could have a negative nuance. Evidence is lacking, however, that the infinitive "to teach" in verse 12 should be construed negatively. Hence, as Andreas Köstenberger has argued, both teaching and exercising authority should be understood as positive activities in verse 12.[2] Belleville proposes two translations for this verse: (1) "I do not permit a woman to teach in order to gain mastery over a man," and (2) "I do not permit a woman to teach with a view to dominating a man." She understands the Greek *oude* to designate in the correlative clause a related purpose or goal. Such a reading is grammatically problematic and misunderstands *oude*, for introducing any notion of purpose here misconstrues the force of the correlative.

Linda also thinks the women in Ephesus were influenced by the Artemis cult, where the female was considered superior to the male. We can simply say in reply that there is no clear evidence in Paul's letter that the Artemis cult played a role. Paul does not mention the cult, nor is there any specific notion in the text that shows the influence of the cult. Linda reads such a background into the text and then interprets the text from the alleged historical situation, an example of arbitrary mirror reading. If we think about it for a moment, Paul could easily have written, "I do not permit women to teach or exercise authority over a man, for they are engaged in false teaching." Or he could have written, "I do not permit women to teach or exercise authority

---

[1]See Al Wolters, "A Semantic Study of *Authentēs* and Its Derivatives," *JGRChJ* 1 (2000: 145–75; H. Scott Baldwin, "A Difficult Word: *Authenteō* in 1 Timothy 2:12," in *Women in the Church: A Fresh Analysis of 1 Timothy 2:9–15*, eds. Andreas J. Köstenberger, Thomas R. Schreiner, and H. Scott Baldwin (Grand Rapids: Baker, 1995), 65–80.

[2]See Andreas Köstenberger, "A Complex Sentence Structure in 1 Timothy 2:12," in *Women in the Church: A Fresh Analysis*, 81–103.

over a man, for they are promoting teachings from the Artemis cult." Instead, the reason Paul gives is rooted in the created order. The reason Paul prohibits women from teaching or exercising authority over men is rooted in God's intention from creation (v. 13). He does not appeal to the cultural argument promoted by egalitarians. Linda passes over what the text actually says and substitutes an alleged background instead.

To sum up, though Linda provides a stirring and thoughtful defense for the egalitarian position, her view fails because it does not provide a convincing interpretation of texts that demonstrate role differentiation between men and women.

A RESPONSE TO LINDA BELLEVILLE

Craig S. Keener

I am pleased Linda's essay complements mine by answering in detail many arguments for the complementarian position I do not address. When the book was originally planned, I understood the audience to be fairly popular and anticipated a shorter length of our essays, precluding the sort of detailed interaction with scholarly debate I had pursued in my earlier book on the subject.[1] I believe that Linda has more than compensated for what is lacking in my own approach.

Her careful response to the complementarian position is important, given the rhetorical strength of the moderate complementarian position that forbids only senior pastors—a view that positions itself as a middle ground between egalitarians and those who prohibit all ministry to women. This position's problem, however, is its exegetical instability, insofar as it depends on the sort of arguments used by egalitarians to limit the full force of the very texts on which it relies (otherwise it would have to aver that women are more easily deceived than men and should not speak at all in church). The complementarian position in all its forms also has another rhetorical advantage in many circles: it remains the dominant view in many evangelical denominations. Some circles where egalitarians are banned from speaking often unfairly paint us with the brush of secular feminism, making it difficult for us to get a fair hearing there. (Given the variety of issues debated in evangelicalism, to be excluded from some fellowships on the basis of a single position is painful

---

[1]Craig S. Keener, *Paul, Women and Wives: Marriage and Women's Ministry in the Letters of Paul* (Peabody, Mass.: Hendrickson, 1992; rev. with new introduction, 2004).

to many of us.) Under such circumstances, we need to make good arguments during whatever hearing we can get!

Linda's treatment of Junia is particularly laudable and detailed. I also concur with her reflections on "the essentially charismatic nature of the NT teaching role" (p. 59). House churches lacked pulpits and were more like large home Bible studies or prayer meetings than the churches most readers might imagine today. The professional pastoral role from which some exclude women today is a far cry from the ancient pastoral role, which was less formal and less authoritative than some roles in which we find women (such as Junia mentioned above). Linda's view that wives were interrupting church meetings with questions fits both the biblical text and what we know of questions in ancient lecture settings; it seems by far the likeliest situation addressed in 1 Corinthians 14:34–35.

Linda's careful arguments on *authentein* (and her and Craig Blomberg's arguments on word pairs) invite me to perhaps reconsider my own understanding of the word pair mentioned in my essay (itself a reversal of my earlier position in my book, where I took a position closer to Linda's). I agree fully with her interpretation of Ephesians 5, where I think the grammar clearly requires mutual submission. I believe that comparing Greco-Roman household codes, which Paul modifies in a more egalitarian direction (especially for wives and slaves), would reinforce her position further. She also treats the false teaching in 1 Timothy carefully, avoiding the excesses of some well-meaning but overzealous reconstructions that have prevailed in recent years.

It should not be surprising that I—a fellow egalitarian exegete—concur with most of her essay. One who has just read her essay would profit little, however, from my simply continuing to rehearse points of agreement. I will thus suggest some areas where I think her argument could be improved. The differences between my approach and Linda's demonstrate that egalitarians do not necessarily share all the same exegetical positions, just as the differences between Craig's and Tom's essays demonstrate that complementarians do not necessarily share all the same exegetical positions. All four of us have sought to do our exegesis as honestly as we can (sometimes crossing party lines), and had the fault lines in the contemporary debate focused on different issues, the four of us might have fallen into different alignments (or, on many issues, all four might have come out on the same side).

Although Linda makes a good case for the meaning "source" in some ancient uses of *kephalē*, I think the case for "authority" is also strong and may be relevant to one or both of the biblical texts under debate (most obviously Eph. 5:22–23). The emerging consensus appears to be that *kephalē* can have either meaning, depending on the context. Her argument for *kephalē* as "prominent part" makes good sense in 1 Corinthians 11, given the emphasis on honor and shame there (though "source" and "authority" could both be defended there as well).

Some views Linda attributes to complementarians (and proceeds to answer capably) are not specifically complementarian views. I am inclined to think that "Your desire will be for your husband" (Gen. 3:16) does involve the judgment of marital conflict, given the proximity of and parallel wording in 4:7. Likewise, the view that the husband "rules" his wife in 3:16 is hardly limited to traditionalist interpreters. As Linda rightly notes, this verse is descriptive rather than prescriptive; a description of human fallenness is not meant to model the kingdom ideal.

Mary and Lydia were hosts (patrons of house churches); this entailed a prominent and influential role but does not specifically indicate that they were what we mean by "overseers" of the congregation. Neither can we be sure of the office of Euodia and Syntyche in Philippi. Further, can we really be sure women leaders outnumber male leaders, especially if we count not just local leaders but Paul's traveling companions (who naturally, in that culture, were male, despite the later fiction of Thecla!)? Women leaders do outnumber male ones in Romans 16, which may be her point.

That women's leadership was more visible in Romanized areas like Rome and Philippi is true, as she points out, but I find much less persuasive the arguments proposed for women's freedoms in Ephesus. The prominence of Artemis in Ephesus no more need have translated into prominence for Ephesian women than the prominence of Athena had done for women in Athens (historically one of the least women-friendly Greek cities, and an ancient influence in Ionian Ephesus). Indeed, the Artemis cult had many male priests. I also doubt that priestesses in the imperial cult provided much of a model for NT ministry.

The woman doorkeeper in Annas's palace (John 18:16) is not significant for a discussion of priestly ministry; porters were commonly servants, but the Levite guards in the temple (e.g., Acts 4:1) were male. While it is true that no OT text commands wives' submission to their husbands, the suggestion that "the law" in 1 Corinthians 14:34 is Roman law runs counter to Paul's use of the phrase scores of times in his letters. I would not cite as supporting evidence for the egalitarian position Noadiah or Athaliah, who lack divine sanction, or Queen Alexandra, for whom the evidence is extrabiblical.

In other cases I would have liked to probe deeper, had more space been available. Is the meaning of "deacon" clear in the NT? Did women clearly fill this role in 1 Timothy 3:11? (Interestingly, I seem to be the least certain on this point of the four contributors. I concur with the occurrence of women deacons in Pliny, am uncertain about 1 Timothy 3:11, and allow that the term in Romans 16:1 may fit its more common ministry sense in the NT. But for all we know, "deacons" even in 1 Timothy may have filled some of the same roles as that more common ministry sense implies, though teaching is not mentioned.) I also would want more support than later tradition for the view that Jesus would have sent a woman among the Seventy-Two for the same reasons I believe Jesus did not include a woman among the Twelve, given traveling conditions and cultural expectations in Galilee. Granted, if this woman was particularly extraordinary or her traveling companion was her husband, this exception is plausible. But we cannot be sure.

The structure of 1 Timothy 5 does seem to suggest that the widows there have some sort of office (as I argued in *And Marries Another*),[2] but while this office may parallel male elders, the responsibilities likely differ. (A primary focus may have been on prayer, as in v. 5; of course this is no insignificant role—cf. Acts 6:4.) One qualification for their office is apparently a pledge to remain single (1 Tim. 5:11–12).

In other cases, Linda's arguments seem to withstand objections. To her observation that Jesus gave the disciples "authority" only to expel demons and heal in Matthew 10:1, some may object that preaching authority is implied in their commission

---

[2]Craig S. Keener, *And Marries Another: Divorce and Remarriage in the Teaching of the New Testament* (Peabody, Mass.: Hendrickson, 1991), 90–91.

to preach the kingdom (v. 7). Even if this is the case, however, such preaching authority is delegated by Jesus to the entire church (28:18–20), in a context where women provide the model (vv. 1–10, contrasted with men in 26:7–8, 45, 56, 75).

In the final analysis, of course, I agree with the thrust of Linda's essay and most of her case. Most important, we balance the particular setting of the prohibitions against some forms of women's ministry with the affirmations of such roles elsewhere in the Bible, where such situations did not prevail. Scripture reveals many women filling ministries more directly influential than most first-century house church elders did. Nevertheless, Linda and I (like Craig and Tom in their complementarian position) would construct our case differently at times.

A RESPONSE TO LINDA BELLEVILLE

Craig L. Blomberg

Linda Belleville and I were students together years ago at Trinity Evangelical Divinity School, and we have kept in touch at academic conferences over the years. I admire her scholarship, highly respect her Christian commitment, and am glad for the opportunity to give this brief response. As in all of my responses in this volume, space constraints prevent me from highlighting in any detail the vast majority of each essay with which I agree. I will try to make very brief remarks to point out broad areas of agreement, but readers have come to expect responses of this genre to focus primarily on disagreements. I will follow that convention but want to underline here in the first of these responses my profound agreement with an appreciation of a large amount of detail in each of my colleagues' chapters.

In reacting to Linda's discussion of Genesis 1–2, I concede that these chapters, taken on their own, might not necessarily lead to a complementarian position. The information in them about gender roles is comparatively meager and susceptible to more than one interpretation. It is only on the basis of later NT use of these chapters that I find myself driven to the position I take. I also agree that Genesis 3 is descriptive rather than prescriptive, though I don't think Linda has felt the full negative force of the sole scriptural parallel (4:7) where both "desire" and "rule" appear together outside 3:16. Although it is grammatically possible that 3:16 could be translated "and *it* [rather than "he"] will dominate her," the translation "he will dominate her" is the much more natural rendering.

Overall, Linda's section on women in leadership is strong and important. Occasionally, I think she pushes the evidence too far. For example, simply to refer to a woman (or man) and the church that meets in their house hardly proves they were the patron, elder, or any other kind of leader, though they certainly may have been; and nothing in Philippians links Euodia and Syntyche to the office of either overseer or deacon.

It is Linda's treatment of NT prophets that seems to be the weakest section in this part of her essay. All three traditionalist points with which Linda takes issue still seem quite solid to me. Apart from those occasions when they were writing inspired Scripture, the NT prophets do not appear to have carried on the "Thus saith the Lord" task of the OT prophets, or Paul would not have commanded the congregation to evaluate them but merely to *obey* them (1 Cor. 14:29)! Second, pointing out that male and female prophetic activity was identical does not contravene the fact that both genders were subject to evaluation. Finally, if NT prophecy was wholly authoritative and not a fallible gift (like all the other gifts of the Spirit), then Paul must have been disobeying God when the Christians in Tyre urged him "through the Spirit" not to go on to Jerusalem (Acts 21:4)—but he went anyway. Despite these minor flaws, Linda does successfully demonstrate there are no roles or functions in ministry forever barred to women. In this way, she debunks one form of traditionalism or complementarianism.

But nothing in Linda's essay defeats my assertion that it is the office of elder/overseer the NT presents as limited to men. She concedes that no women are named as elders but simply points out that many leaders remain unnamed. But the broader pattern of the single "highest" office of religious leadership in each era of salvation history remains intact. Her response to the all-male priesthood in the OT is to blame women's uncleanness, but neither menstruation nor childbirth rendered women perpetually unclean, so this rationale (nowhere hinted at in Scripture) does not seem convincing; after all, men were unclean for various periods of time as well. She attributes Jesus' choice of an all-male apostolate to not wanting to push cultural conventions of the day too far (again a rationale nowhere stated in the Bible). This too seems suspect, given that Jesus was willing to so challenge the religious and political authorities on so many other issues to such an extent that they eventually killed him!

As for whether these various roles truly carry the highest "authority," Linda simply appeals to the nonuse of the term in key contexts. But it is concepts, not terminology, that must prove determinative, and it is hard to read any significant strands of the Bible without seeing priests, apostles, and elders functioning in authoritative ways. Priests mediated between God and humanity, officiating at the sacrifices that enabled them to pronounce the forgiveness of sins over the worshipers as no one else in Israel had the authority to do. Jesus uniquely sent out the Twelve to replicate exactly his ministry of preaching, teaching, and miracle working, an authoritative commission if ever there was one (Matt. 10; Luke 10). And the elders combined responsibilities of teaching and exercising authority most explicitly of all. Even if one denies that 1 Timothy 2:12 refers to elders, 3:3 explicitly links the overseer to teaching, while Titus 1:5–7 clearly equates overseers and elders. An explicit word for "authority" may not appear in 1 Timothy 5:17, but what else can "direct the affairs of the church" in a way worthy of receiving honor—including teaching and preaching—possibly mean?

I agree with Linda, when she turns to her specific texts, that Matthew 10:1–42; 1 Timothy 3:1–7; and Titus 1:5–9 are not terribly relevant to the rest of the debate. I would, however, add 1 Corinthians 11:2–16 into the mix as a passage that is highly relevant. But with respect to the two remaining texts on which she focuses—1 Corinthians 14:34–35 and 1 Timothy 2:11–15—the following points may be noted:

First, as Anthony Thiselton's large NIGTC commentary on 1 Corinthians points out, we need not choose between the complementarian approach to women's silence in the church being understood in the context of the evaluation of prophecy and the egalitarian approach that sees uneducated wives asking disruptive questions. The two may have, in fact, been combined when overseers' wives were challenging the prophecies of their husbands in public. At any event, if these are merely intrusive questions asked by untutored women, then Paul is hopelessly sexist by barring all women from speaking and no men (notwithstanding the fact that there would have been plenty of uneducated men as well).

Second, dozens of times in his letters Paul uses *nomos* without any further qualification, and it almost always refers to the Mosaic law. In no text, to my knowledge, without any contextual clues, does it refer to Roman law. Thus to take the reference in 1 Corinthians 14:34 as denoting Roman law seems an improbable move.

Third, turning to 1 Timothy 2:12, the primary thrust of the present tense in Greek is to refer to ongoing or continual action, not to highlight what is happening only momentarily. Thus it is more likely that Paul's statement "I do not permit . . ." means "I continually do not permit," rather than "I am presently not permitting [but will permit at some later date]."

Fourth, the lexical information Linda presents concerning *authentein* reflects only one side of the debate. The dozens of neutral or positive uses of the term to reflect godly authority from a post-Pauline age in largely Christian literature did not likely stand the older negative use of the term so dramatically on its head without some strongly authoritative warrant for changing the meaning. But if that is how the church fathers understood Paul to have used the term, then the semantic change makes very good sense. Citing English translations that render the verb as "usurp authority" can be a bit misleading, for this expression probably means "usurping the authority that belongs to the men" rather than just "exercising authority in an improper way." Linda's exegesis of this verse doesn't yet convince me, because, despite her very detailed and commendable analysis of the great diversity of relationships between paired elements in similar "neither . . . nor" constructions in her book-length work on our topic, to my knowledge no one has yet discovered an example of a pair of *verbs*, including infinitives, correlated with the Greek conjunction *oude*, in which one of the actions is positive (like the teaching here) and the other negative (as in domineering). Instead, Andreas Köstenberger charts numerous biblical and extrabiblical references in which such paired activities are consistently either both negative or both positive (see p. 98, n. 150). Linda's exegesis of 1 Timothy 2:12 does not seem to jeopardize my understanding of *didaskein oude authentein* as referring merely to the office of elder in the way that her view counters more traditional complementarian interpretations. As for verse 13, virtually 90 percent of all uses of *gar* in Paul are causal, so there would have to be strong contextual evidence to take it in any other way here. And verse 14 need not reflect such evidence, since, as I point out in my essay, it can be separated from verse 13 as the introduction to verse 15 and not seen as the second rationale for Paul's prohibition.

Three final observations merit mention. First, if mutual submission is defined as the same two people deferring to one another in the same way, on the same issue, at the same time, then it is logically incoherent. So egalitarians and complementarians alike, whether they realize it or not, must concede that mutual submission means certain people submitting only to certain others, in certain ways, at certain times. This does not prove the complementarian interpretation of Ephesians 5:21, but it also means that Linda has not refuted it. Second, while support is waning today for the approach to 1 Corinthians 14:33–38 that sees verses 34–35 as a Corinthian slogan rejected by Paul in verses 36–38, throughout much of the 1980s and early 1990s it was by far the most common explanation proffered by evangelical egalitarians. So it was reasonable for the CBMW to have asked about it. Finally as I point out in my chapter (p. 156), Stephen Bedale and other early scholars who studied *kephalē* and argued for the meaning as "source" never denied that it simultaneously carried the sense of "authority."

In closing, I can agree with and admire 90-plus percent of Linda's exegesis. She has ably rebutted a very conservative traditionalist position, but as far as I can see she has not refuted my own brand of complementarianism. I suspect she is right that for many complementarians the issue does boil down to whether women can lead men, but I want to go on record as I conclude that this has never been an issue for me. I have submitted to women leaders in the home, in the church, and in numerous educational contexts throughout my life, often with great joy and harmony. For me, the issue comes down to which position most faithfully represents the totality of the scriptural witness, and it is that task I wrestle with in my essay.

Chapter Two

WOMEN IN MINISTRY: A COMPLEMENTARIAN PERSPECTIVE

Craig L. Blomberg

WOMEN IN MINISTRY:
A COMPLEMENTARIAN PERSPECTIVE
Craig L. Blomberg

The debate about gender roles in ministry is one of the most volatile in the Christian church today. Little wonder—individuals' sense of identity, call, vocation, and service to Christ are deeply wrapped up with the issue. I do not write what I do in order to please any identifiable camp within Christianity, or because it was the view I grew up with (it is not—I was raised in a mainline, egalitarian Protestant denomination), but because repeated, intensive study of this debate for more than twenty-five years has convinced me that my position is the most responsible synthesis of all of the relevant Scriptures. At the same time, I recognize that equally godly scholars who are equally committed to the inerrancy of the Bible come to different conclusions because of the complexity of the data. There is no legitimate place in this debate to impugn fellow evangelicals who differ from one another by using the pejorative labels "liberal" or "fundamentalist," simply because of their views on this topic. All of us who speak and write on gender roles would do well to begin and end every address with the caveats, "I could be wrong" and, "I respect the right of fellow evangelicals and evangelical churches to come to different conclusions, *and I will cooperate with them rather than combat them* for the larger cause of Christ and his kingdom, which so desperately needs such unity."

A helpful analogy for me is the debate between baptists and paedobaptists. I was "sprinkled" as an infant, confirmed as an eighth grader, and did a detailed study of Scripture and the writings of the most highly touted advocates for each side as a twenty-five-year-old Ph.D. student, and I came to the conclusion that the scriptural evidence strongly supported the case for believers' baptism by immersion.[1] Many of the most celebrated proponents of infant baptism, I discovered, agreed with me, conceding that baptizing babies was a post-NT development (even though they argued for its legitimacy).[2] When I decided to be immersed as a believer in a Scottish Baptist church in 1980, I asked my pastor if this step meant I should now aggressively proselytize all my evangelical paedobaptist friends. He chuckled and wisely replied, "No, by no means, but if they ask you why you did what you did or show an interest in the topic, then, of course, share your testimony with them." Over the years this is precisely what I have done, and I have cooperated in many intra-evangelical efforts with Presbyterian, Lutheran, and Episcopalian friends. I believe the gender roles debate should be viewed similarly—clearly important but not one of the non-negotiables of the faith. I have appreciated teaching at Denver Seminary for the past eighteen years for many reasons, one of which is that it deliberately does *not* take a stand on this issue, believing it to be a debate with respect to which Christians should learn to model agreeing to disagree in love. I hope my contributions to this book model that spirit as well, not least because I count Jim Beck, Linda Belleville, Craig Keener, and Tom Schreiner as good friends.

My role in this volume is perhaps more unusual than that of any of the other contributors. In the first edition of this book, I was one of the coeditors;[3] in this second edition, I am a contributor and a respondent. Edition 1 did contain, as a giant appendix, an essay I originally wrote for an anthology on gender roles in Paul, and as such it was somewhat of an odd fit.[4]

---

[1]The classic study remains G. R. Beasley-Murray's *Baptism in the New Testament* (London: Macmillan, 1962). Particularly influential was Paul K. Jewett (*Infant Baptism and the Covenant of Grace* [Grand Rapids: Eerdmans, 1978]), precisely because he argued for believers' baptism from a Reformed perspective, which is normally known to advocate infant baptism.

[2]Particularly influential was Geoffrey W. Bromiley (*Children of Promise: The Case for Baptizing Infants* [Grand Rapids: Eerdmans, 1979]).

[3]James R. Beck and Craig L. Blomberg, eds., *Two Views on Women in Ministry* (Grand Rapids: Zondervan, 2001).

[4]"Neither Hierarchicalist nor Egalitarian: Gender Roles in Paul," in ibid., 329–72. A minimally revised version of this essay has been submitted to Stanley E. Porter in keeping with his hopes that a projected volume on Pauline theology (which he would edit) may still be forthcoming.

Now I must try to say a little something about all of the relevant portions of the Bible. My comments will, therefore, have to be briefer and, to match the other essays, a little less technical, with a few less sources in my footnotes. In fairness to the other contributors, I will not refer to anything they wrote in the first edition of their chapters, although, because all have published elsewhere, I will feel free to cite their views from other published works. Specific interaction with the ways they present their cases here, however, will be limited to my shorter responses after each of their essays.

I'm not really sure what to call my position. Some have seen it as mediating between classic complementarian and egalitarian perspectives (critics would call it fence-sitting!). William Webb refers to it as "ultra-soft patriarchalism,"[5] an expression with which I'm not at all comfortable, because "ultra-soft" doesn't sound like a compliment when used about someone's opinions, while "patriarchal" sounds more conservative and oppressive than even "hierarchical" or "traditional"—the two most commonly used names for the position before "complementarian" was invented a couple decades ago. But I know what Webb means—something like "about as close as you can get to being a full-fledged egalitarian without actually becoming one"—and that is probably an accurate summary of my views. Still, as Tom Schreiner himself points out in a review of my earlier essay, I still do qualify as a complementarian by current nomenclature,[6] which explains the inclusion of my position here.

LARGER ISSUES INVOLVED

Before beginning my survey of Scripture, it is important to acknowledge the number of larger issues that complicate the debate. I have already referred to personal identity; closely related are personal experiences. Almost every egalitarian, and particularly women in church leadership roles, have been personally attacked, often repeatedly, in very sub-Christian ways, by certain complementarians to such an extent that it becomes

---

[5]William J. Webb, *Slaves, Women and Homosexuals: Exploring the Hermeneutics of Cultural Analysis* (Downers Grove, Ill.: InterVarsity, 2001), 242–43.

[6]Thomas R. Schreiner, review of *Two Views on Women in Ministry*, ed. Beck and Blomberg, *SBJT* (forthcoming). From the egalitarian side, Julia Bloom, in her review of our book (*Mutuality* [Winter 2001]: 27), agrees.

hard for them even to consider the possibility that a more restrictive position might be correct. Many complementarians, especially men in church leadership roles, have similarly been attacked by certain egalitarians, or have seen the advocacy of egalitarianism divide fellowships, to such an extent that it becomes hard even to consider the possibility that a more open position might be correct. Somehow we have to overcome the pain of these past (and present) hurts.

A second larger issue is the tendency to see one's views on gender roles as part of a much larger package. If a church moves in a *more* complementarian direction, some will ask if this is the beginning of a move to exclude women from all significant positions in the church. If a church moves in a *less* complementarian direction, some will wonder if this is the first step to full-fledged egalitarianism or, worse still (in their minds), secular feminism. In either case, what is driving the proposed change—is it Scripture, or capitulation to secular trends? And what of church history? The average Christian's knowledge today of what was or wasn't permitted, and why, in each of the major stages and arenas of the history of Christianity is often abysmal. I have frequently heard sweeping claims about what was or wasn't permitted in "almost the whole of church history" on both sides of this debate that simply can't stand up to historical scrutiny.

A third set of larger issues surrounds the ways questions are posed. The most common way the debate has been couched, especially when reported in the secular media, is in terms of the "ordination" of women. Whenever I hear things phrased this way, I want to ask the question "ordained to what?" There are precious few references to ordination in Scripture, and those that do occur do not enable us to answer the questions of for what offices, ministries, or roles is ordination appropriate, and just exactly what does it mean?[7] One of the most common ways egalitarian women justify their quest for church leadership is with reference to the concept of "call." "God called me to be a pastor" becomes the trump card that supersedes all other claims. But how does one evaluate so subjective a conviction? And does Scripture actually support the idea of specific vocational calling for Christians?[8] On

---

[7]See esp. Marjorie Warkentin, *Ordination* (Grand Rapids: Eerdmans, 1982).

[8]See esp. Steve Walton, *A Call to Live: Vocation for Everyone* (London: SPCK, 1994).

the other side, many complementarians, having decided that the office of pastor-elder is limited to men, often jump to the conclusion that therefore women should never preach in a worship service. But what biblical text ever limits preaching to pastors or elders? Noncharismatics typically equate the spiritual gift of prophecy, at least in part, with Spirit-filled preaching (see below, p. 158). But the spiritual gifts (*charismata*) are given indiscriminately by God, apart from gender, as *he* sees fit (1 Cor. 12:11). And 1 Corinthians 11:5 presupposes that women can prophesy when they show appropriate submission to their spiritual heads (see further, pp. 158–61)

A fourth cluster of complicating factors involves what is practiced in different parts of the world today. Countless women from Western cultures have been permitted to preach, teach, evangelize, and in general lead evangelical ministries in non-Western countries—"on the mission field"—when their sending churches would never permit such practices "back home." Can this be anything other than a subtle racism that in essence says other cultures are so inferior that a double standard can be established for them? And what about the diversity in forms of church government? If a complementarian decides that only the "highest" offices of church leadership are reserved for men, what does that mean in an Episcopal or Presbyterian context where the local pastor remains "under" a larger denominational hierarchy? In Baptistic fellowships, in theory (though often not in practice), the congregation holds the final authority. Would this mean that complementarians should make sure that men are always in a majority among the voting membership but that women could be pastors?

Finally, to what degree can we borrow from the various sciences—physiology, psychology, sociology, and anthropology—to try to provide a more thorough rationale for our understanding of Scripture's commands?[9] Western societies have been largely

---

[9]Laudable, detailed attempts on the complementarian side have been made by Stephen B. Clark, *Man and Woman in Christ* (Ann Arbor, Mich.: Servant, 1980), 371–570; and the chapters in *Recovering Biblical Manhood and Womanhood: A Response to Evangelical Feminism,* eds. John Piper and Wayne Grudem (Wheaton, Ill.: Crossway, 1991), represented in pp. 280–331. Supporting egalitarianism, see Mary S. van Leeuwen, *Gender and Grace: Love, Work and Parenting in a Changing World* (Downers Grove, Ill.: InterVarsity, 1990); van Leeuwen, *My Brother's Keeper: What the Social Sciences Do (and Don't) Tell Us About Masculinity* (Downers Grove, Ill.: InterVarsity, 2002).

egalitarian for roughly thirty years; young adults coming to Christ are often shocked to discover that the church is not necessarily an "equal opportunity" employer. Now that women have proved themselves competent in every major occupation in the secular workplace, by what possible logic can the church exclude them from its leadership? Is it enough to say that Scripture requires it, without supplying any convincing rationale? My own view is that we look for all the support we can find, inside or outside the Bible, for any of its commands, but we are still bound to obey them, whether or not irrefutable reasons can be given. Many in our society today find no reason for prohibiting sexual relations outside of marriage among consenting adults, but that does not eradicate all the biblical prohibitions of fornication and adultery.

Too often all five of these categories of questions are never even considered, much less carefully thought through. We will need to keep them all in mind as we embark on a whirlwind tour of Genesis through Revelation.

A SURVEY OF OT SCRIPTURE

Genesis 1–3

After everything else he created, God fashioned ʾādām in his image. Twice the narrator of Genesis uses this term as a collective singular, referring to this new species—humanity (Gen. 1:26, 27a). In verse 26, God is clearly thinking about humankind, because he refers back to ʾādām with a plural pronoun in commissioning "them" to exercise dominion over the rest of creation. Verse 27a refers back to ʾādām with the masculine singular Hebrew pronoun (God created "him"), but the ancient biblical languages (Hebrew, Aramaic, and Greek), like English until about thirty years ago, consistently used masculine forms when they wanted to indicate generic identity (male or female, or male and female together). Only in verse 27b does the text first differentiate ʾādām into "male and female" and shift back to the plural (God created "them"). Men and women alike thus bear God's image equally as his unique stewards over creation.[10]

---

[10]On these verses, cf. esp. Richard S. Hess, "Splitting the Adam: The Use of ʾādām in Genesis i-v," in *Studies in the Pentateuch*, ed. J. A. Emerton (Leiden: Brill, 1990), 1–15.

Genesis 2 proceeds to narrate in much greater detail the creation of the human pair and their brief life in the garden of Eden prior to the fall. The man was created first before the woman (v. 7). Modern readers think little of this and move quickly on, but ancient Jews, accustomed to laws of primogeniture (both in their Scriptures and in surrounding cultures) that gave the firstborn a double share of any inheritance (Deut. 21:17, seemingly illustrated already in Gen. 27:19 and 49:3, spiritualized in 2 Kgs. 2:9 and presupposed in Luke 15:12) might well have seen this as a sign of privilege.[11] At least Paul in NT times seems to do so (1 Tim. 2:13; on which see below, p. 170). It is, of course, obvious that the order of creation in Genesis 1 does not follow the same logic, since humans are created last, not first.[12] But no ancient reader, in a pre-Darwinian world, would ever propose that humans were identical in kind to the animals. It is only when individual humans are compared with one another that questions about orders of rank and responsibility come into play.

One of the first tasks God gives the man is to name each of the animals (vv. 19–20a). This fits his commissioning to exercise dominion; his naming them reflects his authority over them (an understanding that would continue in Judaism subsequently).[13] None of the animals, however, proved to be a sufficiently intimate companion for the man, leading God to declare that it was not good for the man to be alone. An appropriate helper would be created (vv. 18, 20b). The word for "helper" (ʿēzer) suggests one who will play a subordinate role in some sense. It is true that the term is most often used in the Hebrew Bible for God, especially when he helps human leaders in Israel (e.g., aiding kings in battle—Exod. 18:4; Deut. 33:7, Ps. 33:20). Thus an ʿēzer is not inherently an inferior; *in specific contexts* it may refer to someone who is actually in a superior position. In other cases, it is more obviously a subordinate (Isa. 30:5; Ezek. 12:14; Dan. 11:34). But what makes an ʿēzer a "helper" in each context is that he or she comes to the aid of someone else who bears the primary responsibility for

[11]See James B. Hurley, *Man and Woman in Biblical Perspective* (Grand Rapids: Zondervan, 1981), 207–9.

[12]So, e.g., Linda L. Belleville, *Women Leaders and the Church: Three Crucial Questions* (Grand Rapids: Baker, 2000), 103.

[13]See Thomas Finley, "The Relationship of Woman and Man in the Old Testament," in *Women and Men in Ministry: A Complementary Perspective*, eds. Robert L. Saucy and Judith K. TenElshof (Chicago: Moody Press, 2001), 55.

the activity in question.[14] It may be significant that the man is never said to be an ʿēzer of his wife. At any rate, Paul will later derive his understanding of headship, at least in part, from the irreversibility of these created roles: "Man did not come from woman, but woman from man; neither was man created for woman, but woman for man" (1 Cor. 11:8–9; on which see below, p. 159).

On the other hand, in Genesis 2:18 and 20b, the ʿēzer must be someone who is a good match for the man. The English adjective "suitable" renders a Hebrew compound expression made out of three words which, translated separately, could mean "according to," "in front of," and "him" (k plus neged plus ô). "Corresponding to him" is probably as good an idiomatic English rendering as any.[15] Here the equality between the two is stressed, as also in the subsequent description that God formed the woman from one of the man's ribs (vv. 21–22), so that she was made of his very flesh and bone (v. 23a). Now the man can exclaim, "she shall be called 'woman' [ʾiššâ], for she was taken out of man [ʾîš]" (v. 23b), a rare play on words that works in English just as in Hebrew. Just as he "called" out names for the rest of creation, now he exercises his rightful authority and "calls" out the name for his new partner.[16]

The order of creation, the process of naming this second human being, and her role as a helper thus all suggest that she is in some sense subordinate. But this is still a sinless relationship—headship and submission exercised in perfect love. And even then, role differentiation is not what the narrator wants to emphasize the most, so he closes this section with a reminder of their unity in partnership. The first human couple becomes a model for all subsequent marriages in their intimacy (initially without shame) and in being joined together as "one flesh" (vv. 24–25; cf. Matt. 10:7–8 par.; Eph. 5:31).[17]

Paradise, of course, does not last long. Genesis 3 proceeds immediately to the story of the fall of the first human couple into

---

[14]Cf. Bruce K. Waltke with Cathi J. Fredricks, Genesis: A Commentary (Grand Rapids: Zondervan, 2001), 88.

[15]Cf. Kenneth A. Mathews, Genesis 1–11:26 (NAC; Nashville: Broadman & Holman, 1996), 213.

[16]Cf. Gordon J. Wenham, Genesis 1–15 (WBC; Waco: Word, 1987), 70

[17]Cf. Victor P. Hamilton, The Book of Genesis Chapters 1–17 (NICOT; Grand Rapids: Eerdmans, 1990), 179–81.

sin and the consequences that resulted from their disobedience. It is interesting that the serpent approaches only the woman to deceive her (vv. 1–5), and yet God confronts the man first to call him to account for his rebellion (vv. 9–12). Was the woman more vulnerable and the man more responsible?[18] It is hard to be sure. After all, verse 6 shows that both freely committed the same sin; verses 7–8, that they both responded in the same way by covering their nakedness and hiding from God. And God does confront the woman immediately after he addresses the man (v. 13) and pronounces a judgment on both in turn (vv. 16–19). The NT, intriguingly, blames Adam exactly twice (Rom. 5:12–14; 1 Cor. 15:22) and Eve exactly twice (2 Cor. 11:3, 1 Tim. 2:14) in its discussions of the original sin.

What is more significant about Genesis 3 with respect to gender roles is that the harmony between the man and the woman is shattered. He blames her (v. 12), she blames the serpent (v. 13), and God says to the woman, "Your desire will be for your husband, and he will rule over you" (v. 16). This somewhat bland translation masks the full force of the Hebrew. It cannot be that the woman had no desire for the man before their sin—they were created to be "one flesh." Rather, it is that her desire will now be in some way corrupted, distorting their relationship. But if desire preceded the fall, so most likely did the "rule"—the very exercise of authority we have already discussed—only now it too has become warped. In Derek Kidner's memorable words, " 'To love and to cherish' becomes 'to desire and to dominate.' "[19] Tellingly, the only other place in the OT where these words for "desire" (tĕšûqâ) and "rule" (māšal) appear *together* is in the very next chapter of Genesis, when the Lord tells Cain, "Sin is crouching at your door; it *desires* to have you, but you must *rule over* it" (4:7). Clearly the desire here is a twisted one that requires domination, not just loving headship, as a response. God's word to the woman in 3:16 is thus not a prescription of how men and women *should* behave; it is a prediction that this is, sadly, how they often *will* act. Neither is it

---

[18]Leading some to speak of this as the first unfortunate example of sex-role reversal, as, e.g., Raymond C. Ortlund Jr., "Male-Female Equality and Male Headship," in *Recovering Biblical Manhood and Womanhood*, 107.

[19]Derek Kidner, *Genesis* (TOTC; Downers Grove, Ill.: InterVarsity, 1967), 71.

the initial introduction of headship and submission into humanity; it is a description of its distortion due to sin.

After God is done speaking, Adam gives his wife another name, Eve—from a verb for "living"—because she would become the mother of all human life (v. 20). But even though this action more closely parallels later naming formulas when parents would give newborn children their personal names,[20] it is not as parallel to the naming of the animals, since nothing in Genesis 2 ever suggested Adam gave them names like Fido, Spot, Flipper, and so on—he was merely identifying species. Naming began before the fall; it was not just a first-time exercise of newly warped authority after Adam and Eve sinned.

The upshot of our survey of Genesis 1–3 is that there are hints of a divinely intended male headship in God's original scheme of creating man and woman. One cannot relegate this concept merely to the consequences of the fall, which redemption progressively overturns.[21] Without further revelation, however, it would be impossible to determine the implications of this headship, whether for relationships between husbands and wives or for leadership roles among God's people in gathered community, so we must keep reading further along in our Bibles.

The Rest of the Old Testament

No one disputes that the relationship described in the rest of the OT reflects the practice of patriarchy—predominantly male leadership in home, religion, and society. What *is* debated is what the Christian is to make of this observation. Does the NT overthrow patriarchy, as, for example, it supersedes the Jewish dietary laws or sees animal sacrifices as no longer necessary because they were fulfilled in Christ?[22] Obviously, the answer to

---

[20]Cf. G. W. Ramsey, "Is Name-Giving an Act of Domination in Genesis 2:23 and Elsewhere?" *CBQ* 50 (1988): 24–35.

[21]There is, significantly, a broad consensus on this, not only among evangelical complementarians but among nonevangelical scholars as well (who then go on to reject the timeless authority of the pattern they detect). Cf. esp. David J. A. Clines, "What Does Eve Do to Help? and Other Iredeemably Androcentric Orientations in Genesis 1–3," in *What Does Eve Do to Help? and Other Readerly Questions in the Old Testament*, ed. David J. A. Clines (JSOTSup; Sheffield: Sheffield Academic Press, 1990), 25–48.

[22]So esp. Aída B. Spencer, *Beyond the Curse: Women Called to Ministry* (Nashville: Nelson, 1985), 29–42. Cf. throughout Gilbert Bilezikian, *Beyond Sex Roles: A Guide for the Study of Female Roles in the Bible* (Grand Rapids: Baker, 1985).

this question will have to await our survey of the NT material. Meanwhile, we need to determine what women did and didn't (or could and couldn't) do in leadership within the OT itself, and then assess the significance of our observations. Space prevents little more than a mere listing of the most important and representative details.

Scholars agree that one religious leadership role in ancient Israel was uniformly reserved for men—the priesthood (though there is some evidence to suggest the laws may have been disobeyed here and there). Only Aaron and his male descendants could occupy this office (Exod. 28; Lev. 9). The reasons for this restriction, however, are disputed. Traditionally, the Jewish and Christian assumption has been that God wanted to mirror his principle of male headship in creation by reserving the "highest" position among his religious leaders for men.[23] More recently, some have suggested that Israel was merely accommodating itself to the patriarchy of the surrounding cultures.[24] But several ancient Near Eastern societies did have priestesses, and even in the OT, when God wanted his people to be different from others, he knew how to command them to do so. As a result, still other writers wonder if Israel was to appear *different* from nations whose priestesses were regularly bound up in the practice of fertility rites and "mother-goddess" worship.[25] Yet these pagan practices were inculcated by even more male priests than female ones, so it is not clear this ploy would have accomplished its designs. It seems likely the traditional view remains the best one, especially in light of complementary injunctions involving the dominant role for male sacrificial animals (e.g., Lev. 9:3–4) and the stricter marriage laws for priests than for the rest of the people (21:7–15). With additional privilege comes greater responsibility!

Beyond this one office, however, there do not appear to be any other restrictions on women in public leadership in ancient

---

[23]Cf. Thomas Finley, "The Ministry of Women in the Old Testament," in *Women and Men in Ministry*, 74.

[24]Mary Hayter (*The New Eve in Christ* [Grand Rapids: Eerdmans, 1987], 60–79), e.g., thoroughly discusses "Priesthood in the Old Testament," acknowledging numerous factors involved in prohibiting women from officiating. But the heart of the matter remains the cultural framework of pre-Christian patriarchal society far removed from our own.

[25]E.g., Mary J. Evans, *Woman in the Bible* (Downers Grove, Ill.: InterVarsity, 1983), 30.

Israel. While they often remain the exception, women did at one time or another play every other significant role.[26] Deborah represents the one example of a female judge, the leadership office that was a precursor to the kingship (Judg. 4). The text offers no support for the often-held notion that she assumed that position only because no man was able or willing to fill it. What *does* appear is the unwillingness of Barak, the military commander, to go to battle without Deborah alongside him, and Deborah's intriguing response that as a result he will incur the shame of having a woman kill the opposing general, Sisera, rather than accomplishing that feat himself (vv. 8–9). Deborah thus acknowledges the patriarchal context, even while breaking one of its traditional molds and leading her people in exemplary fashion.[27]

Women also appear in the OT as prophets, most notably Miriam (Exod. 15:20–21) and Huldah (2 Kgs. 22:11–20). The prophet could perform very exalted tasks—confronting even kings with their sins (recall Nathan with David or Elijah with Ahab) and directly proclaiming God's word to the people. But the prophets did not seem to perform regular, predictable leadership functions during worship services or in the day-in, day-out administration of tabernacle, temple, or synagogue.[28] So it would seem inappropriate to liken them to Christian pastors or elders.[29]

---

[26]For a detailed survey, see Athalya Brenner, *The Israelite Woman: Social Role and Literary Type in Biblical Narrative* (Sheffield: JSOT Press, 1985). See also the contributions to *Essays on Women in Earliest Christianity*, ed. Carroll D. Osburn (Joplin, Mo.: College Press, 1993–1995), 1:25–39; 2:37–153; Carol L. Meyers, *Discovering Eve: Ancient Israelite Women in Context* (New York: Oxford Univ. Press, 1988).

[27]Cf. K. Lawson Younger Jr., *Judges* (NIVAC; Grand Rapids: Zondervan, 2002), 159.

[28]As Joseph Blenkinsopp (*Sage, Priest, Prophet: Religious and Intellectual Leadership in Ancient Israel* [Louisville, Ky.: Westminster, 1995], 79) summarizes, "The crucial difference between prophet and priest is that the former is called while the latter is appointed to office and therefore dispenses salvation by virtue of the office rather than through personal charismatic endowment." For good introductions to the ministry of prophets, see his pp. 115–65; also David L. Petersen, *The Roles of Israel's Prophets* (Sheffield: JSOT Press, 1981).

[29]Cf., e.g., the chapter in Rebecca M. Groothuis, *Good News for Women: A Biblical Picture of Gender Equality* (Grand Rapids: Baker, 1997), 189–207, titled "The Bible and Women in Leadership," which, while rightly pointing out key roles of women in leadership in both Testaments, fails to engage sufficiently questions of levels of leadership and thus makes it appear that if certain roles are open, all of them must be.

Although women typically did not go out to battle with Israel's troops, they did on occasion play key roles in those conflicts. We have already alluded to Jael, who executed Sisera in the days of Deborah and Barak (Judg. 4:17–24). An anonymous woman similarly ended the battle in Judges 9:53, killing Abimelech by dropping a millstone on him from a tower above him. As in many otherwise patriarchal cultures throughout the history of the world, the daughters of reigning Israelite monarchs could even become queens if there were no sons to inherit the throne. That the one canonical example, Athaliah, proved more wicked than righteous (2 Kgs. 11) can hardly be blamed on her gender; the majority of *kings* in Israel and Judah proved wicked as well. And Esther stands as a wonderful canonical counterexample throughout the book that bears her name, even if her role as queen was "merely" as wife to the king. It was certainly made all the more impressive by the challenging setting of functioning in a foreign, pagan court among a people out to subject their Jewish neighbors to genocide![30]

A tantalizingly vague category of leadership was that of the "wise woman." In 2 Samuel 14, the wise woman of Tekoa serves as adviser to king David in a manner that closely resembles the role of a prophet. The same can be said of the wise woman of Abel Beth Maacah in her interaction with Joab (20:14–22). Nothing suggests a comparison with a NT pastor or elder; if anything, the role of these women is more akin to the leader of a city council.[31]

Other roles for women in OT times bear less directly on the issue of public leadership but still show ways in which the prevailing patriarchy was partially ameliorated. Zelophehad's daughters established the important precedent that women could inherit property in the absence of a legal male heir (Num. 27:1–11). God's Wisdom (like her opposite, "Folly,") is personified as a woman (see esp. Prov. 8–9), an image that continued to develop in the intertestamental period and proved important background for Jesus' claiming divine prerogatives without directly equating himself with Yahweh (e.g., Luke 7:35).[32] The

---

[30]Particularly sensitive to and balanced in interacting with feminist concerns is Karen Jobes, *Esther* (NIVAC; Grand Rapids: Zondervan, 1999).

[31]Joyce Baldwin, *1 & 2 Samuel* (TOTC; Downers Grove, Ill.: InterVarsity, 1988), 280.

[32]See esp. Ben Witherington III, *Jesus the Sage: The Pilgrimage of Wisdom* (Minneapolis: Fortress, 1994).

noble woman of Proverbs 31:10–31 defies a number of the stereotypes of contemporary conservative Christians. She is a strong, influential, and well-respected businesswoman who works hard to provide for her family as well. Nevertheless, that it is her husband who is one of the city's elders (v. 23) suggests at least some traditional role differentiation.[33] One also notes with interest the initiative the unnamed woman of Song of Songs takes throughout the book in her lovemaking,[34] as well as the strong countercultural stands of Rahab in accepting the spies and acknowledging the God of her enemies (Josh. 2) and of Naomi and Ruth in plotting how Ruth should propose marriage to Boaz (Ruth 3:9).[35] Finally, it is important to observe that children are commanded identical obedience to the dictates of both father and mother (Exod. 20:12; Prov. 1:8).

Nevertheless, the majority of OT life clearly left men in most of the prominent leadership roles in society, worship, and the family. And from time to time, practices or passages appear that can deeply trouble modern Christians. How are we to account for God's tolerance of polygamy, even if it was never commanded? (A key part of an answer is that it was actually quite rare. The OT mentions it only thirteen times, twelve of which involve kings or other very wealthy people who could afford multiple wives![36]) Then there are what Phyllis Trible dubbed "texts of terror"[37]—the rape of Dinah (Gen. 34), the seduction of Tamar (2 Sam. 13:1–22), the sacrifice of Jephthah's daughter (Judg. 11:29–40), or the violation and mutilation of the Levite's concubine (Judg. 19). Of course, the context of each of these texts makes it clear that they reflected deeply sinful behavior, but still God permitted them. Even harder to explain may be the legislation that seems to value female lives, whether human (Lev. 12:1–5; 27:1–8) or animal (Num. 15:22–29), somewhat less than their male counterparts.

---

[33]Cf. further Jack P. Lewis, "The Capable Wife (Prov 31:10–31)," in *Essays on Women in Earliest Christianity*, 2:155–80.

[34]Cf. esp. Tremper Longman III, *Song of Songs* (NICOT; Grand Rapids: Eerdmans, 2001).

[35]For defense of this interpretation see Robert L. Hubbard Jr., *The Book of Ruth* (NICOT; Grand Rapids: Eerdmans, 1988), 212.

[36]See Walter C. Kaiser Jr., *Toward Old Testament Ethics* (Grand Rapids: Zondervan, 1983), 182–90.

[37]Phyllis Trible, *Texts of Terror: Literary-Feminist Readings of Biblical Narratives* (Philadelphia: Fortress, 1984).

Of course the Christian can correctly point out that none of these troubling inequities carry over to the NT, though it contains problematic texts of its own, to which we shall shortly turn. But first we should summarize several principles that emerge from this all too rapid survey of OT developments after the fall.

To begin with, nowhere are women viewed merely as property, as was the case in several of the societies surrounding ancient Israel. Despite occasional claims to the contrary, the Hebrew Bible uniformly presents women as full persons, created as much in the image of God as men.[38] Proverbs 19:14, in fact, explicitly contrasts property, which is inherited from parents, with a "prudent wife," who "is from the LORD."

Second, one has to be careful in extrapolating from leadership roles in ancient Israel to the contemporary church. Even in denominations that still refer to pastors as priests, there is no exact correspondence between the roles of Israelite priests and today's pastors. After all, Christ became our priestly mediator for us, and at some level all Christians are priests because of our direct access to God through Christ Jesus (1 Pet. 2:5). Still, as the one established office of minister who led and guided key elements of temple services, the OT priest is a much closer counterpart to today's pastor-elder than, say, the Israelite prophets or judges.[39]

Third, while none of the OT roles of women we have surveyed link as directly with religious leadership as the priesthood, in a theocratic society without separation of church and state, every public or political leader would inevitably teach or legislate certain matters of religion. So if the most central role in the cult leadership was reserved for men, there were certainly numerous other contexts in which women would have taught and/or exercised appropriate authority over men in religious matters.

---

[38]Cf. the detailed survey of Alice O. Bellis (Helpmates, Harlots, and Heroes: Women's Stories in the Hebrew Bible [Louisville, Ky.: Westminster, 1994]), who, as a womanist interpreter, still does not hesitate to point out what she believes are demeaning roles and portraits.

[39]For excellent introductions to the priesthood more generally, see Blenkinsopp, Sage, Priest, Prophet, 66–114; and Richard D. Nelson, Raising Up a Faithful Priest: Community and Priesthood in Biblical Theology (Louisville, Ky.: Westminster, 1993).

Fourth, while undoubtedly the heavy-handed use of patriarchy can be chalked up to human sin and its evil consequences, it is hard to assign every aspect of the system, including even the most loving examples of male headship, simply to life in a fallen world. As it turns out, the pattern of women being permitted to lead in every arena save one will recur in each subsequent major section of our study, by which point it becomes very difficult to attribute this merely to coincidence or accommodation.

Fifth, as Jewish feminist writers have frequently pointed out, it is far too easy for Christian feminists, whether evangelical or liberal, simply to label all OT patriarchy as overturned by the gospel. The OT remains an authoritative book for Christians, which, among other things, means we must be able to affirm God's justice in arranging things the way he did even "back then." More subtly, attributing most or all of ancient Israelite patriarchy to human sinfulness smacks of an anti-Semitism that too quickly wants to make Judaism look bad for the sake of making Christianity look good![40] Nevertheless, and finally, the OT is a decidedly open-ended collection of books. The Latter Prophets look ahead to a new messianic age when God will write his laws on human hearts, make a new covenant, and in general enable greater obedience to his word. Nowhere is this captured as poignantly as in Joel 2:28–32, which also has direct relevance to the debate on gender roles:

> [28]And afterward,
>   I will pour out my Spirit on all people.
> Your sons and daughters will prophesy,
>   your old men will dream dreams,
>   your young men will see visions.
> [29]Even on my servants, both men and women,
>   I will pour out my Spirit in those days....
> [32]And everyone who calls
>   on the name of the LORD will be saved....

Joel emphatically insists that all humanly erected barriers leading to what we would call "discrimination" will be done away with in the gifts of the Spirit in the age of the new covenant. This is precisely the text Peter quotes at Pentecost

---

[40]These themes recur throughout Ross S. Kraemer and Mary R. D'Angelo, eds., *Women and Christian Origins* (New York: Oxford Univ. Press, 1999).

(Acts 2:17–21) to announce that the new day has arrived. So we should expect at least *some* key issues relating to gender roles to differ when we come to the NT.

INTERTESTAMENTAL DEVELOPMENTS

Almost half a millennium elapses between the latest written document of the OT (Malachi—ca. 425 BC) and the earliest NT books (probably James and the earliest Pauline letters—just before AD 50). We need, therefore, to make at least a few comments about relevant developments in Judaism during that period of time and also about prevailing patterns in the Greco-Roman world into which Christianity was born.

Interestingly, while continuing with its prevailing patriarchy, Jewish attitudes toward women in religious leadership were actually more diverse and at times more open than during the rabbinic period (from AD 70 onward for several centuries).[41] Bernadette Brooten has catalogued numerous examples of women in various forms of synagogue leadership, including "rulers" and "elders" (though tellingly absent are any clear references to women as formal religious teachers or rabbis).[42] Moreover, the kind of debate that could take place in the Mishnah (ca. AD 200) concerning whether women were persons or chattel is utterly unparalleled in the Jewish literature of the Second Temple period, in which OT theology remains more dominant.[43] At the same time, even in the pre-Christian period, "all the Jewish sources describe the same ideal picture of society: women provide what is asked of them, be it producing legal heirs, doing housework, remaining faithful to their husbands, avoiding contact with other men unrelated to them, or using their beauty to make their husbands' lives more pleasant. Women who deviate from this perfect behavior are described by all the sources as wicked."[44]

---

[41]See the surveys of Meir Bar-Ilan, *Some Jewish Women in Antiquity* (Atlanta: Scholars, 1998); Leonard J. Swidler, *Biblical Affirmations of Woman* (Philadelphia: Westminster, 1979).

[42]Bernadette J. Brooten, *Women Leaders in the Ancient Synagogue: Inscriptional Evidence and Background Issues* (BJS 36; Chico, Calif.: Scholars Press, 1982).

[43]See Judith R. Wegner, *Chattel or Person? The Status of Women in the System of the Mishnah* (Oxford: Oxford Univ. Press, 1988).

[44]Tal Ilan, *Jewish Women in Greco-Roman Palestine* (Peabody, Mass.: Hendrickson, 1996), 226.

In some respects, Greco-Roman women led less restricted lives in the first century than their Jewish counterparts. Socrates and Plato had developed a philosophical view that granted women far more equality with men, at least in theory, than anything found in intertestamental Jewish literature. Nevertheless, the more traditional views of Aristotle remained far more influential.[45] Roman women were increasingly being granted greater legal freedoms—e.g., to decide for themselves who they would marry. These freedoms had positive and negative consequences.[46] Bruce Winter describes the emergence of what were called "the new Roman women," who often used their sexual liberation to legitimate a promiscuous lifestyle.[47] As in many cultures throughout history, the minority of wealthy Greco-Roman women regularly enjoyed privileges and freedoms that the average woman did not—access to education, civic patronage, leisure time to pursue various hobbies and avocations because slaves did the housework, and leadership in religious circles.

At the same time, the notorious Roman *patria potestas* ("power of a father") gave Roman husbands almost unlimited authority as heads of their households, including the right to inflict corporal punishment on both wives and children (and in the case of slaves even to execute them for disobedience). Nothing like full-fledged modern egalitarianism characterized any significant aspect of Greco-Roman society.[48] If Jesus and the apostles did not learn egalitarianism from the OT or their Jewish upbringing, Greco-Roman influences would not have introduced them to it either. Of course, they may well have broken from *all* relevant backgrounds. But to determine if this is the case, we must proceed to the NT documents themselves.

---

[45]Cf. the surveys in Prudence Allen, *The Concept of Woman: The Aristotelian Revolution, 750 BC–AD 1250* (Grand Rapids: Eerdmans, 1997); Eva Cantarella, *Pandora's Daughters: The Role and Status of Women in Greek and Roman Antiquity* (Baltimore, Md.: Johns Hopkins Univ. Press, 1987); Matthew Dillon, *Girls and Women in Classical Greek Religion* (London: Routledge, 2002).

[46]See esp. Jane F. Gardner, *Women in Roman Law and Society* (Bloomington, Ind.: Indiana Univ. Press, 1986). Cf. also Suzanne Dixon, *Reading Roman Women: Sources, Genres, and Real Life* (London: Duckworth, 2001).

[47]Bruce W. Winter, "The 'New' Roman Wife and 1 Timothy 2:9–15: The Search for a *Sitz im Leben*," TynBul 51 (2000): 285–94.

[48]See esp. the overviews of Deborah F. Sawyer, *Women and Religion in the First Christian Centuries* (New York: Routledge, 1996); Sarah B. Pomeroy, *Goddesses, Whores, Wives, and Slaves: Women in Classical Antiquity* (New York: Schocken, 1975).

A SURVEY OF NT SCRIPTURE

Jesus and the Gospels

When the information in Matthew, Mark, Luke, and John about Jesus' life and teaching is evaluated against the backdrop of OT practice and intertestamental developments, remarkably positive data concerning women stands out.[49] Matthew's genealogy of Jesus contains references to five women, unusual for Jewish genealogies (Matt. 1:1–17). The inclusion of Tamar, Rahab, Ruth, and Bathsheba ("Uriah's wife"—v. 6) proves all the more striking, since all were Gentiles and all came under suspicion (rightly or wrongly) of illicit sexual unions. Mary, the mother of Jesus, likewise lived with the stigma of fornication—the only alternative to the incredible story of a virginal conception that many critics of emerging Christianity could accept. It would seem that even in his genealogy, Matthew wants to stress that Jesus came as the Messiah for all peoples, even the most marginalized (which of course included many women).[50]

Luke's birth narratives (chs. 1–2) likewise give surprising prominence to the roles of the mothers of the two special children being born. It is as if the story is being told from the perspectives of Elizabeth and Mary; perhaps one or both of these women were actually responsible for communicating this information to Luke.[51] It is well known that Luke's presentation of Jesus' adult ministry highlights Jesus' concern to minister to the outcast of Jewish society, including women. In various gospels, a number of Jesus' key miracles are performed specifically for individual women—curing Simon Peter's mother-in-law of a fever (Mark 1:29–31 par.), stopping the flow of blood from the hemorrhaging woman (5:25–34 par.) and raising Jairus's daughter from death (5:21–24, 35–43 par.).

The puzzling episode of Jesus and the Syrophoenician woman (Mark 7:24–30 par.) begins with Jesus shunning the woman in seemingly typical Jewish chauvinist, ethnocentric

---

[49]Cf. Ingrid R. Kitzberger, ed., *Transformative Encounters: Jesus and Women Reviewed* (Leiden: Brill, 2000); and Elisabeth Moltmann-Wendell, *The Women around Jesus* (New York: Crossroad, 1982).

[50]Cf. Craig L. Blomberg, "The Liberation of Illegitimacy: Women and Rulers in Matthew 1–2," *BTB* 21 (1991): 145–50.

[51]Cf. Stephen Farris, *The Hymns of Luke's Infancy Narratives* (JSNTSup 9; Sheffield: JSOT Press, 1985).

fashion. Still, he winds up granting her request, healing her daughter, and praising her great faith (Matt. 15:28). Whatever else is going on in this passage (and there have been many suggestions), he clearly succeeds in bringing the encounter to an exemplary close. Perhaps he deliberately provoked her in order to draw her out and publicly demonstrate the insight and tenacity he knew she had.[52]

A particularly striking encounter is that of the sinful woman at the home of a Pharisee who had invited Jesus to eat with him (Luke 7:36–50).[53] Jesus allows the woman, in her devotion, to "anoint" his feet with perfume and wipe them with her hair, signals that would have suggested to many in her culture that she was a prostitute making sexual advances. But again Jesus knew her heart and used the opportunity to commend her love—a sign of her salvation—and to criticize his host for not having offered even conventional tokens of hospitality.[54] Immediately after this account, Luke explains how Jesus' itinerant troupe included several women, who also helped provide financially for the group's needs (8:1–3). Men and women traveling together in this fashion as coworkers in a teacher's ministry would have scandalized many. But Jesus apparently saw nothing wrong with it.

Much has been made of the famous story of Jesus in Bethany with Mary and Martha (Luke 10:38–42). On the one hand, Jesus is obviously subverting conventional domestic roles. He accepts Mary sitting at his feet (v. 39), the posture of one learning Torah from a rabbi, precisely the role that later rabbinic teachings would normally forbid.[55] Martha's preoccupation with

---

[52]For an overview of options, see Glenna S. Jackson, *"Have Mercy on Me": The Story of the Canaanite Woman in Matthew 15.21–28* (JSNTSup 228; London: Sheffield Academic Press, 2002). Jackson herself suggests the woman becomes like a "psalmist in lament" to be self-empowered with a new identity. Matthew, in turn, uses her story as a paradigm for "enemy women" becoming full members of his Jewish-Christian community.

[53]This passage should not be confused with a later anointing by Mary of Bethany (Mark 14:1–9 par.; John 12:1–8), where there is no hint of sin on the part of the female protagonist and where the symbolism deals with preparation for Christ's death.

[54]Cf. Craig L. Blomberg, "'Your Faith Has Made You Whole': The Evangelical Liberation Theology of Jesus," in *Jesus of Nazareth, Lord and Christ*, ed. Joel B. Green and Max Turner (Grand Rapids: Eerdmans, 1994), 80–82.

[55]Rightly Spencer, *Beyond the Curse*, 58.

household responsibilities is *not* the "one thing" that is needed (v. 42). On the other hand, it goes beyond anything the text says or infers to conclude that a key reason for Mary's (or any other woman's learning from Jesus) was so that she could not only teach others but also "take authoritative leadership positions."[56] Interestingly, John 11 confirms Martha's activism and Mary's contemplation with their various roles in the account of Lazarus's resurrection.

John's detailed account of Jesus' dialogue with the Samaritan woman at Jacob's well (John 4:1–42) illustrates Jesus' concern for the outcast in several unique ways. His conversation partner is not only a woman but a Samaritan and (apparently[57]) one with a dismal sexual history. Yet Jesus guides her with grace and tact to a correct understanding of herself and of him, and she winds up becoming an evangelist to her own people. In similar vein, all of the gospels agree that the first witnesses of the resurrection (both to see Jesus and to tell others of his appearances) were all women (Mark 16:1–8 par.). They stayed by Jesus' side at the crucifixion and watched to see where he was buried, when most of the male disciples had fled. Given that women's testimony was inadmissible in most Jewish legal contexts, this element of the resurrection accounts would scarcely have been fabricated. It also shows Jesus' countercultural confidence in the women as "apostles to the apostles."[58]

Jesus' teaching on marriage and divorce includes strikingly equal treatment of men and women (Matt. 5:32; Mark 10:11–12) in a culture with a clear double standard for the genders with respect to both institutions. Luke's gospel frequently pairs stories about men and women in ways that suggest he is deliberately putting them on equal footing—both Mary and Zechariah

---

[56]Contra ibid., 62.

[57]It is at least possible she was a victim all along of unscrupulous men, since she would not have had the power to initiate the divorces herself and since her current companion may not have wanted to legally marry one with such a past. We have no evidence to say one way or the other; the very fact that few scholars even raise the alternate possibility says something about entrenched, even if unconscious, sexist interpretations! See Alice Mathews, *A Woman Jesus Can Teach* (Grand Rapids: Discovery House, 1991), 24–26.

[58]On this aspect of Jesus' ministry, see further Satoko Yamaguchi, *Mary and Martha: Women in the World of Jesus* (Maryknoll: Orbis, 2002); Richard Bauckham, *Gospel Women: Studies of the Named Women in the Gospels* (Grand Rapids: Eerdmans, 2002).

sing hymns of praise to God for his coming redemption through their children (Luke 1:46–55, 67–79); Simeon and Anna are both righteous elderly Jews who praise God for seeing the newborn Christ child (2:25–35, 36–38). Later on, Luke narrates in close succession Jesus' controversial Sabbath healings of a crippled woman and a man with abnormal swelling of his body (13:10–17; 14:1–6). In each case, Jesus justifies his behavior by appealing to Pharisaic traditions about caring for animals on the Sabbath, so that concern for ailing humans should prove all the more legitimate (13:15–16; 14:5–6). Finally the two pairs of parables known as the mustard seed and yeast (13:18–21) and the lost sheep and lost coin (15:3–10) each present parallel analogies, with one man and one woman as the leading character. At the very least, Jesus wants to relate and appeal to both genders equally within his audience. In the latter pair, he combines a story about a shepherd with one about a woman so that each, in some sense, stands for God![59]

Nevertheless, despite all these remarkable "advances" over his culture, Jesus never promotes full-fledged egalitarianism. Notwithstanding romantic portraits that paint him and his disciples as a company of equals,[60] the Gospels unequivocally depict Jesus as an authority figure instructing others on how to live. He has an inner core of his three closest followers (Peter, James, and John—Mark 5:37; 9:2; 14:33), who in turn form part of the twelve "apostles"—the next circle of leadership moving outward from Jesus himself. Then come a larger group of followers, which grows and shrinks depending on the circumstances, who can be called simply "disciples."[61] Only among this group do women appear. Of course, one can argue that to have a woman as one of Jesus' twelve closest followers would have proved too provocative in his world to gain any adherents for his movement, and thus relegate this restriction on women to a merely cultural phenomenon.[62] But in light of all of the ways just

---

[59]Cf. further Jane Kopas, "Jesus and Women: Luke's Gospel," *ThTo* 43 (1986): 192–202.

[60]Most notably, among recent writers, in J. Dominic Crossan, *The Historical Jesus: The Life of a Mediterranean Jewish Peasant* (San Francisco: HarperSanFrancisco, 1991), esp. pp. 341–44.

[61]See esp. John P. Meier, *A Marginal Jew: Rethinking the Historical Jesus*, vol. 3 (New York: Doubleday, 2001), 19–197.

[62]E.g., Bilezikian, *Beyond Sex Roles*, 236.

surveyed that Jesus *was* willing to scandalize his society, is this argument really credible? Is it just coincidence that the same phenomenon appears here as it did throughout the OT—a surprising openness within a staunchly patriarchal world to the role of women in leadership, including religious leadership, but with one key restriction at what was arguably the most authoritative level among God's people? Increasingly, both liberal feminists and evangelical complementarians are agreeing that Jesus was no full-fledged egalitarian, despite initial enthusiasm among evangelical and liberal feminists alike that perhaps he was.[63] The evangelical feminists who maintain otherwise must shoulder the burden of proof to demonstrate what evidence we have omitted (or skewed) that would prove their case.

The Evidence from the Acts of the Apostles

As we have already noted, Peter sees the arrival of the Holy Spirit at Pentecost as a fulfillment of Joel 2:28–32 (Acts 2:17–21). Whereas the Spirit came and went to empower select people for mighty deeds in OT times, now he would indwell and empower *all* believers, irrespective of gender, age, or status. One of the key manifestations of the Spirit would be prophecy. Numerous studies have scrutinized everything that ancient Jews, Greeks, Romans, and Christians called prophecy, and the one constant that runs through the otherwise diverse phenomena is that prophecy was a message believed to be fairly directly from God or the gods for a specific individual or group of individuals.[64] But, though more disputed, it seems that such a message could be a sudden and spontaneous outburst, a carefully planned speech or many other things in between these two ends of the

---

[63]Cf. Grant R. Osborne, "Women in Jesus' Ministry," *WTJ* 51 (1989): 259–91; John H. Elliott, "Jesus Was Not an Egalitarian: A Critique of an Anachronistic and Idealist Theory," *BTB* 32 (2002): 75–91; Elliott, "The Jesus Movement Was Not Egalitarian but Family-Oriented," *BibInt* 11 (2003): 173–210; Kathleen E. Corley, *Women and the Historical Jesus* (Santa Rosa, Calif.: Polebridge, 2002).

[64]See, e.g., Wayne A. Grudem, *The Gift of Prophecy in 1 Corinthians* (Lanham, Md.: University Press of America, 1982); David E. Aune, *Prophecy in Early Christianity and the Ancient Mediterranean World* (Grand Rapids: Eerdmans, 1983); Christopher Forbes, *Prophecy and Inspired Speech in Early Christianity and Its Hellenistic Environment* (Tübingen: Mohr, 1995); Ben Witherington III, *Jesus the Seer: The Progress of Prophecy* (Peabody, Mass.: Hendrickson, 1999).

spectrum.[65] That women would prophesy, as well as men (Acts 2:17–18), means there must be acceptable contexts within the Christian community for both genders to proclaim to others messages they believe the Lord has given them. As a specific illustration of this phenomenon, Acts 21:9 mentions that Philip's four unmarried daughters all prophesied. Unfortunately, Luke tells us nothing else to explain what this involved, although he does go on immediately to give the contents of a prediction by a male prophet, Agabus (vv. 10–14).

As in the Gospels, women play a surprisingly prominent role in the early Christian movement.[66] Peter raises from death Tabitha (or Dorcas), who was praised as "always doing good and helping the poor," in an account that contains striking parallels to Jesus' resurrection of Jairus's daughter (Acts 9:36–42). Lydia becomes Paul's first European convert, as he ignores the fact that there is no synagogue in Philippi and preaches to a group of women meeting out-of-doors by the river for prayer (16:13–15). Paul exorcises a slave girl in Philippi as well, which leads to his arrest (vv. 16–21). In Thessalonica and Berea a number of "prominent" Greek women respond to Paul's preaching by becoming believers (17:4, 12). Similarly, one of the visitors to the Areopagus in Athens, when Paul addresses the philosophers there, is a woman, Damaris, who becomes one of his comparatively few converts in that setting (17:34). A lone negative model is Sapphira, who is judged equally along with Ananias (5:7–10). Significant here is the fact that she is treated independently of her husband and given a chance to confess their sin and avert judgment. But when she fails to use her opportunity, the punishment is not lifted simply because she was submitting to her husband. Human authorities must always be *dis*regarded when they command or model something that violates Christian

---

[65]Denied by those listed in the previous note. But see Anthony C. Thiselton, *The First Epistle to the Corinthians* (NIGTC; Grand Rapids: Eerdmans, 2000), 960–61; Thomas W. Gillespie, *The First Theologians: A Study in Early Christian Prophecy* (Grand Rapids: Eerdmans, 1994), 23–28; and esp. David Hill, *New Testament Prophecy* (London: Marshall, Morgan & Scott, 1979), 213: Christian prophets are "those who have grasped the meaning of Scripture, perceived its powerful relevance to the life of the individual, the Church and society, and declare that message fearlessly."

[66]See esp. Ivoni R. Reimer, *Women in the Acts of the Apostles: A Feminist Liberation Perspective* (Minneapolis: Fortress, 1995), who concludes that Acts's portrait remains "androcentric," even while introducing with varying degrees of emphasis important liberating motifs.

ethics—in this case lying about how much money they received for the sale of their property (vv. 1–2).

Doubtless the most controversial episode in Acts with respect to gender roles is the enigmatic account about Priscilla and Aquila (18:18–26). Fellow tentmakers with Paul, this couple is referred to six times in the NT (18:2, 18, 26; Rom. 16:3; 1 Cor. 16:19; 2 Tim. 4:19). Four of the times, Priscilla's name appears first (Acts 18:18, 26; Rom. 16:3; 2 Tim. 4:19), whereas one would normally have expected her husband to be listed first in every instance. Presumably, she was the more prominent partner in some respect, perhaps in their ministry. The only thing we learn here about this ministry is that, after hearing Apollos preach in Ephesus and recognizing deficiencies in his knowledge of the Christian message, the two "invited him to their home and explained to him the way of God more adequately" (Acts 18:26). Even if their home was a house church, nothing in the text suggests this was some kind of formal, public instruction, though we cannot exclude the possibility. On the other hand, at the very least we have a positive example of a Christian woman helping to teach an adult Christian man in the area of religious doctrine, a practice some very conservative complementarians wrongly exclude altogether.[67]

Descriptive Material from the Epistles

When one turns to the Epistles, one thinks immediately of a handful of didactic texts that place restrictions on women. Before turning to them, however, it is important to see what positive roles for women leaders in ministry appear.[68] In Romans, Paul commends Phoebe, calling her both a *diakonos* and a *prostatis* (Rom. 16:1–2). The term *diakonos* is the identical word that is translated "deacon" in most English Bibles when it refers to a man occupying the office of helper to the elders or overseers (esp. Phil. 1:1; 1 Tim. 3:8–13). The feminine equivalent *diakonissa* is not attested in the Greek language until a later date, so in

---

[67]A balanced analysis appears in Wendell Willis, "Priscilla and Aquila—Coworkers in Christ," in *Essays on Women in Earliest Christianity*, 2:261–76.

[68]For a brief review of every reference to a named woman in the Pauline Epistles, see Andreas Köstenberger, "Women in the Pauline Mission," in *The Gospel to the Nations: Perspectives on Paul's Mission*, eds. Peter G. Bolt and Mark Thompson (Downers Grove, Ill.: InterVarsity, 2000), 221–47.

Paul's day the masculine form would have functioned generically for men or women in this position.[69] In other contexts, a *diakonos* can be a more informal helper of many different sorts, but given that Paul calls Phoebe a *diakonos* "of the church in Cenchreae" (Rom. 16:1), it is likely she is one of its deacons.[70] More and more complementarian scholars are acknowledging this, even though at times it has had little effect on the polity of the denominations to which they belong.[71] We know from early church history that the office of deaconess was common for several centuries, granting women church leadership roles, including the responsibility to care pastorally for, catechize, and baptize other women—tasks it was felt it was inappropriate for men to perform.[72] One wonders if there would be fewer disqualifications from the ministry these days if male pastors would reinstate something along these lines (e.g., referring long-term female counselees to women counselors whenever possible)!

The word *prostatis* is a bit more controversial. Most English Bibles render it somewhat along the lines of the NIV's "a great help." A few feminists have tried to argue, on the basis of cognate words, that it means "leader" or even "pastor."[73] But a growing consensus of complementarians and egalitarians alike are recognizing its widespread use as "patron"—a well-to-do person who helps finance various projects.[74] This fits Romans 16:2 very well, since Phoebe will have travel costs the Corinthians are asked to help defray, just as she has proved generous in supporting many others, including Paul himself.

---

[69]See Joseph A. Fitzmyer, *Romans* (AB; New York: Doubleday, 1993), 729.

[70]E.g., Douglas J. Moo, *The Epistle to the Romans* (NICNT; Grand Rapids: Eerdmans, 1996), 914.

[71]E.g., Thomas R. Schreiner, *Romans* (BECNT; Grand Rapids: Baker, 1998), 787. Schreiner teaches at The Southern Baptist Theological Seminary but, sadly, very few Southern Baptists allow for women deacons.

[72]See Anne Jensen, *God's Self-Confident Daughters: Early Christianity and the Liberation of Women* (Louisville, Ky.: Westminster, 1996), 59–73; Clark, *Man and Woman in Christ*, 117–23.

[73]Spencer (*Beyond the Curse*, 115–16) goes so far as to call Phoebe a leader over Paul! Cf. also Groothuis, *Good News for Women*, 196.

[74]E.g., Thomas R. Schreiner, "The Valuable Ministries of Women in the Context of Male Leadership," in *Recovering Biblical Manhood and Womanhood*, 219–20; Caroline F. Whelan, "*Amica Pauli*: The Role of Phoebe in the Early Church," *JSNT* 49 (1993): 67–85.

Less well known in the list of people in Romans 16 to whom Paul sends greetings is Junia (v. 7). Many English translations spell the name "Junias," as if it were male. But the first thirteen hundred years of church history overwhelmingly recognized this as a woman's name; over 250 occurrences of it appear in ancient documents and inscriptions, and for it to be masculine it would have to be a contraction of Junianus—a form that has yet to be attested anywhere.[75] By greeting Andronicus and Junia together, Paul may be indicating they were husband and wife. At any rate, he calls them "outstanding among the apostles." Despite attempts of some complementarians to make this mean merely "well known to the apostles,"[76] the use of *en* followed by a plural object is far more naturally and commonly rendered "among."

But then egalitarians sometimes jump in prematurely and argue if a woman could be an apostle, surely we have all the proof we need that they could function in the highest roles of church leadership. At this point, however, we have to define our terms carefully. The gospel writers regularly refer to the Twelve as apostles, and throughout his ministry Paul takes pains to stress that his apostolic authority is on a par with theirs. But Paul also includes "apostle" in two of his lists of spiritual gifts (1 Cor. 12:28; Eph. 4:11) that God's Spirit gives to whomever among his people he chooses (1 Cor. 12:11). Thus Paul can also call Epaphroditus (Phil. 2:25), Titus (2 Cor. 8:23), and James, the Lord's brother (Gal. 1:19), *apostoloi*, presumably implying, as in the term's broader Greek usage, "someone sent on a mission." In contemporary Christian parlance, we would call these people "missionaries" or, if they don't travel too far from home, "church planters."[77] This too is clearly an authoritative role of Christian

---

[75]Cf. Schreiner, *Romans*, 795–96; Köstenberger, "Women in the Pauline Mission," 229–31.

[76]Most recently, Michael H. Burer and Daniel B. Wallace, "Was Junia Really an Apostle? A Re-examination of Rom 16.7," *NTS* 47 (2001): 76–91. Evaluating this study is difficult because the evidence presented is highly selective, the numbers of true parallels to *episēmos* plus *en* plus the dative are limited, and, even in their so-called closest parallel (from *Pss. Sol.* 2:6), Burer and Wallace translate "among" in a locative sense, even though the first noun is not a subset of the second.

[77]Cf., respectively, Robert Saucy, "The Ministry of Women in the Early Church," in *Women and Men in Ministry*, 178; Belleville, *Women Leaders and the Church*, 54.

leadership that includes teaching doctrine to adult men and women, but it was not designed to be an office of local, ongoing church administration and instruction.[78] Properly functioning missionaries should, in fact, be appointing (or perhaps even ordaining) elders to perform this task, thus working themselves out of a job so that they can move on to a new location (Acts 14:23).

There are numerous other women coworkers in Christian ministry whom Paul commends in various contexts. Approximately one-third of the people Paul greets in Romans 16 are women, a striking statistic by the standards of ancient letter writing. Among them are Mary, "who worked very hard for" the Romans (v. 6); Tryphena and Tryphosa, "those women who work hard in the Lord" (v. 12); and Paul's "dear friend Persis, another woman who has worked very hard in the Lord" (v. 12). Elsewhere we are introduced to messengers from Chloe's household (1 Cor. 1:11) and to Nympha's house church (Col. 4:15). That families and fellowships would be described with women's names suggests that these were currently single adult Christian women and thus leaders of their homes, including at least their children but possibly slaves as well. In Philippians 4:2–3, Paul entreats Euodia and Syntyche "to be of the same mind in the Lord," and he asks an unnamed friend in the church there to "help these women since they have contended at my side in the cause of the gospel." From all of these references, we may conclude that women played important leadership roles in Paul's ministry and in his churches. But it outruns the evidence to claim we know they were formal pastors or elders or, for that matter, that they held any identifiable position. Paul simply doesn't give us enough information for that.[79]

Two texts that some have claimed *do* justify us thinking that Paul countenanced female elders are 1 Timothy 5:2 and Titus 2:3.[80] The first of these is typically translated as referring to "older women," but the form is the feminine plural of *presbyteros*, which frequently in the NT, and especially in the Pastoral Epistles,

[78]Cf. further John Thorley, "Junia, A Woman Apostle," *NovT* 38 (1996): 18–29; Richard S. Cervin, "A Note Regarding the Name 'Junia(s)' in Romans 16.7," *NTS* 40 (1994): 464–70.

[79]A classic study remains E. Earle Ellis, "Paul and His Coworkers," *NTS* 17 (1971): 437–52.

[80]E.g., Groothuis, *Good News for Women*, 197; Spencer, *Beyond the Curse*, 107–8.

means "elder" in the sense of church leader. On the other hand, the context here strongly supports a simple reference to age. The masculine *presbyteros* appears in 1 Timothy 5:1 and is widely recognized to mean merely "an older man." Verses 1–2 also enjoin correct treatment of "younger men" and "younger women" (from *neōteros*), and it is highly unlikely these terms refer to any kind of office. Moreover, in Titus 2:3 a different word is used (*presbytis*), which does not refer to a leadership role but merely to age, yielding "teach the older women to be reverent in the way they live." It is true that Paul was addressing elders as church leaders in 1:5–9 (just as he did in 1 Tim. 3:1–7), but the more immediate context again is dealing with old and young, men and women (2:1–8).[81]

As with the other parts of Scripture we have surveyed, there are more tangential texts that bear only indirectly on our question, but they are worth mentioning briefly. A few egalitarians have tried to argue that the "lady chosen by God" to whom 2 John is addressed (v. 1) is the female pastor of a house church.[82] But, given the reference to her children as fellow addressees and the closing greetings from "the children of your sister, who is chosen by God" (v. 13—despite the fact that John is writing), it is far better to accept the dominant belief throughout church history that the ladies are metaphors for two house churches, with their children as their members, just as Revelation can speak of the church as the "bride" of Christ more generally (Rev. 21:2, 9; 22:17).[83] In 1 Thessalonians 2:7 and 11, it is interesting to observe how Paul likens his pastoral ministry both to the tenderness of a *mother* caring for her little children and to the encouragement, comfort, and instruction of a *father* as he "deals with his own children." Much like feminine metaphors for God in the OT,[84] there is a side to male leadership that must reflect the gentle, nurturing qualities stereotypically associated with women.

---

[81]On both texts, cf. I. Howard Marshall, *A Critical and Exegetical Commentary on the Pastoral Epistles* (ICC; Edinburgh: T&T Clark, 1999), 243, 574.

[82]E.g., Spencer, *Beyond the Curse*, 109–12.

[83]See, e.g., Marianne M. Thompson, *1–3 John* (IVPNTC; Downers Grove, Ill.: InterVarsity, 1992), 151.

[84]On which, see esp. Virginia R. Mollenkott, *The Divine Feminine: The Biblical Imagery of God as Female* (New York: Crossroad, 1983). To recognize these metaphors does not commit us actually to using terms like "mother" or the feminine pronoun "she" for God, which Scripture does *not* do.

Finally, 1 Timothy 5:3–16 introduces us to the prominent role some widows played in prayer and good deeds; criteria were established for admitting them to the "church rolls," much like those for overseers and deacons (vv. 9–10).[85] But again this scarcely makes them equal in authority to these groups.

One final theme in Paul's letters must be unpacked before we turn to the explicitly prescriptive passages in the Epistles that generate so much controversy. That is the nature of several of the spiritual gifts. Included on Paul's lists, in addition to apostles and prophets, which we have already treated, appear teachers and administrators (Rom. 12:7; 1 Cor. 12:28), different kinds of leaders (Rom. 12:8), evangelists, and pastor-teachers (Eph. 4:11).[86] Virtually every thoughtful Bible student today agrees that when these terms are used of spiritual gifts, women may receive and exercise them just as powerfully as men may. Here it is helpful to distinguish spiritual gifts from church offices (or, for those who find the term "office" too institutionalized a concept for first-generation Christianity,[87] substitute something like "a settled or consistent function, role, or position"). At heart, the term "pastor" simply means "shepherd"— one who comes alongside one or more other people to care for them in any of a myriad of ways. The teacher is one who instructs others, especially in Paul's world, in the fundamental doctrines of the faith. Evangelists are those who share their faith with the goal of leading others to the Lord. Administrators guide and organize, while the term "leader" is a very broad one in Greek (as in English) that encompasses numerous supervisory roles.[88] When God's people recognize that any given woman has been given one or more of these leadership gifts, they should work as hard as they would for any man to give her abundant opportunity to cultivate those gifts in the church.

---

[85]For a thorough study, see Bonnie B. Thurston, *The Widows: A Women's Ministry in the Early Church* (Philadelphia: Fortress, 1989).

[86]The lack of repetition of the definite article suggests to most commentators that this is an example of Granville Sharp's rule loosely applied. "Pastors" and "teachers" are not entirely separate gifts; each involves some element of the other.

[87]E.g., Walter L. Liefeld, *1 and 2 Timothy, Titus* (NIVAC; Grand Rapids: Zondervan, 1999), 116–17.

[88]On the nature of the various spiritual gifts, see esp. Kenneth Hemphill, *Spiritual Gifts: Empowering the New Testament Church* (Nashville: Broadman, 1988); Siegfried Schatzmann, *A Pauline Theology of Charismata* (Peabody, Mass.: Hendrickson, 1987).

At the same time, all of these gifts can be exercised without a person holding any formally designated church leadership role, so their presence in Paul's lists does not settle the larger debate between complementarians and egalitarians.

The Classic Controversial Passages in Paul

It is finally time to turn to the most commonly cited Pauline texts that seem to bear most directly on the gender roles debate. We will proceed in the probable chronological order of the epistles in which they appear.

Galatians 3:28

A text that forms a bridge between the merely descriptive and the purely prescriptive texts is Galatians 3:28: "There is neither Jew nor Gentile, neither slave nor free, neither male nor female, for you are all one in Christ Jesus." Most discussions of this passage either claim too little or too much from this one text. On the one hand, complementarians often correctly point out that the larger context is about the principle of salvation by faith rather than works and the resulting role of the law in salvation history (chs. 3–4). Thus they argue that all Paul is stressing is that men and women (like Jews and Gentiles or slaves and free-persons) come to Christ on identical terms; there is no discrimination when it comes to being saved.[89] On the other hand, egalitarians often cite this text as a "manifesto" of sorts that proves Paul could not have envisioned any timeless restrictions on women in leading in the church or home. All other passages that at first seem to teach otherwise must have been misinterpreted, or else Paul was providing merely situation-specific guidelines.[90]

Neither of these approaches can be sustained after careful exegesis. It is true that men and women come to Christ on identical terms. But the most immediate context is 3:26–29, which also talks about baptism. Baptism was the outward sign of an inward repentance and faith in Christ. We often forget today

---

[89]E.g., Timothy George, *Galatians* (NAC; Nashville: Broadman & Holman, 1994), 282–92.

[90]E.g., Stanley J. Grenz with Denise M. Kjesbo, *Women in the Church: A Biblical Theology of Women in Ministry* (Downers Grove, Ill.: InterVarsity, 1995), 99–107.

how egalitarian a ritual it was, replacing the Jewish initiation rite of circumcision that applied only to men.[91] If baptism no longer automatically communicates that symbolism, contemporary churches should ask themselves what other outward signs they can use to demonstrate the absolute equality of men and women in God's eyes at the very essence of their being. Serving Communion, for example, is one of those practices that unfortunately got bound up in church history with ordination, despite no text of Scripture ever suggesting the Lord's Supper could be administered only by a certain category of Christian. Complementarians and egalitarians alike should thus be able to agree that women and men both will serve Communion (the Lord's Supper, Eucharist). In churches where this has not previously been the practice, the symbolism of such a simple gesture has proved extraordinarily meaningful to women in ways men may never fully appreciate, simply because (like baptism in Paul's world) it represents so significant a break from past chauvinism with one of the church's central ordinances (or sacraments).

On the other hand, more than twenty years ago Ben Witherington pointed to texts in later rabbinic literature with striking parallels to Galatians 3:28 that nevertheless went on to include far more restrictions on women than anything even typical Christian complementarians propose (see esp. *Seder Eliyahu Rabbah* 7 and *Yalkut Lech Leka* 76). So to conclude from this one programmatic statement that Paul could not have consistently imagined any role differentiation between the genders in church or home throughout the whole "church age" simply violates the standard canons of logic.[92] The word "one" (*eis*) in this passage does not obviously mean "equal in all respects" in any of its 344 other NT usages; "equal" is not even a definition found in the standard lexica.[93] Equality may be suggested

---

[91]Ben Witherington III, "Rite and Rights for Women—Galatians 3.28," *NTS* 27 (1981): 601. For Christians from Roman backgrounds, there may have been a contrast with the rite of passage for adolescent boys in which they donned a fancy new toga as a sign of adulthood. See J. Albert Harrill, "Coming of Age and Putting on Christ: The *Toga Virilis* Ceremony, Its Paraenesis and Paul's Interpretation of Baptism in Galatians," *NovT* 44 (2002): 252–77.

[92]See Witherington, "Rite and Rights," 593–94. Cf. also Ed L. Miller, "Is Galatians 3:28 the Great Egalitarian Text?" *ExpTim* 114 (2002): 9–11.

[93]See Richard W. Hove, *Equality in Christ? Galatians 3:28 and the Gender Dispute* (Wheaton, Ill.: Crossway, 1999), 69–76, 107–21.

in certain contexts, as with Galatians 3:28, but then we dare not infer more about the kind of equality envisioned than each given context warrants.

First Corinthians 11:2–16

Now we come to the first of several texts in which Paul gives varying commands to men and women in the contexts of Christian worship.[94] A few scholars have attempted to argue that this passage is a non-Pauline interpolation or a Corinthian slogan (vv. 3–7 or 3–10), which Paul then rebuts in verses 11–16.[95] But there are no manuscripts anywhere that omit or relocate this passage, and there is nothing "sloganlike" (a one-sided, concise proverb that Paul would need to qualify) about verses 3–7. We will have to come to grips with the text where it is, as it stands.

The specific problem involves what men and women are or are not wearing on their heads while praying or prophesying (vv. 4–5). So Paul grounds his instructions for what should or shouldn't cover one's physical head by drawing an analogy with one's spiritual head: "the head of every man is Christ, and the head of the woman is man, and the head of Christ is God" (v. 3). A firestorm of controversy, however, has surrounded the meaning of this word "head" (*kephalē*). Complementarians argue vigorously for the traditional understanding of head as an "authority," while egalitarians promote the concept of "source" or "origin." Complicating matters is the infrequency of *any* nonliteral use of *kephalē* in ancient Greek usage; the word normally means the anatomical head on a person or animal. After earlier allegations on each side that the word *never* meant what the other side claimed it did,[96] there is a growing consensus that there are at least a handful of

---

[94]For a rare attempt to deny this is the context, see Harold R. Holmyard III, "Does 1 Corinthians 11:2–16 Refer to Women Praying and Prophesying in Church?" *BSac* 154 (1997): 461–72. For seven reasons for assuming this *is* the correct context, see Craig Blomberg, *1 Corinthians* (NIVAC; Grand Rapids: Zondervan, 1994), 219.

[95]See, respectively, William O. Walker Jr., "The Vocabulary of 1 Corinthians 11.3–16: Pauline or Non-Pauline," *JSNT* 35 (1989): 75–88; and Thomas P. Shoemaker, "Unveiling of Equality: 1 Corinthians 11:2–16," *BTB* 17 (1987): 60–63.

[96]See, e.g., Wayne Grudem, "Does *Kephalē* ('Head') Mean 'Source' or 'Authority Over' in Greek Literature? A Survey of 2,336 Examples," *TJ* 6 (1985): 38–59 (arguing for only "authority over"); and Berkeley and Alvera Mickelsen, "What Does *Kephalē* Mean in the New Testament?" in *Women, Authority and the Bible*, ed. Alvera Mickelsen (Downers Grove, Ill.: InterVarsity, 1986), 97–110 (arguing for only "source").

uses of *kephalē* meaning primarily either "authority" or "source."[97] But what has not been demonstrated is that the singular form (the plural *kephalai* can mean the headwaters of a river, and hence its source) ever means "source" without simultaneously implying some dimension of authority.[98]

Many egalitarians have cited Stephen Bedale's pioneering study a half century ago that argued for "source" as a crucial part of Paul's meaning in texts with *kephalē* especially Ephesians 5:23. But they have either not gone on to read or not bothered to concede that Bedale concluded, "The male is *kephalē* in the sense of *archē* (beginning) relative to the female; and, in St. Paul's view, the female in consequence is 'subordinate' (cf. Eph. 5:23)."[99] Likewise, some writers have suggested translating *kephalē* as "preeminent" or "prominent"—and perhaps therefore "representative."[100] But again it is unclear if an entity can be most or even more prominent without implying at least some kind of functional superiority in the context at hand.

Egalitarians often point to the unusual order of 1 Corinthians 11:3 as further proof that Paul is not establishing a hierarchy here. If he were, so they say, one would have expected to read, "The head of the woman is man, the head of man is Christ, and the head of Christ is God," thus moving from most subordinate to most authoritative (or vice-versa).[101] Instead we get the sequence of man-Christ, woman-man, Christ-God. But in fact

---

[97]Authors defending "authority" draw especially on the Septuagint, Philo, and Plutarch; those favoring "source" draw on Philo (again), Herodotus, Artemidorus, the Orphic literature, and *L.A.E.* See Andrianjatovo Rakotoharintsifa, *Conflits à Corinthe* (Genève: Labor et Fides, 1997), 208.

[98]Most meticulous of all in rebutting those who would cite texts claiming "source" without "authority" as the full meaning of the word is Wayne Grudem, "The Meaning of *Kephalē* ('Head'): An Evaluation of New Evidence, Real and Alleged," *JETS* 44 (2001): 25–65.

[99]Stephen Bedale, "The Meaning of *Kephalē* in the Pauline Epistles," *JTS* 5 (1954): 214. See also the "matriarch" of modern liberal Christian feminism, Elisabeth Schüssler Fiorenza, *In Memory of Her: A Feminist Theological Reconstruction of Christian Origins* (New York: Crossroad, 1983), 229.

[100]See Walter L. Liefeld, "Women, Submission and Ministry in 1 Corinthians," in *Women, Authority and the Bible*, 134–54; Andrew C. Perriman, "The Head of a Woman: The Meaning of *Kephalē* in 1 Corinthians 11:3," *JTS* 45 (1994): 602–22; Richard S. Cervin, "Does *Kephalē* Mean 'Source' or 'Authority Over' in Greek Literature? A Rebuttal," *TJ* 10 (1989): 85–112.

[101]E.g., Bilezikian, *Beyond Sex Roles*, 137–38.

this makes good sense if Paul is leading up to commands to Christian men and women. It would be natural to refer to their heads first and then draw the comparison between Christ and God. It is also important to note that the terms *anēr* and *gunē* could just as easily be translated "husband" and "wife" as "man" and "woman." This ambiguity will recur in 1 Corinthians 14 and 1 Timothy 2 as well; in each context, a minority of scholars has argued that Paul's commands apply only to married persons as a sign of authority and submission in marriage that does not have any human counterpart with adult singles.[102]

What kind of head coverings, then, is Paul so concerned about in verses 4–5, and what causes his concern? It is possible that he is describing a veil, shawl, or some other external head covering he wants women to wear, although it is interesting that by the time he gets to verses 14–16, he is unambiguously talking about long and short *hair*. Verses 4–7a could be translated quite differently than in most Bibles, as the NIV text note demonstrates, so that Paul is talking about long hair on women and short hair on men throughout the whole passage.[103] The ambiguity is generated because the Greek literally speaks just of having something "down from the head." There are a host of possible cultural phenomena that could have explained Paul's concern with head coverings or hair length—Roman priests covering their heads with their togas while officiating at pagan services; shoulder-length hair on many Greek men, suggesting homosexuality; overly short hair on Greek women, suggesting lesbianism; lack of a veil or shawl on some Jewish or Greek women, suggesting a wife was not "attached" but "available"; and more. What all these phenomena share is that Paul was concerned that Christian men and women at worship not appear as though they were either religiously unfaithful to God or sexually unfaithful to their spouses.[104] In cultures where such head

---

[102]Cf., respectively, Jason D. BeDuhn, "'Because of the Angels': Unveiling Paul's Anthropology in 1 Corinthians 11," *JBL* 118 (1999): 300–301; E. Earle Ellis, "The Silenced Wives of Corinth (1 Cor. 14:34–5)," in *New Testament Textual Criticism*, ed. Eldon J. Epp and Gordon D. Fee (Oxford: Clarendon, 1981), 213–20; Jerome D. Quinn and William C. Wacker, *The First and Second Letters to Timothy* (ECC; Grand Rapids: Eerdmans, 2000), 199–200.

[103]See, e.g., David E. Blattenberger, *Rethinking 1 Corinthians 11:2–16 through Archaeological and Moral-Rhetorical Analysis* (Lewiston, N.Y.: Mellen, 1997).

[104]Cf. further Blomberg, *1 Corinthians*, 210–11, 215.

coverings (or their absence) do not send similar mixed signals, one need not obey these commands literally. But then Christians must ask what other outward forms of dress, appearance, or behavior could send the wrong messages in their cultures, and make sure to abstain from those practices.

In the midst of these primary concerns, the significance of verse 5 for the gender roles debate dare not be missed. Paul does take it for granted that women will pray and prophesy in public Christian worship. And we must recall that one of the forms of Christian prophecy was akin to what we today would call a sermon, delivered by a Spirit-filled preacher convinced he or she was passing along a message from God (above, p. 127). To date, the only restriction on women in ministry we have discovered in either Testament is what we may call, admittedly with a little anachronism, the "highest office" of authority and responsibility in the settled religious life of the community. One could thus be completely faithful to 1 Corinthians 11:5 by allowing a woman to preach, while at the same time insisting that the elders of a local congregation all be men, and that her authority to preach is a delegated one, with the elder board as the ultimate body of human leaders to whom the entire church (preachers included) is accountable. One should, in fact, phrase things more strongly: not to encourage a woman who appears to have the gift of prophecy to cultivate it in the context of preaching God's word to his people is to fight against God's purpose in giving spiritual gifts to all his followers—especially for the edification of the entire body (Eph. 4:13).[105]

Verse 7b, however, reaffirms the ultimate hierarchy Paul does envision: the man "is the image and glory of God; but woman is the glory of man." Tragically, especially in past eras of church history, the lack of symmetry in this half verse has

---

[105]For a wonderfully tactful and successful model of implementing this within a complementarian church structure, see Sarah Sumner, *Men and Women in the Church* (Downers Grove, Ill.: InterVarsity, 2003), 311–18. Prayer and prophecy, in fact, sum up the essence of Christian worship. As Francis Watson ("The Authority of the Voice: A Theological Reading of 1 Cor 11.2–16," *NTS* 46 [2000]: 525) phrases it, "In prophecy one articulates the word of God to the congregation, in prayer one articulates the word of the congregation to God; and in the conjunction of these activities there occurs the divine-human dialogue that lies at the heart of the Christian community's life and worship."

been taken to mean the woman was not created in the image of God, a flagrant contradiction of Genesis 1:26–28. In fact, the lack of symmetry functions precisely to safeguard against the conclusion that "woman is the *image* and glory of man," which would be blasphemous.[106]

Verses 8–9 continue an argument from irreversibility, pointing to the order and purpose of creating men and women (see above, p. 130). Coming as they do immediately after a half verse that reaffirms the hierarchy stated in verse 3, verses 8–9 ground male headship in the way God created things—not a changeable principle depending on the specific circumstances. Verse 10 is difficult, but it probably refers to the concept that angels watched over and even participated with God's people at worship, in part to ensure proper decorum.[107] The NIV gratuitously adds "sign of" before "authority" in this verse;[108] the Greek literally reads, "therefore the woman ought to have authority over her head because of the angels." Every other NT use of the three-word expression *exousian echein epi* means "to have authority (or control) over."[109] So, far from giving the woman permission to do what she wants with her head, this verse simply reinforces Paul's earlier teaching that she should keep the appropriate covering on it.[110]

In verses 11–12, Paul introduces an important qualification to his argument from the created order in verses 8–9. "In Christ"—as believers grow in sanctification—men and women become more and more mutually interdependent. It makes no sense to say this caveat altogether cancels out the force of verses 8–9;[111] why then did Paul bother to write them at all? Rather, with Judith Gundry-Volf, Paul can appeal "to creation to support instructions which presume a hierarchicalist relationship of

---

[106]Rakotoharintsifa (*Conflits à Corinthe*, 219–20) stresses that the notion that the man is not fully honored without the woman's glory also guards against the view that does not ascribe equal dignity to the woman.

[107]See esp. Joseph A. Fitzmyer, "A Feature of Qumran: Angelology and the Angels of 1 Corinthians xi.10," *NTS* 4 (1957): 48–58.

[108]But following the influential article by Morna D. Hooker, "Authority on Her Head: An Examination of 1 Corinthians xi.10," *NTS* 10 (1966): 410–16.

[109]Matt. 9:6 (par. Mark 2:10; Luke 5:24); Rev. 11:6; 14:18; 16:9; 20:6. Cf. also the similar constructions with synonyms for *epi* (Luke 19:17; 1 Cor. 7:37) or without forms of the verb "to have" (Luke 9:1; Rev. 2:26; 6:8; 13:7).

[110]Cf. Raymond F. Collins, *First Corinthians* (SP; Collegeville, Minn.: Liturgical, 1999), 411.

[111]E.g., Bilezikian, *Beyond Sex Roles*, 133–34.

man and woman as well as undergird their new social equality in Christ without denying the difference."[112] Male headship among Christians should never be authoritarian or heavy-handed, as one often experiences in the non-Christian world. Tragically, it is often in complementarian churches where one finds a *greater* authoritarianism than in the secular workplace!

In verses 13–16, Paul returns to the particular cultural manifestations of headship and subordination that triggered this instruction in the first place. Tellingly, all of Paul's rationales are culture bound. Verse 13 asks rhetorically if it is "proper" (or "fitting"—*prepon*) for a woman to pray or prophesy with an uncovered head—a question that would be answered quite differently from one culture to the next. Verse 14 at first glance seems to appeal to something more fundamental—"the very nature of things." But Paul himself knew his OT well enough to know that one kind of man proved obedient to God when he refused to cut his hair—the Nazirite (Num. 6—of whom Samson is the most famous, though scarcely most virtuous, example [Judg. 13–16]). Paul himself had taken temporary Nazirite vows as a Christian (Acts 18:18). So it is inconceivable he could have used *physis* ("nature") here to mean "God's timeless will in every culture throughout human history," even though he regularly uses it that way in other contexts. Here it must have simply meant the way the people in the Corinthians' culture evaluated "the nature of things."[113] Likewise, verse 16 appeals to "practice," or "custom"(*synētheia*), and when Paul says the churches of God have no other custom, he means simply in his day, in his culture.

In short, 1 Corinthians 11:2–16 teaches the timeless principles of male headship and female subordination, at least among husbands and wives; it also reveals that appearance or demeanor during worship (or anywhere else, for that matter, but especially during worship) should in no way send the wrong cultural signals that one is unfaithful—either to God or to one's spouse. How that played out in Paul's day involved head coverings, including hair length. What it means for Westerners today may

[112]Judith Gundry-Volf, "Gender and Creation in 1 Corinthians 11:2–16: A Study in Paul's Theological Method," in *Evangelium, Schriftauslegung, Kirche*, eds. J. Ådna, S. J. Hafemann, and O. Hofius (Göttingen: Vandenhoeck & Ruprecht, 1997), 152.

[113]Cf. Thiselton, *First Epistle to the Corinthians*, 844–46. Moreover, the "natural" thing for hair to do is to grow long if it is not cut! Thus, Khiok-Khng Yeo, "Differentiation and Mutuality of Male-Female Relations in 1 Corinthians 11:2–16," *BR* 43 (1998): 20.

be quite different—not revealing too much skin, not behaving flirtatiously, not dressing or acting like members of some other religion just for the sake of "contextualizing" the gospel, and so on. The passage does not address the issue of whether there are certain roles reserved for men in church, but it tacitly approves one key role for women—Spirit-filled preaching, which the contemporary church neglects to its detriment, inappropriately squelching the gifts of numbers of women and often damaging them psychologically in the process by telling them unbiblical things about what they can't or shouldn't do.

First Corinthians 14:33–38

Unless we assume Paul gratuitously contradicted himself in the space of three chapters, however we account for this passage, we cannot take it to mean Paul was telling women never to utter a word in church![114] What then did he mean by "silencing" the women? At least five main options have been suggested. I will treat them in what I believe to be an increasing order of probability.

To begin with, many liberal and a handful of evangelical scholars have argued that Paul did not write these verses; they were added into the manuscript tradition by more conservative scribes.[115] It is true that a few very late manuscripts move verses 34–35 to the end of the chapter, but this is different from omitting them altogether.[116] Plus it makes perfect sense to see why someone

---

[114]Contra Marlene Crüsemann ("Irredeemably Hostile to Women: Anti-Jewish Elements in the Exegesis of the Dispute about Women's Right to Speak [1 Cor. 14.34–35]," *JSNT* 79 [2000]: 21), who calls the text "a comprehensive prohibition of public speaking, applying to all Christian women"!

[115]For one example from each perspective, see, respectively, Winsome Munro, "Women, Text and the Canon: The Strange Case of 1 Corinthians 14.33–35," *BTB* 18 (1988): 26–31; and Gordon D. Fee, *The First Epistle to the Corinthians* (NICNT; Grand Rapids: Eerdmans, 1987), 699–708.

[116]Philip B. Payne ("Fuldensis, Sigla for Variants in Vaticanus, and 1 Cor 14.34–5," *NTS* 41 [1995]: 240–62; and "Ms. 88 as Evidence for a Text without 1 Cor 14.34–5," *NTS* 44 [1998]: 152–58) has argued that marginal additions and symbols in a handful of manuscripts that do contain these verses nevertheless provide evidence of knowledge of a manuscript tradition that lacked them, but his arguments prove unconvincing. See Curt Niccum, "The Voice of the Manuscripts on the Silence of Women: The External Evidence for 1 Cor 14.34–5," *NTS* 43 (1997): 242–55; D. W. Odell-Scott, "Editorial Dilemma: The Interpolation of 1 Cor 14:34–35 in the Western Manuscripts of D, G and 88," *BTB* 30 (2000): 68–74.

might think they were dislocated—they seem to interrupt a discussion of tongues and prophecy that spans verses 26–40. So it is highly probable that Paul's original did contain these verses right where we read them in English translations.

Second, a number of egalitarians have proposed that verses 34–35 reflect a Corinthian slogan that Paul, in fact, rebuts in verses 36–38. Just as 6:12; 7:1; 8:1; and 10:23 can all be plausibly taken as views some people in the Corinthian church are promoting but which Paul cannot accept without qualification (see the use of quotation marks in TNIV for each of these verses), so also some in Corinth want to silence the women. According to this view, verse 36 ("Did the word of God originate with you?") begins Paul's reply, in which he challenges this overly zealous conservatism.[117] This option too seems highly unlikely. Verses 34–35 do not form a short, pithy proverb, as "slogans" inevitably do. And if they reflect a slogan Paul refutes, they would have to represent an ultraconservative, legalistic Jewish approach not reflected in any of the other probable slogans in the letter, all of which represent an overly libertine, or at least a very Hellenistic, perspective. Unlike Paul's "yes, but" logic elsewhere, Paul would have to be understood as not affirming *any* part of this supposed slogan. Add to all these arguments the observation that almost all of its adherents have written only in the last thirty years or so, and it seems to be only slightly more probable than the suggestion that Paul did not write these words at all.

Third, a more plausible option suggested periodically throughout church history is that these verses apply merely to a specific situation in Corinth not replicated in all churches everywhere. Verse 33b ("as in all the congregations of the Lord's people") can be plausibly taken as the end of the previous paragraph rather than as an introduction to verses 34–35. Given the lack of education of most women in Paul's world, and given possible parallels with segregated synagogue seating that relegated women more to the periphery of the congregation, making them prone to chattering or gossip rather than full involvement in worship, one can see how Paul might have wanted to silence particularly disruptive behavior in Corinth. Perhaps the questions these women were asking were very elementary ones that distracted

---

[117]E.g., recently, Collins, *First Corinthians*, 514–17. A flurry of studies proposed and discussed this view in the 1980s; today one finds little support for it.

from the flow of teaching or worship and were better dealt with privately (v. 35). On this interpretation, unless similar phenomena are present, there is no need for women today to speak any less in church than men.[118] One problem with this view is that the support for segregated synagogues comes from centuries later; no archaeological or literary evidence suggests such a practice was in place in the first century. More seriously, as D. A. Carson phrases it, this approach becomes "unbearably sexist."[119] We know from Paul's own writings that there were at least a handful of gifted and educated women in his churches and plenty of uneducated men. Silencing *all* women and *no* men scarcely addresses this problem satisfactorily. Finally, the appeal to "the law," which teaches women's submission, suggests Paul is again grounding his instruction in some more culture-transcending principle. Attempts to limit this *nomos* ("law") to extrabiblical Jewish tradition or Greco-Roman legislation require Paul to have used this term, without explanatory qualification, in a very uncharacteristic way, since normally he means *Torah* (any or all of the Hebrew Bible) by the term.[120] Attempts to limit his reference to post-fall arrangements in the OT, no longer incumbent on believers, makes Paul's instruction incoherent.[121] Why would he appeal to a principle he recognizes no longer supports his ethic?

A fourth option recognizes that the context of Paul's teaching is an entire chapter on problems with the exercise of spiritual gifts in Corinth, especially prophecy and tongues. Since

---

[118]For the most persuasive versions of this option, cf. Craig A. Keener, *Paul, Women and Wives: Marriage and Women's Ministry in the Letters of Paul* (Peabody, Mass.: Hendrickson, 1992), 80–88; Belleville, *Women Leaders and the Church*, 152–62. A new version has recently been proposed by Terence Paige, "The Social Matrix of Women's Speech at Corinth: The Context and Meaning of the Command to Silence in 1 Corinthians 14:33b–36," *BBR* 12 (2002): 217–42. Paige argues that the only kind of speaking Paul is forbidding is ordinary conversation between women and men to whom they are not related, which still would have been seen as dishonorable in Greek society. But this is precisely *not* what *laleō* consistently means in 1 Corinthians 14 (see below, p. 164).

[119]D. A. Carson, "'Silent in the Churches': On the Role of Women in 1 Corinthians 14:33b–36," in *Recovering Biblical Manhood and Womanhood*, 147.

[120]See Douglas J. Moo, "'Law,' 'Works of the Law,' and Legalism in Paul," *WTJ* 45 (1983): 73–100.

[121]Esp. Gen. 3:16, common among older commentators. E.g., A. T. Robertson and Alfred Plummer, *A Critical and Exegetical Commentary on the First Epistle of St Paul to the Corinthians* (ICC; Edinburgh: T&T Clark, 1914), 325.

tongues seem to have gotten most out of hand, and by analogy with Greco-Roman religions in which women at times exhibited ecstatic or out-of-control forms of public speaking, perhaps Paul is merely telling the women in Corinth not to speak in tongues (glossolalia).[122] This approach moves us close to the best of available options by noting that in 1 Corinthians 14, the verb for "speak" (*laleō*) appears twenty-one times outside of its puzzling uses in verses 34–35, and in twenty of these instances it refers to a very limited kind of speech—prophecy, the evaluation of prophecy, tongues, or the interpretation of tongues. And a sizable majority of these uses do refer to glossolalia. But speaking in tongues, like its interpretation and like prophecy, is a spiritual gift given by God to whomever he wills, irrespective of gender. This leads us to the final and best option.

The evaluation of prophecy is not a spiritual gift. At one level, it is incumbent on all listeners to evaluate the truthfulness of messages allegedly from God (v. 29). But it would ultimately have devolved to the leadership of the church to render a verdict on any disputed messages. If Paul believed the highest level of church leadership was reserved for men (even if one should argue that such a view was not timeless but culture specific), then it could be that he is telling the women (at least in his day) to be silent merely in that one specific context. They are not to usurp the authority of the male leaders in pronouncing authoritatively on any disputed prophecy. It is significant that the very last topic Paul addressed before these seemingly intrusive comments about women is prophecy and its evaluation (vv. 29–33a).[123] It is even possible to combine this interpretation with elements of the third view surveyed above and envision that women were asking disruptive questions as part of the evaluation of prophecy. Among other problems, this could have led to wives contradicting their husbands, including their husbands' prophecies, in a way that compromised their submission

---

[122]See esp. Ralph P. Martin, *The Spirit and the Congregation: Studies in 1 Corinthians 12–15* (Grand Rapids: Eerdmans, 1984), 87.

[123]Cf. further Hurley, *Man and Woman in Biblical Perspective*, 188–93; Simon J. Kistemaker, *Exposition of the First Epistle to the Corinthians* (NTC; Grand Rapids: Baker, 1993), 511–15. On this view it is important to distinguish the task of rendering an authoritative evaluation on alleged prophecy—if its contents are true or not—from the charism of discerning spirits—recognizing, e.g., the presence of the demonic. See esp. Grudem, *The Gift of Prophecy*, 58–67.

(v. 34).[124] On this view, the "law" in verse 34 would be the entire Hebrew Bible, including the pre-fall arrangements of authority and subordination. But the only unambiguous timeless principle would be wives' submission to husbands.[125] It is possible, though, that a second culture-transcending principle is presupposed—reserving the highest leadership role in the church for men—but if so, it is not explicitly stated. It is, in fact, the next passage to which we must turn that remains the primary battleground for debating that issue.

First Timothy 2:8–15

There is no question that the context of 1 Timothy is the presence of false teaching in Ephesus, against which Paul urges Timothy to stand fast.[126] Most scholars see some combination of Jewish and Gnostic elements in this heresy. First Timothy 1:6–11 makes sense only against the background of Jewish debates over the role of Torah; forbidding marriage (4:2) is best understood against a Hellenistic backdrop, particularly the kind of asceticism that later full-blown Gnosticism would promote. Egalitarians correctly stress that Paul's restrictions on women in 2:11–12 must be interpreted in light of the dangers of heresy afoot in the church. But some reconstructions read back into the first century developments for which we have secure evidence only from one or two centuries later,[127] and it is telling that none of the references to false teachers in the Pastoral Epistles ever explicitly number women among them. It is true the heretics

---

[124]Thus Thiselton, *First Epistle to the Corinthians*, 1150–61. Cf. James D. G. Dunn, *The Theology of Paul the Apostle* (Grand Rapids: Eerdmans, 1998), 592.

[125]So even Keener, *Paul, Women and Wives*, 86–87.

[126]Contra J. M. Holmes, *Text in a Whirlwind: A Critique of Four Exegetical Devices at 1 Timothy 2.9–15* (JSNTSup 196; Sheffield: Sheffield Academic Press, 2000), 117–39.

[127]Most notably Richard Clark Kroeger and Catherine Clark Kroeger, *I Suffer Not a Woman: Rethinking 1 Timothy 2:11–15 in Light of Ancient Evidence* (Grand Rapids: Baker, 1992). For a response, more historically nuanced, see Steven M. Baugh, "A Foreign World: Ephesus in the First Century," in *Women in the Church: A Fresh Analysis of 1 Timothy 2:9–15*, eds. Andreas J. Köstenberger, Thomas R. Schreiner, and H. Scott Baldwin (Grand Rapids: Baker, 1995), 13–52. Cf. also Sharon H. Gritz, *Paul, Women Teachers, and the Mother Goddess at Ephesus: A Study of 1 Timothy 2:9–15 in Light of the Religious and Cultural Milieu of the First Century* (Lanham, Md.: University Press of America, 1991), 157–58, conclusions that are almost always overlooked by the egalitarians who cite her.

seem to have an inordinate influence over certain particularly gullible women (5:15; 2 Tim. 3:6–9), but it is a big jump from men teaching women heresy to the conclusion, never stated in the text, that those women in turn became (false) teachers, so that the *only* thing Paul is forbidding in 2:11–12 is the teaching of heresy.[128] As with 1 Corinthians 14:33–38, one could fairly ask how silencing *all* women and *only* women would solve this particular problem!

It is also true that there are culture-specific elements in the immediate context of verses 11–12. The passage begins with verses 8–10 and first addresses the men (v. 8) in church (cf. 3:15 for this limitation of venue). They must "lift up holy hands in prayer, without anger or disputing." Presumably, it is always right to pray and always wrong to do s o in a quarrelsome fashion, but lifting up hands is just one of several acceptable postures. Interestingly, the Greek syntax supports this understanding, since the only actual command emerges from the statement "I want the men everywhere to pray . . . without anger or disputing." "Lifting up" translates a participle that could be purely modal: "as they lift up [holy hands]." In other words, this *is* the particular posture they are employing; now they *must* be sure to do it in the right spirit.

At first glance, verses 9–10 seem to include numerous situation-specific elements. Surely, for example, there can be nothing intrinsically wrong with braided hair! On closer inspection, it seems better to take both verses as fundamentally timeless in outlook. No one disputes that decent, appropriate, and modest dress (v. 9a), while varying in specifics from one culture to another, is still appropriate for all Christian women (and men!). Likewise, all believers should metaphorically clothe themselves with good deeds (v. 10). But what about the braided hair and jewelry of verse 9b? The Greek here in fact reads, "not with braids *and* gold or pearls or costly garments." James Hurley has observed how wealthy Greco-Roman women often invested hours in daily coiffure, intricately weaving their hair and holding it together with costly gems.[129] This emphasis on ostentation

---

[128] As, e.g., with Keener, *Paul, Women and Wives,* 111–12.

[129] Hurley, *Man and Woman in Biblical Perspective,* 199. With a few exceptions, such adornment would be limited to the tiny but influential minority of wealthy women in town. Thus, Alan Padgett, "Wealthy Women at Ephesus: 1 Timothy 2:8–15 in Social Context," *Int* 41 (1987): 19–31.

is surely always wrong. It is unfortunate that in some wings of the contemporary church there is still an emphasis on "dressing to the hilt."[130] Far too readily, even if unwittingly, this becomes a temptation to flaunt one's wealth, to distract other worshipers, and to make the less well-to-do feel like second-class citizens in God's household. Fortunately, in many Christian contexts today there no longer is the same pressure to dress up there once was.

Despite first appearances, then, when we come to verses 11–12, there is little momentum for assuming we will find context-specific mandates.[131] Verse 11 commands women to learn in quietness (*hēsychia*) and all submission (*hypotagē*). It is important to observe that the sole imperative in this verse is the command to learn. In Paul's day, this was the countercultural element that would have stood out: women are obliged to learn the word of God every bit as much as men, despite regular Jewish prohibitions against teaching women Torah.[132] *Hēsychia* does not mean "silence" (cf. its only other NT uses outside this passage in Acts 22:2 and 2 Thess. 3:12). The cognate adjective *hēsychios* has appeared as recently as in 2:2 to refer to the kind of lives all believers are to live—"peaceful and *quiet*," cooperative and caring, *not* never speaking! *Hypotagē* is cognate to the verb for "submission" (*hypotassomai*) in 1 Corinthians 14:34 and suggests some form of subordination. Again, this is behavior for students, male or female, that is always appropriate, even though what is considered submissive or cooperative may vary from one culture to the next.

---

[130]Dressing elaborately for church, of course, is not always a flaunting of wealth. In African-American communities, dressing well for church is important for other reasons; many persons who are very poor dress well for church. The quality of clothing in black communities often serves a different cultural role than it does in white suburbia.

[131]Neither do three additional arguments relativize the passage, despite some claims to the contrary. (1) Paul's use of "I" remains authoritative—he regularly understands his instructions to come from the Lord; (2) his use of "permit," by being negated, leaves the command an absolute "I do *not* permit"; and (3) the present tenses do not mean that Paul's lack of permission is only for the present moment—given the use of infinitives (moods outside the indicative), the force is "I am *continually* not permitting ..."

[132]The observation that Paul's main concern lies with the *way* women learn (as in Thomas R. Schreiner, "An Interpretation of 1 Timothy 2:9–15: A Dialogue with Scholarship," in *Women in the Church: A Fresh Analysis*, 122) does not undermine the force of this observation.

With verse 12 we come to what may be the single most scrutinized verse of Scripture in recent scholarship. Here the meaning of Paul's command to the women seems initially obvious: they are not to "teach" or "have authority over" a man (still, of course, in the context of the worshiping community—recall 3:15). But while the word for "teach" is the very common verb *didaskō*, used throughout the NT, the word normally translated "exercise authority" (*authenteō*) is found nowhere else in Scripture and is quite rare in Greek literature more generally. Leland Wilshire's survey of the 329 known uses of the term in Greek literature spanning the five centuries before and the five centuries after the time of Christ shows that prior to the first century the term often had the negative overtones of "domineer" or even "murder." After the first century, especially in Christian circles, it was frequently used more positively for the appropriate exercise of authority.[133] Was that because believers were following Paul's break from tradition and a more positive use of the term?[134] It is hard to be sure.[135]

But an important study by Andreas Köstenberger has shown that pairs of infinitives, as we have here in verse 12, without exception throughout the NT and very consistently in extrabiblical Greek as well, join together either two positive concepts or two negative concepts.[136] Thus the only way for *authentein* (the infinitival form of *authenteō* used here) to mean something pejorative like "dominate" or "domineer" is if *didaskein* likewise is negative. This presents one immediately obvious option: Paul is prohibiting the *false teaching* that clearly was afflicting Timothy's church in Ephesus. But elsewhere in his letters, when Paul wants to refer to false teaching he calls it that, with the verb *heterodidaskaleō* (1 Tim. 1:3; 6:3), or he at least qualifies *didaskō* with words that make it obvious the teaching is false (Titus 1:11). The other fifteen unqualified uses of *didaskō* in Paul all clearly refer to positive

---

[133]See Leland E. Wilshire, "The TLG Computer and Further Reference to *Authenteō* in 1 Timothy 2.12," *NTS* 34 (1988): 131.

[134]Cf. Paul W. Barnett, "Wives and Women's Ministry (1 Timothy 2:11–15)," *EvQ* 61 (1989): 225–38.

[135]Wilshire himself later clarified that he was opting for one of the earlier meanings—"to initiate violence." Thus Leland E. Wilshire, "1 Timothy 2:12 Revisited: A Reply to Paul W. Barnett and Timothy J. Harris," *EvQ* 65 (1993): 52. But this meaning scarcely fits this context!

[136]See Andreas J. Köstenberger, "A Complex Sentence Structure in 1 Timothy 2:12," in *Women in the Church: A Fresh Analysis*, 81–103.

teaching.[137] So it seems we should give both "teaching" and "exercising authority" their ordinary, positive sense in 1 Timothy 2:12.

At this juncture, a second grammatical study comes into play. Philip Payne has demonstrated that the conjunction *oude* ("nor") that connects the two key verbs in verse 12 regularly joins together expressions that in some sense are mutually defining.[138] In formal terminology this is called a "hendiadys" (from Greek words that mean "one through two"). In other words, Paul is not forbidding two separate actions here; rather, the two verbs together define one specific function or role. The larger context of 1 Timothy 2 further supports this interpretation. While not always employing formal hendiadys and while using conjunctions other than *oude*, Paul seems to have a propensity to use pairs of largely synonymous words to say just about everything important twice (or, occasionally, four times)! Thus we find in verse 1 "petitions, prayers, intercession and thanksgiving"; in verse 2a, "kings and all those in authority"; in verse 2b, "peaceful and quiet," and "godliness and holiness"; in verse 3, "good and acceptable" (KJV; TNIV, "pleases God"); in verse 4, "to be saved and to come to a knowledge of the truth"; in verse 7a, "a herald and an apostle"; in verse 7b, "I am telling the truth, I am not lying"; in verse 8, "without anger or disputing"; in verse 9, "decency and propriety"; and in verse 11, "quietness and full submission." With this many examples of the pattern, we might well expect to find a similar pair in verse 12.

But if Paul is not prohibiting women from all forms of teaching men in church, and if he is not prohibiting women from exercising all forms of authority over men in church, what might the *one* role of "authoritative teaching" be that he has in mind? We do not have to look very far to find a convincing answer. In the very next chapter of 1 Timothy, Paul sets forth criteria for the two leadership offices of the church—overseers and deacons (3:1–13). Note the two most obvious distinctions between the two groups of leaders: (1) Only in his instructions for elders must candidates

---

[137]Marshall's objection (*Pastoral Epistles*, 458, n. 157) that if the text had read *heterodidaskalein* it would have been implying "but I do allow men to [give false teaching]" does not carry force, because the prohibition still could have been clearly framed to avoid this conclusion (e.g., "I do not permit the women to continue their false teaching").

[138]See Philip B. Payne, "*Oude* in 1 Timothy 2:12," paper presented at the meeting of the Evangelical Theological Society (Atlanta, November 1986).

be "able to teach" (v. 2), and (2) Only in his instructions for deacons do women appear (v. 11). It is true that the ordinary word "women" (from *gynē*) could mean the deacons' "wives," but why would Paul be concerned about the character of deacons' wives and not insist on similar qualifications for overseers' wives? But if Paul envisioned only male overseers, while wanting men and women alike to share in the diaconate (recall the discussion of Phoebe, pp. 147-48), then the distinction makes perfect sense.[139] In Titus 1:5–7 it is clear he uses the terms "overseer" and "elder" interchangeably, and in 1 Timothy 5:17 the elders are described distinctively as those who "direct the affairs of the church." Thus, the two important responsibilities that set apart the elder, or overseer, from the rest of the church are their teaching and their exercising of authority—precisely the concepts involved in 2:12. It appears probable, therefore, that the only thing Paul is prohibiting women from doing in that verse is occupying the office of overseer or elder. This fits what we saw in our survey of Acts and the nonprescriptive material in the Epistles—women filling every major role in church life and leadership except that of elder.

We still have to ask, however, if this prohibition is timeless, or if it is dictated by certain unique circumstances in the first century. Verses 13 and 14 appear to give us an answer. Verse 13 once again grounds Paul's commands in the order of creation—Adam was created first. Attempts to argue that the word for "for" (*gar*) at the beginning of this sentence means something other than "because" fly in the face of Paul's overwhelmingly consistent use of this adverb.[140] As we noted earlier (p. 129), while foreign to modern sensibilities, this kind of argument would have made perfect sense in ancient cultures familiar with the practice of primogeniture. That the OT presents several striking exceptions to this pattern (e.g., Ishmael, Esau, Ephraim) does not invalidate the rule; the exceptions would not stand out if there were not a regular pattern in the first place.[141]

Verse 14 proves more difficult. Most in the history of the church have seen it as a second reason for Paul's principle of

---

[139]There is a growing scholarly consensus that women deacons are in view here. See Jennifer H. Stiefel, "Women Deacons in 1 Timothy: A Linguistic and Literary Look at 'Women Likewise ...' (1 Tim. 3.11)," *NTS* 41 (1995): 442–57.

[140]See Douglas J. Moo, "The Interpretation of 1 Timothy 2:11–15: A Rejoinder," *TJ* 2 (1981): 202–4.

[141]Cf. George W. Knight III, *The Pastoral Epistles* (NIGTC; Grand Rapids: Eerdmans, 1992), 143.

male headship in the church—Eve was deceived rather than Adam. Most, too, believed that women were inherently more gullible than men, even ontologically inferior to them,[142] but those convictions have rightly been abandoned by virtually all complementarians as well as egalitarians. There is simply too much physiological, social-scientific, and experiential evidence to the contrary. Furthermore, Adam ate freely of the forbidden fruit and sinned just as much as Eve did. So if he was not deceived, this means he sinned "with his eyes wide open," knowing full well what he was doing. That scarcely inspires hope in assigning ultimate leadership responsibility to the man rather than to the woman![143] The argument that carries over the adjective "first" from verse 13, making Paul say Eve sinned first, is true to Genesis 2 and is a grammatical possibility,[144] but it is hard to see what Paul's point would be. There were no ancient institutions like the laws of inheritance that were based on order of deception! The claim that "Eve was deceived by the serpent in the Garden (Genesis 3:13) precisely in taking the initiative over the man"[145] founders on the fact that she was tricked by Satan and sinned by eating the fruit *before* turning to Adam and thus only afterwards played a role in helping him to fall.

I therefore stand by my suggestion, offered nearly fifteen years ago, that verse 14 may not have been intended as a second rationale for Paul's prohibition at all.[146] It does not begin with a "for," merely an "and" (*kai*), while verses 14 and 15 are linked more closely with a *de* ("but"), suggesting a mild contrast. Having

---

[142]A key point, though probably overstated, throughout Kevin Giles, "A Critique of the 'Novel' Contemporary Interpretation of 1 Timothy 2:9–15 Given in the Book *Women in the Church*," *EvQ* 72 (2000): 151–67, 195–215. Cf. Andreas Köstenberger, "Women in the Church: A Response to Kevin Giles," *EvQ* 73 (2001): 205–24; Kevin Giles, "Women in the Church: A Rejoinder to Andreas Köstenberger," *EvQ* 73 (2001): 225–45.

[143]Cf. the tortuous logic Hurley (*Man and Woman in Biblical Perspective*, 214–16) uses to get around this.

[144]See Barnett, "Wives and Women's Ministry," 234.

[145]Douglas Moo, "What Does It Mean Not to Teach or Have Authority over Men? 1 Timothy 2:11–15," in *Recovering Biblical Manhood and Womanhood*, 190.

[146]Craig L. Blomberg, "Not Beyond What Is Written: A Review of Aída Spencer's *Beyond the Curse*," *CTR* 2 (1988): 414. William D. Mounce (WBC; *Pastoral Epistles* [Nashville: Nelson, 2000], 142) is the only scholar to my knowledge who has interacted in any detail with my proposal. For his objections and my response to them, see my "Neither Hierarchicalist nor Egalitarian," 367.

alluded to Genesis 2 in verse 13, it would have been natural for Paul to think next of Genesis 3 and the fall of Adam and Eve, along with God's subsequent punishment of the first couple. In essence, verse 14 then functions to set up verse 15 by recalling that things got worse before they got better.

Verse 15 is an enormously difficult verse to translate but is probably best understood as combating the heresy and its anti-marriage stance (4:3). A literal translation would yield, "But *she* will be saved by childbirth, if *they* remain in faith and love and holiness with propriety." While not all women marry or give birth, this remains an important role for the gender overall (the generic "she"), whereas the responsibility of every Christian woman is to exercise saving faith (the distributive "they"). Tellingly, the verb "save" in the Pastorals elsewhere can mean part of the process of "restoring" the cosmos to God's intended ideals (cf. 1 Tim. 4:16 and 2 Tim. 4:18), and this is probably how Paul is using the word here. As I have written previously, one may thus paraphrase the flow of thought from 1 Timothy 2:12–15 as follows:

> Women are not to hold the authoritative teaching position in the church because that is not a role for which they were created. Moreover, things subsequently deteriorated for the woman, after creation, when she fell, through the deception of the serpent. But there is a bright side. Women, collectively, will be preserved/restored as they exercise in a godly fashion their distinctive role of rearing children.[147]

To this should be added: but spiritual salvation proceeds only from faith in Christ as evidenced by a transformed lifestyle of faith, love, and holiness.

---

[147]Blomberg, "Not Beyond What Is Written," 415. My approach combines the strengths of two studies—M. D. Roberts, "'Women Shall Be Saved': A Closer Look at 1 Timothy 2:15," *TSFBul* 5.2 (1981): 4–7; and Andreas J. Köstenberger, "Ascertaining Women's God-Ordained Roles: An Interpretation of 1 Timothy 2:15," *BBR* 7 (1997): 107–44. The next most likely alternative may be that *dia* ("through") refers to difficult circumstances through which women must pass (cf. similar grammar in 1 Cor. 3:15 and 1 Pet. 3:20), thus yielding the sense of "women will be saved *despite* suffering the pain of childbearing, so long as they continue in faith. . . ." So Simon Coupland, "Salvation through Childbearing? The Riddle of 1 Timothy 2:15," *ExpTim* 112 (2001): 303.

Texts in the Epistles Relating to
Husbands and Wives in the Family

Strictly speaking, the debate about male headship in the home lies outside the purview of this volume. Still, while a few writers entirely separate the issues of home and church,[148] most agree that the latter was initially modeled on the former. If we can learn more about God's design for husbands and wives, we should be able to make some valid inferences about men's and women's roles in the gathered community of believers. Our space is limited, so we will just touch on some key highlights.

Colossians 3:18–19 and Ephesians 5:21–33

These two passages appear as part of Christian *Haustafeln*, or domestic codes. We have numerous similar examples of Jewish, Greek, and Roman discussions of the proper roles of various family members.[149] When we recall that slaves were included as part of an extended family, it is clear that Paul is adopting (and adapting) this established literary form in addressing instructions to wives and husbands, children and parents, slaves and masters.

The Colossians passage is quite brief, commanding wives to submit to their husbands, "as is fitting in the Lord" (3:18). At the very least, this comparative clause implies that submission is an appropriate behavior for Christian wives, but it probably also implies, "only that degree of subjection to the husband which is 'fitting in the Lord' is to be countenanced."[150] Paul does not call for wives to follow their husbands in ungodly behavior or in non-Christian belief. (Thus the *en panti* in Eph. 5:24 cannot mean literally "in every single request," but is a broader generalization like "in every area of life."[151]) Yet what would have stood out

---

[148]E.g., Richard M. Davidson, "Headship, Submission, and Equality in Scripture," in *Women in Ministry: Biblical and Historical Perspectives*, ed. Nancy Vyhmeister (Berrien Springs, Mich.: Andrews Univ. Press, 1998), 259–95.

[149]For texts and analyses of arguably the closest parallels, see Angela Standhartinger, "The Origin and Intention of the Household Code in the Letter to the Colossians," *JSNT* 79 (2000): 117–30.

[150]James D. G. Dunn, *The Epistles to the Colossians and to Philemon* (NIGTC; Grand Rapids: Eerdmans, 1996), 248.

[151]Peter T. O'Brien, *The Letter to the Ephesians* (PNTC; Grand Rapids: Eerdmans, 1999), 417.

most against the other ethical systems of Paul's day is nothing in verse 18 but all of verse 19: "Husbands, love your wives and do not be harsh with them."[152] No authoritarian Roman *patria potestas* should be allowed in the Christian community!

The Ephesians text expands in considerable detail. The specific commands to wives and husbands are introduced by the overarching command to "submit to one another out of reverence for Christ" (5:21), which in turn is one of several participial clauses defining what it means to be filled with the Spirit (v. 18). Here, even more clearly than in the previous epistolary passages treated, Paul grounds his commands not merely in creation but in *re*-creation. The wife submits, just "as the church submits to Christ" (v. 24). And, again far more counterculturally, the husband loves his wife, "just as Christ loved the church and gave himself up for her" (v. 25). It is not merely a creation ordinance (as in 1 Tim. 2:13), not merely a vestige of post-fall patriarchy; it is a *Christian* responsibility—grounded in Jesus' sacrificial atonement for the sins of humanity—for husbands to exercise *loving* leadership to which wives should want to submit.[153] The same debated *kephalē* ("head") reappears here, as in 1 Corinthians 11:3, but when paired with the verb for submission, there should be no debate that a hierarchy of authority is being established. The husband has at least some kind of leadership role. At the same time, it is probably significant that Paul commands children and slaves to "obey" the authorities over them (Eph. 6:1, 5), yet never uses this term for wives (despite countless Christian marriage ceremonies). Commanding and obeying do not foster healthy relationships among voluntary adult partnerships like marriage. What is needed, rather, is "love" and "respect" (5:33).[154]

What is more, Paul *radically redefines* the authority husbands and fathers retain. Their authority is not one of privilege but of

---

[152]Andrew T. Lincoln (*Ephesians* [WBC; Dallas: Word, 1990], 374) notes that commands to husbands to love their wives are infrequent outside the NT (citing only the Jewish sources *Pseudo-Phocylides* 195–97 and *b. Yevamot* 62b), and that *agapaō* is never used in Greco-Roman household codes as a husband's duty.

[153]Points made convincingly throughout Stephen F. Miletic, *"One Flesh"—Ephesians 5.22–24, 5.31: Marriage and the New Creation* (AnBib; Rome: Biblical Institute Press, 1988).

[154]Cf. further Klyne Snodgrass, *Ephesians* (NIVAC; Grand Rapids: Zondervan, 1996), 285–318.

responsibility. They are to be as concerned for their wives' well-being as Christ was for lost humans. Husbands must give of themselves sacrificially to serve their wives' best interests (vv. 25–30).[155] There is scarcely any support here for the common complementarian claim that the husband ultimately makes the decisions for the family, usually those that are in his best interest, trusting that God will beautifully work things out for his wife (and children) in the process. If anything, Paul's model is that the husband chooses what is in his *wife's* best interest, even if it comes at great cost to himself and his aspirations![156] In other contexts, where there is no logistical requirement that anyone lead, Paul can be remarkably egalitarian—compare especially his identical commands to wives and husbands scattered throughout 1 Corinthians 7.

If male headship in the family provided the model for male headship in the church, then we discover profound implications here for Christian leadership. Far from aspiring to become the strong, dynamic, visionary leader to whom God uniquely speaks and then expecting the "flock" to follow relatively passively, the overseer-elder must ask what it means to become a servant to his people (cf. Mark 10:35–45 par.; John 13:1–17). Far more biblical are those definitions of leadership that involve seeking to discern what God is already doing among a group of believers and then determining how best to encourage them in those directions.[157] Sadly, there is precious little of this being taught in either complementarian or egalitarian circles these days.

First Peter 3:1–7

The one key passage in the non-Pauline epistles we have thus far neglected appears in the middle of a Petrine *Haustafel*. Here for the first time we learn that Christian wives have a responsibility to submit even to non-Christian husbands, though

---

[155]Cf. Ian A. McFarland, "A Canonical Reading of Ephesians 5:21–33: Theological Gleanings," *ThTo* 57 (2000): 344–56.

[156]Cf. the very thoughtful applications throughout Sumner, *Men and Women in the Church*.

[157]Cf. Craig Williford, president of Denver Seminary (class lecture, 2003), who defines spiritual leadership as "influencing a group of people to effectively complete their God-given task in a way that contributes to the whole movement of God worldwide."

again "submission" must be distinguished from unquestioning obedience. The very fact that these women refuse to maintain the religion of their husbands sets them off as "highly insubordinate" in the eyes of most of their non-Christian peers.[158] Peter is concerned rather with these wives not putting *unnecessary* stumbling blocks in the way of their husbands coming to Christ (v. 1). This raises the interesting applicational question of what wives (or women in church) should do in cultures where their *not* functioning in an egalitarian fashion becomes the stumbling block to the unsaved world. Some egalitarians argue, for precisely this reason (and others), that we must abandon male headship in home and church in today's Western cultures.[159] On the other hand, it is interesting how a little book like Titus can include similar evangelistic motive-clauses for right role relationships (2:5, 8, 10) and yet also recognize that such behavior is simply "good" in and of itself (2:3, 7; 3:1).[160] Perhaps the answer to the question of contemporary application, therefore, is not to give up the principle of male headship but to take every possible step to demonstrate to a watching world how loving and self-sacrificing it can be. Imagine the potential evangelistic effect of an unsaved world seeing Christian men in general and leaders in particular truly and consistently looking out for others' interests, and especially women's interests, more than their own (Phil. 2:4).

First Peter 3:7 shows how high the stakes are at this point. Here Peter addresses *Christian* husbands, commanding them to live considerately with their wives, "treating them with respect" (lit., "showing them honor"), so that their prayers may not be hindered. To the extent that loving headship in the home provides the model for the church, we may state bluntly that unless male Christian leaders show enough concern for the complete well-being of the women in their congregations, they should not count on God answering their prayers as consistently as he would otherwise! The woman is, after all, the "weaker vessel," a description that should not be equated with psychological, emotional, or even physical weakness but that reflects her more "vulnerable" position in a marriage, in church, and in society.[161] Even

---

[158]J. Ramsey Michaels, *1 Peter* (WBC; Waco, Tex.: Word, 1988), 157.

[159]See esp. John H. Elliott, *1 Peter* (AB; New York: Doubleday, 2000), 585–99.

[160]See esp. throughout Knight, *Pastoral Epistles*.

[161]Cf. Peter H. Davids, *The First Epistle of Peter* (NICNT; Grand Rapids: Eerdmans, 1990), 123.

in an increasingly egalitarian secular world, women are taken advantage of in hurtful ways far more often than men, in situations that largely remain outside their control. The church should be known as a refuge against such behavior; tragically, it often perpetrates it, at times even more than in the outside world.[162]

All three major NT *Haustafeln* pair the apostles' commands to husbands and wives with partially parallel instructions for masters and slaves. (Ephesians and Colossians add teaching for parents and children, while 1 Peter also addresses government and citizens.) This raises huge interpretive questions that go far beyond the scope of this chapter. But the following are crucial points to make. First, Ephesians 5:21 must be seen as an introduction to all three sets of commands that follow in 5:22–6:9. It makes no sense to command every Christian to submit to every other Christian; no one would ever lead on anything! It *does* make sense if Paul is saying that here are three situations in which certain categories of believers should submit to other categories of Christians.[163]

Second, this observation raises immediately the issue of the parallelism between the nineteenth-century debate on slavery and the current debate on gender roles. There *are* striking parallels in many respects,[164] but it does not follow that the laudable abolition of slavery entails the abolition of role differentiation between men and women. (The "in the same way" of 1 Pet. 3:1 cannot mean that every aspect of women's submission and slaves' submission is identical, because Peter uses the same adverb (*homoiōs*) in verse 7 when he addresses the husbands and does not command them to submit at all.) Complete parallelism between the slavery and gender roles debates would mean that, just as Christians helped to abolish the entire institution that made having masters and slaves possible, they must also abolish the institution of marriage that makes having husbands and wives possible—a goal I hear *no* evangelical supporting!

Third, neither does it follow that, because Christians went beyond any explicit command of Scripture in abolishing the

---

[162]See esp. Catherine Clark Kroeger and James R. Beck, eds., *Women, Abuse, and the Bible* (Grand Rapids: Baker, 1996).

[163]See Hurley, *Man and Woman in Biblical Perspective*, 139–41; O'Brien, *Letter to the Ephesians*, 400–404.

[164]See esp. Willard M. Swartley, *Slavery, Sabbath, War and Women* (Scottdale, Pa.: Herald, 1983).

entire institution of slavery, they should go beyond any explicit Bible text in adopting full egalitarianism.[165] First Corinthians 7:21, after all, does explicitly tell individual slaves to gain their freedom if they can,[166] whereas there is no corresponding verse anywhere telling any women to overthrow male headship if they can.

Finally, slaves and masters are humanly created categories of people that can be eradicated (in theory at least) with one stroke of legislation. Women and men are genders God established in creation to reflect his image in the world. Gender is something with which humans are born, and, except in a very few pathological cases, it remains unalterable. Thus, while recognizing the parallels among the different pairs of people addressed in the NT domestic codes, we must also recognize that no two pairs present complete parallelism. Each must be treated somewhat uniquely.

✳

Much more could and probably should be said about all of the texts surveyed in this chapter, as well as others not discussed at all. Hopefully, we have highlighted the most important passages and said the most significant things about them. Before turning to conclusions and additional applications, however, it is important to make at least a few brief remarks about the role of church history.

THE SIGNIFICANCE OF CHURCH HISTORY

Although evangelical Protestants rightly stress that Christian doctrine and ethics should be based ultimately on the witness of Scripture as the only inerrant guide for belief and behavior, every Christian has a personal history, a denominational (or nondenominational) history, and certain theological traditions to which they have been exposed rather than others. The handful of Christians today who have studied significant amounts of church history recognize how complex the treatment

---

[165]As with the "redemptive movement" hermeneutic of Webb (*Slaves, Women and Homosexuals*).

[166]That this is the correct translation of this controversial verse has been decisively established by S. Scott Bartchy (*Mallon Chrēsai: First-Century Slavery and 1 Corinthians 7:21* [SBLDS 11; Missoula, Mont.: Scholars Press, 1973]).

of any doctrine or practice quickly becomes. One of the best and most even-handed presentations of key developments bearing on women in ministry over the nearly twenty centuries of Christianity's existence is Ruth A. Tucker's and Walter Liefeld's *Daughters of the Church: Women and Ministry from New Testament Times to the Present* (Grand Rapids: Zondervan, 1987).[167] I have had students read the book and ask me if the authors were complementarian or egalitarian, because they treat the evidence in so balanced a fashion. As it turns out, both are egalitarians, but what comes through the most to me as I read their survey is how compatible their overview of church history is with my somewhat limited form of complementarianism.

It is beyond dispute that the early church for several centuries had deaconesses (see above, p. 148); they reemerged occasionally in later eras, including at times in Protestantism. When they disappeared in the early church it was because their roles were being swallowed up by abbesses and nuns (and the corresponding institutions of abbeys and convents). It is beyond dispute that women have functioned in almost every age as evangelists and missionaries, regularly (though not always) with their churches' blessings. It is beyond dispute that God has raised up extraordinary women, even in some of the most androcentric times and places, to challenge the institutionalized male leadership of the church with Bible-based teaching in what might be considered to be prophetic ministries. Indeed, the less institutionalized the form of Christianity, the more likely for women to have emerged in key leadership roles. The Pentecostal and charismatic movements have provided numerous modern examples of this phenomenon. In contemporary complementarian evangelicalism, women may almost always teach from Scripture in certain limited contexts (though the reasons for keeping them from the pulpit, speaking the identical words to an identical cross section of believers, are usually based on confusing function with office). But what has never been conclusively demonstrated is that any significant wing of the established church over any significant period of time ever permitted women in the highest office of elder-overseer (or "priest" in Catholic and Orthodox traditions). Is it merely a coincidence that this is exactly the pattern we have discovered in the

---

[167]The rest of this section is heavily indebted to their survey, which documents the generalizations made here.

Scriptures as well—the one (and only one) most authoritative role in each period of God's dealings with humanity being reserved for men?

How often I have heard more conservative complementarians criticize my view as being comparatively new in the annals of church history and thus not likely to be accurate. I suspect it is their knowledge of church history that, in fact, is inadequate. Yet, at the end of the day, it is a bit disingenuous for anyone, complementarian or egalitarian, to protest that a certain view cannot be true because it reflects a small, minority perspective in church history. By that logic, the Reformation could never have been justified; by that logic, slavery could never have been abolished. What must prove ultimately decisive for establishing any Protestant evangelical doctrine is the most accurate synthesis of *biblical* teaching possible, irrespective of where this puts an individual on any theological or historical spectrum.

CONCLUSIONS AND ADDITIONAL APPLICATIONS

A consistent pattern emerges from all of the main sections of our study. In the first two chapters of Genesis, there are hints (we dare not put it more strongly) of male headship. After the fall, patriarchy is clearly the norm, but with sin in the world what was intended as a loving and gracious arrangement too often becomes abusive. As we look at what God specifically commands or commends throughout the OT, however, we see women in all roles of religious leadership (even if at times rarely), save one—the priesthood. As the office overseeing the sacrifices that mediated forgiveness of sins to humanity, priests could fairly be described as the most central or important human religious leaders in ancient Israel. In the Gospels, Jesus encourages and nurtures women in numerous countercultural ways, again with one exception: he does not choose any to form part of his closest circle of twelve apostles. In the book of Acts, women play significant leadership roles in the early church, with one notable exception: none are ever portrayed as elders-overseers. The same is true of the descriptive portions of the Epistles. When we come, finally, to the prescriptive texts in Paul about women's roles in church, we discover that the most plausible synthesis is that Paul restricted women from only one position—again that of elder or overseer. While not as directly relevant, the prescriptive texts in Paul and Peter about marriage likewise enjoin male headship, and a vast majority of scholars believe this provided the model for male headship in church. But the apostolic writers radically redefine headship, by the standards of their world, so that it becomes fundamentally self-giving rather than self-serving. Even church history, prior to the last few decades, while not normative as Scripture is, gives no clear evidence of any sustained conviction that women should occupy the highest office in a given church or ecclesiastical structure, while more often than many realize allowing and even encouraging them in numerous subordinate leadership roles.

In light of this consistent pattern, it is hard to escape the twin conclusions that (1) male headship is a timeless, God-ordained principle for home and church, but (2) unlike its manifestation in secular society or other religions, among God's people it is limited to the highest office and even then transformed into a model of loving servanthood that puts others, especially women, above self. One can find occasional articulations and incarnations of this model in the contemporary church; perhaps there has been no more well-known, eloquent spokesperson and personal embodiment of this balance than John Stott, for many years rector of All Souls Church in London.[168] But unfortunately, egalitarians by definition disagree with conclusion 1 above, and many complementarians (including some who claim to agree with it) never actually implement conclusion 2.

A number of related issues clamor for brief attention before this study draws to a close. What specifically is the "highest office" in churches today? There is no way to give only one answer to this question because of so many competing ecclesiologies. In the episcopal model, a bishop, archbishop, patriarch,

---

[168]See John R. W. Stott, *Issues Facing Christians Today* (London: HarperCollins, 1990), 254–84. Fairly close to this perspective is the combined presentation of chapters in Saucy and TenElshof, eds., *Women and Men in Ministry.* See also Ann L. Bowman, "Women in Ministry," in *Two Views on Women in Ministry*, 239–99, which in turn built on her earlier discussions in "Women in Ministry: An Exegetical Study of 1 Timothy 2:11–15," *BSac* 149 (1992): 193–213; and "Women, Spiritual Gifts and Ministry," *FaithMiss* 14 (1996): 57–74. On the domestic side, a fairly equivalent treatment is Ronald and Beverly Allen, *Liberated Traditionalism: Men and Women in the Balance* (Portland, Ore.: Multnomah, 1985).

or pope fills that slot. In the presbyterian model, it is the local presbytery. In the congregational model, it is the pastor, or in a multiple-staff church (except for the Plymouth Brethren model of a plurality of elders who are truly interchangeable in role and function) it is the senior pastor. Presumably valid application of Scripture's teaching could permit and even encourage women to fill all other positions in each of these settings except the ones just named.[169] Even better, reflecting my conviction (some would say bias!) that the congregational model is the most scriptural of the three,[170] one could seek to reestablish a small group of male elders in each local church who all have equal authority and roughly equal responsibility for the authoritative teaching of the church.[171]

However this issue is decided, it then becomes crucial to have gifted, godly women in all of the remaining levels of leadership. And the male pastor or board of elders needs regularly to consult these women in all matters of significance for the life of the church; how else can he or they function as servant leaders, implementing what is best for the whole congregation, including the women?[172] When one recognizes the biblical restrictions on women exclusively to involve an *office* (or specific position or role), it becomes clear there are no *tasks* or ministry gifts they cannot or should not exercise—including preaching, teaching, evangelizing, pastoring, and so on. Given the countercultural role of much of the Scriptures in both Testaments on gender roles, and recognizing that in a fallen world we *won't*

---

[169]It is common, but fairly hypocritical, of complementarian churches to employ women in professional staff roles, give them the identical job descriptions as men called "pastors" who have held the same positions, but then call them merely "directors" (or some other alternative). It *does* appear that "pastor" in various NT contexts is interchangeable with "overseer" and "elder," but, unlike the latter two titles, "pastor" is also a spiritual gift, given to men and women alike, so that churches should not hesitate to call anyone a pastor who is exercising such a gift in a consistent, recognized church position.

[170]For support, see Robert Saucy, *The Church in God's Program* (Chicago: Moody Press, 1972), 127–65.

[171]On the probability of multiple elders per church in each NT community, originally most likely one per house church, see Bradley Blue, "Acts and the House Church," in *The Book of Acts in Its Graeco-Roman Setting*, ed. David W. J. Gill and Conrad Gempf (Grand Rapids: Eerdmans, 1994), 119–222.

[172]See esp. the practical advice in Judith TenElshof and Robert Saucy, "The Complementary Model of Church Ministry," in *Women and Men in Ministry*, 325.

agree on our forms of church government and that complementarians will continue to disagree among themselves, a key test for any church or male church leader is as follows: *Once you have decided, as best as you can understand it, what Scripture does permit women to do, can any reasonably objective observer of your church and your ministry quickly recognize you are bending over backwards to encourage and nurture women in these roles?* If not, then you can't possibly be obeying Scripture adequately, *even on your interpretation of it.* Interestingly, over the years, I have had a number of outspoken egalitarian women, some of them well known in evangelical circles, confide in me privately and tell me that if complementarians would just do this much consistently, they could live with the remaining areas of disagreement and even stop lobbying for further privilege.

I return to where I began. It is important for me to end by saying again, "I could be wrong." One of the wonderful merits of William Webb's recent study of the similarities and differences in the biblical teaching and current debates on slaves, women, and homosexuals is to address an entire chapter to the question "What If I Am Wrong?" Interestingly, as a cautious egalitarian, Webb's answer to this question is in essence that he would adopt a position virtually identical to mine.[173] I have to make a similar confession. If I am wrong, then I suspect the cautious (or centrist) egalitarian is correct. Having been immersed in the evangelical subculture since I was fifteen (in 1970), I have seen far too many women deeply hurt by uncaring attitudes and actions or by rude remarks (sometimes intended, unsuccessfully, to be humorous) by male (and occasionally female!) complementarians, normally alleged to be justifiable by their theological perspectives, for me to ever imagine adopting a more restrictive form of complementarianism than the one I now hold. On the other hand, I have only somewhat less often seen egalitarian spokespersons communicate much of anything besides an "I demand my rights" kind of attitude. On both sides, it seems that quests for power rather than biblical obedience dominate the behavior of many. Thankfully, there are growing numbers of exceptions to these sweeping generalizations, including many of my colleagues and students at Denver Seminary and the other contributors to this volume! And I sense a spirit among the

---

[173]See Webb, *Slaves, Women and Homosexuals*, 236–44.

twentysomethings in our churches and seminaries that is becoming less combative on these issues and more appreciative of efforts like the one this book represents. Meanwhile, I do all I can to bracket my experiences, good and bad, return to Scripture, ask what it really says, and then try to follow it. May God help all the readers of this volume to do the same, whatever position it may lead them to embrace.

A RESPONSE TO CRAIG BLOMBERG

Craig S. Keener

I deeply appreciate the generosity and open-mindedness of this essay by my friend (and fellow Craig). I appreciate both his scholarship and his Christian integrity, and I can attest that he models the charity (both inside and outside this book) that the book is meant to convey. I also agree with many of his exegetical arguments; for the sake of honoring my word allotment in this response, however, I will focus on areas of disagreement.

Craig finds a consistent limitation of the "highest" position in all three sections of Scripture, providing a neat outline. Unfortunately for the argument, however, each of these sections addressed patriarchal societies, a factor we all take into account for less controversial matters (like parental arrangement of marriages). More damaging, these are hardly parallel samples. The OT argument, for example, is surprisingly weak. (He can argue in the creation narrative at best from inference, and priests' gender reflects ritual purity considerations hardly relevant to the case.) His parallel between apostles and pastors might prove more persuasive did they not overlap chronologically, with pastors a much less authoritative calling in the NT period. I contend below that none of his arguments are strong enough to prohibit particular ministries to women today.

Regarding the creation narrative, the creation sequence of genders hardly parallels the issue of rank by birth order (which would primarily determine the inheritance in any case, and that usually for males only). That Genesis repeatedly rejects the pervasive custom of primogeniture (Gen 25:23; 48:19; 49:4) also does not help the argument. The naming formula used for animals (2:20) has a clear literary parallel with Eve—but only after the

185

fall (3:20), in contrast to the differently worded phrase before-hand (2:23). After acknowledging that ʿēzer does not mandate subordination, Craig appeals to Paul to establish subordination anyway. Yet if the narrative is not clear enough without Paul, why not simply focus on Paul? And what does Craig's text in 1 Corinthians 11:8–9 (which Paul balances in 11:11–12), which in context supports only head coverings, have to do with women pastors?

The priesthood was a ritual office connected with purity regulations, far less related to proclamation than prophetic ministry was. The law's stricter purity restrictions for women (esp. regarding menstruation) made women priests impracti-cal (in a system which would disqualify them from service for considerable periods of time). Hopefully, most pastors today are more concerned with speaking God's message and leading (like prophets and judges) than with satisfying purity regula-tions. (We recognize that OT laws generally raise their envi-ronment's moral standard, but not to the fullest ideal; cf. Matt. 19:8.) Further, Deborah's role as not only a judge but also a prophet suggests spiritual authority comparable to apostles as well as kings.

It was not inconsistent for Jesus to be countercultural in some ways (allowing women disciples) but to accommodate his culture in others (choosing males for the Twelve, whom he would send out to evangelize). Ministry in any culture requires decisions on which priorities we must fight for. Sending out women on evangelistic travels, either as two women alone (regarded as unsafe) or a woman and a man (scandalous) was impractically provocative and counterproductive to the mission. For practical reasons, Jesus also chose no Gentiles (impossible) and possibly no Judeans (for geographic reasons).

Craig's distinction among different kinds of apostles (to evade the implications of Junia) is arbitrary; apart from "apostles of churches" (in both cases clearly identified as such), Paul uses "apostles" without explanation for those who performed the same sorts of "missionary" tasks he as an apostle did, a circle larger than the Twelve (1 Cor. 15:5–7). Certainly they exercised more authority (charismatic, but continuous) than local elders.

His distinction between a "settled function" and a gift is too ambiguous in the text (cf., e.g., "prophets" being those who prophesy in 1 Cor. 14:29–31) to disallow women from the former. He argues that women never filled the "highest" office of pastor or elder or overseer. Since we know the names of few, if any, pastors in Paul's day, we cannot say women never filled this office (though I think it safe to infer from Paul's wording in 1 Tim. 3:2 that Paul assumed that the vast majority would be men, especially given the local situation). The examples of women in civic or (perhaps more commonly) synagogue administration are so few (compared to men in such offices) that it seems unlikely that women felt encouraged to pursue such offices or had many opportunities to develop the skills requisite for them—quite in contrast to today.

More important, pastors, who were probably teams of supervising members within house churches, were not the "highest" office; as I show in my essay, we do have examples of women exercising "higher" authority than this. (This is even aside from Linda Belleville's appropriate challenge to much of our thinking about authority in ministry.)

I agree that "head" has a wider semantic range than "source," its meaning determined by the context. But this agreement does not resolve other questions. Does superior prominence (here emphasizing cultural honor) require superior rank? Even if Paul refers to rank, does he assume a first-century cultural or a universal situation? He never appeals to the husband's authority in 1 Corinthians 11 but at most assumes it for his argument. Paul uses headship (via a wordplay) to argue for women's head coverings—something Craig does not regard as transcultural. The same is true with his argument for woman as man's glory—Paul indicates nothing about authority, only about head coverings! To assert that the transcultural principle behind head coverings is wifely submission is assuming what one hopes to prove. (Ancients used head coverings to express sexual modesty and marital fidelity.)

Craig challenges egalitarian arguments that Paul addresses a particular situation in 1 Corinthians 14:34–35 by rightly rejecting the proposal of segregated synagogues. This is, however, only one of many proposals for the particular situation; my view, which he describes as more persuasive in a footnote, he neither explains nor refutes! Paul commonly uses *laleō*, which (contrary to some arguments on both sides) need not specify a particular kind of speech. The one kind of speech explicitly referred to in verses 34–35 is asking questions, and ancient texts offer relevant conventions for appropriate questions and for who could ask them. Even in first-century culture, many continued to find women's speech in public meetings inappropriate; that most women were unlearned would make their questions appear all the more improper. Paul sometimes states general principles (here about women) that admit exceptions (such as their prophesying in 11:5 demands).

Craig claims that Paul's appeal to the law teaches women's submission. To which law does Paul refer? If it is (most usefully for complementarians) the creation order that mandates women's silence or submission here, it mandates head coverings a few chapters earlier. Claiming that wifely submission is the transcultural principle here is again assuming what one hopes to prove.

Craig himself appeals to a specific situation to explain 14:34–35, namely evaluating prophecies (v. 29). But asking questions in verse 35 is much closer context than verse 29; evaluating prophecies is only one among many kinds of speech in the context. Further, evaluation of prophecy may be a gift (cf. the cognate in 12:10), and in 14:29 itself is the domain of either all who prophesy or of the entire congregation. It carries no greater connotation of rank than prophecy itself.

Craig argues that "it is a big jump from men teaching women heresy" to making Paul's prohibition of women teaching in 1 Timothy 2 depend on this (p. 166). Is it merely coincidence that the one setting in the Bible where we *know* that false teachers were targeting women (5:13; 2 Tim. 3:6) provides the one passage that forbids women to teach? Again, this is a general rule that might admit exceptions, just like Paul's requirement of "husband of one wife." Against the false teachers (1 Tim. 4:3; Titus 1:11), Paul emphasizes stable families, but "husband of one wife" allows exceptions for someone single like Paul. Paul's argument from creation order here is no different from his argument that creation order supports head coverings— which Craig regards as a culture-specific application.

Likewise, we cannot ignore the cultural setting of Ephesians 5, despite transcultural relational principles of submission (v. 21) and love (v. 2). Paul closely follows the format of Aristotle's widely used household codes but varies them in a specifically egalitarian direction. I am inclined to agree with Craig that context would lead wives to associate "head" here with its common sense of "authority"; but Paul wanted husbands to hear it differently. In contrast to

Aristotle's model, Paul does not tell the husband how to "rule" his wife but only how to love her (v. 25); the husband must use his "headship" as opportunity to serve his wife.

Paul summons the wife to submit to her husband as to Christ—just as two paragraphs later slaves must serve their masters as they would Christ (6:5). The fact that Christians submit to authority structures (Rom. 13:1–7) does not mean we must retain the same authority structures today (such as masters or kings [1 Pet. 2:13]). We retain marriage, of course, but not necessarily the authority structure of ancient patriarchal marriages, which is the point at issue in the ancient analogy with slaves. Evangelical egalitarians do not support abolishing distinctions between genders; we can retain distinctions without these distinctions being hierarchical. (In fact, few complementarians today would divide gender roles in precisely the ways common among various of Paul's contemporaries.) We all agree that all of Scripture includes timeless principles, but this agreement does not resolve what these timeless principles are—this is the debate in question.

Craig points out that most of the church throughout history (excluding the first century, of course, the point under debate!) has failed to ordain women as pastors or "priests." But an appeal to the church's example on leadership throughout history (and today, for that matter) is more questionable than its example on many theological points. How often have church leadership models followed Jesus' instructions that the least is the greatest and that true leaders are servants (Luke 22:25–26)? If our leadership models have not reflected Jesus' most basic teaching on leadership, to what degree can we trust them to reveal other biblical patterns?

A RESPONSE TO CRAIG BLOMBERG

Thomas R. Schreiner

Craig Blomberg always impresses me with how much he has read, and his essay here is no exception. The coverage of secondary literature is masterful, and yet Craig does not depend on secondary sources in setting forth his view but establishes his case by a careful exegesis of the text. Since Craig is a complementarian, readers will not be surprised to learn I am in basic agreement with his position. He rightly concludes that a diversity of ministry positions are open to women, but the office of pastor or elder is confined to men.

I also agree with Craig that complementarians need to work especially hard at including women in ministries that are permitted by Scripture. For instance, there is no scriptural basis to prevent women from serving during Communion or from leading in prayer or Scripture reading when we gather to worship.

Craig rightly detects in Genesis 2 suggestions of a difference in role between men and women, while also arguing that the text teaches the fundamental equality of males and females. The only qualification I would add is that Scripture traces the impact of sin on the entire human race to Adam rather than Eve (Rom. 5:12–19). Craig does not clarify this important truth when he says that both Adam and Eve are blamed twice for sin.

I concur with the distinction he establishes between priests and prophets. Women never served in the former capacity, but a number of women are identified as prophets in the OT. Blomberg observes that the parallel between priests and pastors is not exact, and yet he sees a pattern in that women are allowed to serve in every office but one. This pattern carries over to the NT, where Jesus encourages women to learn Scripture and regularly treats them as fully human and equal to men. Still, women are not appointed as apostles. Craig is on target again when he maintains that the restriction cannot be chalked up to cultural accommodation. Jesus boldly contravened cultural norms, and it is hard to believe he accommodated to the conventions of his day when the appointment of a female apostle would have signaled so clearly a new pattern for the people of God.

More and more scholars recognize that women served as deacons in the NT (Rom. 16:1; 1 Tim. 3:11), and such a view is confirmed by a reading of early church history. Craig presents the case for women deacons persuasively. Women share every spiritual gift, and men and women are one in Christ (Gal. 3:28). Craig proposes the common complementarian view that the truth of Galatians 3:28 does not erase role distinctions between men and women. At the same time, he helpfully insists there are social ramifications in this verse for how men and women relate to one another as believers.

Craig sees some role differentiation between men and women in 1 Corinthians 11:2–16, and he rightly argues that head coverings or hairstyle do not carry the same cultural equivalent today and hence are not normative. More controversial is his claim that the gift of prophesy, which women exercised, may include the activity of Spirit-inspired preaching, and that women should be allowed to preach today as long as they are accountable to the elders of the church. He does not provide convincing evidence that preaching is equivalent to the gift of prophecy. Prophets certainly exhorted and spoke the word of the Lord to people. But those who prophesied received spontaneous revelations from God and mediated those revelations to God's people (1 Cor. 14:29–33). For example, Agabus received two revelations in the book of Acts, in which he predicted a famine (11:27–28) and the arrest of Paul (21:11). God's people received instruction and encouragement from such words, but it is doubtful that prophecy should be equated with preaching, which is a combination of the gift of teaching and exhortation (1 Tim. 4:13). Those who prophesy are, in a sense, passive vehicles who transmit the revealed word of God. Teaching draws on the apostolic tradition and explains that tradition to those gathered. Still, I agree with Craig that there are contexts in which women can address both men and women where there is no violation of the prohibition of 1 Timothy 2:12, and some have wrongly ruled out any churchly words from women on the basis of this verse.

The meaning of 1 Corinthians 14:34–35 continues to be debated, and Craig carefully surveys the various views, concluding that Paul forbids women from judging prophecies, for in doing so they would be exercising a final authority. This text cannot command center stage in the debate, for however it is interpreted, Paul cannot be forbidding women from speaking at all. This would clearly contradict the encouragement in 1 Corinthians 11:5 and many other texts of Scripture that allow women to prophesy. Craig sees a transcendent principle in this text in that women are to be submissive to their husbands and perhaps to the male leaders in the church. Craig may be correct in saying that the women are prohibited from judging prophecies. Such a view would support my overall view of the relationship between men and women quite well. Nevertheless, it seems that clear evidence is lacking for the view Craig prefers. I tend to think there was great confusion in the congregation because some of the wives were asking questions and disrupting meetings (not because they were sitting in a separate section). Hence, Paul was not absolutely forbidding all women from speaking in the assembly. He already permitted them to pray and prophesy in 1 Corinthians 11:5! What Paul rules out here is the asking of disruptive questions by wives in a rebellious spirit. Such a spirit contradicts the submissive spirit wives are to display in their relationship to their husbands.

My reading of 1 Timothy 2:8–15 is not dramatically different from Craig's. We both agree that women are not clearly identified as purveyors of the heresy. The principle regarding clothing is that women should dress modestly and without ostentation. Andreas Köstenberger's reading of 2:12 is accepted, so that both teaching and exercising authority represent positive activities women should not engage in. I concur that the text implies that women should not serve as elders. It seems to me, though, that the text cannot be restricted to this truth. The functions of teaching and exercising authority are excluded for women. I would conclude from this that women should not regularly teach a mixed Sunday school class composed of adult men and women. And yet Craig and I agree that the clearest truth communicated is that only men should serve as elders, and that verse 13 demonstrates that the prohibition transcends the situation addressed in 1 Timothy, since it is rooted in creation.

Craig's suggestion regarding 2:14 is provocative, but there are at least three weaknesses with this view. First, the *kai* in verse 14 naturally connects the verse with verse 13. Second, the structure of verse 13 matches verse 14, for both verses compare and contrast Adam and Eve in an "a-b-a-b" pattern. Third, Craig's view does not explain well the reference to Adam in verse 14. Any reference to Adam is unnecessary if the concern is only the salvation of women. But the reference to both Adam and Eve fits with the argument in verse 12 that women are not to teach men.

Craig rightly sees a difference of role in the marriage texts (e.g., Eph. 5:22–33) and correctly emphasizes the countercultural call for husbands to love their wives sacrificially. Marriage cannot be equated with slavery, for marriage is established by God at creation, whereas slavery is an evil institution regulated by the Scriptures (like divorce). Furthermore, Paul encourages slaves to gain freedom in 1 Corinthians 7:21.

Contrary to Craig, I think the Ephesian text implies that, if there is disagreement between a husband and wife, the husband has the ultimate responsibility to make a decision for the family. I don't agree with those who say that, in a good family, disagreements will always be resolved through discussion. Sometimes good Christians end up disagreeing (like in this book!), and then a decision has to be made. Craig rightly warns that husbands should not use this responsibility selfishly, and he is surely right in saying that husbands have often sinned in this way. On the other hand, I think Craig is slightly off-kilter in saying that good leaders seek to determine what God is already doing with a group and then lead them in the direction they are going. In a sinful world, a church or a family may not be heading in a positive direction, and biblical leadership may require a church or family to be lovingly directed in a new and perhaps radically different direction.

I conclude by saying that my disagreements with Craig are not major. I believe we are in substantial agreement in terms of the meaning of the biblical text, and I found his essay to be a helpful and convincing defense of the complementarian position.

A RESPONSE TO CRAIG BLOMBERG
Linda L. Belleville

There is much to appreciate about Craig's essay. The author describes his position as "about as close as you can get to being a full-fledged egalitarian without actually becoming one" (p. 125). This means all ministries are open to women—even ones that involve women leading men as preachers and teachers. But that this makes the author a borderline egalitarian is to be questioned. For while he grants the idea of women leading men, he does not affirm women as pastors or elders. Women can lead men occasionally and exceptionally, he says, and only in the context of showing "appropriate submission to their spiritual heads" (p. 127). This places the author squarely in the traditionalist camp. According to Craig, "we are still bound to obey" (p. 128) those Scriptures which state that women cannot officially teach or exercise authority over men.

FIVE FUNDAMENTAL FALLACIES

Rather than nitpick at the details of the exegesis, I will target the fundamental fallacies of the position.

1. Generalizing Fallacies

Life is rarely black-and-white. So we are taught early on to avoid "never" and "always." It is disappointing, therefore, to find them here in Craig's chapter. For example, it is said that "all the Jewish sources describe the same ideal picture of society. . . . Women who deviate . . . are described by all the sources as

194

wicked" (p. 139). No one contests that Judaism for the most part was a patriarchal culture. Even so, perception and reality can vary substantially. Attitudes varied even in Jewish literary circles. Philo opined that "a woman is more accustomed to being deceived than a man" (*QG* 1.33). But the book of Judith (by a slightly earlier author) lifted up a woman (Judith) as the model of scrupulous devotion to the Mosaic law and as the deliverer of Israel. The rabbis varied as well. One rabbi (Rabbi Eliezer) states that any man who would give his daughter knowledge of the law teaches her lechery (*m. Soṭah* 3:4). But another credits the redemption of God's people from Egypt to the righteousness of the women of Israel (*b. Soṭah* 11b).

Greco-Roman attitudes were not as uniform as the author presents either. While it was true that Classical and Hellenistic Athenian women stayed in seclusion, Classical Spartan and Greco-Roman women did not. They moved about freely in public, participating in politics, public offices, and civic projects. Land registers show that women owned 40 percent of all Spartan real estate. The Spartan model toward which Alexander the Great gravitated held cultural sway for six hundred years. The Romans went even further. So while Paul is more restrictive in an Asian context (Eph. 5:22; Col. 3:18 ["Wives, submit yourselves"]), he is more expansive in Greece (1 Cor. 7:5 ["by mutual consent"]) and even more so in Italy, where he commends women—married and otherwise—as coworkers (Rom. 16). Such varying counsel and practice points to sensitivity to local practices and social norms.

There are further instances of sweeping generalizations:

- "Jesus never promotes full-fledged egalitarianism" (p. 144). This really is a red herring. Jesus simply used common sense in navigating outreach in a Jewish patriarchal culture.
- "The notorious Roman *patria potestas* ("power of a father") gave Roman husbands almost unlimited authority" (p. 140). What the author neglects to note is that by the first century, the Roman husband's power was largely nominal. Roman women were increasingly opting for *sine manus* ("without power"), which radically limited the power of the husband.

2. Anachronism Fallacies

Craig distinguishes between the "regular, predictable leadership functions" (p. 134) of priest/rabbi and pastor/elder and the ad hoc exercise of gifts such as teaching and preaching. He sees a pattern of women leading in every area save official, regular roles that he finds very difficult to attribute "merely to coincidence or accommodation" (p. 138). For instance, the author observes that Israel had no female priests. Yet scholarship has shown why this was so. Israel's purity laws excluded such a possibility (i.e., anyone with a discharge of blood). But then they also excluded a man who had a nocturnal emission (Deut. 23:10; cf. Lev. 15) or a sore that would not heal (Lev. 13–14), the blind, lame, disfigured, deformed, injured, hunchback, and dwarfed (Lev. 21). Yet such would hardly exclude someone from ministry today. Also, the priesthood was a hereditary role, and priests served in rotation (Luke 1:8–9). So there was nothing *regular* about the role. The OT prophet, on the other hand, *was* a regular ministry—more comparable than the priesthood to that of the pastorate today. And women *did* serve as prophets.

The author also notes that no women rabbis (the equivalent of a theology professor today) are found in the literature of Paul's day. Yet, culture offers the explanation. The education of ancient women (Jewish, Greek, and Roman alike) typically ceased at puberty; hence they could not obtain the education needed to be a rabbi. Craig recognizes that NT women did exercise authoritative roles—including "teaching doctrine to adult men and women," as long as it was not in the capacity of "an office of local, ongoing church administration and instruction" (p. 150). He states, "It outruns the evidence to claim that we know [women] were formal pastors or elders or, for that matter, that they held any identifiable position" (p. 150). A Priscilla can instruct an Apollos, but she can't be a teaching elder in her local church. A Junia can plant a church, but she can't provide the ongoing pastoral leadership.

The author is quick to distinguish spiritual gifts from church offices (p. 152); the apostle Paul was not so quick to do so. In fact, there is nothing settled or consistent about leadership in the early church apart from the possession of leadership gifts, whether it was Italy (Rom. 12:4–8), Asia Minor (Eph. 4:7–13), or Greece (1 Cor. 12:7–12, 27–30). Yes, the apostle Paul appointed elders as part of the church-planting process in Asia (Acts 14:23; cf. 1 Pet. 1:1; 5:1–4). But there is no indication he did so in Greece. There is no mention of elders (or any other settled function) in the church at Corinth. Ephesian church leaders are called *elders* (Acts 20:17; cf. 1 Pet. 5:1). But the Philippian leaders are identified as *overseers* and *deacons*—with no elders in sight. Phoebe is identified as a *deacon* of the Cenchreaen church, Paul urges the Thessalonians to respect those who work hard among them, and the Roman church had many leaders Paul recognized as *coworkers* and *colaborers*. But the language of *elder*, *deacon*, and *overseer* is missing entirely.

This makes the language of "office," or "settled or consistent function, role, or position" (p. 152) anachronistic—a figment of our modern imagination. The pastoral office is even more dubious. The single time the term "pastor" arises in the NT, it is as a gift, combined with the gift of teaching and in the plural (Eph. 4:11). So like a house of cards, without "office"—or formal capacities—the traditionalist argument collapses.

3. Ecclesial Fallacies

That ecclesiology is at the heart of Craig's view of women in ministry is clear from his insistence that "the elders of a local congregation all be men" (p. 158). An *elder board* is the polity of some churches today, but is it normative for all? A particular ecclesiology also informs his insistence that the elder board is "the ultimate body of human leaders to whom the entire church (preachers included) is accountable" (p. 158). Yet, church government typically falls into the category of *adiaphora*—matters about which believers agree to disagree because Scripture is not clear.

Although the author takes the ecclesial office of elder as a NT given, it is something debated by most and rejected by some. Just as ordination is a later ecclesial development, so with offices. It would be fairer to speak of church offices as a later development and to speak of "leadership roles" taken up by those God has gifted for those roles. The same is true of *submission*. When there is a call for submission, it is *not* because of an "office" but because of the effort expended (1 Cor. 16:16). This would include both men and women, as the comparable male and female coworkers in Romans 16 demonstrate.

4. Male Prerogative Fallacies

There is an assumption in Craig's essay that male is the gender of privilege. God created a him to be the decision maker (*kephalē*) and a her as a subordinate helper (*ʿēzer* [p. 129]). Yet, this is only so if the meanings of "CEO" and "helper" are correct. If one translates *ʿēzer* as "partner" (versus "helper") and *kephalē* as "source of nourishment" (versus "CEO"), then the house of hierarchical cards collapses. Indeed, one is hard-pressed to squeeze subordination out of the underlying Hebrew term *ʿēer*. It would entail ignoring other equally viable translations such as "partner" (NRSV), as well as the unwavering "help" God or a military ally provides (GNT, KJV, ASV; see *TDOT*, *HALOT*, BDB). The author also claims that it has not been demonstrated that *kephalē* "ever means 'source' without simultaneously implying some dimension of authority" (p. 156). But this ignores texts such as *Life of Adam and Eve* 19.11, where "desire is the *source* [*kephalē*] of every form of sin" demonstrates just the opposite.

Genesis 3 is rightly acknowledged as the record of when and how things went awry. But then the author goes on to argue that what went wrong is that the woman's desire becomes "a twisted one that requires domination, not just loving headship, as a response" (p. 131). Genesis 4:7 becomes the definitive support, but without being the needed parallel. For while it is true that the terms "desire" and "master" are the same, the pronoun is the neuter *it*, not the masculine *he*. Genesis 4:7 provides a parallel only if the pronoun *hûʾ* in 3:16 is translated "it": "Your yearning will be for your man and *it* [not he] will rule over you" (AT). The Hebrew pronoun permits either. And frankly, "it" [the woman's yearning] better fits the context.

If male prerogative were the divine intent, one would have expected Jesus to concede the point—"Yes, God created the male to be in charge." Yet, when the opportunity arose, Jesus handled Pharisaic assumptions about male prerogative as *misperception*, citing Genesis 1:27 (Matt. 19:4) and Genesis 2:24 (Matt. 19:5). Plus, he repeats it: "So they are no longer two, but one" (19:6). In fact, Jesus goes a step further in emphasizing that God has the sole prerogative ("What God has joined together"), and human beings (male and female alike) have none ("let no one separate" [v. 6]). Instead, male prerogative is attributed to hardness of heart (not the female's attempt to subvert the male's leadership [vv. 7–8]).

The author counters with the incontrovertible fact that the Twelve were all males. Jesus all too willingly scandalized his Jewish contemporaries by eating with prostitutes and "sinners," so why not choose a woman apostle? One could also argue that Jesus scandalized his society by touching a leper. Yet he did not choose a leper to be in his cadre—or a eunuch, or a non-Jew, or a slave. Does that mean that lepers, eunuchs, non-Jews, and slaves are excluded from leadership positions in the church too?

The author further counters with the fact that the apostle Paul used creation order in a hierarchical way: "For Adam was formed first, then Eve" (1 Tim. 2:13). No one denies Paul's use of the creation narratives. How and for what purpose are the key questions. The historical particulars that led to the writing of 1 Timothy are critical to answering these questions, yet traditionalists become strangely quiet at this point. Instead 1 Corinthians 11:8–9 is invoked as settling the question of male prerogative ("an argument from irreversibility" [p. 159]). And 1 Timothy 2:13 is invoked as support for a male prerogative reading of Genesis 2 ("the laws of primogeniture" [p. 129]). The result is an unhelpful hermeneutical circle.

Perhaps most disturbing is the automatic step Craig takes from the husband as the decision maker in the marriage to the man as the decision maker in all male-female relationships. Indeed, it is his belief that male headship in the family provides "the model for male headship in the church" (p. 175). So the more we learn about male headship in the family, the better we will understand male headship in the church. The assumption of hierarchy is clear from the author's treatment of 1 Corinthians 11, where "the *kephalē* of a woman is the man" (v. 3) is read in light of the created order of male first, female second. "Ultimate hierarchy," "irreversible creation order," and "female subordination" is the pervasive language in this section of the essay (pp. 155–61)—and anything contrary to this conclusion is explained away. Can 1 Corinthians 11 really get a fair reading from an author who assumes it teaches "the timeless principles of male headship and female subordination" (p. 160)?

5. Cultural Fallacies

There is an inclination in Craig's essay to draw on first-century culture when it supports hierarchy, and to eschew it when it runs counter. This is evident in his treatment of 1 Corinthians 11, which overlooks an important head-covering practice of Paul's day. It is not headship in marriage that enlightens this passage (as the author claims) but the unisex dress of male and female Greco-Roman religious leaders that is key. Paul is not teaching that women are forsaking male headship and submissive roles and so going down the slippery slope to lesbianism (so Craig), for Paul gives equal attention to the dress of female *and male* worship leaders. What carried a stigma was a *woman* who cut her hair short or shaved her head (1 Cor. 11:6), a *woman* praying with her head uncovered (v. 14), a *man* praying with his head covered (v. 4), and long hair on a *man* (v. 14).

To treat such matters at length—as Paul does here—leads one to think that some sort of sexual-identity confusion lurks in the background. I believe it is plausible to think that the Corinthians took "there is neither male nor female in Christ" (Gal. 3:28) to mean they should do away with gender distinctions. It may well be, as Murphy-O'Connor and others have suggested, that Paul is concerned the Corinthians' actions would be read by outsiders in a homosexual light (see O'Connor's "Sex and Logic in 1 Corinthians 11:2–16," *CBQ* 42 ([1980]): 482–500). Paul may have felt the Roman religious practice of both male and female priests covering their heads with their togas blurred the sexual distinctions implicit in the creation of ʾādām as male and female (Gen. 1:27).

The flaws in Craig's treatment of 1 Corinthians 14:34–35 and 1 Timothy 2:11–15 are most disappointing. For example, the author rejects the placement of verses 34–35 after verse 40 on the basis of very late manuscripts (pp. 161–62), when in fact the Western text tradition from early on supports the location (second-century Old Latin version; fourth-century Latin father Ambrosiaster; sixth-century Western manuscript Claromontanus). The author also overlooks the evidence presented by NT scholar Philip Payne and textual critic Bruce Metzger of a bar-umlaut sign in codex Vaticanus (B) and breaking mark at the beginning of verse 34 and at the end of verse 35 in p^{46}, A, D, and 33, indicating that copyists were aware of a textual problem.

Equally disappointing is the author's conclusion that verses 34–35 have to do with women "usurp[ing] the authority of the male leaders in pronouncing authoritatively on any disputed prophecy" (p. 164). This seems to contradict the text's implication that the women in question were those seeking to learn (not render prophetic judgments). The author goes even further. The evaluation of prophecy, he states, is not a spiritual gift and so is forbidden to women. Yet, Paul pairs the gifts of prophecy and "distinguishing between spirits" (1 Cor. 12:10), and he instructs the *entire* Thessalonican congregation (not male leaders) to stop treating prophecies with contempt but seek to prove their genuineness instead (1 Thess. 5:20–21).

First Timothy 2:12 is approached as a marriage text (despite the worship context), and the resources are dated—citing a 1988 article by Leland Wilshire on *authentein* that was subsequently revised by Wilshire and a different conclusion drawn—one that does not support the traditionalist position. Craig concludes that the prohibition has to do with women being elders on the basis of a meaning of *authentein* ("hold authority over") that did not exist at the time Paul wrote. The basis is a grouping of English translations that render the Greek *authentein* as "have or exercise authority over," in contrast with Greek dictionary definitions of "usurp" or "domineer." Indeed, there is no instance in the Greek of Paul's day (or earlier) of *authentein* having a meaning like the NIV's routine exercise of authority. This is why all early Latin, Coptic, and Syriac versions of this verse have "domineer." Indeed, in the Old English (and subsequently in the KJV), women are prohibited from "usurping" authority versus "exercising or holding" it.

How one correlates "teaching" and *authentein* is actually the key unanswered question in Craig's essay. This is because he gives Ephesian culture short shrift. The reason early versions have "domineer" is because it best fits the cultural context of the Ephesian cult of Artemis and the presence of false teaching within the Ephesian church. The cult of Artemis (woman's supremacy) was at the heart of the city's prestige and at the center of its economy—as the two-hour chant "Great is Artemis of the Ephesians" indicates (Acts 19:28, 34).

Chapter Three

WOMEN IN MINISTRY: ANOTHER EGALITARIAN PERSPECTIVE

Craig S. Keener

WOMEN IN MINISTRY:
ANOTHER EGALITARIAN PERSPECTIVE

Craig S. Keener

Most Christians do not realize how much our backgrounds and traditions affect the ways we read the Bible. Having held both egalitarian and complementarian (or hierarchicalist) views on women's ministry with sincerity at different times in my life, in both cases dependent on my desire to be faithful to God's Word, I recognize the sincere reasons for which many believers stand on either side of the issue. I am firmly convinced the Bible supports women's ministry, but I have good friends (some of whom are women) who disagree.

A major reason believers have come to hold different views on the matter, however, is that different passages, taken by themselves, seem to point in different directions. Christians with equally high views of Scripture thus often end up with different ways of understanding how God intends us to fit these varied texts together.[1]

THE PROBLEM

Some passages in the Bible support a wide variety of women's ministry, especially those that give explicit examples

---

[1]Because this essay is intended for a more general audience and because I have provided detailed documentation for most of my points elsewhere (see my *Paul, Women and Wives: Marriage and Women's Ministry in the Letters of Paul* [Peabody, Mass.: Hendrickson, 1992, rev. with new introduction, 2004]; articles on gender roles in InterVarsity's *Dictionary of Paul and His Letters; Dictionary of the Later New Testament and Its Developments;* and *Dictionary of New Testament Background* [esp. "Marriage," 680–693]), I document relatively lightly in this essay.

of women prophetesses, a judge with authority over all of God's people, a probable apostle, and women who shared in Paul's ministry of the gospel. Another passage (1 Tim. 2:11–14) appears to forbid women from teaching Scripture in the presence of men, and it is one of two passages that actually can be understood to prohibit women's public speech in church altogether. Sadly, some Christians who start with one group of texts view with suspicion Christians who start with the other group of texts, sometimes even questioning their evangelical commitments. I am thus grateful to my colleagues in this volume for the opportunity to dialogue with them as fellow evangelicals working together to understand God's Word better.

If some texts seem to point in one direction and others in a different direction, it leaves us several options:

1. One group of texts is mistaken. (This is not an option for conservative evangelicals, including the contributors to this book.)
2. The Bible permits to women some kinds of ministries but prohibits others.
3. The Bible prohibits women's ministry under most circumstances but allows exceptions in specific cases, in which case we should allow such ministry today in exceptional cases.[2]
4. The Bible permits women's ministry under normal circumstances but prohibits it in exceptional cases, in which case we should allow it under most circumstances today.

The second position appeals to many Christian interpreters today, but those who hold this position must make many of the same interpretive judgments made by those who affirm women's ministries more generally. The texts to which this position appeals do not specify one kind of verbal ministry but actually enjoin complete silence on the part of women in church, and one text explicitly speaks against any teaching in the presence of men. If these texts mean all they sound like they mean, then

---

[2]Combining positions 2 and 3, Robert W. Yarbrough ("The Hermeneutics of 1 Timothy 2:9–15," in *Women in the Church: A Fresh Analysis of 1 Timothy 2:9–15*, eds. Andreas J. Köstenberger, Thomas R. Schreiner, and H. Scott Baldwin [Grand Rapids: Baker, 1995], 195, n. 181) recognizes that Scripture shows that God could use women as prophets or judges, though not explicitly as pastors.

they prohibit women's public ministry altogether (indeed, their apparent demand for absolute silence would prohibit even singing in the choir or reading publicly a list of announcements). If, by contrast, they do not mean all they sound like they mean, views 3 and 4 are as legitimate an option as view 2. What's more, as I argue below, some of the roles by which women carried out ministry in the Bible were more authoritative than the offices from which they are often now restricted.

I argue in this essay for the fourth view, namely, that the Bible permits women's ministry under normal circumstances and prohibits it only under exceptional circumstances. Because Paul's letters to Timothy address a specific situation (women were, in fact, vehicles for propagating false teaching, as we can demonstrate from the letters themselves), the nature of the exceptional circumstance seems fairly clear. The one Bible passage that explicitly prohibits women from teaching the Bible—in contrast with numerous passages that endorse various women communicating God's message—is addressed to the one church where we specifically know that false teachers were effectively targeting women. Is this a coincidence?

BIBLICAL EVIDENCE FOR WOMEN'S MINISTRY

I start with the passages that appear to support women's involvement in various forms of ministry.

Prophetesses (Exod. 15:20; Judg. 4:4; 2 Kgs 22:14; 2 Chr. 34:22; Isa. 8:3; Luke 8:36; Acts 2:17–18; 21:9; 1 Cor. 11:4–5)

A ministry frequently described in Scripture as promoting women's direct involvement is that of *prophesying*. Today most people think first of pastors when they hear the word *ministers*, but in the OT the most common form of ministry with respect to declaring God's word was the prophetic ministry.[3]

---

[3]Some distinguish *gifts* from *offices*, but in Ephesians 4:11, the role of prophet stands alongside apostles, evangelists, and pastors-teachers as one of the ministries of the word that equips God's people for ministry. We should avoid distinguishing offices from gifts too arbitrarily, especially when someone receives a title (as in Exod. 15:20; Judg. 4:4; 2 Kgs 22:14; Isa. 8:3; Luke 2:36) and our term for "office" does not exist in Scripture (Eph. 4:8, 11 calls ministers "gifts"; "prophets" in 1 Cor. 14:29, 32 seems to refer to any who prophesy).

In the OT, true prophetesses included Miriam (Exod. 15:20), Deborah (Judg. 4:4), Huldah (2 Kgs 22:14; 2 Chr. 34:22), and apparently Isaiah's wife (Isa. 8:3). In the NT, they included Anna (Luke 2:36) and Philip's four virgin daughters (Acts 21:9; in that culture, their virginity probably also suggested their youth). Paul seems to assume that prophetesses were a regular phenomenon in the early Christian churches; in fact, he affirms women both praying and prophesying publicly, provided their heads are covered (1 Cor. 11:4–5).[4] Luke, who throughout both his gospel and the book of Acts shows particular gender sensitivity in reporting about women almost as often as about men, recounts Peter's inspired interpretation of Joel 2:28–29: When God pours out his Spirit once the Messiah has come, women and men will both prophesy (Acts 2:17–18). This passage is as paradigmatic for Acts as Isaiah 61:1–2 was for Luke (Luke 4:18–19). The NT church's witness (cf. Acts 1:8) is characterized by the OT prophetic mantle (in a general sense), irrespective of class, gender, age, or (most surprisingly to the Jerusalem church) race.[5]

To be sure, most prophetic voices (especially in the OT) were male, but this was to be expected in a culture where most public voices were male. Even in the OT, however, the prophetic office was not exclusively male, like the priestly office was. The priestly office provides some lessons for ministry but not necessarily the conclusion that ministers must be male; Protestants apply the priestly analogy to all believers (cf. 1 Pet. 2:5, 9; Rev. 1:6; 5:10; 20:6). Further, if we restrict ministry to men because priests were male, why should we not restrict it also to a particular tribe, as the law clearly did? Many of the regulations God gave the priesthood would have communicated well to his people in an ancient Near Eastern setting—Hittite ritual purity customs, Egyptian architectural features in the tabernacle, and so forth. An exclusively male priesthood made sense in view of

---

[4]Rather than devote space here to what head coverings mean, see my article on "head coverings" in *Dictionary of New Testament Background* (Downers Grove, Ill.: InterVarsity, 2000), 442–47; in less detail, my *Paul, Women and Wives*, 19–69. Gender segregation was impossible in house churches (see Bernadette J. Brooten, *Women Leaders in the Ancient Synagogue: Inscriptional Evidence and Background Issues* [BJS 36; Chico, Calif.: Scholars Press, 1982], 103–38), so men would invariably hear women's prophecies.

[5]Concerning this passage, see my earlier work in *The Spirit in the Gospels and Acts* (Peabody, Mass.: Hendrickson, 1997), 190–213.

some of the ancient Near Eastern cults surrounding Israel and ancient purity customs.

The prophetic office, however, depended on personal calling and on gifts.[6] I address in greater detail below the issue that men prophets outnumbered women prophetesses in Bible times, but suffice it to point out here that fewer women would have had the mobility and social respect to be effective prophetic voices; further, prophetic leaders like Samuel and Elisha would probably not mix genders in the bands of prophets they were mentoring. These factors make the activity of some prophetesses all the more noteworthy.

Some may argue that the prophetic office is irrelevant today because, in their perspective, prophecy has ceased. In my opinion, various texts suggest that prophecy, like other gifts, will continue until Christ's return, even in the narrowest sense of prophecy (1 Cor. 13:8–12; Eph. 4:11–13; Rev. 11:3–7). Moreover, Acts 2:17–18 must remain decisive, for it describes the Spirit-filled church from Pentecost forward, all whom God would call (vv. 38–39) in the era of salvation (v. 21). But even if this gift of prophecy did continue today only in a more restrictive sense, the text at the least indicates that women as well as men must speak God's message with the Spirit's power. Let us, however, grant for a moment the claim some make that prophecy has ceased. Even if this claim were correct, it would not erase the record that in the biblical period some women held an office more directly influential than offices now frequently denied them.

Wishing to allow women to prophesy but not to teach, some claim that from the time of Ezra onward the prophets were on a level less authoritative than the scribes, because scribes handled the Scriptures. This distinction, however, is not quite accurate. Although prophecy is not the same gift as teaching, hearers can learn from it (1 Cor. 14:31). Most of the prophets whose messages are contained in the Bible do interpret and apply earlier biblical messages, especially the law but also images from earlier prophets. (In keeping with this genre, the book of Revelation contains more OT allusions than any other

---

[6]Against the distinctions some make between prophets and those who prophesy, Paul seems to apply the former title to those who fulfill the latter function, at least on a frequent basis (1 Cor. 14:29, 32).

NT book, though it lacks specific quotations.)[7] Indeed, most of the OT was *written* by prophets. In any case, prophets delivered God's message; to voice the objection that women are allowed to deliver God's message in prophecy but not by teaching Scripture is essentially to claim they can minister as long as they do it *without* using Scripture!

A prophetic commission connotes some sort of authority or authorization (Rev. 11:3). Of course, not all prophets exercised the same measure of authority. Samuel, Elijah, and Elisha supervised prophetic movements that recognized their authority. But at least some women, such as Deborah (see comment below), exercised significant authority in this prophetic office. In any case, prophets of either gender had no authority outside of their message. Nathan, for example, had to retract his counsel to David when he discovered it contradicted what the Lord was actually saying (2 Sam. 7:3–5). If the authority inheres in the message proclaimed, Huldah exercises great authority to apply the Book of the Law to her generation (2 Kgs 22:14–20). There was also undoubtedly a reason Josiah sent messengers to her (22:13) rather than to other prophetic figures; perhaps hearing the law forced him to recognize truths she had already been proclaiming.[8]

A Judge (Judg. 4:4)

Along with her brother Aaron, Miriam overstepped her authority when she challenged the greater prophetic office of Moses (Num. 12:1–14), who functioned as the closest OT model for NT apostolic ministry (2 Cor. 3:6–18; cf. John 1:14–18).[9]

---

[7]For my comments on biblical allusions in Revelation, see my commentary (*Revelation* [NIVAC; Grand Rapids: Zondervan, 2000], various pages); Gregory K. Beale provides more detail in *The Book of Revelation* (NIGTC; Grand Rapids: Eerdmans, 1999), various pages.

[8]Jeremiah was still very young (2 Kgs 22:3; Jer. 1:2, 6). In any event, 2 Kings draws numerous parallels between the revivals under Josiah and, a century earlier, under Hezekiah—and Huldah's role in this narrative precisely parallels that of Isaiah in Hezekiah's day in 2 Kings 19:2–7.

[9]For the Moses allusion in John 1:14–18, see Marie-Emile Boismard, *St. John's Prologue* (London: Blackfriars, 1957), 136–39; Anthony Hanson, "John I.14–18 and Exodus XXXIV," *NTS* 23 (1976): 90–101; Henry Mowvley; "John 1.14–18 in the Light of Exodus 33.7–34.35," *ExpTim* 95 (1984): 135–37; Craig Keener, *The Gospel of John: A Commentary* (2 vols.; Peabody, Mass.: Hendrickson, 2003), 405–26.

Moses was not only a prophet but also a chief leader, and occasionally he was even compared to a king (Deut. 33:5). The closest equivalents after Moses and before the apostles would be prophets who also led Israel (Deborah, Samuel, and David—see Acts 2:30) and perhaps those who led the remnant in times of great wickedness (like Elijah and Elisha). Of the two explicit prophetic judges (Samuel and Deborah), one was a woman—an obvious biblical example of an authoritative prophetess.

In the entire era of the judges, only one woman was a judge, and the book of Judges makes a point of showing this was noteworthy. The Hebrew is emphatic: "a *woman* prophet [prophetess], the wife of Lappidoth" (Judg. 4:4). But while its rareness made it remarkable, the text offers no note of condemnation. One of the main features of Judges is its insistence that Israel regularly turned from God's commandments, and that God, rather than the judges he raised up, was the real hero. Most of the judges whose stories are narrated in detail exhibit significant problems in their personal lives (8:27; 11:30–39); the book even skips over twenty years of Samson's ministry to reveal his sexual entanglements (15:20–16:31), rooted in what we might today call his earlier dysfunctional relationships (14:2–3)! Even Samuel may have had some problems (1 Sam. 8:3; cf. 2:12–17, 29), although they were not serious enough to sidetrack his ministry.

Yet Deborah, who does not grasp for power but shares it willingly with Barak, comes off pretty much squeaky-clean—as, in fact, a woman would have had to in order to have maintained leadership in her era.[10] In any case, she clearly exercised authority over Israel. She apparently even shared Barak's military leadership, though this was because Barak refused to accept his commission alone (Judg. 4:6–10). Some object that God appoints women only when men are not getting the job done. Even if one were to grant this premise, it would hardly provide an argument against women's ministry today, given the fact that perhaps over half the world's population has yet to hear the gospel of Jesus Christ in a culturally intelligible way and that most of Christ's church, and presumably many of its teachers, remain too asleep to rise to his call.

---

[10]Deborah perhaps once took the opportunity to affirm members of her gender in a distinctive way when she warned Barak—perhaps to shame him—that God would give Sisera into the hands of a woman; in any case, God fulfilled this prophecy when Jael put a spike into Sisera's head (Judg. 4:9, 21).

An Apostle (Rom. 16:7)

If Moses and the prophetic leaders were the closest OT equivalent to the NT apostles, Deborah merits a place among them. Clearly a number of NT women also continued the prophetic office, as noted above. But were there any explicit women apostles in the NT? Because of apostles' special rank and their role in breaking new ground for God's kingdom, women would have faced special obstacles in that culture, as they would in many cultures even today. Thus, we should not expect great numbers of women apostles in Scripture, but if we have even one woman apostle, its occurrence would confirm our suspicion (based on Deborah and what I have noted from the prophetesses) that a woman could hold this office.[11]

Paul does not hand out the title lightly; he applies the title explicitly only to a handful of leaders in his day, besides the Twelve and (often) himself (1 Cor. 9:5–6; Gal. 1:19; cf. 1 Thess. 2:5 with 1:1). But neither does he restrict the title to the Twelve; in fact, he clearly distinguishes it from them (1 Cor. 15:5–7). Even Luke, who usually restricts the term to the Twelve, allows it for Paul and Barnabas in at least one passage (Acts 14:4, 14). By "apostles" I do not mean those who write Scripture or speak with canonical authority; most apostles did not contribute to the Bible, nor were all NT writers apostles. But a survey of every use of "apostle" in the NT (a survey I have done but can only summarize here) includes in most cases special authority that stemmed from a special commission and message (rather than purely administrative authority), a ministry that typically included signs and wonders and broke new ground for God's kingdom (whether in founding the Jerusalem church or other churches).

In Romans 16:7 Paul speaks of Andronicus and Junia, who are "of note among the apostles" (KJV). Some think "of note among the apostles" means simply that the apostles thought well of them. While this position is grammatically possible, Paul nowhere refers to "the apostles" as a group to whose opinion he appeals. Indeed, the most natural and common sense of "among" a group means they are members of that group (see, e.g., Rom. 1:13; 8:29), hence here "well-known apostles," which

---

[11]For comments about those who wish to distinguish official ministry roles from gifts, see n. 3 above. When the title is applied, as in Romans 16:7, we have good reason to see a ministry role there!

was how the Greek fathers (and most modern scholars) take the phrase. Less persuasively, some try to circumvent the implication of this phrase by arguing that they are a special kind of nonauthoritative apostle, like the "messengers of the churches" in 2 Corinthians 8:23 (KJV; cf. also Phil. 2:25). This attempt also has little to commend it; for one thing, we do not know that the "messengers of the churches" lacked authority (they were probably often Paul's ministry companions—cf. Acts 20:4). More important, it is unsound interpretive methodology to read a more specific meaning into a phrase than its use in that context and situation warrants. Paul does not qualify "apostles" in Romans 16:7 as "apostles of the churches" or "your apostles," and everywhere else in the NT where the phrase remains unqualified, it refers to apostles with rank. Would Paul commend them for being something less than what an unqualified *apostle* means in every other NT instance and yet expect Roman Christians to understand what he means?

An even less plausible way to get around Junia's being an apostle is to claim that Junian (the direct object form of the common female Junia, not of the male Junius) is really a contraction for the male name Junianus. But this contradiction never appears in Greek literature (including in Rome's inscriptions). Indeed, because of the way Latin names are transcribed into Greek, *Junia* grammatically *can* be nothing other than a woman's name here, though many earlier scholars failed to notice this.[12]

The only reason someone would deny that Junia is a woman here, against the otherwise plain reading of the text, is the assumption that Paul cannot describe a woman as an apostle. If we know that Paul would never allow a woman to be an apostle,

[12]See Richard S. Cervin, "A Note Regarding the Name 'Junia(s)' in Romans 16.7," *NTS* 40 (1994): 464–70 (an article brought to my attention by Michael Holmes). For a woman apostle here, see, e.g., Wayne Meeks, *The First Urban Christians: The Social World of the Apostle Paul* (New Haven, Conn.: Yale Univ. Press, 1983), 47. J. B. Lightfoot (*Saint Paul's Epistle to the Galatians* [London: Macmillan, 1910], 96, n. 1), who thought Junia to be male, doubts that any would have taken the phrase "as esteemed *by* the Apostles" were it not to circumvent the extension of the apostolate beyond the Twelve. The best defense of the minority view that the apostles merely thought well of them is Michael H. Burer and Daniel B. Wallace, "Was Junia Really an Apostle? A Re-examination of Rom. 16:7," *NTS* 47 (2001): 76–91 (esp. 84–91), but the evidence can be sorted differently, and Richard Bauckham (*Gospel Women: Studies of the Named Women in the Gospels* [Grand Rapids: Eerdmans, 2002], 166–180 (esp. 172–180) refutes this position.

one might be forced to make the inference that Junia is not what Paul normally means by an *apostle* and that perhaps the Roman believers could be expected to know what he might mean based on their knowledge of Junia. But such an argument merely assumes what one hopes to prove, for nothing in the text itself points to Junia being anything other than a woman apostle, as even the later church father John Chrysostom recognized. At the least, those who deny women's public ministry should admit that the simplest reading of Romans 16:7 is a "hard" case for their position, as many egalitarians would admit the simplest reading of 1 Timothy 2:11–12 is for theirs.

Because an unmarried man and woman working together (as this couple apparently does) would generate scandal, Andronicus is probably either Junia's brother or, far more likely in that culture, her husband. We know that some married male apostles took their wives with them when they traveled (1 Cor. 9:5), but this text claims more than that she simply traveled with him. The shared title indicates she actually shared in his ministry in a special way, the way many couples in other professions also worked together.[13]

Laborers in the Word (Rom. 16:1–12; Phil. 4:2–3)

Although today we often think of ministry especially in terms of senior pastors, apostles and prophets were in some sense the highest-ranking ministers of the NT church; whenever Paul lists them among gifts or ministries he lists them first, including on the one occasion where he enumerates some ministries (1 Cor. 12:28). As I will observe later, they were more prominent than local pastors, and, in at least some churches, "prophets and teachers" apparently *were* the pastors (Acts 13:1). I'll return to the issue later, but for now let me note that women are mentioned in some of the highest offices of early Christianity and are abundant at least as prophetesses. Although less dramatic than testimony to prophetic and apostolic roles, two passages provide further evidence for their ministry in God's

---

[13]On husband-wife teams in other professions, see Jane F. Gardner, *Women in Roman Law and Society* (Bloomington, Ind.: Indiana Univ. Press, 1986), 240. To say Andronicus and Junia are both simply called by the husband's proper title is to deny that Paul stated correctly what he meant, for he specifically employs a plural pronoun and verb in making the point.

word—Romans 16:1–12 and Philippians 4:3. Especially in the former passage Paul employs the same terms to describe the ministry of women that he commonly uses to describe that of men.

Paul conveys personal greetings to more men than women in Romans 16. Some insist that the greater number of male ministers in the NT suggests that ministry is an exclusively male vocation, so when we come to a discussion of Romans 16, I sometimes joke with my students that we should greet only men in public. But while Paul greets more men than women here, he commends the ministries of women much more often than the ministries of men.[14] He commends for ministry most of the women he cites but fewer than one-quarter of the men. (I sometimes tell my students that on the basis of this commendation we should institute a quota in which most ministers should be women! I am, of course, only joking in order to provoke some interpretive observations.) Paul may very well be going out of his way to commend the women because, in a culture biased against their ministry, they needed special encouragement. But I use the fact of the larger percentage of women commended to illustrate how our conclusions about women's ministry often stem from the particular texts we read most closely.

The nature of some of the ministries commended in Romans 16 is ambiguous: Mary, Tryphena, Tryphosa, and Persis "worked very hard in the Lord" (vv. 6, 12). This phrase implies ministry, probably especially in evangelism and discipling (1 Cor. 15:10; Gal. 4:11; Phil. 2:16; Col. 1:29). It does not need to connote administrative authority (the most frequent matter of debate today), although the language does not at all rule out this possibility (1 Cor. 16:16; 1 Thess. 5:12; 1 Tim. 5:17; 2 Tim. 2:6). I state these conclusions cautiously, but it should be noted the same language is used for many male ministers in the NT, and so our conclusions about the ministries of both genders should be equally cautious. That Euodia and Syntyche shared Paul's struggle for the cause of the gospel in Philippi (Phil. 4:2–3) likewise implies their involvement in ministry, probably evangelism, though this is a call for which all believers are responsible (1:27).

---

[14]This is still true even if, as is probable, Paul's greetings to some men alongside their households imply that these men held some positions in the churches that met in their homes.

Priscilla and her husband, Aquila, are Paul's "co-workers" (Rom. 16:3), a frequent term in Paul's letters. He especially applies it to those who shared his ministry labors (v. 9; 1 Cor. 3:9; Phil. 4:3; Col. 4:11)—including fellow itinerants like Timothy (Rom. 16:21; 1 Thess. 3:2), Titus (2 Cor. 8:23), Epaphroditus (Phil. 2:25), and others (Phlm. 24), as well as house church leaders like Philemon (Phlm. 1). The possible more general sense of the term ("work with you" [2 Cor. 1:24]) does not fit the particular commendation of this passage. Other passages may fill in a few more particulars of this married team's ministry, which included instructing ministers and leading a house church (Acts 18:26; 1 Cor 16:19; cf. Phlm. 1–2).

The nature of certain other women's ministries in Romans 16 is clearer. Junia was, as I noted above, an apostle (v. 7), most likely as part of a husband-wife apostolic team. The chapter opens with mention of Phoebe, who carried Paul's letter to Rome, hence plainly functioning as Paul's agent. Given his commendation, it is possible Paul expects her to be able to explain to the Roman Christians details of his letter if she is questioned (vv. 1–2), as letter bearers sometimes were.[15] Would she have been qualified to answer questions about the content of Paul's teaching in that letter? Paul provides her qualifications. She will depend on the hospitality of the Roman Christians but has provided such hospitality to many others (v. 2); the term used for her providing help customarily referred to patrons, including sponsors of religious groups that met in wealthy homes. In ancient inscriptions, as many as 10 percent of these sponsors were women, and Paul has no objections to the church continuing this practice. Phoebe is a well-to-do woman— probably a businesswoman, perhaps a widow or freedwoman— in whose home the church could meet (similarly Nympha in Col. 4:15). The person in charge of synagogue buildings held an important role in the synagogue, and most hosts of house churches held prominent roles in the churches.

A position of prominence and responsibility might not necessarily require Phoebe to explain Scripture, so let's examine Romans 16:1, where Paul calls her a *diakonos* of the church in Cenchreae, Corinth's port town on the Aegean Sea. The term translated "servant" here (NIV; TNIV, "deacon") is a term Paul sometimes used for Jesus (15:8) but most often for Paul himself

---

[15]See, e.g., Xenophon, *Cyr.* 4.5.34. Bearers might also communicate a letter's spirit (e.g., 1 Macc. 12:23; Cicero, *Fam.* 12.30.3; Eph. 6:21–22; Col. 4:7–8).

(2 Cor. 11:23; Eph. 3:7; Col. 1:23, 25), his other fellow ministers of the word (Eph. 6:21; Col. 1:7; 4:7), or Paul and other ministers of the word together (1 Cor. 3:5; 2 Cor. 3:6; 6:4). The term can mean "deacon" (Phil. 1:1; 1 Tim. 3:8, 12)—but the NT nowhere specifically defines what this title means. It may relate to the more common usage of *diakonos* (ministry of the word noted above). Yet those who fill the office of "deacons" must be committed to sound doctrine (1 Tim. 3:9), so we cannot rule out that even they may have taught others, even if they possessed an office distinct from Paul's normal usage. But there is no reason to make the term here mean something different from its most common sense in Paul (and its almost exclusive sense in Paul in this period of his writings).

Some churches today have redefined Phoebe's role as a deaconess on a level of authority lower than deacons, but Paul does not employ any special feminine form of *diakonos* here. There is no reason to assume Paul means by Phoebe's title something other than what he normally means by the term (that is, a minister of God's message, such as Paul himself)—unless we presuppose that he does not allow women's ministry (by reading an interpretation of another passage into this one).[16] But as I've noted, he clearly allows women some speaking ministry as prophets and, very likely, at least sometimes as apostles. It is natural that most of Paul's fellow ministers, especially his traveling companions such as Timothy and Titus, would be male; but the fact that Paul can employ the same title for a woman challenges the prejudice that women cannot fill the same sorts of ministry roles.

One could argue that because Paul instructs women to teach women (Titus 2:3–4), his other counsel about women's ministry applies only to ministering to women. Given first-century social conditions, I suspect that in evangelism and teaching, Paul's female collaborators probably *did* regularly minister, both privately and corporately, to other women—though there are some explicit exceptions (Acts 18:26, e.g., which at least allows a married couple to privately tutor a prominent minister!).[17] But given

---

[16]For more detailed documentation, see my *Paul, Women and Wives*, 238–40.

[17]On a somewhat entertaining note, Rebecca Merrill Groothuis (*Good News for Women: A Biblical Picture of Gender Equality* [Grand Rapids: Baker, 1997], 222–23) points out that those who prohibit women from teaching men because "women are more easily deceived" often allow women to teach other women—the very people they would most easily lead into further deception.

what we know about the house churches, it is also impossible to completely restrict women's ministry of God's message in this manner, even in the first century. Women and men met together in the largest room in the house churches, and even if they were seated separately (a situation for which we lack early evidence), it would hardly be possible for women to pray and prophesy without men hearing them![18]

If we do not read 1 Timothy 2 into the earlier texts, whose original readers had no access to Paul's first letter to Timothy, we have no reason to doubt that Paul accepts women in ministry. Paul describes the ministries of women in the same language that he employs to describe those of men.

Does Paul Permit Only Some Ministry Roles?

Some argue that 1 Timothy 2 (treated below) prohibits not every kind of Bible teaching role but only those kinds of teaching exercised "with authority," namely, that of a senior pastor. Thus, women can teach Sunday school; direct the Christian education department; and do youth ministry, worship ministry, evangelism work, community ministry, and counseling ministry—virtually anything except be "in charge." Because in many circles most women in ministry are not senior pastors anyway, this perspective may be closer in practice to the one that accepts all women's ministries than to the one that restricts all women's ministries. (In fact, when a male senior pastor propounds this view, he is usually not restricting women's ministries in his particular congregation at all, because in his congregation he holds the senior pastor position himself.)

But this view actually represents something of an accommodation between the traditional restrictive position and the customary egalitarian position. The problem with this accommodation, of course, is that the words in 1 Timothy restrict women from speaking altogether; whether or not we read this text as a universal prohibition, the text says nothing about senior pastors. The most probable way to take the grammar of 2:12 is not that women may not teach in an authoritative way (as I once took it), but that they may not teach or hold (or usurp) authority,

---

[18]On the lack of early evidence for further gender segregation even in the synagogues, see Brooten, *Women Leaders*, 103–38; Shmuel Safrai, "The Synagogue," in *The Jewish People in the First Century* (Philadelphia: Fortress, 1974), 908–44.

as some complementarian scholars have argued.[19] Once you protest that Paul did not mean to prohibit *all* speaking, you have already raised the interpretive question of what he actually did mean in his historical context and how it might be applied in our context today.

Consider some of the problems with this mediating position, close as it is in many respects to a fully egalitarian position. First, it is not, as I have noted, a description of what this text *says*, taken at face value and without appeal to the local situation, any more than the full egalitarian position is. The text does not specifically mention senior pastors; rather, it seems to suggest all kinds of (Bible) teaching and all kinds of authority. No more Sunday school teachers in gender-mixed classes! But if the text's words should be qualified, what prevents one from qualifying them toward a full egalitarian position, which makes the other texts we have examined easier to explain?

Second, reducing this text to the issue of rank or authority does not answer the question of other texts that appear to support women's ministry. Paul seems to think apostles and prophets are the highest-ranking leaders in the body of Christ (1 Cor. 12:28; Eph. 4:11; cf. Rom. 12:6), yet he apparently endorses a woman apostle (Rom. 16:7) and certainly endorses prophetesses (1 Cor. 11:5; cf. Acts 2:17–18; 21:9). At least in exceptional circumstances, some prophetesses held supreme administrative authority (Judg. 4:4). Once we admit that, at least in exceptional circumstances, women can exercise authority, we are moving toward the third and fourth views articulated at the beginning of this chapter.

Finally, this view risks imposing a modern understanding of church leadership on the NT setting. Only a small portion of what the Bible teaches about ministry actually focuses on pastors.

---

[19]See esp. the argument in Andreas J. Köstenberger, "A Complex Sentence Structure in 1 Timothy 2:12," in *Women in the Church: A Fresh Analysis*, 81–103, which, though not foolproof, is on the whole persuasive (see my review in *JETS* 41 [1998]: 513–16, against my earlier position in *Paul, Women and Wives*, 109). One could take both expressions as negative (false teaching and domineering), but I believe I can make my case, even granting the complementarian reading of much of the evidence. One could link "teaching" with elders (1 Tim. 3:2; 5:17), but that association is not always explicit (1 Tim. 1:3; 4:11, 13, 16; 6:2; 2 Tim. 2:2, 24; 3:10, 16; cf. especially Titus 2:3), and even if this passage prohibits women elders, we would still have to address whether the prohibition is local or universal.

What's more, "senior pastors" did not exercise the same kind of authority in Paul's day that most do today. Typically, local churches in Paul's day held at most around fifty members, since they met in homes. Fifty members on average probably represented several families and a number of individuals who attended without families, meeting in the spacious home of a well-endowed family. Church leaders were chosen from among the members, and following the model of the synagogues, churches probably often had a plurality of elders (Acts 13:1; 14:23; 1 Tim. 4:14; 5:17; Titus 1:5), who were also called "overseers" (Acts 20:17, 28; Titus 1:5, 7; probably 1 Pet. 5:1–2). Thus it is possible that a significant percentage of family leaders were also in church leadership of some sort! Our modern emphasis on pastoral authority may read our modern situation into early Christian house churches. Many women Sunday school teachers may in fact be exercising more teaching authority today than many first-century elders did!

Paul's ideal for the church was that everyone would exercise their spiritual gifts in these house churches (1 Cor. 14:26). Among these gifts, Paul emphasizes prophecy no less than teaching (v. 1). (To be sure, prophecy can be abused, for we "prophesy in part," but so also can teaching, for we also "know in part" [13:9, 12].) Pastors had very important roles as supervisors in local congregations, but it seems doubtful they exercised the sort of authority pastors do in many modern evangelical churches. This is not to say that all churches must reinstitute the specific forms of church leadership practiced in the first century. The early church often adapted forms of leadership from the synagogue and used structures that best fit their culture; our situation differs from theirs, as does what is practical to apply in our setting. But many aspects of gender roles have also changed in our culture, and we ought to take this into account when we consider appropriate leadership forms.

In Greco-Roman culture and in the house church setting, it is hardly surprising that most leaders in the church were men—probably most often older men who were respected heads of stable families (1 Tim. 3:2–5; 5:17–19).[20] At the same time, we

---

[20]Despite the use of the word *man* in many translations of this verse, 1 Timothy 3:1 uses a gender-neutral term, not the gender-specific *anēr*, to designate one seeking the office of elder.

know not all church leaders were older heads of families—Paul himself was not, and Timothy was young (4:12; from Acts we can deduce he may have been in his thirties).

Furthermore, although we have no women pastors named in the NT, in the most specific sense we have no male pastors named either. To be sure, we do know that most elders were male (1 Tim. 3:2), but this appears to be the text's assumption (reflecting a given cultural situation) rather than its exhortation: Paul may have been specifying marital infidelity in language applicable to the majority of elders in his day. Again, it is doubtful that ancient readers would have considered Paul himself literally the husband of one wife (or a "one-woman man"), but as a church leader he fit the basic sense of the requirement because he was not unfaithful to a wife.[21]

In addition to this text, we have the names of some of Paul's male traveling companions whom he appointed to oversee local churches and church leaders in certain areas—men such as Timothy and Titus. But Paul lived in a culture where female traveling companions would have proved scandalous, hence counterproductive for spreading the gospel.[22]

Nevertheless, the most common terms that Paul uses to describe himself and his male fellow laborers—*diakonos* (1 Cor. 3:5; 2 Cor. 3:6; 6:4; 11:23; Eph. 3:7; 6:21; Col. 1:7, 23–25; 4:7) and *synergos* ("co-worker" [cf. Rom. 16:9, 21; 1 Cor. 3:9; 2 Cor. 1:24; 8:23])—he also uses to describe women colleagues, though they probably did not travel with him (Rom. 16:1, 3; perhaps Phil. 4:3). Other phrases he uses to describe his male colleagues he

---

[21]Besides the smaller pool of educated women, the majority of people "respectable" enough to be leaders in that culture (1 Tim. 3:2, contrast 2:9) would be men; part of the culture also mistrusted religions that liberated women from traditional roles (see my *Paul, Women and Wives*, 139–56). On the meaning of "one-woman man" in its first-century context, see my *And Marries Another: Divorce and Remarriage in the Teaching of the New Testament* (Peabody, Mass.: Hendrickson, 1991), 83–103; even if Paul had been married before, it is unlikely that anyone in the first century would have applied the phrase to him at this point. On the widespread understanding that general principles might sometimes be qualified, see my *And Marries Another*, 21–28.

[22]Jesus' disciples did have female traveling companions (Mark 15:40–41; Luke 8:1–3), despite probable scandal (see Lucian, *The Runaways* 18; Ben Witherington III, *Women in the Ministry of Jesus*, SNTSMS 51 [Cambridge: Cambridge Univ. Press, 1984], 117), but Paul had to exhibit greater concern for the scandal factor because he was trying to establish a church within Greco-Roman society. Jesus, by contrast, was deliberately moving toward confrontation with the authorities and his execution.

also applies to some women in Romans 16, as we have seen ("work hard" in vv. 6, 12; cf. 1 Cor. 16:16; 1 Thess. 5:12). We can frame our questions so narrowly that we exclude the value of the evidence we do have (as scholars frequently do to prove a variety of positions), but the evidence we have is certainly abundant when we consider that it comes from occasional documents. Women filled these ministry roles less frequently than men, but they did fill them. If Paul acknowledges women apostles and prophets, who communicate God's word with authority,[23] need we suppose he rejected all women *pastors*— especially since this is not what he actually says?

Why More Men Than Women?

Some allow that women may minister under exceptional circumstances but argue that male church leadership is the norm. Those who hold this view often allow all the successful women ministers they know to be "exceptions," and thus do not restrict women's ministry. In practice, then, those who hold this technically nonegalitarian position may *function* as egalitarians. It is nevertheless important to consider the question they raise: If God supports women's ministry, why do most of the ministers in the Bible happen to be men?

The question is legitimate, but some knowledge of the biblical world is helpful in answering it. Social conditions do affect both people's responses to God's call and the areas to which God will call people for the most effective ministry. Thus, for example, most of the women Paul mentions as sharing with him in the gospel in some way (apart from prophecy, which seems more widespread) are in Rome or Philippi (Rom. 16:1–12; Phil 4:3)— locations in which women appear to have exercised greater social mobility than in Greece or in much of the parts of urban Asia Minor influenced by Hellenistic culture.[24]

---

[23]I follow my own research on the nature of apostles and prophets here (summarized in *The Spirit in the Gospels and Acts*, as well as "The Function of Johannine Pneumatology in the Context of Late First-Century Judaism" [Ph.D. diss., Duke University, 1991]) rather than that of Wayne Grudem (*The Gift of Prophecy in 1 Corinthians* [Lanham, Md.: University Press of America, 1982]), though I respect all and affirm most of Grudem's work on the subject.

[24]See, e.g., Valerie Abrahamsen, "The Rock Reliefs and the Cult of Diana at Philippi" (Th.D. diss., Harvard Divinity School, 1986).

Some people question why Jesus, who often showed himself to be countercultural, chose only men for his twelve most prominent disciples. Jesus was indeed countercultural in advancing the status of women (Luke 8:1–3; 10:38–42), but even Jesus did not directly challenge every detail of his culture, choosing his closest workers most strategically for the culture he intended to reach. None of the Twelve was a Gentile, a slave, or, as far as we know, a peasant or even a Judean. Most were Galileans, and the five whose occupations we know apparently came from the top 10 percent of wage-earning occupations in Galilee.[25] Does this mean Jesus would never choose Gentiles to follow him later? Shall we restrict the ministries of Gentiles today or impose a quota system to make sure the majority of ministers are Jewish? One suspects that we would quickly experience a leadership shortage in our churches!

Conclusions in Support of Women's Ministry

Women appear at least occasionally in most ministry positions in which men are attested frequently in the NT. Paul normally traveled with men, but while he often sent his male traveling companions, he could also send a woman like Phoebe (Rom. 16:1–2). Most apostles and prophets were men, but at least one apostle and many prophetic figures were women. We have few specific leaders of house churches named, whether male or female; we do have the names of some in whose homes church members met, as well as the names of those with titles like *diakonos* ("servant," "minister") or *synergos* ("co-worker"), but these homeowners and titles apply to women as well as to men.

We cannot list many specifically titled senior pastors of either gender in the first century, but if we can accept women as prophets and other ministers, there is no reason to exclude women from the pastoral office. Men clearly predominated— but so did free persons and, in the earliest period, Jews. Today we can recognize a different social setting—one that allows more Gentiles to minister; today's different setting also invites more women to embrace the roles some had begun to embrace already in the NT.

[25]I summarize the data more fully in *A Commentary on the Gospel According to Matthew* (Grand Rapids: Eerdmans, 1999), 151, 311.

BIBLICAL EVIDENCE POSSIBLY AGAINST WOMEN'S MINISTRY

If one could win the debate on women's ministry simply by the number of Bible passages one could cite, the clear weight of the debate would favor women's ministry. But for those who hold the entire Bible to be God's inspired word, we cannot dismiss any passage. Our goal must be to understand what each one says in its historical context, not simply to count texts. Two texts can be used to prohibit women's ministry, of which one (and only one) explicitly addresses women's ministry in particular. While this one is indeed rather explicit, if it means all it could possibly mean, it would represent a radical departure from everything else Paul taught on the subject—and it would restrict women even more than today's most conservative voices on the subject do.

One question that this apparent contradiction invites is this: Could these passages have been addressing specific situations?

Might These Passages Address Specific Situations?

Some people conclude we must accept as transcultural everything Paul says, regardless of the situations that prompted it. They are partly right. Everything the Bible says is for all time; but not everything the Bible says is for all circumstances, and there is not a single Christian in the world today, regardless of his or her views on the issue of women in ministry, who applies every text to all circumstances—not even all the straightforward commands.

Our theological backgrounds often shape what we characterize as cultural. Thus, a nonegalitarian scholar (an esteemed friend of mine) cited approvingly my treatment of head coverings in 1 Corinthians 11:2–16 (for which I am grateful), acknowledging that head coverings are not a transcultural requirement. He then curiously proceeded, however, to deny without debate that one could approach 1 Timothy similarly (which makes an identical argument from the creation order)!

Others more consistently not only prohibit women from teaching but require them to wear head coverings to church in *all* cultures. Close to half my students in one class in northern Nigeria, where head coverings are part of the culture, held this view, so after they had finished debating with the other half, I asked why none of them had greeted me with a holy kiss—and they laughed! The holy kiss is an explicit command repeated in Scripture five times as often as head coverings (Rom. 16:16; 1 Cor. 16:20; 2 Cor. 13:12; 1 Thess. 5:26; 1 Pet. 5:14), but the usual response is, "That was merely a cultural form of greeting." Indeed it was, but covering the head (technically, all the hair) was also merely a cultural expression of sexual modesty, as can be demonstrated from a massive number of ancient sources.[26] Yet a few of my students bordered on calling other students "liberal" because they did not insist on head coverings as a transcultural requirement! Who determines where to draw the line? Is everyone liberal who holds as cultural something we hold as transcultural?

But some demand to know whether Paul could have addressed a specific situation in such broad, sweeping terms. When one reads the rest of Paul's letters, one can only answer, "Definitely!" Paul regularly writes in the language and figures of speech of his day; he also uses cultural images presupposed in his day.[27] More to the point, Paul's letters are full of statements that are locale specific and cannot possibly have meaning apart from the local situation.[28] Sometimes Paul even alludes to matters known only to local congregations (see, e.g., 1 Cor. 1:16; 3:4–6; perhaps 15:29; 2 Thess 2:5).

To be sure, Paul's letters are full of principles directly applicable to today's situations; the practices of complaining and arguing, for instance, are probably not much different today than they were when Paul wrote Philippians. At the same time, other passages require some sensitivity to the original situation in order to be able to translate the principles into our contemporary situation—matters like head coverings or food offered to idols, for instance. Even in these cases Paul works with transcultural

---

[26]See my articles on "kissing" and "head coverings" in *Dictionary of New Testament Background*, 628–29; 442–47; or, less thoroughly, my *Paul, Women and Wives*, 19–69.

[27]I sought to provide (albeit on a relatively popular level) much of the background that illustrates this point in *The IVP Bible Background Commentary: New Testament* (Downers Grove, Ill.: InterVarsity, 1993), 407–646.

[28]See Rom. 1:7, 10, 13; 15:22–24; 16:1–27; 1 Cor. 1:2, 11–12; 4:17; 5:1–6; 6:6–8; 7:5; 8:9; 11:17–22; 16:5–12; 2 Cor. 1:1, 15–17; 1:23–2:13; 6:11–13; 7:5–16; 9:2–5; 10:6–16; 11:1–21; 12:11–13:10; Gal. 1:2, 4:12–20; Phil. 1:1, 4–8, 19; 4:2–3, 10–19; Col. 1:2; 2:1; 1 Thess. 1:1; 2:1, 17–18; 2 Thess. 2:1.

principles, but he articulates them in specific ways that address specific situations, and if we choose to ignore these situations when we interpret his writings, it follows that we must greet each other with holy kisses in church (in keeping with ancient family customs, they may have often been light kisses on the lips) or risk disobeying the apostles!

Some people conclude that, whereas some texts are culture specific, texts that give specific commands are universally applicable.[29] I would respond that *all* Scripture is universally applicable (2 Tim. 3:16). But all Scripture is also articulated in culture-specific and language-specific ways (e.g., in Hebrew or Greek). Often biblical writers addressed specific situations in specific churches, inviting us to read their letters as case studies directly applying to specific situations so we can identify their more indirect, universal principles, which we will then reapply in other situations. Inspiration does not change a writing's *genre*, or type of literature. Psalms are still psalms, narrative is still narrative, and epistles are still epistles. Pastoral letters, like sermons addressed to local congregations, can contain both universal and culture-specific exhortations side by side; this should be true, whether they are inspired or not.

This character of the genre of pastoral letters seems evident. Consider this: I sometimes write letters of exhortation containing mainly universal principles that are also relevant to the particular situation I am addressing. Yet in those same letters I may include some exhortations directly relevant only to those situations I am specifically addressing. Unless I consciously write with the expectation that there will be other future readers who are *outside* the particular situation, I may never stop to differentiate my universal and situation-specific exhortations. Because I intend all my exhortations to be relevant to my immediate audience, I do not write these two kinds of exhortations in different ways or express them in different literary forms. A later reader may therefore distinguish which I thought was which only by reconstructing the situation and comparing my other writings that addressed specific situations. Thus it is significant that the Bible always portrays complaining attitudes and homosexual behavior as wrong; eating food sacrificed to idols as often wrong; and

---

[29]Cf., e.g., T. David Gordon ("A Certain Kind of Letter: The Genre of 1 Timothy," in *Women in the Church: A Fresh Analysis*, 53–63), who argues from some universal instructions in the Pastoral Epistles.

women's authority as ministers of the word as sometimes limited but sometimes commended, as noted above.[30]

Paul provides many direct commands that we do not observe today, and some that we cannot observe. How many Christians today put money into savings the first day of every week for a collection for the saints in Jerusalem (1 Cor. 16:1–3)? Paul commands his readers to receive Epaphroditus (Phil. 2:29), but because Epaphroditus is no longer living, we cannot fulfill this command literally. Paul exhorts his readers to pray for him and his companions (2 Thess. 3:1–2), but we who reject prayer for the dead cannot fulfill this command today. Instead, we learn from these passages general principles about giving generously, being hospitable, and praying for God's servants.

Must a transcultural application be absurd before we will limit it? Or do these "absurd" examples point out the way we consistently ought to read Paul's letters? To claim that only the *obviously* culturally limited passages are in fact culturally limited is simply to beg the question of interpretation methods. When slaveholders read Paul's command to slaves to obey their masters (Eph. 6:5), they did not think this command absurd for other settings, so they took it as a transcultural endorsement of slavery.[31] Because Paul always sought to be sensitive to his readers' situations (1 Cor. 9:19–23; 10:31–33), we dare not presume that every command applies to all circumstances.[32]

---

[30]On passages commending women's ministry, see my *Paul, Women and Wives*, 237–57 (citing other sources); for the hermeneutical principle, see Gordon D. Fee and Douglas Stuart, *How to Read the Bible for All Its Worth*, 3d. ed. (Grand Rapids: Zondervan, 2003), 72–76. See also William Webb, *Slaves, Women and Homosexuals: Exploring the Hermeneutics of Cultural Analysis* (Downers Grove, Ill.: InterVarsity, 2001); essays in Ronald W. Pierce, Rebecca Merrill Groothuis, and Gordon D. Fee, eds., *Discovering Biblical Equality: Complementarity without Hierarchy* (Downers Grove, Ill.: InterVarsity, 2004), 355–428; cf. F. F. Bruce, *A Mind for What Matters* (Grand Rapids: Eerdmans, 1990), 259–325.

[31]On the different interpretations undergirding and opposing slavery, see Glenn Usry and Craig S. Keener, *Black Man's Religion: Can Christianity be Afrocentric?* (Downers Grove, Ill.: InterVarsity, 1996), 98–109; my *Paul, Women and Wives*, 184–224; and esp. Willard M. Swartley, *Slavery, Sabbath, War and Women* (Scottdale, Pa.: Herald, 1983), 31–64, 198–204 (my *Paul, Women and Wives* would have profited had I read Swartley first).

[32]Even some general principles in Paul's letters, like many general exhortations in antiquity, could admit exceptions. To his call to submit to governing authorities (Rom. 13:1–7) Paul nowhere adds an explicit exception for disobeying immoral

First Corinthians 14:34–35

This passage enjoins "silence" without explicitly specifying the silence being addressed. If it means silence in every situation (the way we must interpret it if we cannot take the situation into account), then women cannot sing in the choir, sing in the congregation, pray aloud, or prophesy. Whatever else Paul may mean, however, he cannot mean *complete* silence, because earlier in the same letter he allowed women to pray and prophesy (11:5); most likely he would also allow them to sing (14:15, 26; cf. Eph. 5:19; Col. 3:16). So what particular kind of speech is he restricting?

Interpreters have approached this passage from a variety of angles, which I have surveyed and addressed in detail elsewhere.[33] The context may suggest spiritual gifts, but as I've noted, Paul permitted women to prophesy (1 Cor. 11:5). Some have suggested that Paul opposes women's evaluating other prophecies, but this proposal makes little sense of both the text itself (which speaks of asking questions) and Paul's suggestion that all those who prophesy are to participate in evaluating prophecies (14:29). Some have suggested that the passage means women cannot teach, but nothing in the context or elsewhere in Paul's Corinthians correspondence indicates this is the issue he is addressing here.

The problem seems not to be women *teaching* but rather that the women are *learning*—too loudly. Unless Paul changes the subject from women's general silence in church (v. 34) to their asking questions to learn (v. 35, first part) and then back to women's general silence in church (v. 35, last part), Paul is addressing their asking questions in church in an effort to learn. That the two ideas are connected is clear from the grammar of verse 35; he bases women's silence regarding questions on the

commands (see Acts 5:29), but his emphasis and priorities throughout his letters make it clear he would expect us to recognize such exceptions. For the same reason, even those who hold that husbands have a transcultural right to rule their families cannot ignore the general rules summoning all Christians to serve one another, submit to one another, and seek one another's good—exhortations that at the very least qualify any Christian's use of authority.

[33]See my survey of views in *Paul, Women and Wives*, 74–80, where I also offer more detailed responses to the views cited in the next paragraphs. See also (more briefly but more current) my *1–2 Corinthians* (New York: Cambridge Univ. Press, 2005), 117–21; my "Learning in the Assemblies: 1 Corinthians 14:34–35," in *Discovering Biblical Equality*, 161–71.

statement (*gar* ["for"]) that it is "shameful" (a term that can mean culturally inappropriate) for women to speak in church.

Throughout the first-century Mediterranean world, novices were expected to learn quietly, but advanced students were expected to interrupt all kinds of public lectures with questions.[34] What was wrong with the women interrupting with questions? Perhaps the issue was the church's witness in terms of cultural propriety; it was culturally shameful for the women to ask questions.[35] (Their prophesying would probably prove no more culturally unusual than that of the men.)

But why was it shameful for the women to be asking questions? Perhaps it was because of the commonly expected submissive role of their gender in antiquity;[36] if we conclude this was Paul's reasoning, it would not require us to prevent women from asking questions today. Another (and partly compatible) possibility, however, is that they were asking unlearned questions. Whereas questions at public lectures were expected, ancient literature testifies that unlearned questions were considered foolish and rude—and women generally possessed inadequate education and were most often unlearned. (Although there were always exceptions, anyone who has read through numerous pages of ancient literature without reading simply the collected exceptions will recognize that, in the vast majority of cases, men were more educated than women of the same social class).[37] Jewish women could learn the law by listening in the synagogue, but in the overwhelming majority of cases, they were not trained in it. Unlike boys, girls were not normally taught to recite Torah. In

---

[34]See Plutarch, *On Listening to Lectures* various passages; Aulus Gellius 18.13.7–8; 20.10.1–6; *Tosefta Sanhedrin* 7:10.

[35]For documentation of Roman concern with Eastern cults subverting Roman traditional values, see my *Paul, Women and Wives*, 139–56.

[36]See Heliodorus, *Aeth.* 1.21. Further on women's expected submission (increasingly ignored by Roman aristocrats but still ideal), see, e.g., Livy, *Hist. Rome* 34.2.9–14 (Cato's extreme view); 34.7.12; Valerius Maximus, *Facta* 3.8.6; Philo, *Hypoth.* 7.3; Josephus, *Ag. Ap.* 2.200–201; Plutarch, *Bride* 19, 33, *Mor.* 140D, 142E; Artemidorus, *Onir.* 1.24; more fully, my "Marriage," 687–90. A few women pled cases, but they are reported as exceptional (Valerius Maximus, *Facta* 8.3); on criticisms of publicly vocal women, see, e.g., Musonius Rufus (in C. E. Lutz, "Musonius Rufus: The Roman Socrates," *YCS* 10 [1947]: 3–147 [at 42.14–15]).

[37]On rude questions, see Plutarch, *On Listening to Lectures* 4, 11, 13, 18, *Mor.* 39CD, 43BC, 45D, 48AB; on women's lesser education (as a general rule), see documentation in my *Paul, Women and Wives*, 83–84, 126–27; also my "Marriage," 680–93.

the first-generation church in Corinth, most women were novices and therefore obligated to learn quietly.

Paul's short-range solution, then, is to call for an end to the women's public questions. (This would not be the only place where Paul would address a group—even gender—with a general rule, even though it might not apply to every member; see 1 Tim. 4:7; 5:11, 14; Titus 1:12.) At the same time, however, he provides a long-range solution: These women should ask their husbands at home to explain matters. In today's culture this may sound repressive, but in Paul's day it expressed the opposite attitude. Ancient writers testified that most husbands thought their wives incapable of learning academic disciplines. Those who thought husbands should provide private tutoring for their wives who had less education opportunities were a more progressive minority, and Paul's language here is more progressive even than most of their own.[38] His long-range solution to their being uneducated novices is that they should be allowed to learn, and their marriage partners should be committed to furthering their learning.

First Timothy 2:11–14

This passage is part of a broader set of instructions about decorum in public worship in the Ephesian church. After briefly addressing a problem with the men (v. 8), Paul focuses on what seems to be a more pervasive problem with the women, who are given to outward adornment (vv. 9–10) and apparently are seeking to teach rather than to learn (vv. 11–12).

Paul's instructions are firm: The women must remain silent. Again, if pressed to mean all that it could mean, this demand would prohibit even singing in public worship, but the specific issue at hand is probably simply the explicit prohibition of teaching. Pressing even this more specific prohibition to mean all it could mean, however, women should not even teach Sunday school classes in which men are in attendance. (Though most churches today do not meet in homes, saints presumably remain the church whenever and wherever they gather.) Whether Paul prohibits women from having authority altogether or simply

---

[38]Plutarch urges taking an interest in one's wife learning, against what he regards as the common view (*Bride* 48, *Mor.* 145BC), though he (unlike Paul) explicitly regards women as intellectually inferior (*Mor.* 145DE).

from usurping authority (which would be prohibited for men as well) remains a matter of debate.[39] In contrast to my former position on this issue, however, I believe Paul probably prohibits not simply "teaching authoritatively" but both teaching Scripture at all and having (or usurping) authority at all. In other words, women are forbidden to teach men—period. (How one teaches Christians Scripture without exercising the authority involved in instructing others how to live, seems difficult to understand in any case!)

Is this a universal rule? If so, it is a rule with some exceptions, such as for a husband-wife team teaching a ministerial student (Acts 18:26) and for Spirit-directed utterances, like prophecy (1 Cor. 11:4–5), from which people could also learn (14:31). But it is also possible this text is the exceptional one, which can be argued if it can be shown to address a particular situation. After all, if it were to be a universal rule, one should have expected Paul to pause when praising women's ministry earlier to note that these were exceptional cases. One might also have expected Timothy, who had worked with Paul for many years, to be aware of this rule already, perhaps contrary to the way Paul now frames its wording ("I am permitting"—present tense).[40]

Ultimately, the question of universality must be tested by two issues: First, are there, in fact, exceptions to the general prohibition here, despite the fact that such exceptions would

---

[39]For usurping authority, which neither men nor women should do, see David M. Scholer, "1 Timothy 2:9–15 and the Place of Women in the Church's Ministry," in *Women, Authority and the Bible*, ed. Alvera Mickelsen (Downers Grove, Ill.: Inter-Varsity, 1986), 205; Carroll D. Osburn, "*Authenteō* (1 Timothy 2:12)," *ResQ* 25 (1982): 2–4 (this interpretation was argued as early as the 1800s; "usurp authority over" appears earlier in the KJV). "Have authority over" seems supported by the thorough and careful survey of H. Scott Baldwin ("A Difficult Word: *Authenteō* in 1 Timothy 2:12," in *Women in the Church: A Fresh Analysis*, 65–80), but this makes the somewhat controversial move of omitting the noun cognates and leaves only *two* pre-Christian references. It seems precarious to hinge the prohibition of half of Christians from acknowledging a call on such a disputed term. But in any event, the passage also prohibits teaching.

[40]These arguments merely establish the possibility; one could conversely argue that Paul *does* draw on a more common rule from the stricter wording in 1 Corinthians 14:34 (the only other Pauline passage using this word for "permitting")— except that another Corinthian passage reveals that this passage must allow public prayer and prophecy (1 Cor. 11:4–5). In the same way, other statements within the Pastoral Epistles must qualify our understanding of this one.

contradict the tendency of the broader culture? As noted above, there *are* exceptions, in contrast to genuinely universal biblical rules like those prohibiting homosexual behavior. Second, do Paul's letters to Timothy, who is caring for the church at Ephesus, reveal a situation that would elicit such instructions as these?

The latter question is relatively easy to answer. The one passage in the Bible that specifically prohibits women from teaching is addressed to the one church where we know false teachers were effectively targeting women. A primary problem in Ephesus was false teaching (1 Tim. 1:3–20; 4:1–7; 6:6–10, 20–21; 2 Tim. 2:16–26; 3:5–13; 4:3–4), and the primary false teachers (who were men—1 Tim. 1:20; 2 Tim. 2:17) were exploiting the women in order to spread their false teaching. How do we know this? If women as a rule were less educated then men, they would become a natural target as those particularly susceptible to such false teaching. Thus, it isn't surprising to learn that these false teachers targeted women in the households (2 Tim. 3:6) who were proving to be incapable of learning correctly (3:7; cf. 1 Tim. 4:7).

Churches met in homes, so false teachers needed large homes that would welcome them; the homes headed by women were usually those of widows. Thus, it would not be at all unexpected for some widows to go from house to house spreading "nonsense" (1 Tim. 5:13). As Gordon Fee has demonstrated to me, a survey of every use in extant Greek literature of the word translated "busybodies" in 5:13 reveals that the word was used for those speaking nonsense, and in moral and philosophical contexts it typically refers to those spreading false or improper teaching.[41] In this case, as in some of Paul's other social instructions in the Pastoral Epistles (6:1; Titus 2:8, 10), Paul is concerned that social improprieties may turn people away from the gospel's eternal truth (1 Tim. 5:14–15). The church was being persecuted and slandered, and its reputation was important for the gospel's sake.[42]

Two objections are typically raised at this point. The first (raised especially on a popular level) is that, even when provoked by specific situations, Paul's situation-specific instructions

---

[41]Gordon Fee provided me both a list of all the occurrences in extant Greek literature and copies of the fuller context of most of these texts, and the evidence is, as he points out, overwhelming.

[42]On slander against the church for social roles, see full documentation in my *Paul, Women and Wives*, 139–56.

must retain permanent force—yet no one holds this position consistently. The second (maintained by scholars and popular readers alike) is more compelling on the surface, namely, that Paul grounds his case in Scripture (2:13–14); I address each objection in turn in more detail below.

Dare We Appeal to Local Situations to Interpret 1 Timothy?

Let's grant that Paul addresses a concrete local situation. Dare we argue that he might have given different instructions to address a different local situation or culture elsewhere? His letters to Timothy do invite us to take account of the specific situations addressed. When in the context of 1 Timothy 2:11–12 Paul exhorts men to pray properly (v. 8), shall we assume that Paul does not care whether women pray properly? Or should we assume instead that, just as Paul had a specific situation to address with the women (vv. 9–15), he also had a specific problem in mind regarding the behavior of the Ephesian men (v. 8)?

If the problem with the Ephesian women was their lack of education and consequent susceptibility to false teaching, the text provides us a concrete local example of a more general principle: *Those most susceptible to false teaching should not teach.* But are women always the ones most susceptible to false teaching today? And can interpreters who insist on maintaining the "straightforward sense" without taking into account dramatic cultural differences be consistent in how they apply different biblical texts? This is a crux in the debate; whereas egalitarian interpreters like Gordon Fee and Catherine Clark Kroeger may approach 1 Timothy 2 with radically different understandings of the background, they share a common approach of recognizing that a passage's background can actually affect the meaning we find there.[43]

Some object to this way of approaching 1 Timothy, but the Pastoral Epistles, like Paul's other letters, summon us to read them this way. Paul specifically writes to Timothy (1 Tim. 1:2; 2 Tim. 1:2) and Titus (Titus 1:4) in these letters. Paul specifically

---

[43]See the different interpretations in Gordon D. Fee, *1 and 2 Timothy, Titus* (NIBC; Peabody, Mass.: Hendrickson, 1988); Richard Clark Kroeger and Catherine Clark Kroeger, *I Suffer Not a Woman: Rethinking 1 Timothy 2:11–15 in Light of Ancient Evidence* (Grand Rapids: Baker, 1992). Much of what I say in this section is borrowed from my article "Interpreting 1 Timothy 2:8–15," in *Priscilla Papers* 12 (Summer 1998): 11–13.

left Timothy in Ephesus to oppose those who were teaching false doctrines (1 Tim. 1:3), and he exhorts Timothy to do so in keeping with the prophecies given him (v. 18; 4:14; cf. 2 Tim. 1:6); he also addresses specific false teachers (1 Tim. 1:20) who are no longer living today. Although Paul did not leave *us* in Ephesus, as he did Timothy, nor did *we* receive Timothy's prophecies, there are plenty of transcultural principles here to embrace, such as the need to oppose dangerous doctrines and to heed words of wisdom and properly tested prophecy. But again, noting that specific exhortations can have more general relevance does not allow us to simply assume we know what the transcultural relevance is before we have studied the situation carefully.

How many would regard as transcultural the warning that widows younger than sixty will speak nonsense (1 Tim. 5:11–13) or that fables circulate especially among older women (4:7)? If we must follow all commands in 1 Timothy as transcultural, even the most conservative churches are falling woefully short. Most do not prohibit the exclusive drinking of water for those with stomach ailments or compel them to use wine (5:23). Similarly, if we are to obey 2 Timothy, each of us should come to Paul quickly, making sure we pick up his cloak and books from Troas before coming to him (4:9–13)—a command that may prove difficult to fulfill for anyone after Paul's death, especially if Timothy *already* collected Paul's belongings in Troas. (That Paul also calls Titus to come to him in Titus 3:12 surely attests this as a transcultural requirement for God's servants: We all should try to visit Paul in Rome.) We should also beware of Alexander the coppersmith (2 Tim. 4:14–15), despite the fact that he is most assuredly dead—the mortality rate for people over 1,500 years old being what it is.[44]

Perhaps more significant are passages providing instructions not merely to Timothy but to the church as a whole. Here, for example, widows must not be put on the list for church support unless they are at least sixty years old, have been married only once (1 Tim. 5:9), and have brought up children and washed saints' feet (v. 10). Apart from our general neglect of caring for widows to begin with (to some degree influenced by differences between today's welfare system and that of ancient Judaism), so few widows today have washed saints' feet that our churches can

---

[44]For other unquestionably situation-specific allusions, see 2 Timothy 1:2–6; 3:14–15; 4:20; Titus 1:4–5.

claim to be obeying Paul's teaching even when they don't include them on their list for monetary support! Younger widows are encouraged to remarry, not taking the pledge of membership in the order of older widows supported by the church (vv. 11, 14). How widows today can obey this precept if they fail to find another husband is not quite clear, but in Paul's day men outnumbered women by a considerable margin; remarriage for women was much easier than it is today.[45]

Paul is clear that some of his commands in the Pastoral Epistles relate to avoiding apostasy (v. 15) and—a matter related to the views of the broader culture—public reproach (3:2, 6–7, 10; 6:1; Titus 1:6–7; 2:8, 10). This explicitly includes not only some of his exhortations concerning gender roles (Titus 2:5) but also concerning the obedience of slaves (1 Tim. 6:1–2; cf. Titus 2:9–10), which most evangelicals today would admit addressed a specific cultural situation. If the principles are more binding than the situation-specific exhortations that illustrate them, we may wish to consider how today's situation differs from that of the first century and how the act of diminishing women's opportunities rather than strengthening them challenges the church's witness.[46]

Rebecca Merrill Groothuis summarizes this point well:

> If 1 Timothy 2:11–15 can legitimately be understood as a prohibition relevant only for women in a historically specific circumstance (which it can), and if there is no other biblical text that explicitly forbids women to teach or have authority over men (which there is not), and if there *are* texts that assert the fundamental spiritual equality of women with men (which there are), then women who are not in the circumstance for which the 1 Timothy 2:12 prohibition was intended may safely follow whatever call

[45]Even in Paul's day, this was probably one of his general principles to which he might permit exceptions; thus, church leaders should be husband of one wife (1 Tim. 3:2; Titus 1:6), possibly directed against teachers who advocated mandatory celibacy (1 Tim. 4:3; see my *And Marries Another*, 83–103, though also noting the emphasis may be marital fidelity). But Paul himself was unmarried and probably had never married (he was too young to have been a member of the Sanhedrin, even if the marriage rules were in force in his day). Paul warned Timothy not to rebuke others harshly (1 Tim. 5:1–2), but under different circumstances Paul rebuked Peter publicly (Gal. 2:14), which was normally considered inappropriate behavior (even by Paul himself—see 1 Tim. 5:19–20).

[46]See Alan Padgett, "The Pauline Rationale for Submission: Biblical Feminism and the *hina* Clauses of Titus 2:1–10," *EvQ* 59 (1987): 39–52.

they have to ministry. In other words, it ought at least be acknowledged that the traditionalist interpretation is debatable on biblical grounds. This being the case, we should give the benefit of the doubt to any woman who is called to and qualified for pastoral leadership.[47]

But Paul Cites the Old Testament

If we could stop here, there might be little debate about 1 Timothy 2:11–12, hence about any level of women's ministry in the church. The evidence for a specific situation behind 1 Timothy 2 is clear enough in Paul's letters to Timothy, and the evidence that Paul elsewhere affirmed ministries of women is compelling enough that evangelical scholars as a whole might well agree, but for one problem—the fact that Paul goes on to base his argument on the OT, citing biblical authority for what he says. Surely this means he intends it for all situations!

Or does it? Does Paul apply all OT texts universally, or does he sometimes apply them to local situations? Before we can determine how Paul uses Scripture in 1 Timothy 2, we must first ask how he uses Scripture in general. (I'll return to a specific discussion of Genesis 1–2 later.) If he always uses it in a straightforward manner, then presumably 1 Timothy 2 *must* silence all women after all. His arguments here are that God created men first, women are more easily deceived than men, and therefore women should not teach men. We should make sure that if we universally prohibit women from teaching, we should do so for the reason the text on which we base our practice cites; that is to say, for Eve's deception to constitute a universal argument, we must assume that all women are easily deceived (presumably always more deceived than most believing men are)—the usual historic interpretation of the verse. Thus this analogy between Eve and women would tell us something about their *nature* rather than about first-century women's educational status. If we say that only *most* women are easily deceived, then we can prohibit only most women from teaching by this argument. If we say that the women in Ephesus were deceived like Eve because they were uneducated, the principle is simply that the untrained are more susceptible to deception. But if it is a universal prohibition based on gender, it is a statement, not about

---

[47]Groothuis, *Good News for Women*, 211.

first-century women's education, but about all women's ontological inferiority in discerning truth. This is a claim we ought
to be able to verify or refute empirically, yet most empirical
research suggests that, when educational opportunities are the
same, women are as adept in discerning deception as men are.

But what if Paul is simply drawing a local analogy between
Eve and the easily deceived women in Ephesus (or the majority
of women in his day who were uneducated, hence easily
deceived)? What if Paul is simply making a local analogy, as he
did elsewhere when he drew an analogy between Eve and all the
Corinthian Christians (male and female alike [2 Cor. 11:3])? Is this
possible? If Paul often argues by analogy and sometimes uses
Scripture in an ad hoc manner, there is no reason to doubt that
Paul may be doing so in 1 Timothy 2—which would undercut
the main pillar for applying this text to women transculturally.[48]

Often, perhaps even usually, Paul reads the OT in a straightforward manner, just as we typically do. For instance, he often
applies commands given to Israel to all believers who have
accepted Israel's Bible (see, e.g., Rom. 13:9); principles from
Israelite law can help guide the church (see, e.g., 2 Cor. 13:1). But
what happens when we must address an issue that no specific
biblical text addresses? In these cases we customarily look for texts
that address similar principles and draw analogies between those
texts and the situation we must address; Paul did the same thing.

Arguments by Analogy. Paul often universalizes biblical texts
by analogy. Because his contemporaries, both Jewish and Gentile,
customarily drew on both positive and negative models in history to make their points, Paul's audience would have followed
his approach easily. Thus, for example, an ox that treads out the
grain provides an analogy for a minister of the gospel (1 Cor. 9:9–
10; 1 Tim. 5:18). In many cases, Paul could have applied his analogies to situations other than those to which he specifically applied
them.[49] Thus, as God gives to the poor (Ps. 112:9), so he would also

---

[48]Here I have used parts of my article "How Does Paul Interpret Eve in 1 Timothy 2?" *Priscilla Papers* 11 (Summer 1997): 11–13.

[49]E.g., in Galatians 4:22–31, Paul specifically applies Hagar and Sarah to spiritual Ishmaelites (who want to circumcise Gentiles) and spiritual descendants of
Abraham, but these are hardly the only analogies one might draw from these biblical characters, nor would he condemn today's medical circumcision of Gentile
infants (which differs from the situation he addressed). Other inspired interpreters
use Sarah as a model for Christian wives (1 Pet. 3:6) or for all believers (Heb. 11:11).

provide for the Corinthians if they give sacrificially (2 Cor. 9:9).[50]
Paul's specific applications are often christological, because Christ
is rightly his focus.[51]

Sound arguments by analogy depend on correct exegesis
but are not themselves intended as exegesis. Some of Paul's
analogies are closer to the original sense of the texts he cites than
others. Those that are more distant from the original sense of the
text should not be pressed beyond their immediate application,
and sometimes we can recognize that Paul himself would not
wish us to press his analogies beyond the immediate service to
which he puts them. Creation's proclamation in Psalm 19:4, for
instance, parallels the gospel proclamation in Romans 10:18. The
incomprehensible language of the Assyrian invaders was a
divine message of judgment toward Israel after they had rejected
God's other attempts to get their attention (Isa. 28:11; cf. 33:19;
Deut. 28:49); Paul applies the incomprehensible nature of this
language to speaking in tongues (1 Cor. 14:21), perhaps because
it also functions as a warning to unbelievers (14:22). Hosea tells
of Israel's rejection and their restoration (Hos. 1:10); perhaps
because Paul believes that the conversion of the Gentiles will
provoke Israel to repentance (Rom. 11:13–14), he applies this text
to the salvation of the Gentiles (Rom. 9:25–26). The primary
analogy between Psalm 116:10 and 2 Corinthians 4:13 is the need
to speak in accordance with what one believes. Paul even quotes

---

[50]Given Paul's mission, it is not surprising many of his analogies concern the
era of salvation he proclaims. Paul draws a natural analogy between the law of
Moses and the gospel he preaches (Rom. 10:6–8); both, after all, are God's word.
Likewise, the proclamation of Israel's restoration is an analogy for the gospel message (Rom. 10:15). He draws an analogy between the preservation of a remnant from
the Assyrian judgment (Isa. 10:5, 21–24) and the ultimate future restoration of the
survivors of his people (Rom. 9:27–29). Likewise, by faith the righteous would live
through the impending Babylonian invasion (Hab. 2:4 in context); Paul applies the
principle to the day of judgment (Rom. 1:17; Gal. 3:11). Perhaps for similar reasons,
he applies imagery for Israel's future salvation (Isa. 49:8) to the present offer of salvation through his gospel (2 Cor. 6:2). Paul can draw a large-scale analogy between
Moses and the apostolic ministry of the new covenant (2 Cor. 3:6–16), in which
Moses' transforming revelation "of the Lord" in the exodus narrative corresponds
to believers' transforming experience of the Spirit (vv. 17–18).

[51]Thus, Paul can draw analogies between Israel's provision in the rock and
spiritual drink in Christ, between God's provision of food in the wilderness and the
Lord's Supper, and between Israel's crossing the sea and the experience of Christian
baptism (1 Cor. 10:1–4).

one of Job's comforters to make a point (1 Cor. 3:19), in spite of the fact that, on the whole, these comforters' specific application of their wisdom was wrongheaded (Job 42:8).

Like other Jewish teachers Paul will on occasion even rephrase a text. For instance, Psalm 68:18 speaks of a conqueror *receiving* gifts. Because conquerors would normally distribute such plunder among their troops, Paul and some other Jewish traditions on this passage can apply it to *giving* gifts, and Paul applies it to the ascended Jesus giving ministers to his church (Eph. 4:8). When Paul wants to, he can argue that "seed" is singular and must refer to Christ (Gal. 3:16), even though he knows very well (contrary to his modern detractors) that it can refer to "descendants" in the plural; indeed he uses it in this manner elsewhere (Rom. 4:13, 16, 18; 9:7–8; 11:1), and even in the same chapter in Galatians (3:29)! In the polemical context of Galatians 3:16, where Paul may be responding to his opponents by using their own methods, he employs a standard interpretive technique of his contemporaries: Apply the text the way you need to in order to make your point.

While some of us may not want to accept that Paul uses Scripture in an ad hoc way at times (it makes it difficult for us to teach sound hermeneutics to our students), respect for Scripture requires us to revise our preconceptions in light of what we find in the text rather than forcing the text to fit philosophical assumptions about what we think it *should* say. Those who wish to maintain, on the basis of Paul's allusion in 1 Timothy 2:13–15 to a passage from Genesis, that verses 11 and 12 *necessarily* contain a transcultural principle should reread Paul's other letters carefully with respect to his use of the OT. To be sure, Paul often uses Scripture with a universal import; often, however, he makes analogies to argue points he intends only for a specific situation. Given Paul's support of women's ministry in other passages, as well as the presence of occasional authoritative models like Deborah in Scripture, I believe the burden of proof should rest on those who argue that he intends his biblical allusion to be understood more universally here.

Creation Order and Fall in 1 Timothy 2:13–14. Some of Paul's analogies may be more relevant than others for his comparison of women with Eve in 1 Timothy 2. Although he can make general comparisons with Eve (see, e.g., 1 Cor. 6:16; Eph. 5:31–32), the two most relevant comparisons are in 1 Corinthians 11:6–10 and 2 Corinthians 11:3. In these texts Paul can use the Eve analogy in an ad hoc manner.

In 1 Corinthians 11:6–10, Paul states that Eve was created for Adam's sake; therefore women should wear head coverings. Having offered this argument, however, he reminds us that, in the end, neither men nor women are independent of the other (vv. 11–12). The "creation order" argument applied to women's silence in 1 Timothy 2 is precisely one of the arguments Paul employs in 1 Corinthians 11:8–9 to admonish wives to cover their heads in church. We cannot consistently require a transcultural application prohibiting women's teaching or holding authority based on 1 Timothy 2:11–12 without also requiring all married women to cover their heads in keeping with 1 Corinthians 11:2–16 (a point Paul, in fact, argues at much greater length).

Second Corinthians 11:3, however, is more relevant, referring specifically to Eve's deception, as in 1 Timothy 2:14. Paul draws an analogy between Eve and the Corinthian Christians in 2 Corinthians 11:3; the basis for the comparison is that both were easily deceived. This example indicates that he could apply the image to anyone easily deceived, including most of the women in the Ephesian church, but that Paul does not always make this analogy on the basis of gender. As we have seen, some of his other analogies are also situation specific.

Some interpreters today appeal to the creation order argument by noting that Adam, not Eve, names the animals (Gen. 2:20)—but of course Eve hadn't yet been created at this point (v. 22). Some claim that Adam names Eve the way he names the animals he rules, but Genesis distinguishes his recognition of Eve (v. 23) from the naming formula used for the animals (v. 20)—until after the fall (3:20). Others apply to Adam's prior creation the ancient principle of primogeniture (the state of being the firstborn), but this would work only if the passage implied that Adam and Eve were both children expecting an inheritance (in which case, Adam gets twice as much; but compare 1 Pet. 3:7), and only if inheritance rights controlled all rank; it would also work better if Genesis did not elsewhere specifically challenge the custom of primogeniture (25:23; 48:19; 49:4).

The fall introduced marital tension into the world (3:16), but it is surely not wrong for us to work to reduce marital conflict, as with most other aspects of the fall (pain in childbirth, the hardship of toil, and ultimately sin and death in the world).[52] In the creation order, man and woman together comprised "man" in God's image and together ruled the earth (1:26–28; 5:1–2). Likewise, given the use of the Hebrew terms elsewhere (which anyone may check with the help of a concordance), "suitable helper" (2:18, 20) points to male and female correspondence, not to one partner's subordination.

Some interpreters today will ultimately object that we must find Eve's subordination in the creation order because Paul does, but this brings us back to our original point: Does Paul in fact subordinate all women (more specifically, demanding their silence in church) because Eve was created second? Would he use chronology as a transcultural argument? Elsewhere in his writings, the first can be inferior to the second, a mere prototype of God's plan (1 Cor. 15:45–47). Adam is not a mere prototype of Eve, but neither does Paul use chronological priority as a universally self-evident argument; his argument here is constructed for a specific situation.

OTHER CONSIDERATIONS

In the space that remains, I now turn briefly to some other considerations.

What about the Biblical Pattern of Male Headship in the Home?

Because the question of gender relations in the home is a separate issue (and space is limited here), I mention this objection only in passing and offer two brief responses. First, I have argued elsewhere at considerable length that in his most detailed exposition of the matter, Paul's ideal is *mutual submission* and *servanthood*. Various interpretive assumptions lead interpreters to

---

[52]Genesis 3:16 and 4:7 are the only two OT texts that use these terms for "desire" and "rule" together (and two of only three using this term for "desire"); their proximity and identical construction invite us to interpret their construction together and to view 3:16 as a statement of marital contention in which the husband, being stronger, will prevail. An inspired, accurate *description* of the fall is not necessarily prescriptive, in contrast to inspired apostolic *affirmations* of women's ministry (see Rom. 16:1–2, a letter of recommendation, as is widely recognized—see, e.g., Meeks, *The First Urban Christians*, 109). On Genesis 2–3, see further Joy Elasky Fleming, "A Rhetorical Analysis of Genesis 2–3 with Implications for a Theology of Man and Woman" (Ph.D. diss., University of Strasbourg, 1987).

differ as to whether the husband should always lead the home in all respects. But even granted such differences, I believe that it is biblically impossible to doubt that Christian husbands and wives should practice mutual submission and servanthood (Eph. 5:21), even if it is specified more explicitly for the wives (v. 22), just as all Christians should practice mutual love (v. 2), even if it is specified here more explicitly for the husbands (v. 25). Moreover, Paul believes in submitting to authority structures within the culture, yet he no more mandates as permanent the ancient patriarchal marriage patterns (vv. 21–33) than he mandates as permanent the practice of urban household slavery (6:5–9), both of which are part of the same section of household codes (5:21–6:9).[53] Paul addresses the roles as they existed in his day, but the principle is *submission to those in authority, and becoming servants even when we hold authority*.[54] "Helper" (Gen. 2:18) is usually a term of strength, often used even of God as our helper; wives' subordination probably stems from the fall (3:16; see above).

Second, the issues of women's ministry (affirmed by many passages, apparently limited in, at most, two) and gender roles in the home *are* distinguishable. A person may have different roles in different situations; for example, I have taught students in an academic setting who, in a church setting, were my pastors. Further, the question of how these two issues relate would prove less relevant for a single woman. Likewise, I know evangelical couples whose bishops assigned the husband and wife each to serve as pastors of separate (though nearby) churches. Some nineteenth-century evangelical missionary couples similarly divided their ministry outreach in order to reach more people. In other words, even a person who does not accept the egalitarian or "mutual submission" arguments for the home need not prohibit women's ministry.

What about the History of Interpretation of the Biblical Evidence?

As biblically faithful Christians, we accept the views of the Bible over tradition because we view the Bible as God's most

---

[53]As I noted in *Paul, Women and Wives* (208), the point of this comparison is not whether marriage is God-ordained (of course it is), but whether the particular patriarchal structures of marriage that undergird Greco-Roman household codes are God-ordained.

[54]I have argued this at length, with fuller documentation than possible here, in *Paul, Women and Wives*, 139–224.

direct revelation of his will (cf. Mark 7:7–13). We are, therefore, less concerned with how others have interpreted the Bible—often in light of their own cultures and church traditions—than in the biblical message itself. But because we ourselves are part of specific cultures and church traditions, the history of interpretation does help us gain perspective.

The most common view on women's ministry in the history of the church has been that women could not minister God's word to men. This was, of course, no mere restriction of women in the pastorate! But this view rested on a premise that was almost equally widespread, namely, that women cannot teach the Bible to men because women are more easily deceived than men and ontologically inferior to men, at least in those gifts most necessary for the practice of church leadership and doctrinal scrutiny.[55] Is it fair to appeal to the conclusion (on the basis of historical precedent) without accepting the logic behind that conclusion (on the basis of the same precedent)? This view of women's nature reflects Aristotelian premises and a consensus from the larger culture—a culture that I believe reflects male-female relations that are a result of the fall (Gen. 3:16).

To be sure, the burden of proof rests on any person who advocates a view no one ever thought of before, because if it were obvious in Scripture, it should surprise us that we would be the first to discover it! Often, however, the church has missed or suppressed truths that are clear enough in Scripture to allow us to accept the burden of proof and advocate a position previously not widely accepted, such as justification by faith. At many points, Martin Luther, for instance, challenged the status quo of traditions in his day. For strategic purposes, however, he felt it necessary to maintain many traditional practices, so that most of his people would find familiarity in many aspects of church worship.[56] Other Reformers sought to "reform" traditions further, and this often led to conflict among early Protestant leaders.[57] Most Protestants today recognize that the Reformation did not settle all questions of

---

[55]See the data in Daniel Doriani, "A History of the Interpretation of 1 Timothy 2," in *Women in the Church: A Fresh Analysis*, 213–67.

[56]See Luther's conservative but critical use of the Roman liturgy (Paul J. Grime, "Changing the Tempo of Worship," *ChrHist* 39 [1993]: 16–18); bear in mind, though, that Luther's views on gender roles were progressive in his historical setting (see Steven Ozment, "Re-inventing Family Life," *ChrHist* 39 [1993]: 22–26).

[57]See Robert D. Linder, "Allies or Enemies?" *ChrHist* 39 (1993): 40–44.

which particular church traditions may still require revision. I believe we have sufficient biblical evidence in favor of women's ministry to accept the burden of proof. I would argue that the majority view in the church throughout history—the view that came down to most of us through tradition—reflects the restrictive cultures of human history in which the tradition was formed rather than the clearest reading of the biblical evidence. (One might compare the anti-Jewish ideas that many church fathers absorbed from Greek culture in a manner foreign to the generally Jewish-Christian writers of the NT.)

Having acknowledged the dominant historical testimony of the older churches, however, it should be noted that some reform movements have always affirmed the ministry of women. One group that sought reform during the Middle Ages was the Waldensians; they ultimately incurred persecution from the medieval Roman church. But alongside justification by faith and an appeal to Scripture's authority, the earliest Waldensians were accused of letting women preach.[58] Women's ministry also became increasingly accepted in many times of revival, including the Wesleyan revival that changed the course of spiritual life in Britain and the Second Great Awakening in the United States. Pentecostal and Holiness groups were ordaining women long before modern secular feminism and unbiblical arguments for women's ordination made it a divisive issue in some circles. Many Baptist and other evangelical churches permitted more freedom for women's ministries until the fundamentalist-modernist controversy of the 1920s; Freewill Baptist churches and the Christian and Missionary Alliance (in its earlier years) also affirmed women's ministry. The oft-repeated charge in some circles that even among evangelicals women's ministry carries a thinly veiled secular agenda may be well-meaning, but it is certainly misinformed historically. Revivals brought to the fore women's spiritual gifts and a fresh reading of Scripture in settings where no one had thought of modern secular feminism.[59]

---

[58]See "Did You Know?" *ChrHist* 30 (1991): 3; also the more radical Hussites in Elesha Coffman, "Rebels to Be Reckoned With," *ChrHist* 68 (2000): 39–41.

[59]For some surveys, see Stanley J. Grenz with Denise Muir Kjesbo, *Women in the Church: A Biblical Theology of Women in Ministry* (Downers Grove, Ill.: InterVarsity, 1995), 36–62; Nancy Hardesty, *Women Called to Witness: Evangelical Feminism in the Nineteenth Century* (Nashville: Abingdon, 1984); Catherine Booth, *Female Ministry: Women's Right to Preach the Gospel* (New York: Salvation Army, 1975; 1st. ed.,

Some Relevant Principles

Few evangelicals on either side of the women's ministry debate would dispute that Jesus' acceptance of women in many respects proved unusual in his day (e.g., Luke 8:1–3). What is more striking is his acceptance of women as actual disciples—something few, if any, other rabbis did.[60] People of any means usually sat on chairs or, at banquets, reclined on couches. To sit at a teacher's feet, however, was to adopt the posture of a disciple.[61] This is the posture that Mary adopts, and Jesus defends her adoption of this role against Martha's preference for traditional matronly roles (Luke 10:38–42). All disciples—male and female—best learn discipleship by following Jesus. But it is easy for modern readers to forget that rabbis restricted women from being disciples (albeit not from listening in the synagogues) largely because, after the elementary levels, disciples became rabbis-in-training. Mary might have been learning simply for herself—but she also might have been learning partly in order to share Jesus' message with others who would listen.

What do such acts of Jesus indicate in the broader context of his ministry? Jesus regularly crossed the boundaries of clean and unclean (Mark 1:41–42; 2:16; 5:30–34, 41–42; 7:2, 19), even though many of those boundaries were grounded in the OT (Lev. 11:2–47; 13:45–46; 15:25–27; Num. 19:11–13; Ps. 1:1). He did not oppose the OT teachings (Matt. 5:17–20; Luke 16:17), but he interpreted them in such a way as to reflect on and reapply their purpose in fresh situations (Matt. 5:21–48). He also demanded that we keep first things first, not missing the forest for the trees; broader principles like justice, mercy, and faith took precedence over biblical details adapted for specific situations (Matt. 23:23–24; Mark 10:5–9). In our commendable attention to grammatical details in some passages addressing specific situations, we must

---

1859); articles in *ChrHist* 82 (2004). See esp. the lengthy treatment in Ruth A. Tucker and Walter L. Liefeld, *Daughters of the Church: Women and Ministry from New Testament Times to the Present* (Grand Rapids: Zondervan, 1987). Note the expectation suggested by Acts 2:17–18.

[60]See Leonard Swidler, *Women in Judaism: The Status of Women in Formative Judaism* (Metuchen, N.J.: Scarecrow, 1976), 97–111; my *Commentary on Matthew*, 689–90.

[61]See Acts 22:3; *m. Avot* 1:4; *Avot of Rabbi Nathan* 6; 38a; 11, §28B; *b. Pesahim 3b; Palestinian Talmud Sanhedrin* 10:1, §8. For sitting on chairs normally, see Safrai, "Home and Family," in *The Jewish People in the First Century*, 737.

remain vigilant against the temptation to ignore broad principles about what matters most to God.

To issue a warning about such a temptation is not to answer to everyone's satisfaction which positions, in fact, reflect such principles, but to fail to ask the question is to ignore a dynamic principle of interpretation to which Jesus' ministry summons us. Given even a few clear examples of women's ministry in the Bible, is one text (or at most two)—which may be situationally conditioned—enough to deny or substantially restrict a group of laborers for the kingdom?

Some say they do not have enough certainty in order to permit women's ministry, but should those who are less than absolutely certain deny the calling of others, or should they perhaps keep silent on the issue? If these women claim to be called and bear the same sort of fruit on average as men (criteria we typically use to evaluate a man's calling), how objectively can we evaluate men's calls to ministry while rejecting women's? Some people tell me they reject women's callings because they have seen women fail at ministry, but have they never seen men fail at ministry? Some have never witnessed effective public ministry by a woman. On the other hand, I have seen more male ministers fall into sexual sin than women ministers. A few years ago I worked under a woman pastor who led more people to Christ in one year than I've seen any male pastor of a comparably sized congregation achieve. Our personal experiences may differ, but in the end is it not as dangerous to risk forbidding what God endorses as to risk promoting what he forbids?

A Personal Note

I mentioned earlier that I have been on both sides of the issue at different times in my life. After my conversion to Christianity, I spent my earliest years in conservative evangelical circles that had affirmed women's ministry since the early twentieth century (when women in ministry was even more accepted in some evangelical circles than it is today). In such circles the "conservative" position supported women's ordination, and some of my most effective Bible teachers were women. At the same time, however, I believed that 1 Timothy 2 prohibited women's ministry, and I found myself in the uncomfortable situation of appreciating the divinely blessed ministry of people whom I did not think should be involved in such ministry! When I gently engaged in dialogue with female friends who were preparing for ministry, I struggled to square my view of 1 Timothy 2 with their seemingly strong sense of calling and with everything else I knew about God from the Bible.

Such a setting sparked my interest in the question, but it took several years before I could resolve it. I continued to believe 1 Timothy 2 excluded women from Bible teaching, as gently and humbly as I desired to express it. Yet, as I read forty chapters of the Bible each day, I increasingly began to recognize the way the Bible was inviting me to read it. I labored to develop a fresh, consistent interpretive method from studying Scripture itself. The Bible summoned me to understand it in the light of the world it first addressed (which its first audiences assumed), and as I studied the background of the Bible, I grew increasingly convinced that the Bible did, in fact, affirm women's ministries.

By this time, however, I was spending time in different evangelical circles, where the "conservative" view was that women could *not* be ministers! Thus—being the "brave" young scholar I was—I planned to keep my convictions to myself. In time, however, several factors combined to convince me I needed to speak out. First, by this point I was seeing the way many godly evangelical friends of mine—women who were in ministry—were being regularly mistreated, and my wanting to support them came to matter more than my reputation. (I should hasten to add, however, that many complementarians do not mistreat women in ministry, and that, like myself in my complementarian days, they wish to be *personally* supportive.)[62] Second, the church's treatment of women in general had become a major apologetics issue on many university campuses, and I was heavily involved in campus ministry and apologetics. Certainly the credibility of the gospel mattered more than my reputation! Third, I saw this as an opportunity to demonstrate the importance of cultural background in Bible interpretation, hence a useful test case for promoting the importance of sound interpretation. Fourth, as I continued to pray about what books to start with, I felt that God wanted me to articulate the evidence I had found.

---

[62]For one commendable example, see Thomas R. Schreiner, "An Interpretation of 1 Timothy 2:9–15: A Dialogue with Scholarship," in *Women in the Church: A Fresh Analysis*, 105.

Finally, being a young scholar, I did not yet have much of a reputation to lose!

It was only after I published on the issue, however, that I realized how vitriolic the debate was becoming. Some evangelicals were denying the genuine evangelical commitment of those who did not share their views on the subject, and some trivialized rather than responded to our scholarship. They had every right to disagree charitably, as many of my friends do even today, but when some people misrepresented us and resorted to political power plays, they stooped to non-Christian methods of engaging in the debate. Disagreement on matters secondary to the gospel invites dialogue; slander, however, is a sin that must be addressed by means of repentance. This is true for whichever side is guilty of the slander, no matter how deeply our personal passions run on this or any other issue.

CONCLUSION

A number of passages clearly support women sharing God's word—and sometimes sharing it in more authoritative ways than the passages most often in dispute appear to suggest. Paul applies the same titles to ministries of women as to those of men, and he explicitly affirms women in the most prominent ministry roles of the early church. Context and background demonstrate that the two passages used to argue against women's ministry apply to particular situations within the two particular congregations; these texts, therefore, do not contradict those that support women's ministry. Of these two passages, the one specifically prohibiting women from teaching the Bible (1 Timothy 2) is also addressed to the one congregation where false teachers were specifically targeting women with their views. We should, therefore, not allow our traditions or an (at best) uncertain (and most likely mistaken) interpretation of a single passage to deny the calling of women who otherwise prove themselves fit for ministry.

A RESPONSE TO CRAIG KEENER
Craig L. Blomberg

Once again I am grateful for the opportunity to respond to a detailed, thoughtful essay reflecting one of the stronger contributions from the egalitarian position. Like Linda, Craig is a good friend—a humble, godly scholar and a person who meticulously researches each topic on which he writes. Again, there is much with which I agree, but space constraints require me to focus primarily on areas about which I have questions.

In an early footnote, Craig rejects the distinction between gifts and offices based on the overlap between the two for such terms as "apostles," "evangelists," and "pastors-teachers." I agree that each of these terms can be used in two different ways, but it remains possible to distinguish them. For example, Luke normally uses "apostles" to refer only to the Twelve, whereas Paul regularly uses the term much more broadly as a spiritual gift. But it is telling that the key role or office in debate—that of elder or overseer—is never used in any other way. That is to say, it never appears as a spiritual gift. Therefore, it is possible to argue that God gives all his gifts indiscriminately to both genders without settling the debate over who may hold the office of elder/overseer.

As in Linda's essay, Craig does a fine job highlighting the many women leaders in both Testaments. But when he comes to his section "Does Paul Permit Only Some Ministry Roles?" he misses some points. It is true that typical English translations of 1 Timothy 2:12 ("do not permit to teach or to exercise authority over") seem to suggest all kinds of teaching and all kinds of authority. But I argue this is not the meaning in the Greek. Unlike Linda, Craig does acknowledge and even agrees with Andreas Köstenberger in his study of paired infinitives. But

249

Köstenberger's work needs to be supplemented by Philip Payne's study of constructions involving *oude* (see p. 169). Payne has convincingly shown that pairs of expressions linked by this conjunction usually refer in the NT to mutually defining activities, not to entirely separate or independent ones. Thus the argument that Paul is referring only to "authoritative teaching," and, as I would argue, even more specifically to the office of elder or overseer, remains a probable interpretation.

Just as Linda replied to the observation that we have no reference to any female elders merely with the comment that we have many unnamed males as well, so, too, Craig offers the identical response with respect to pastors. But it appears to me no stronger than when it appeared in Linda's chapter. Linda argued that Jesus selected no women apostles because there were limits as to how much he dared to confront his culture, to which I queried if that was really likely, given the confrontations he was willing to make, even sacrificing his life in the process. Craig seems in part to acknowledge my point by arguing that Paul had to exhibit greater concern for the scandal factor because he was trying to establish a church within Greco-Roman society, whereas Jesus was moving toward confrontation with the authorities. If accurate, this point undercuts Linda's argument that Paul would have had greater freedom in the Greco-Roman world than Jesus in the Palestinian-Jewish world. On the other hand, Jesus did travel with women disciples in the supposedly more conservative culture of Israel, and there is no record of that being one of the issues that got him in trouble with the authorities! So one wonders how strong the argument about Paul's having to avoid female travel companions really is.

Craig makes a good point that no one generalizes from the makeup of the twelve apostles to forbid Gentiles, slaves, or peasants from the highest levels of church leadership today. If the only argument we had for gender restriction from "highest" offices were the apostolate, I would agree that the case would remain unproved. But Craig does not deal with the pattern throughout the ages that moves from priest to apostle to elder/overseer (and even throughout church history, notwithstanding the exceptions he itemizes to women's more itinerant or unofficial leadership roles). It is harder to reject the entire pattern as culturally determined than it is to dismiss any one portion of that pattern.

Craig argues that since both 1 Corinthians 11 and 1 Timothy 2 appeal to the order of creation, then if one denies women the office of elder, one must insist on head coverings as equally transcultural. But this misses what the appeal to creation in 1 Corinthians 11 most immediately supports. The appeal in verses 8–9 comes right after verse 7, which contrasts man as the glory of God and woman as the glory of man, a clear allusion back to the order of headship in verse 3. Head coverings are simply the situation-specific outworking in the first century of the timeless principle of male headship; we have other applications today. On the other hand, 1 Timothy 2:13 does come immediately after verse 12. Thus the appeal to the order of creation directly supports the prohibition of women elders in the preceding verse.

On 1 Corinthians 14:34–35, Craig argues that the interpretation that sees women's silence as pertaining only to the evaluation of prophecy makes little sense of the text, which, in fact, refers to asking questions while also containing Paul's injunction that all who prophesy are to participate in evaluating prophecies. As I point out in my essay, Anthony Thiselton has made a very plausible suggestion as to how this interpretation makes sense in this context: Wives may well have been challenging their husbands' prophecies, and the most likely exegesis of 1 Corinthians 14:29 is not that all who prophesy are to evaluate their prophecies but that the "others" (i.e., in the whole congregation) must do so. But inevitably, such broad-based evaluation would lead to various opinions, and ultimately it would devolve to the highest level of church leadership to make an authoritative decision. Once again, as in Linda's chapter, as attractive as the idea is that Paul was merely silencing uneducated women asking foolish or rude questions, it is not convincing that Paul would silence all women and no men, given the possibilities of at least some of the women in Greco-Roman circles gaining considerable education and plenty of the men not receiving one.

Again, as in my response to Linda's piece, one must appeal to the translation of *authentein* in 1 Timothy 2:12 as "to usurp authority" with care. Craig argues this is something neither men nor women should do, which would be true if the point means that some from either gender tried to take authority that had not been delegated to them. But if it refers to one gender seeking to acquire that which God intended only for the other, then the translation "to usurp authority" does not support the egalitarian interpretation at all. Likewise, when Craig cites Rebecca Groothuis, who argues that 1 Timothy 2:11–15 is the only prescriptive text on this topic and that there are situation-specific ways to interpret it, both authors miss the recurring pattern throughout Scripture, which I have pointed out. In fact, there is no OT text with a verb in the imperative mood that explicitly forbids women from being priests. But no one would argue from this that appointing women priests was a legitimate option in pre-Christian Judaism (the requirement that priests be "sons" of Aaron takes care of that, even if it is phrased as a declaration rather than a command).

Perhaps the most creative and fascinating part of Craig's essay deals with the way Paul cites the OT, especially with his arguments by analogy. There is no doubt Paul appeals to numerous OT passages in less than straightforward ways to marshal support for both theological and ethical maxims of the gospel. But Craig is mixing apples and oranges here. What he seems to want to argue for is that not all appeals to the OT in Paul support timeless or transcultural injunctions (irrespective of how straightforward or creative the use of the OT is). In fact, as far as I can tell, every single example he gives leads to a statement in the NT that indeed remains timeless: providing support for ministers of the gospel, giving sacrificially to the poor, proclaiming the gospel throughout creation, tongues having the potential to "scare people off" if uninterpreted, the conversion of the Gentiles provoking Israel to repentance, the need to speak in accordance with what one believes, the fact that God catches the self-styled wise in their craftiness, the Holy Spirit's giving gifts to his people, and Jesus as the climactic seed of Abraham. Paul makes some very creative analogies, to be sure, in supporting these points from the OT, but not one of the texts Craig cites provides a parallel to what he is trying to demonstrate, because none of them support situation-specific injunctions in the NT.

Again, there appears to be some uncharacteristically careless reading of Scripture in Craig's comments on page 240. First Corinthians 11:8–9 does not argue that "Eve was created for Adam's sake; therefore women should wear head coverings" (as I've already noted above). Further, the comparison in 2 Corinthians 11:3 between Eve and the Corinthian Christians concerning the ease of their deception is beside the point, since Paul derives no command or proscription from this comparison. Next, Paul does not subordinate all women because Eve was created second. First Timothy 2:12 speaks only of the office of elder. Finally, Paul certainly doesn't demand women's silence in church because Eve was created second. Genesis 2 is not even referenced in 1 Corinthians 14:34–35.

As I point out in my chapter, there are differences, as well as parallels, between Paul's treatments of slavery and gender roles. But even if we concede, with Craig, that Paul addresses the roles as they existed in his day with the timeless principles being submission to those in authority and becoming servants even when we hold authority, then it is worth pointing out that in a majority of the cultures of our world today, including most non-Christian cultures, patriarchal marriages, often exercised in a far more repressive fashion than they ever were in Christianity, remain the norm. Thus, by Craig's logic, wives' submission to their husbands, at least in these cultures, should still prevail.

In Craig's closing personal note, he recognizes, as do I, that God gifts women in all the same areas in which he gifts men. He also calls women to a wide variety of roles, as he does men. Like Linda, Craig effectively rebuts those more conservative forms of complementarianism that would deny women opportunities to exercise all their gifts or functions in ministerial roles. But I don't see that my more limited complementarian position is in any way undermined. Indeed, one of the attractive features of understanding the biblical restrictions as limited to one specific office is that there are opportunities apart from serving in that office for men and women to exercise every gift and fill every ministerial role, including other forms of spiritual leadership, including pastoral ministry, and including preaching. No person of either gender should ever feel they have too few opportunities to use their gifts to minister for God's kingdom or to fulfill their calling.

A RESPONSE TO CRAIG KEENER

Linda L. Belleville

It is a pleasure to respond to this finely crafted essay. Although done independently, our essays parallel one another very closely. So I will highlight and expand on what I feel to be the distinctive contributions. Craig's thesis is that "the Bible permits women's ministry under normal circumstances but prohibits it in exceptional cases, in which case we should allow it under most circumstances today" (p. 206).

Craig targets the methodological fallacies that are endemic to typical traditionalist argumentation. For example, traditionalists argue that women could be prophets but not teachers because the prophet did not hold a formal "post" like the rabbi or scribe and hence not an authoritative one. Craig points to the inherent inconsistency in this line of thought. It is hard to imagine anything more authoritative than the "Thus saith the Lord" proclamation of the prophet and the *didactic* character of the prophetic word. As Craig notes, most of OT Scripture was written by prophets. On the other hand, scribal and rabbinic authored works such as Sirach and Wisdom, while deemed profitable, were *not* accorded the status of Scripture and hence do not have a place in our canon.

Craig also targets the "unsound interpretive methodology [that] read[s] a more specific meaning into a phrase than its use in that context and situation warrants" (p. 213). To speak of *pastoral authority* and *senior pastor* is to impose a modern understanding of church leadership onto early church practice. As Craig points out, the early house churches had fifty members on average (the maximum size a house atrium could accommodate), probably representing several families and a number of individuals, and met in the homes of well-endowed families—a setting hardly requiring a senior pastor and staff.

Also, for traditionalists to say that Jewish *priests* were the religious CEOs of Judaism is to read antiquity in terms of modern Catholic or Episcopal polity. The priesthood of Israel was a hereditary position that handled the cult of sacrifice. Not only were women excluded, but anyone not in Aaron's family line was as well. The ability to complete one's priestly tour of duty was dependent on physical purity—something that automatically excluded women due to their monthly menstruation, as well as anyone with an unhealed wound, sore, infirmity, or physical disability.

What all this points up is that the Bible is, as Craig states, "for all time; but not everything the Bible says is for all circumstances" (p. 224). We do a tremendous disservice to the church when we bypass the step of interpreting texts in their respective cultural contexts. "Do not cook a young goat in its mother's milk" (Exod. 23:19; 34:26; Deut. 14:21) is one of my favorite examples. Without understanding the fertility rites of Israel's neighboring cultures, the command is absurd. These kinds of "statements that are locale specific . . . cannot possibly have meaning apart from the local situation" (p. 225).

The question, then, is where to draw the line. The rule of thumb is as follows: Transculturally applicable are (1) OT teachings that are reaffirmed by the NT, (2) prohibitions that reappear in Scripture, and (3) affirmations that repeatedly occur throughout Scripture. For example, the prohibitions of the Decalogue—do not murder, commit adultery, steal, give false testimony, and covet—are affirmed throughout Scripture despite the changing cultural panorama. The affirmation throughout Scripture of marriage as one male and one female forsaking all other loyalties, cleaving and becoming "one," combined with the prohibitions against same-sex unions, provide a clear transcultural ethic as well.

Women in ministry, however, is not in this category. The culture may be patriarchal and hierarchical, but what matters is the *explicit teaching* of Scripture—teaching that is affirmed and reaffirmed throughout. Jesus nowhere says that the Twelve he chose to be with him during his earthly ministry (and then sent out) had to be male because of the creation order of male first, female second. Yet traditionalists lift up his practice at a given point as normative for all time. Could Jesus' practice have been determined by *cultural sensitivity*? Truth be told, Jesus also chose and sent out the Seventy-Two with the same scope of authority as the Twelve (Luke 10:1–17). The church fathers had no difficulty calling the Seventy-Two "apostles" and including at least one female (Junia). Will excluding women as "apostles" to an Islamic missionary field be understood by subsequent generations as cultural sensitivity? Or will it be misinterpreted as due to a so-called *biblical prohibition*?

Was Paul being culturally sensitive when he commanded that "wives should submit to their husbands in everything" (Eph. 5:24)? Let's apply our rule of thumb: (1) It is *not* an OT teaching that is reaffirmed by the NT. This command is not even found in the OT. (2) Nor is it a prohibition that consistently appears throughout Scripture. In fact, this is the first time Paul invokes gender specific submission in marriage. This command doesn't appear in letters prior to Ephesians and doesn't reappear in letters addressed to churches outside of the particular locale (the Lycus Valley [Eph. 5:22, 24; Col. 3:18; 1 Pet. 3:1]). (3) Is the converse—"[Your husband] will rule over you" (Gen. 3:16)—an affirmation that consistently appears throughout Scripture? Not only does Genesis 3:16 not consistently appear; it doesn't reappear at all. When the "rules" of marriage appear, they are the pre-fall mutuality ones of Genesis 1–2. Indeed, the affirmations of mutual intimacy, mutual authority, and mutual consent found in 1 Corinthians 7:1–5 are in flat contradiction with Ephesians 5:22–24 (par. Col. 3:18; Titus 2:5; 1 Pet. 3:1). All this points to *cultural sensitivity* in the case of Ephesians 5:22–24 (and par.). In the case of the Cretan church plant, cultural sensitivity is what drives Paul as well. Wives are to be submissive "so that no one will malign the word of God" (Titus 2:5). The same is true of 1 Peter 3:1. Wives are to be submissive so that their unbelieving husbands "may be won over."

Was Paul being culturally sensitive in commanding Ephesian widows to remarry and have children (1 Tim 5:14)? The same rule of thumb applies. Remarriage does not appear in earlier letters and flatly contradicts Paul's counsel elsewhere that widows do well *not* to remarry and that singleness for the unmarried is preferable to marriage for the sake of full-time ministry (e.g., 1 Cor 7:8, 11, 25, 40); indeed, it is preferable for the same reason for men too (vv. 32–35). So why the command to the Ephesian church? *Situational sensitivity* is what drives Paul. As Craig points out (pp. 232–35), false teachers were prohibiting marriage as something outside of God's will (1 Tim 4:3), and they were targeting wealthy widows who were proselytizing on their behalf (5:13). So it is not surprising that *in this situation* Paul counsels remarriage.

What about 1 Timothy 2:11–15? According to Craig, it is one of these exceptional cases. It was a church in which "false teachers were effectively targeting women" (p. 232). So it is not unexpected that Timothy is urged to muzzle them (1:3). But what about Paul's use of the creation order ("Adam was formed first, then Eve" [2:13])? Doesn't this make 2:12 transcultural? Craig rightly observes that the so-called "creation order" argument is precisely one of the arguments Paul uses in 1 Corinthians 11:8–9 to admonish wives to cover their heads in church. As Craig points out, "We cannot consistently require a transcultural application prohibiting women's teaching or holding authority based on 1 Timothy 2:11–12 without also requiring all married women to cover their heads in keeping with 1 Corinthians 11:2–16" (p. 240).

A RESPONSE TO CRAIG KEENER

Thomas R. Schreiner

Craig Keener, like Linda Belleville, argues well for the egalitarian position. I have profited much from his scholarship, especially his work in historical background. In this essay, many of his conclusions are convincing. Women did function as prophets, deacons, evangelists, and missionaries. Complementarians must encourage women to pursue the variety of ministries endorsed by Scripture. Craig also rightly raises the issue of hermeneutics. How do we apply the words of the biblical text to our setting when our culture differs from biblical times?

Despite the strength of Craig's essay, he is not persuasive in maintaining that no restrictions are placed on women in terms of ministry. Contrary to Craig, Jesus did not conform to the culture of his day in appointing only male apostles. Elsewhere, Jesus overturns cultural conventions, and we have every reason to think he would have done the same if he believed women should be apostles. It is difficult to believe Paul was bold enough to appoint (in Craig's view) a female apostle a few years after Jesus' ministry (Rom. 16:7), but Jesus lacked the courage to blaze the trail. Craig thinks it is clear that Junia served as an apostle according to Romans 16:7, but the term more likely designates a missionary and church planter and does not convey the idea that Junia and Andronicus were equal to Paul and the Twelve.

Craig's exegesis of 1 Timothy 2:11–14 and 1 Corinthians 11:2–16 does not account well for Paul's argument from creation. The primary objection he raises is hermeneutical, maintaining, for instance, that if 1 Corinthians 11:2–16 is transcultural, we should require women to wear something on their heads in church. Craig's argument at first glance may seem compelling, but it does not finally succeed. Most scholars today rightly argue that the *principles* of God's word apply to our culture today. In fact, Craig is helpful in distinguishing between what is cultural and what is transcultural. We are not trying to reproduce the culture of the Bible in today's world. We do not believe we must greet one another with a holy kiss because it is what the Bible literally says (Rom. 16:16). Nor do we demand that those with stomachaches must drink wine in accordance with 1 Timothy 5:23. We derive *principles* from these texts, concluding that we are to greet one another warmly and with affection, and that those with stomach problems should take an appropriate remedy for their discomfort. Similarly, most complementarians believe that the point of 1 Corinthians 11:2–16 is not the literal issue of head coverings. Head coverings (or hairstyles—scholars do not even agree on what the cultural practice was!) or the lack thereof sent a particular message to those who lived in the Greco-Roman world of the first century.

In applying the text to today's world, we seek to discern the principle of the passage. We do not try to reproduce the cultural world addressed. I would argue that the principle here is that women should prophesy in a way that supports male leadership, since Paul introduces the text by appealing to man as the head of the woman (v. 3), and he also grounds his argument in the creational differences between men and women (vv. 8–9). Complementarians are not saying, therefore, that we must invariably reproduce the customs of the biblical text in our culture. We are arguing that there are *contextual indicators* (the order of creation in vv. 8–9 and 1 Tim 2:13) that the principles in these passages are transcultural.

Craig, somewhat surprisingly, endorses the conclusions of Andreas Köstenberger in his study of 1 Timothy 2:12. Köstenberger demonstrates from parallels in both extrabiblical Greek and biblical materials that Paul prohibits two activities here—teaching and exercising authority. Both activities are legitimate, i.e., there is nothing inherently wrong with teaching and exercising authority. Nevertheless, Craig thinks the prohibition against women teaching is not universal because of cultural factors in the text. He thinks women were prohibited from teaching because they were less educated and more prone to false teaching. Such a claim is unconvincing, for Paul could have easily said that women are prohibited from teaching because they were spreading the false teaching or because of their lack of education. Instead he appeals to the created order. In addition, no clear evidence exists in 1 Timothy that women promulgated the heresy, for the only false teachers mentioned are men (1:20). First Timothy says nothing at all about women spreading false teaching, for in context 5:13 refers to gossip, not false teaching. Moreover, if egalitarians are correct and both men and women were spreading false teaching, why does Paul only restrict women from teaching? If Paul only banned women from spreading the heresy, his advice seems rather sexist.

Craig also argues that not all proof texts from the OT are transcultural, and that the OT could be used analogously, without any notion of a transcultural application. Craig raises an important and complex issue that deserves more discussion than is possible here. It should be said in reply that an argument from the OT based on the created order is almost certainly transcultural. Jesus argued from creation in defending monogamy and God's intention that husbands and wives should not divorce (Matt. 19:3–9); Paul argued from creation in prohibiting homosexuality (Rom. 1:26–27). There is no reason, in the case of 1 Timothy 2:13, to think Paul is only arguing analogically. Paul prohibits women from teaching and exercising authority over men because of God's intention in creating men and women.

Craig rightly sees that the prohibition in 1 Corinthians 14:34–35 stems from the confusion spread by women who were asking questions when the church was gathered. I believe he is correct in saying that Paul is not prohibiting women from speaking in tongues, from prophesying, or even from judging prophecies. He fails to see, however, that the text does not merely address matters of cultural propriety or rudeness. It was noted earlier that we must discern the principle in texts addressed to specific cultural situations. The principle in this case is enunciated in 1 Corinthians 14:34. The women "are to subject themselves, just as the Law also says" (NASB). The transcultural principle, then, is that wives are to be submissive to their husbands. In this situation their submission manifests itself in how they conduct themselves in worship. Paul locates the principle of submission in the "Law." Paul almost certainly uses the term here to refer to the OT Scriptures, and most likely he refers to the creation narratives, especially Genesis 2, where a role differentiation between men and women is implicit in the narrative.

Wives are to quit being disruptive because their disruptive speech shows they are not being submissive. The principle from the text, therefore, is not that women should be absolutely silent in church (as some conservatives allege). Such an admonition would contradict 1 Corinthians 11:5, where women are encouraged to pray and prophesy.

Craig's argument from prophecy is one of the strongest in support of his position, but it fails to persuade for several reasons. First, we should observe the pattern of biblical revelation. Women served as prophets in the OT but never as priests. Similarly, in the NT women served as prophets but never as apostles or elders. Second, the gift of prophecy should be distinguished from the gift of teaching. Those who prophesy receive revelations from God that are then transmitted to believers (1 Cor. 14:29–33). The gift is therefore more passive in nature than the gift of teaching. Prophets transmit the word of the Lord; they do not study, prepare, and then deliver the word of the Lord. I am not denying that the prophetic word delivered by women is authoritative, though whether a prophecy is truly from God must be discerned by the church (v. 29; 1 Thess. 5:20–21). Third, 1 Corinthians 11:2–16 casts important light on the prophetic ministry of women. Women are encouraged to pray and prophesy in the church, but Paul enjoins the women to adorn themselves in a certain way because of male headship. Significantly, he begins the section by reminding his readers that "the man is the head of a woman" (v. 3). In other words, women are permitted to pray and prophesy in the assembly, but they are to do so in a way that indicates they are submissive to male leadership. I conclude that the possession of the prophetic gift by women does not lead to the conclusion that they can serve as pastors and teachers today.

Craig makes a good case for the egalitarian view, but his view does not successfully explain Paul's argument from creation, which supplies a transcultural grounding for the prohibition against women's teaching or exercising authority over men. Women served as prophets, deacons, and patrons but not as priests, apostles, and pastors.

WOMEN IN MINISTRY: ANOTHER COMPLEMENTARIAN PERSPECTIVE

Thomas R. Schreiner

Chapter Four

WOMEN IN MINISTRY:
ANOTHER COMPLEMENTARIAN PERSPECTIVE

Thomas R. Schreiner

WOMEN IN MINISTRY: ANOTHER COMPLEMENTARIAN PERSPECTIVE

Thomas R. Schreiner

I believe the role of women in the church is the most controversial and sensitive issue within evangelicalism today. This is not to say that it is the most important controversy, for other debates—the openness of God, and inclusivism versus exclusivism, for example—are more central. Nonetheless, "the women's issue" generally sparks more intense debate, probably because women who must defend their call to pastoral ministry feel their personhood and dignity are being questioned by those who doubt the validity of their ordination. Men who support the ordination of women are often passionate about the issue, both for exegetical reasons and because they feel compassion for women who have shared their stories with them.[1] Most women who feel called to ministry have experienced the pain of speaking with men who have told them their desires are unbiblical.

I am as affected by our cultural climate as anyone, and thus I would prefer, when speaking with women who feel called to pastoral ministry, to say they should move ahead and that they have God's blessing to do so. It is never pleasant to see someone's face fall in disappointment when they hear my view on this matter. On the other hand, I must resist the temptation to please people and instead must be faithful to my understanding of Scripture. And I understand Scripture to forbid women from teaching and exercising authority over a man (1 Tim. 2:12). In

---

[1]It is clear, e.g., that Craig Keener (*Paul, Women and Wives: Marriage and Women's Ministry in the Letters of Paul* [Peabody, Mass.: Hendrickson, 1992], 3–4, 120) is influenced significantly by the sense of call many women feel.

this essay I will try to explain what is involved in this prohibition. Following the lead of others, I will call my view the *complementarian* view, and I will call the view that believes all ministries should be open to women the *egalitarian* view.

HISTORY, HERMENEUTICS, AND TERMINOLOGY

Before I undertake an explanation of the biblical text, I want to say something about history, hermeneutics, and accurate terminology.

History

Throughout most of church history, women have been prohibited from serving as pastors and priests.[2] Thus, the view I support in this essay is "the historic view." I readily admit that those supporting the historic view have sometimes used extreme and unpersuasive arguments to defend their views, and that low views of women have colored their interpretations. Nor does the tradition of the church prove that women should be proscribed from the pastorate, for as evangelicals we believe in *sola scriptura*. Nonetheless, evangelicals must beware of what C. S. Lewis called "chronological snobbery."[3] The tradition of the church is not infallible, but it should not be discarded easily. The presumptive evidence is against a "new interpretation," for we are apt to be ensnared by our own cultural context and thus fail to see what was clear to our ancestors. An interpretation that has stood the test of time and been ratified by the church in century after century—both in the East and the West and in the North and the South—has an impressive pedigree, even if some of the supporting arguments used are unpersuasive.[4]

---

[2]See Daniel Doriani, "A History of the Interpretation of 1 Timothy 2," in *Women in the Church: A Fresh Analysis of 1 Timothy 2:9–15*, eds. Andreas J. Köstenberger, Thomas R. Schreiner, and H. Scott Baldwin (Grand Rapids: Baker, 1995), 23–67.

[3]C. S. Lewis, *Surprised by Joy* (New York: Harcourt, Brace, and World, 1955), 207.

[4]Karen Jo Torjeson (*When Women Were Priests: Women's Leadership in the Early Church and the Scandal of Their Subordination in the Rise of Christianity* [San Francisco: HarperSanFrancisco, 1993], 9–87) argues that women actually functioned as priests in the earliest part of church history. Ruth A. Tucker and Walter L. Liefeld (*Daughters of the Church: Women and Ministry from New Testament Times to the Present* [Grand Rapids: Zondervan, 1987], 63, 89–127), who are egalitarian scholars, are more careful and persuasive in their analysis of the evidence.

Moreover, the view that women should not be priests or pastors has transcended confessional barriers. It has been the view throughout history of most Protestants, the various Orthodox branches of the church, and the Roman Catholic Church. All of these groups could be wrong, of course; Scripture is the final arbiter on such matters. But the burden of proof is surely on those who promote a new interpretation, especially since the new interpretation follows on the heels of the feminist revolution in our society. Despite some of the positive contributions of feminism (e.g., equal pay for equal work and an emphasis on treating women as human beings), it is scarcely clear that the movement as a whole has been a force for good.[5] The final verdict is not in, but I am not optimistic about the outcome.

Hermeneutics

A brief word on hermeneutics is also necessary. We are keenly aware that all interpreters are shaped by their previous experience and culture.[6] No one encounters a text with a blank slate, without presuppositions. A detached objectivity is impossible, for we are finite human beings who inhabit a particular culture and a specific society. On the other hand, we must beware of thinking we can never transcend our culture. Otherwise, we will always and inevitably read into texts what we already believe. If we are ensnared by our own histories and social location, then we can dispense with reading any books, though we may enjoy reading those that support our current biases. If we can never learn anything new and if we invariably return to our own worldview, then there is no "truth" to be discovered anyway. Every essay in this volume would simply represent the cultural biases of the contributors, and your response as a reader

---

[5]See Mary A. Kassian, *The Feminist Gospel: The Movement to Unite Feminism with the Church* (Wheaton, Ill.: Crossway, 1992); Robert W. Yarbrough, "The Hermeneutics of 1 Timothy 2:9–15," in *Women in the Church: A Fresh Analysis*, 155–96; Harold O. J. Brown, "The New Testament Against Itself: 1 Timothy 2:9–15 and the 'Breakthrough' of Galatians 3:28," in *Women in the Church: A Fresh Analysis*, 197–211. From a secular point of view, see Nicholas Davidson, *The Failure of Feminism* (Buffalo, N.Y.: Prometheus, 1988).

[6]For a helpful analysis of common hermeneutical errors on both sides, see Andreas J. Köstenberger, "Gender Passages in the New Testament: Hermeneutical Fallacies Critiqued," *WTJ* 56 (1994): 259–83.

would be your own particular cultural bias. If we are trapped by our past, we may as well relish who we are—and conclude we're simply wasting our time in reading anybody else's opinion.

The idea that we are completely bound by our past is hermeneutical nihilism. Instead, awareness of our cultural background and presuppositions may become the pathway by which we transcend our past. People do change, and we can with diligent effort understand those who are different from us. Similarly, comprehending texts that are distant from us is possible, and we may even accept such a "foreign" world as the truth. Indeed, hermeneutical nihilism is really a form of atheism, for evangelicals believe in a God who speaks and who enables us to understand his words. The Spirit of God enables us to comprehend and embrace the truths of his word (1 Cor. 2:6–16), truths we rejected when we were unregenerate. Christians are confident that God's word is an effective word, a word that creates life (John 6:63). Naturally, this does not mean Christians now have perfect knowledge, nor does it imply we will agree on everything; neither am I denying that some texts are difficult to interpret. We "know in part" (1 Cor. 13:12) until the day of redemption.[7] And yet we can gain a substantial and accurate understanding of the Scriptures in this age. I approach this issue, therefore, with the confidence that God's word speaks to us today and that his will on the role of women can be discerned.

Another hermeneutical matter must be discussed at this juncture. Occasionally the debate between the complementarian and egalitarian views is framed as a choice between fundamental texts. For example, one author using the ordination of women as an illustration in discussing the millennium declares the following about the role of women: "The crucial question becomes which passages control the discussion: the passages where no limits seem to be expressed or those that do. Different sides take different positions based on whether they regard the nonrestrictive texts to be more fundamental to determining the view or the restrictive texts."[8]

---

[7]Unless otherwise noted, Scripture citations are taken from the New American Standard Bible (NASB).

[8]Darrell L. Bock, "Summary Essay," in *Three Views on the Millennium and Beyond,* ed. D. L. Bock (Grand Rapids: Zondervan, 1999), 280. Incidentally, this is not a criticism of Bock's overall view, for I believe he is a complementarian.

Let me simply say at the outset that I reject the dichotomy expressed here. I do not believe the issue relates to which texts are "more fundamental" or which texts "control the discussion." Such a view assumes that one set of texts functions as a prism by which the other set of texts is viewed. All of us are prone, of course, to read the Scriptures through a particular grid, and none of us escape such a tendency completely. But this way of framing the issue assumes that the decision on women's ordination is arrived at by deciding which set of texts is more fundamental. If this perspective is correct, it is hard to see how one could possibly say that 1 Timothy 2:11–15 is more fundamental than Galatians 3:28. The game seems to be over even before it begins. I am convinced the complementarian view is correct, not because 1 Timothy 2:11–15 is "more fundamental" or that it "controls the discussion" when interpreting Galatians 3:28. Rather, complementarians, in my opinion, have done the most justice to both Galatians 3:28 and 1 Timothy 2:11–15 when these texts are interpreted in context. Neither text should have priority over the other; both must be interpreted carefully and rigorously in context.

I have often heard egalitarians make another hermeneutical statement quite similar to what is noted above. They will say Galatians 3:28 is a clear text, and the texts that limit women from some ministries are unclear.[9] Then they proceed to say that clear texts must have sovereignty over unclear ones. Who could possibly disagree with this hermeneutical principle when it is abstractly stated? I also believe clear texts should have priority. However, the claim that Galatians 3:28 is the clear text begs the question. Both Galatians 3:28 and texts that limit women in ministry yield a clear and noncontradictory message. Those who preceded us in church history did not think that 1 Timothy 2:11–15 was unclear and that Galatians 3:28 was transparent. Our ancestors did not perceive the same tension between the two texts that many feel today. The texts strike us as polar because a modern notion of equality is often imported into Galatians 3:28. My own position is that the main point in both Galatians 3:28 and the texts that limit the role of women is clear. I am not arguing that every detail in texts like 1 Corinthians 11:2–16 and 1 Timothy 2:11–15 is transparent, but the basic teaching is not

---

[9]So Gretchen Gaebelein Hull, *Equal to Serve: Women and Men in the Church and Home* (Old Tappan, N.J.: Revell, 1987), 183–89.

hard to understand, nor is the main truth in Galatians 3:28 difficult to grasp.

Terminology

A word about terminology is also in order. Even though I use the phrase "ordination of women" for convenience, the real issue is not ordination but whether women can function in the pastoral office. The language of ordination is not regularly used in the NT of those who serve as leaders in the church.[10] The NT refers to *presbyteroi* ("elders") and *episkopoi* ("overseers") who serve as leaders in the early church. That elders and overseers constitute the same office is evident from Paul's address to the Ephesian leaders at Miletus (Acts 20:17–35). In verse 17 they are designated as "elders," while in verse 28 the same group is described as "overseers." The term "elders" probably designates the office, while the term "overseers" refers to function—the responsibility to watch over the church. Verse 28 also contains a pastoral metaphor, for the overseers are responsible to *poimainein* ("shepherd") God's flock. Here we have an indication that pastors, overseers, and elders refer to the same office.

Titus 1:5–9 also supports the idea that "elders" and "overseers" refer to the same office. Paul charges Titus to appoint elders in every city (v. 5) and then proceeds to describe the requisite character (v. 6). In verse 7 he shifts to the word "overseer." The singular use of the word "overseer" (*episkopon*) does not designate another office but is generic. The "for" (*gar*) connecting verses 6–7 indicates a new office is not in view, since Paul continues to describe the character required of leaders. Indeed, the very same word (*anenklētos*, "above reproach") is used in both verses 6 and 7, functioning as further evidence that "overseers" and "elders" refer to the same office. Peter's first letter (5:1–4) provides confirmatory evidence as well. Peter addresses the elders (*presbyterous*) in verse 1, calling on them to shepherd (*poimanate*) the flock. The participle *episkopountes* ("overseeing") is also used (verse 2), and so I conclude that shepherding (pastoring) and overseeing are the responsibilities of elders.[11]

---

[10]For a study of ordination, see Marjorie Warkentin, *Ordination: A Biblical-Historical View* (Grand Rapids: Eerdmans, 1982).

[11]Contra the normal Presbyterian view that distinguishes ruling and teaching elders in 1 Timothy 5:17. Of course, whether "elders" refers to an office is also

Nor is it the case that elders and overseers were exceptional in the NT. Paul and Barnabas appointed elders in every church planted on their first missionary journey (Acts 14:23).[12] "Overseers and deacons" (Phil. 1:1) comprise the two offices in Philippi. Leaders in the church at Jerusalem are designated as "elders" (Acts 15:2, 4, 6, 22, 23; 16:4). We have already seen that Paul instructed Titus to appoint elders in Crete (Titus 1:5). The qualifications and responsibilities of overseers and elders are explained in 1 Timothy 3:1–7 and 5:17–25. Peter's reference to "elders" (1 Pet. 5:1) indicates that elders were appointed in the churches in Pontus, Galatia, Cappadocia, Asia, and Bithynia (1 Pet. 1:1). When James refers to the leaders of the church, he calls them "elders" (Jas. 5:14). This brief survey reveals that elders and overseers were common in the NT church. Elders are not limited to Paul's letters but are also found in the writings of James, Peter, and Luke. Geographically, elders and overseers stretch from Jerusalem to Philippi to Crete. The terminology, of course, is not fixed. Leaders of churches are also referred to without the use of the titles "elders" or "overseers" (1 Cor. 16:15–16; Gal. 6:6; 1 Thess. 5:12–13).

My thesis in this essay is that women were not appointed to the pastoral office. Sometimes we ask, "Are women called to the ministry?" I used that very language in introducing this essay. But such language is too imprecise. *All* believers, including women, are called to ministry. There are a multitude of ministries women can and should fulfill. Similarly, the question is not whether women should be ordained, since ordination is not the central issue in the NT. The question I want to raise is quite specific: Are women called to function as pastors, elders, or overseers? My answer to this question is no, and this essay will explain why.

THE DIGNITY AND SIGNIFICANCE OF WOMEN

We are apt to misunderstand the Scriptures if we immediately delve into texts that limit women from the pastoral office,

---

debated. R. Alastair Campbell (*The Elders: Seniority within Earliest Christianity* [Edinburgh: T&T Clark, 1998]) has recently proposed that an office is not designated by the term. Supporting the notion that an office is in view is Benjamin L. Merkle, *The Elder and Overseer: One Office in the Early Church* (New York: Peter Lang, 2003).

[12]The appointing of elders in "every church" indicates a plurality of leadership in local churches. So also Acts 20:17 refers to *presbyterous tēs ekklēsias*, showing that there were plural elders for a single church. This is the most plausible way of reading Philippians 1:1, as well as the other texts regarding elders.

for the dignity and significance of women is constantly taught in the Bible. Genesis 1:26–28 teaches that both men and women are made in God's image, and together they are to rule over the world God created. Not only are both males and females made in God's image, but also they are *equally* made in his image. No evidence exists that males somehow reflect God's image more than females. Stanley Grenz provides no evidence for saying that contemporary complementarians deny that both men and women equally share God's image.[13] Anyone who has read the literature knows that such an allegation is not true of the vast majority of complementarians.

The dignity of women is often portrayed in the OT. We think of the courageous life of Sarah (Gen. 12–23), the faith of Rahab (Josh. 2), the commitment of Hannah (1 Sam. 1–2), the devotion of Ruth (Ruth 1–4), Abigail's gentle but firm rebuke of David (1 Sam. 25), the humble faith of both the widow of Zarephath (1 Kgs. 17) and the Shunammite woman (2 Kgs. 4), and the risk-taking faith of Esther (Esth. 1–10). As the author of Hebrews writes, "time will fail me" (Heb. 11:32) were I to narrate the lives of these OT women and others I have skipped over.

It has been noted often and rightly that Jesus treated women with dignity and respect and that he elevated them in a world where they were often mistreated. He displayed courage and tenderness in speaking to the Samaritan woman when it was contrary to cultural conventions (John 4:7–29). The compassion of Jesus was evident when he raised from the dead the only son of the widow of Nain (Luke 7:11–17), for that son would likely have become her sole means of support. He lovingly healed the woman who had suffered from a hemorrhage of blood for twelve years (Mark 5:25–34) and delivered the woman who had been unable to stand up straight for eighteen years (Luke 13:10–17), even though he was criticized in the latter instance for performing such a healing on the Sabbath. Jesus' tender firmness toward women in bondage to sin was remarkable, as is evidenced in the stories of the woman caught in adultery (John 8:1–11) and the sinful woman who washed his feet

---

[13]Stanley J. Grenz with Denise Muir Kjesbo, *Women in the Church: A Biblical Theology of Women in Ministry* (Downers Grove, Ill.: InterVarsity, 1995), 169. Amazingly, Grenz cites Ruth Tucker, who is an egalitarian, in support but cites no primary sources to prove his charge.

with her tears and dried them with her hair (Luke 7:36–50). Jesus healed women who were hurting, such as the daughter of the Syrophoenician woman (Mark 7:24–30) and Peter's mother-in-law (1:29–31). When suffering agony on the cross, he was concerned for his mother's welfare and requested John to care for her (John 19:26–27).

Jesus often used women or the world of women as examples in his teaching. He commended the queen of Sheba (Matt. 12:42), likened the kingdom of heaven to leaven which was put in dough by a woman (13:33), told the parable of the ten virgins (25:1–13), and defended his ministry to sinners with the parable of the lost coin of a woman (Luke 15:8–10). The necessity of steadfastness in prayer is illustrated by the widow who confronted the unjust judge (18:1–8). Jesus upheld the dignity of women by speaking out against divorce, which particularly injured women in the ancient world (Mark 10:2–12). Nor are women simply sex objects to be desired by men, for Jesus spoke strongly against lust (Matt. 5:27–30). Jesus also commended the poor widow who gave all she owned—more than the rich who gave lavish gifts out of their abundance (Luke 21:1–4).

Women were also prominently featured in the ministry of Jesus. His ministry was financed by several women of means (Luke 8:1–3), and it is likely that some of these women traveled with him during at least some of his ministry. Jesus commended Mary for listening to his word, in contrast to Martha, who was excessively worried about preparations for a meal (10:38–42). The account is particularly significant because some in Judaism prohibited women from learning Torah, but Jesus encouraged women to learn the Scriptures.[14] His close relationship with Mary and Martha is illustrated by the account of the raising of Lazarus (John 11:1–44) and his anointing for burial by Mary (12:1–8). The devotion of women was also apparent in their concern for Jesus, even on his way to the cross (Luke 23:27–31; cf. Mark 15:40–41). Finally, Jesus appeared to women and entrusted them to be his witnesses when he was raised from the dead (Matt. 28:1–10; Mark 16:1–8; Luke 24:1–12; John 20:1–18), even though the testimony of women was not received by courts.

---

[14]On the topic of women learning Torah, see the balanced appraisal of Ben Witherington III, *Women and the Genesis of Christianity* (Cambridge: Cambridge Univ. Press, 1990), 6–9.

What is particularly striking is that Jesus appeared to women first, showing again their significance and value as human beings.

The importance of women was not nullified by the early church after Jesus' ministry. Women participated with men in prayer before the day of Pentecost (Acts 1:12–14). Widows who were lacking daily provisions were not shunted aside, but specific plans were enacted to ensure their needs were met (6:1–6; 1 Tim. 5:3–16; see also Jas. 1:26–27). Tabitha was commended for her loving concern for others (Acts 9:36–42), and Luke features the conversion of Lydia, who worked as a merchant (16:14–15). Concern for women is illustrated in the eviction of the demon from the slave girl (vv. 16–18); her owners were concerned for profits (vv. 19–21), but Paul desired her salvation and deliverance.

All of these texts confirm the teaching of Galatians 3:28, "There is neither Jew nor Greek, there is neither slave nor free man, there is neither male nor female; for you are all one in Christ Jesus."[15] Both women and men, slave and free, are valuable to God. Women are made in God's image and thus possess dignity as his image bearers. The fundamental purpose of Galatians 3:28 in context is to say that both men and women have equal access to salvation in Christ. The Judaizing opponents had rocked the Galatian churches, causing them to wonder if one had to be circumcised to be saved (5:2–6; 6:12–13). Paul reminded them that one belongs to the family of Abraham by faith alone (3:6–9, 14, 29). One does not need to become a Jew and receive circumcision in order to qualify for membership in the people of God. Nor are the people of God restricted to males. Anyone who believes in Christ, whether male or female, is part of God's family.

Klyne Snodgrass argues that Galatians 3:28 cannot be confined to salvation but also has social implications.[16] Jews and Gentiles, for instance, now relate to each other differently because of their oneness in Christ. I believe Snodgrass is correct. The main point of this verse is that all people, including both men and women, have equal access to salvation in Christ.

---

[15]Some scholars see this verse as containing an early baptismal formula, but the prehistory of the text need not detain us here.

[16]Klyne R. Snodgrass, "Galatians 3:28: Conundrum or Solution?" in *Women, Authority and the Bible*, ed. Alvera Mickelsen (Downers Grove, Ill.: InterVarsity, 1986), 161–81.

Nonetheless, it is also true that such a truth has social consequences and implications. However, we must read the rest of what Paul says to explain accurately what these social implications are. It is extraordinarily easy to impose on the biblical text our modern democratic Western notions of social equality.[17] As we proceed, we will attempt to discern Paul's own understanding of the social implications of Galatians 3:28.

The late F. F. Bruce's understanding of Galatians 3:28 was fundamentally flawed, for he read into it his own philosophical conception of equality: "Paul states the basic principle here; if restrictions on it are found elsewhere in the Pauline corpus ..., they are to be understood in relation to Galatians 3:28, and not vice versa."[18] Bruce's assertion begged the question. He assumed all the verses were to be interpreted through the lens of Galatians 3:28, but thereby he ensured that his own notions of equality would be read into the verse. Nothing Paul writes elsewhere can qualify or limit his view of Galatians 3:28.

Let me apply Bruce's logic to the issue of homosexuality.[19] What if I were to say, "Galatians 3:28 is Paul's fundamental statement on what it means to be male and female. Any verse written elsewhere on the matter must be read in light of Galatians 3:28. Therefore, those verses in Paul's letters that proscribe homosexuality are to be read in light of Galatians 3:28. Paul says

---

[17]Rebecca Merrill Groothuis (*Good News for Women: A Biblical Picture of Gender Equality* [Grand Rapids: Baker, 1997], 46) falls into this very error in defining equality. She does not derive her definition from Scripture but from classical liberal thought. For a persuasive critique of Snodgrass and egalitarian interpretations of Galatians 3:28, see Köstenberger, "Gender Passages," 274–79; and the insightful work of Richard W. Hove, *Equality in Christ? Galatians 3:28 and the Gender Dispute* (Wheaton, Ill.: Crossway, 1999).

[18]F. F. Bruce, *Commentary on Galatians* (NIGTC; Grand Rapids: Eerdmans, 1982), 190. Judith M. Gundry-Volf would draw different conclusions than I would from Galatians 3:28, but she rightly argues that this verse does not abolish all gender differences. See "Christ and Gender: A Study of Difference and Equality in Galatians 3:28," in *Jesus Christus als die Mitte der Schrift: Studien zur Hermeneutik des Evangeliums*, eds. C. Landmesser, H. J. Eckstein, and H. Lichtenberger (BZNW 86; Berlin: Walter de Gruyter, 1997), 439–77.

[19]I am not saying that the issues of women in ministry and homosexuality are of equal clarity or importance, for I am persuaded that anyone who thinks homosexuality is acceptable is no longer an evangelical. The scriptural teaching on homosexuality is clearer than its teaching on the role of women. Nonetheless, the very principle propounded by F. F. Bruce could logically lead to the result I point out above.

that whether one is a male or female is of no significance to God. Therefore, whether one marries a male or female is irrelevant." Evangelicals would rightly protest that such an exegesis reads modern notions of sexual relations into the text. My point is that precisely the same kind of question-begging exegesis is being employed in egalitarian interpretations of Galatians 3:28. Women have equal access to salvation, and there are social consequences to this truth, to be sure, but we need to read Paul and the rest of the Scriptures to determine what these implications are.

At this juncture we need to remind ourselves of the teaching of Galatians 3:28. The Bible does not teach that men or masters or Jews are somehow closer to God. Males and females, masters and slaves, and Jews and Gentiles all have equal access to salvation. It certainly follows that we should treat every human being, whether male or female, with dignity and respect. We also proclaim the gospel to all people groups and both genders in the hope of their salvation.

Since men and women have equal access to salvation, they are also joint heirs "of the grace of life" (1 Pet. 3:7). Peter teaches here that both men and women have an equal destiny; both will receive an inheritance on the day of the Lord. The Bible does not teach that women will have a lesser reward than men, that men will somehow rule over women in heaven, or that women will have a lesser place in heaven. Men and women are equally heirs of the salvation God has promised.

WOMEN IN MINISTRY

It would be a fundamental mistake to so concentrate on the Scripture passages that limit women in ministry that we fail to see the many ministries in which women were engaged during Bible times. My purpose in this section is to show the variety of ministries involving women and also to explain how such participation in ministry does not contradict the view that women are prohibited from serving in the pastoral office.

The Scriptures clearly teach that women functioned, at least occasionally, as prophets. In the OT, Miriam (Exod. 15:20–21), Deborah (Judg. 4:4–5), and Huldah (2 Kgs. 22:14–20) are prominent. Anna in the NT also functions like an OT prophet, since she exercised her gift before Jesus' public ministry (Luke 2:36–38). In Peter's Pentecost sermon he emphasizes that Joel's prophecy has been fulfilled and that the Spirit has been poured out on both men and women (Acts 2:17–18). Philip's four daughters were prophets (21:9), and women in Corinth apparently exercised the gift as well (1 Cor. 11:5). The spiritual gift of prophecy belongs to women as well as men (Rom. 12:6; 1 Cor. 12:10, 28; Eph. 4:11). Egalitarians often argue that prophecy is actually ranked above teaching (1 Cor. 12:28), and thus if women have the right to prophesy, they must also be able to teach and preach because they possess all the spiritual gifts.

To handle this issue adequately, we must define the gift of prophecy. Some define prophecy as preaching.[20] It is true that those who prophesy proclaim and declare God's word to the people of God. On the other hand, identifying prophecy as preaching is misleading, since those who preach the Scriptures use the gift of teaching in their exposition. Women are banned from the pastoral office, since one of the fundamental roles of elders is preaching that involves teaching men (1 Tim. 3:2; 5:17; Titus 1:9). Even though prophets declare the word of God, the gift of prophecy should not be equated with the regular teaching and preaching of God's word.

In 1 Corinthians 14:29–32, Paul indicates that prophecy involves the spontaneous reception of revelation or oracles from God.[21] This is evident from verse 30, for a revelation is suddenly given to a prophet who is seated. Clearly a prepared message is

---

[20]See, e.g., J. I. Packer (*Keep in Step with the Spirit* [Old Tappan, N.J.: Revell, 1984], 215), who essentially defines prophecy as "preaching." Packer is a complementarian. For this notion of prophecy, see also David Hill, *New Testament Prophecy* (London: Marshall, Morgan & Scott, 1979), 213; Anthony C. Thiselton, *The First Epistle to the Corinthians* (NIGTC; Grand Rapids: Eerdmans, 2000), 960–61; Craig L. Blomberg, "Neither Hierarchicalist nor Egalitarian: Gender Roles in Paul," in *Two Views on Women in Ministry*, eds. James R. Beck and Craig L. Blomberg (Grand Rapids: Zondervan, 2001), 344–45.

[21]For studies of prophecy that support this basic view, see David E. Aune, *Prophecy in Early Christianity and the Ancient Mediterranean World* (Grand Rapids: Eerdmans, 1983); Wayne A. Grudem, *The Gift of Prophecy in 1 Corinthians* (Lanham, Md.: University Press of America, 1982); Graham Houston, *Prophecy: A Gift for Today?* (Downers Grove, Ill.: InterVarsity, 1989), 82–86; Christopher Forbes, *Prophecy and Inspired Speech in Early Christianity and Its Hellenistic Environment* (WUNT 2/75; Tübingen: Mohr, 1995), 218–21; Max Turner, *The Holy Spirit and Spiritual Gifts*, rev. ed. (Peabody, Mass.: Hendrickson, 1996), 185–220.

not involved, for the person sitting down receives a revelation from God without warning and stands to deliver this spontaneous word of God to the congregation. Such a definition of prophecy fits with Agabus's prophecies in Acts. The Lord revealed to him that a famine would spread over the world (11:27–28), and he also prophesied that Paul would be tied up and handed over to the Gentiles (21:10–11). These prophecies are hardly prepared messages but are oracles that come supernaturally from God.

The oracular nature of prophecy is also evident in the prophecies of Deborah (Judg. 4:4–9) and Huldah (2 Kgs. 22:14–20), for they deliver God's specific word in response to particular situations. From this I conclude that prophecy is not to be equated with the teaching required of those serving as elders/overseers/pastors. It also follows that prophecy is distinct from the gift of teaching. Teaching involves the explanation of tradition that has already been transmitted, whereas prophecy is *fresh* revelation.[22]

It is not the purpose of this essay to resolve whether prophecy still exists as a gift today.[23] What must be observed is that the presence of women prophets does not neutralize the prohibition against women serving as pastors. God has raised up women prophets in the history of the church, but it does not follow that women should serve as elders or overseers of God's flock. In the OT, women served occasionally as prophets but never as priests.[24] Similarly, in the NT, women served as prophets but never as pastors or overseers or apostles. Not a single NT example can be adduced that women served as pastors, elders, or overseers. When we examine 1 Corinthians 11:2–16 in more detail later, we will also see that Paul instructs women to exercise their prophetic gift with a submissive demeanor and attitude, since man is the head of a woman (v. 3).

Another difference between prophecy and teaching must be noted. Prophecy is a passive gift in which oracles or revelations are given by God to a prophet. Teaching, on the other hand, is a gift that naturally fits with leadership and a settled office,

---

[22]See *TDNT*, 6:854, s.v. *"prophētēs"*; Heinrich Greeven, "Propheten, Lehrer, Vorsteher bei Paulus," *ZNW* 44 (1952–53): 29–30; Forbes, *Prophecy and Inspired Speech*, 225–29; Turner, *Holy Spirit and Spiritual Gifts*, 187–90, 206–12.

[23]For a discussion of this issue, see *Are Miraculous Gifts for Today? Four Views*, ed. Wayne A. Grudem (Grand Rapids: Zondervan, 1996).

[24]For development of this argument, see Gordon J. Wenham, "The Ordination of Women: Why Is It So Divisive?" *Chm* 92 (1978): 310–19.

for it involves the transmission and explanation of tradition.[25] I am not arguing that prophecy is a lesser gift than teaching, only that it is a distinct gift.

Isn't there a flaw in the above argument? For women have the gift of teaching, just as men do. When the spiritual gifts are listed (Rom. 12:6–8; 1 Cor. 12:8–10, 28–30; Eph. 4:11; 1 Pet. 4:10–11), no hint is given that women lack the gift of teaching. In fact, Priscilla and Aquila together instructed Apollos more accurately about the things of the Lord (Acts 18:26), and the listing of Priscilla first may signal that she was more learned than her husband. Paul also testifies to the powerful ministry of this couple, calling them fellow workers in the gospel and referring to a church that met in their home (Rom. 16:3–5; 1 Cor. 16:19; cf. 2 Tim. 4:19). Some egalitarians also point to Titus 2:3, where the teaching of women is commended.

In many respects I agree with egalitarians here. Sometimes complementarians have given the impression that women are unintelligent and that they lack any ability to teach. Such a view is clearly mistaken, for some women unquestionably have the spiritual gift of teaching. Men should be open to receiving biblical and doctrinal instruction from women. Otherwise, they are not following the humble example of Apollos, who learned from Priscilla and Aquila. Moreover, women should be encouraged to share what they have learned from the Scriptures when the church gathers. The mutual teaching recommended in 1 Corinthians 14:26 and Colossians 3:16 is not limited to men. Sometimes we men are more chauvinistic than biblical.

Nonetheless, the above Scripture texts do not indicate that women filled the pastoral office or functioned as regular teachers of the congregation. All believers are to instruct one another, both when the church gathers and when we meet in smaller groups of two or three (1 Cor. 14:26; Col. 3:16). To encourage and instruct one another is the responsibility of all believers. But such mutual encouragement and instruction is not the same thing as

---

[25]Previously I argued that women's gift of prophecy was not exercised as publicly as it was by men (see my "The Valuable Ministries of Women in the Context of Male Leadership: A Survey of Old and New Testament Examples and Teaching," in *Recovering Biblical Manhood and Womanhood: A Response to Evangelical Feminism*, eds. John Piper and Wayne Grudem [Wheaton, Ill.: Crossway, 1991], 216). I now have some reservations about the validity of this argument.

a woman's being appointed to the pastoral office or functioning as the regular teacher of a gathering of men and women.

Complementarians can easily go too far and think that women cannot teach them anything from Scripture, when the example of Priscilla says otherwise. On the other hand, a single occasion in which Priscilla taught Apollos in private hardly demonstrates that she filled the pastoral office. Let me use an example from today. If a member of my church named Jim took aside another person in my congregation and explained something from the Bible to him, it does not follow that Jim was actually functioning as a teacher or a pastor in our church. Other information would be needed to clarify Jim's precise role. Egalitarians can be tempted to read more into the Priscilla account than it actually says. And egalitarians are sometimes disingenuous about Titus 2:3, for the context reveals that Paul encourages the older women to instruct *younger women*.[26] It is eisegesis to use this text to defend the belief that women can teach men in pastoral ministry, for the ministry of older women to younger women is what is commended here.

Paul celebrates the contributions of women in ministry. One of his favorite terms for those who assist him in ministry is *synergos* ("coworker," "fellow worker"). The lineup of coworkers is impressive: Timothy (Rom. 16:21; 1 Thess. 3:2; Phlm. 1), Apollos (1 Cor. 3:9), Urbanus (Rom. 16:9), Titus (2 Cor. 8:23), Epaphroditus (Phil. 2:25), Aristarchus (Col. 4:10; Phlm. 24), Mark (Col. 4:11; Phlm. 24), Jesus Justus (Col. 4:11), Epaphras (Phlm. 24), Demas (Phlm. 24), and Luke (Phlm. 24). But coworkers are not limited to men. Priscilla is called a *synergos* ("fellow worker") in Romans 16:3. Euodia and Syntyche are commended as coworkers in Philippians 4:3, and Paul says they struggled together with him in spreading the gospel.

Paul also often uses the verb *kopiaō* ("to labor") to designate those involved in ministry (1 Cor. 16:16). Indeed, the term *kopiaō* often describes his own ministry (1 Cor. 4:12; 15:10; Gal. 4:11; Phil. 2:16; Col. 1:29; 1 Tim. 4:10). In some texts, leaders are said to labor, or work hard (1 Cor. 16:16; 1 Thess. 5:12; 1 Tim. 5:17). What is remarkable is that a number of women are noted by Paul as having worked hard: Mary (Rom. 16:6) and Tryphaena, Tryphosa, and Persis (v. 12). Egalitarians conclude from this that women functioned as leaders in the early church.

---

[26]See Grenz, *Women in the Church*, 129.

We ought not to miss a point both egalitarians and complementarians can agree on: women were obviously significantly involved in ministry. And they worked hard in their ministries. But the evidence does not clearly indicate that women functioned as leaders, for the terms are fundamentally vague on the matter of leadership. We know women worked hard in ministry, but these terms do not tell us they functioned as pastors. The flaw in such reasoning is easily apparent if we consider the case of the apostle Paul. Let me construct a simple syllogism:

> Paul the apostle often describes his ministry as labor, or hard work.
> A number of women are said to labor in ministry.
> Therefore, women functioned as apostles.

The logical flaw here is immediately apparent, for "labor" is not unique to or distinctive of apostles. People can labor in ministry without being apostles. Similarly, women labor in ministry without necessarily functioning as leaders. In my own church, many women are working hard and laboring in the ministry, but they do not fill pastoral leadership roles. The reader should note carefully what I am not saying. I am not arguing that the terms "fellow worker" ("coworker") and "labor" ("work hard") clearly exclude women from pastoral leadership. I am merely saying the terms do not demonstrate they functioned as such.

Did women serve as deacons in the NT period? The debate centers on Romans 16:1 and 1 Timothy 3:11. Many complementarians are persuaded that women were not deacons. Unfortunately, the text is unclear, so certainty is precluded, and we are limited to a study of two verses! On balance, I think women did serve as deacons, and I believe we should encourage them to fill this office in our churches. The word for "deacon" (*diakonos*) often refers to service in general, with no specific office being intended. Nevertheless, it seems that Phoebe filled an office in Romans 16:1, for she is spoken of as a "deacon of the church at [TNIV, "in"] Cenchreae" (NRSV). The addition of the words "of the church at Cenchreae" after *diakonos* suggests an official position, for it appears she filled a particular role in a specific local church.

It is possible 1 Timothy 3:11 refers to the wives of deacons instead of women deacons, but a reference to women deacons is more likely for a number of reasons. First, the women in verse 11 are introduced with the term "likewise"—the same term used to introduce male deacons in verse 8, so it is most reasonable to think Paul is continuing to describe offices in the church. Second, some English versions translate the word *gynaikas* ("women") here as "wives" (KJV, NKJV, NIV), but the Greek language does not have a separate word for "wives" and the term could just as easily be translated "women" (NASB, NRSV, RSV, TNIV). In fact, the reference would clearly be to wives if Paul had written "their wives" (requiring simply the addition of the Greek *autōn*) or "the wives of deacons" (requiring simply the addition of the Greek *diakonōn*). Since neither of these terms is used, women deacons rather than wives are probably in view.[27] Third, the qualifications for these women are identical or similar to the qualifications of male deacons and elders. The similarity of the qualifications suggests an office, not merely a status as the wives of deacons. Fourth, why would Paul emphasize the wives of deacons and pass over the wives of elders, especially if elders (see below) had greater responsibility in the act of governing the church? Failure to mention the wives of elders is mystifying if that office carried more responsibility. A reference to women deacons, however, makes good sense if women could serve as deacons but not as elders (more on this below).

I conclude that women did serve as deacons in the NT and that they should serve as such in our churches today. We see once again that women were vitally involved in ministry during the NT era, and churches today are misguided if they prohibit women from doing what the Scriptures allow.

But if women served as deacons when the NT was written, how can they be prohibited from governing and teaching roles today? One of the problems in the contemporary church is that many churches have deviated from the biblical pattern in which there were two offices: elders/overseers and deacons (Phil. 1:1; 1 Tim. 3:1–13). In many modern churches the deacons function as the governing board of a church. This is unfortunate, for deacons are nowhere identified with or made a subcategory of elders in the NT. The offices of deacon and elder are distinct.[28] And appointing women as deacons does not affect the validity of the complementarian view at all, for elders/overseers—*not* deacons—are responsible for leadership and teaching in the

---

[27]In support of a reference to wives, see George W. Knight III, *The Pastoral Epistles* (NIGTC; Grand Rapids: Eerdmans, 1992), 170–73.

[28]I discussed the evidence for elders previously in this essay (pp. 270–71).

church. Two qualities demanded of elders, namely, being able
to teach (1 Tim. 3:2; 5:17; Titus 1:9) and governing the church
(1 Tim. 3:5; 5:17; Acts 20:28), are nowhere required of deacons.
The elders, not the deacons, have the responsibility for the doctrinal purity and leadership of a church. The deacons are responsible for ministries of mercy and service in the church, and they
do not exercise leadership in teaching and in governing the
church. It is significant, then, that 1 Timothy 2:12 prohibits
women from teaching and exercising authority over men. Notice
that women are prohibited from doing the two activities that distinguish elders from deacons (teaching and exercising authority). I conclude, then, that women can and should serve as
deacons, but they should not occupy the pastoral office, which
involves teaching and exercising authority.[29]

Egalitarians are convinced women did serve as leaders in
the early church. They identify Junia as a woman apostle in
Romans 16:7. Some believe women functioned as leaders
because John wrote in his second letter to "the chosen lady"
(2 John 1), and this lady is understood to be an individual
woman leading the church.[30] Others think women served as
elders because Paul refers to women elders in 1 Timothy 5:2 (cf.
Titus 2:3). Many egalitarians point to Phoebe in Romans 16:2,
understanding the word *prostatis* to refer to a leader.[31] Still others
say women must have functioned as leaders because churches
met in their houses, and as the patrons of these houses they
would have been leaders—for example, Mary the mother of

---

[29]Some people appeal to the NT accounts of Stephen and Philip and argue that
their ministries show that deacons functioned as leaders and were not restricted to
"service" ministries (Acts 6:1–8:40). Let me make a few brief comments. First, we're
not absolutely sure Stephen and Philip functioned as deacons, for the title is not used
of those appointed in Acts 6:1–6, though the noun *diakonia* is used of the need (v. 1)
and the verb *diakonein* (v. 2) of the task to be fulfilled. On balance, I think the Seven
were deacons, but certainty eludes us. Second, the preaching ministry of Stephen
and Philip hardly proves it is part of the ministry of deacons to preach, for the Seven
are appointed so that the Twelve will not abandon the ministry of the word (vv. 2,
4). Third, simply because some deacons did more than required (Stephen and Philip
served *and* preached), it does not follow that *all* deacons can or should teach and
preach. Luke features Stephen and Philip precisely because they were exceptional.

[30]See Aída B. Spencer, *Beyond the Curse: Women Called to Ministry* (Nashville:
Nelson, 1985), 109–12; Tucker and Liefeld, *Daughters of the Church*, 74–75.

[31]See Keener, *Paul, Women and Wives*, 238–40; Spencer, *Beyond the Curse*, 113–17.

John Mark (Acts 12:12–17), Lydia (16:13–15), Chloe (1 Cor. 1:11), Priscilla (Rom. 16:3–5), and Nympha (Col. 4:15).[32]

The arguments of egalitarians in the preceding paragraph are unconvincing. Some argue that women should preach because they bore witness to the resurrection. We should not reason, however, that Mary Magdalene was qualified to be a leader because Jesus appeared to her.[33] Nor is there any evidence elsewhere that she functioned as such. Seeing the risen Lord and bearing witness to his resurrection was a great joy and privilege, to be sure, but it doesn't logically follow that such women should serve as leaders or teachers. Indeed, if Jesus had appointed female apostles, then it would be clear that all ministry roles are open to women. We know, however, that Jesus appointed only male apostles. Now I do not believe a male apostolate settles the issue on the role of women. But if Jesus were as egalitarian and bold and radical as egalitarians make him out to be, it is passing strange he did not appoint any female apostles, especially since these same egalitarians see Paul as commending female apostles (Rom. 16:7). Jesus seems to accommodate to the culture more than Paul—when he could have made a bold statement that would have resolved the whole issue definitively. A male apostolate does not prove that women should not serve as leaders, but when combined with the other evidence, it does serve as confirmatory evidence for the complementarian view.

Nor is it at all compelling to say that women patrons functioned as leaders of house churches. No convincing evidence supports such a view. Does anyone really believe that Mary the mother of John Mark was one of the leaders of the church in Jerusalem simply because the church met in her house (Acts 12:12)? Acts makes it clear that the leaders were Peter, John, and James the brother of the Lord (in addition to the other apostles and elders). No correlation can be drawn between the church's meeting in Mary's house and the assuming of a leadership role.

Similarly, not even a hint is given of Chloe's functioning as a leader in Corinth. The church, in fact, is exhorted to be subject to the house of Stephanas (1 Cor. 16:15–16), and Chloe is left out. Nor is it persuasive to define *prostatis* as "leader" in Romans

---

[32]This appears to be the view of Grenz, *Women in the Church*, 90–91.

[33]Contra Grenz (*Women in the Church*, 79), who also supports women as leaders on the basis of Rhoda's telling the others that Peter was at the door of the house (Acts 12:14)!

16:2. What Paul says in this verse is that the Romans should *parastēte* ("assist") Phoebe wherever she needs help because she has been a *prostatis* ("helper") of many, including Paul himself.[34] The play on words between *parastēte* and *prostatis* is obvious. Phoebe is commended here as a patroness. Paul is scarcely suggesting she functioned as his leader or as the leader of the church. Paul did not even agree that the Jerusalem apostles were his leaders (Gal. 1:11–2:14), and so it is impossible to believe he would assign such a role to Phoebe!

The evidence that women served as elders is practically nonexistent and unpersuasive. For example, it is obvious in Titus 2:3 that the office of elder is not in view, for Paul refers to older men (v. 2), older women (v. 3), younger women (vv. 4–5), and younger men (v. 6). The mention of the various age groups reveals that Paul refers to age rather than office. The same argument applies to 1 Timothy 5:2. In verses 1–2 Paul gives Timothy advice about how to relate to older men, older women, younger men, and younger women. Any notion of office has to be read into the text here, and virtually all commentators agree that age (not office) is intended. Nor does "chosen lady" in 2 John refer to a woman leader or elder.[35] Almost all commentators agree it is a reference to the church as a whole. The plurals in verses 6, 8, 10, and 12 indicate that John writes to the church as a whole, not simply to one person. Referring to the church as a "lady" comports with the rest of Scripture, for both Paul and John describe the church as Christ's bride (Eph. 5:22–23; Rev. 19:7). And Israel is also portrayed as a woman in the OT (Isa. 54:1; Jer. 6:23; 31:21; Lam. 4:3, 22). Readers would naturally understand the metaphor of the church as a lady to refer to Christ's church. The distinction between the lady and her children should not be used to say a woman was the leader and the children were the congregation.

---

[34]For further discussion on Phoebe, including a bibliography citing alternative views, see my *Romans* (BECNT; Grand Rapids: Baker, 1998), 786–88.

[35]Grenz, *Women in the Church*, 91–92. Grenz admits the evidence is ambiguous, but he fails to inform the reader that virtually all the commentators agree a specific woman is not in view. The sources he mentions (see his p. 242, nn. 95, 96) are a commentator from 1888, another commentary without a date, and Spencer, *Beyond the Curse*. The standard commentaries all stand in agreement against him. See, e.g., Raymond E. Brown, *The Epistles of John* (AB; Garden City, N.J.: Doubleday, 1982), 651–55; Stephen S. Smalley, *1, 2, 3 John* (WBC; Dallas: Word, 1984), 318; John R. W. Stott, *The Epistles of John* (TNTC; Grand Rapids: Eerdmans, 1964), 200–201.

The lady designates the church as a whole, and the children refer to the individual members of the church.

The support for women serving as elders or leaders vanishes when closely examined. The most plausible argument for the egalitarian view comes from the example of Junia, for she and Andronicus are identified as apostles in Romans 16:7.[36] But the verse is far too ambiguous to make a case. It is hermeneutically akin to finding support for baptism for the dead from 1 Corinthians 15:29, for the purpose of the verse is not to speak to women in leadership roles. The text is ambiguous at three levels: First, is Paul referring to a man or a woman? Second, are Andronicus and Junia(s) outstanding in the eyes of the apostles, or are they outstanding apostles themselves? Third, is the term "apostle" used as a technical term, or is it used nontechnically to refer to missionaries?

Scholars continue to debate whether the reference is to a man or a woman (Junias or Junia). If it is the male Junias, then we have a contraction of the name Junianus. Personally, I believe a woman is in view. This was the majority view in the history of the church until at least the thirteenth century. Moreover, a contraction of Junianus is nowhere else found in Greek literature, and so I think we can be confident Junia was a woman.

Second, is Paul saying Andronicus and Junia were "outstanding among the apostles," or "outstanding in the eyes of the apostles"? The former is the view of almost all commentators. Michael Burer and Daniel Wallace, however, recently conducted an intensive search and analysis of the phrase, compiling evidence to support the idea that "noteworthy in the eyes of the apostles" is the best translation.[37] Their research indicates it is unlikely that Junia is identified as an apostle here, and hence the verse says nothing about women serving in the apostolic office.

---

[36]For a careful assessment of the evidence, see Andreas J. Köstenberger, "Women in the Pauline Mission," in *The Gospel to the Nations: Perspectives on Paul's Mission*, eds. Peter G. Bolt and Mark Thompson (Downers Grove, Ill.: InterVarsity, 2000), 221–47. For further discussion on Junia see John Thorley, "Junia, A Woman Apostle?" *NovT* 39 (1996): 18–21; Richard S. Cervin, "A Note Regarding the Name 'Junia(s)' in Romans 16.7," *NTS* 40 (1994): 464–70; Schreiner, *Romans*, 795–97.

[37]Michael H. Burer and Daniel B. Wallace, "Was Junia Really an Apostle? A Reexamination of Romans 16:7," *New Testament Studies* 47 (2001): 76–91. See now Richard Bauckham who has raised serious objections about the interpretation of the evidence proposed by Wallace and Burer in his *Gospel Women: Studies of the Named Women in the Gospels* (Grand Rapids: Eerdmans, 2002), 172–80.

Further research, however, may indicate Burer and Wallace are mistaken, and support the conclusion that Junia is identified as an apostle. If women served as apostles, can any leadership role be ruled out for them?

But here a third consideration arises. Paul is not assigning Andronicus and Junia a place with the Twelve. The term *apostolos* is not always a technical term (e.g., 2 Cor. 8:23; Phil. 2:25).[38] It can also be used in a nontechnical sense to refer to missionaries. Biblical commentator Rudolf Schnackenburg wrote, "The apostles referred to in Romans 16:7, without further qualification, could hardly have been anything else but itinerant missionaries."[39] In the Apostolic Fathers, *apostolos* is used of itinerant evangelists.[40] If Junia was an apostle, she probably functioned particularly as a missionary to women. Ernst Käsemann observed that "the wife can have access to the women's areas, which would not be generally accessible to the husband."[41] In the culture of Paul's day, the reading of Käsemann and Schnackenburg is much more likely than the modern view that Junia was an apostle in the technical sense. To sum up, the verse does not clearly identify Junia as an apostle, and even if this view is incorrect, "apostle" is not used in a technical sense.

Egalitarians, however, detect a contradiction when complementarians say women can function as missionaries but not as pastors. I think Romans 6:7 and Philippians 4:2–3 indicate that women did indeed function as missionaries, and complementarians should celebrate and encourage such a ministry. But I fail to see the contradiction, for the very same Paul who celebrated women missionaries also prohibited them from serving as pastors/overseers/elders. If there is a contradiction, it exists in Paul himself, and no evangelical would want to say this. Paul,

---

[38]See Wolf-Henning Ollrog, *Paulus und seine Mitarbeiter: Untersuchungen zu Theorie and Praxis der paulinischen Mission* (WMANT 50; Neukirchen-Vluyn: Neukirchener Verlag, 1979), 79–84.

[39]Rudolf Schnackenburg, "Apostles before and during Paul's Time," in *Apostolic History and the Gospel*, eds. W. W. Gasque and R. P. Martin (Grand Rapids: Eerdmans, 1970), 294; so also E. Earle Ellis, *Pauline Theology: Ministry and Society* (Grand Rapids: Eerdmans, 1989), 66.

[40]*Did.* 11:3–6; Herm. *Vis.* 13.1; Herm. *Sim.* 92.4; 93.5; 102.2.

[41]Ernst Käsemann, *Commentary on Romans* (Grand Rapids: Eerdmans, 1980), 413; so also Peter Stuhlmacher, *Paul's Letter to the Romans* (Louisville, Ky.: Westminster, 1994), 249.

moved by the Holy Spirit, barred women from the pastoral office and permitted them to be missionaries.

Many women missionaries in the history of the church have agreed with the complementarian view, and once a church was planted in a particular mission field, male leaders were appointed. I am not, however, baptizing everything women missionaries have done in the field throughout history. Very likely some roles were fitting and others questionable. We derive our view of what women missionaries can and should do from Scripture, not from what they have actually done. We would not want to claim that everything male missionaries have done has been right either. Nonetheless, many women missionaries throughout history have actually held the complementarian view and ministered and preached the gospel in such a way that this view was not violated.

DIFFERENT ROLES FOR MEN AND WOMEN IN THE FAMILY

Established in Genesis 1–3

We have already seen that men and women equally are made in God's image (Gen. 1:26–27) and are thus of equal value and significance as God's creatures. But I would also contend there are six indications in Genesis 1–3 of a role differentiation between men and women. By role differentiation I mean Adam has the responsibility of leadership and Eve has the responsibility to follow his leadership. Before explaining these six points I must make a crucial comment: *Equality of personhood does not rule out differences in role.* For moderns, the tension between these two truths (equality of personhood and differences in role) is nearly unbearable. For instance, the basic point of Rebecca Merrill Groothuis's book *Good News for Women* is that one cannot logically posit both equality of personhood and differences in role. Groothuis, however, simply reveals that she imbibes the modern enlightenment view of equality, which insists that equality must involve equality of *function.* Anyone familiar with American society knows that this notion of equality continues to exert tremendous influence.

The biblical view, however, is very different. God is not an equal opportunity employer—at least as far as installation into ministry is concerned. God decreed that priests could come *only from the tribe of Levi*, but all Israelites had equal worth and dignity before God.[42] Similarly, the pastoral role is reserved for men only, and yet women have equal dignity and value as persons created in God's image. Groothuis and other egalitarians are faced with the daunting prospect of saying that Israelites who could never serve as priests are of less dignity and value than those who were qualified for the priesthood.[43] Complementarians are spared such a problematic conclusion, for we acknowledge that a permanent difference in role (the tribe of Joseph could never serve as priests) does not mean those who cannot fill that role (descendants of Joseph) are of lesser worth or dignity.

The six indications Adam had a special responsibility as a leader are these:

1. God created Adam first, and then he created Eve.
2. God gave Adam the command not to eat from the tree of the knowledge of good and evil.
3. God created Eve to be a helper for Adam.
4. Adam exercised his leadership by naming the creature God formed out of Adam's rib "woman."
5. The serpent subverted God's pattern of leadership by tempting Eve rather than Adam.
6. God approached Adam first after the couple had sinned, even though Eve sinned first.

I am not suggesting every one of these arguments is of equal weight or clarity. Arguments two and five, for example, are plausible only if the other arguments are credible. They cannot stand alone as decisive arguments for the interpretation proposed. Each argument needs to be investigated briefly.

Adam Was Created before Eve

First, the responsibility for leadership belonged to Adam (and hence to males) because Adam was created before Eve (Gen. 2:7, 21–24). I am unpersuaded by those who argue that Adam was neither male nor female—a sexually undifferentiated

---

[42]See James B. Hurley, *Man and Woman in Biblical Perspective* (Grand Rapids: Zondervan, 1981), 44–45.

[43]Grenz (*Women in the Church*, 152) faces the same problem.

being—before the creation of Eve.[44] When Yahweh fashioned the woman out of the man, he made a person who was suitable for the man (v. 18), and Adam recognized her as a fitting counterpart (v. 23). What the text emphasizes is the creation of Adam first and the act of the woman being formed from the man's rib (vv. 21–23). Nothing is said about *ha-ʾādām* suddenly becoming male. Nor does the creation account in Genesis 2 abandon the theme of equality, for, as Adam said, the woman was "bone of my bones, and flesh of my flesh" (v. 23). The man and woman were united in a love relationship as partners (v. 24).

The narrative in Genesis 2, however, adds a dimension that is missing in chapter 1.[45] Contemporary scholars rightly emphasize that the narrative was written carefully and artistically to convey a message to readers.[46] The discerning reader observes that the man was created before the woman and that the woman was even fashioned from part of the man. The narrator writes with great skill, summoning us to ponder thoughtfully the elements of the story. Why does the narrator bother to tell us the man was created first and then the woman? That the woman shares full humanity and personhood with the man is evident, as we have already seen, from 2:23–24. But if the only point of the story were the equality of men and women, then creation at the same point in time would be most fitting. An egalitarian message would be communicated nicely by the creation of man and woman at the same instant. I believe the narrator relays the creation of man *first* to signal that Adam (and hence males in general) had a particular responsibility to lead in his relationship with Eve. Correspondingly, Eve had a responsibility to follow Adam's leadership.

Egalitarians object to this interpretation by saying such logic would lead us to think that animals should rule over human beings, since animals were created before humans.[47] This objection has always struck me as a clever debating point instead of a substantive argument. The narrator did not worry about readers drawing such a conclusion, since it is patently obvious

---

[44]So Phyllis Trible, *God and the Rhetoric of Sexuality* (Philadelphia: Fortress, 1978), 80, 98.

[45]I believe the two creation accounts are complementary, not contradictory.

[46]See Robert Alter, *The Art of Biblical Narrative* (New York: Basic Books, 1981).

[47]So Paul Jewett, *Man as Male and Female: A Study of Sexual Relationships from a Theological Point of View* (Grand Rapids: Eerdmans, 1975), 126–27.

human beings are distinguished from animals, insofar as humans are the only creatures made in God's image (1:26–27). But readers *would* be inclined to ask this question: "Why is the human race differentiated into male and female, and why is the male created first?" A more serious response could be that females were created last as the crown of creation, and if anything, females rather than males would assume leadership. Such a reading would fit the pattern of Genesis 1, where human beings are created last and are responsible to rule the world for God. This latter reading suffers, however, from imposing the narrative pattern of Genesis 1 on Genesis 2. Instead, the Hebrew reader would be disposed to read the second creation account in terms of *primogeniture*.[48] The firstborn male has authority over the younger brothers after the father dies. The reversal of primogeniture explains why the stories of Jacob's primacy over Esau (chs. 26–36) and Joseph's rule over his brothers are so shocking (chs. 37–50).

Egalitarians, of course, face another problem with their particular reading of Genesis 2—a canonical one. Paul forbids women to teach and exercise authority over a man because Adam was created before Eve (1 Tim. 2:12–13). Many egalitarians, when interpreting Genesis 2, fail to mention 1 Timothy 2:12–13. The most natural reading of the words of Paul in 1 Timothy 2:11–15 supports the complementarian interpretation of Genesis 2: men bear the responsibility to lead and teach in the church *because* Adam was created before Eve (see also 1 Cor. 11:8–9).

The Command Was Given to Adam, Not Eve

Second, the command to refrain from eating from the tree of the knowledge of good and evil was given to Adam, not to Eve (Gen. 2:16–17). This argument for male leadership is not decisive but suggestive. God likely commissioned Adam to instruct Eve about this command, signaling Adam's responsibility for leadership and teaching in the relationship. Closely connected is the injunction given to Adam to cultivate and take care of the garden of Eden (v. 15). It is possible, of course, that nothing should be made of the fact that the prohibition in verses 16–17 was given only to Adam. On the other hand, the story

---

[48]See Hurley, *Man and Woman in Biblical Perspective*, 207–8.

could have been constructed so that the command was given to the husband and wife. I believe the narrator is providing a hint of male leadership by revealing the restriction was communicated only to Adam.

Eve Was Created to Be a Helper

The third indication of male leadership is that Eve was created as a "helper" (ʿēzer) for Adam (vv. 18, 20). The standard egalitarian objection is that Yahweh is often designated as Israel's helper, and yet he is clearly not subordinate to Israel.[49] Yahweh surely is Israel's helper in that he saves and delivers Israel—so how can complementarians possibly think that describing Eve as Adam's helper *supports* the case for male headship? If anything, it seems the argument could be reversed. Yahweh was Israel's helper *and leader*. The objection appears to be a strong one, and it has the merit of precluding a simplistic argument for the complementarian view.

The egalitarian interpretation, however, is also in danger of promoting a simplistic argument that is not contextually grounded. Anyone who has read the OT knows that Yahweh was often portrayed as Israel's helper, and thus the term "helper" alone does not signify male leadership in Genesis 2. And yet words are assigned their meanings in context, and in the narrative context of Genesis 1–3, the word "helper" signifies that Eve was to help Adam in the task of ruling over creation. Indeed, in some contexts in the OT, the word "help" designates those who assist a superior or ruler in accomplishing his task.[50] For instance, in 1 Kings 20:16, thirty-two kings who have less power than Ben-hadad helped him in war. Indeed, the verb "to help" is used of warriors who helped David militarily (1 Chron. 12:1, 22–23), and it is clear David was the leader and they were assisting him. Similarly, David exhorted leaders to help Solomon when he was king (22:17), in which case there is no doubt these leaders were assisting Solomon in his leadership over the nation. An army also helped King Uzziah in a military campaign (2 Chr.

---

[49]So Trible, *God and the Rhetoric of Sexuality*, 90.

[50]See David J. A. Clines, "What Does Eve Do to Help? and Other Irredeemably Androcentric Orientations in Genesis 1–3," in *What Does Eve Do to Help? and Other Readerly Questions in the Old Testament*, ed. David J. A. Clines (JSOTSup; Sheffield: Sheffield Academic Press, 1990), 31–32.

26:13). Yahweh pledged he would nullify those who helped the prince in Jerusalem (Ezek. 12:14; cf. 32:21), and those who helped were obviously subordinates of the prince. These examples show that context is decisive in determining whether the one who helps has a superior or inferior role. Egalitarians cannot dismiss the complementarian view simply by saying that Yahweh helped Israel, for in other texts it is clear that leaders were helped by those who were under their authority.

I believe there is contextual warrant in Genesis 1–3 for the idea that women help men by supporting the leadership of the latter. If we read Genesis carefully, we see that the rule of human beings over creation, which is a call to careful stewardship (not exploitation), is combined with the injunction to have offspring who will, in turn, exercise dominion over the earth for God's glory (1:26, 28). One of the ways women help men, therefore, is by bearing children, as David J. A. Clines rightly argues. I am not suggesting this is the only way women function as helpers, but the difference in roles between men and women is established at creation in that only women bear children. We are not surprised to learn that the curse on Adam focuses on his work in the fields, so that thorns and thistles grow as a consequence of his sin (3:17–19). Correspondingly, Eve is cursed in her sphere, so that she experiences pain in the bearing of children (v. 16).[51] It is important to notice that the distinct role of women—bearing children—is *not* the result of the fall. The consequence of the fall is an *increase in pain* during childbirth, but the actual bearing of children, which is the distinct task of the woman, was established before sin entered the world.

A contemporary observation is appropriate here. The support of abortion rights by radical feminists is closely linked with the goal of changing the role of women. Radical feminists rightly perceive that pregnancy and giving birth to children distinguish women from men. If women are liberated so that sexual relations are severed from motherhood, then women can enjoy the same rights as men. I would contend that such feminist aspirations run counter to God's created intention, for God himself decreed that women, and not men, would bear children.

Once again, a canonical reading of Scripture confirms the interpretation adopted here. In 1 Corinthians 11:8–9, Paul reflects

---

[51]Ibid., 33–36.

on the narrative in Genesis 2, for in 1 Corinthians 11:8 he observes that man did not come from woman, but woman from man. Then in verse 9 he declares, "For indeed man was not created for the woman's sake, but woman for the man's sake." How do we explain Paul's words in this verse? I think it is quite likely he was reflecting on the word "helper" in Genesis 2:18, 20. We know the creation account in Genesis 2 was in his mind, and the notion that woman was created "for the man's sake" is almost certainly a Pauline commentary on the word "helper." The woman was created for Adam's sake to help in ruling the world for God's glory. Such an interpretation of 1 Corinthians 11:9 fits the context of that chapter nicely, since man is designated here as the "head" of the woman (v. 3). We have strong Pauline evidence, therefore, that "helper" refers to the subordinate role of women.

The Woman Was Named by the Man

I am now prepared to assert my fourth argument from Genesis—the naming of the woman by Adam. A prefatory comment is in order. For clarity each of the arguments presented is separated from the other, but we need to remember that each one is closely linked in the narrative. For example, the narrator linked the naming of the animals with the man's need for a helper (2:18–20). The narrator wanted us to perceive that a suitable helper was not found among the animals. Adam needed a partner who was bone of his bones and flesh of his flesh (v. 23) to assist him in his task of cultivating and caring for God's garden. A unique creative work of God was needed in order to provide a woman for him. Adam perceived, when naming the birds, wild animals, and domestic animals, that none of these were suitable partners. The intertwining of the various parts of the narrative actually functions as an argument for the complementarian view, for we must see that the word "helper" appears in a context in which animals are named by Adam.

What is the significance of the naming of the creatures God made (vv. 18–20)? The link in the text is obvious, for this was certainly one of the means by which Adam exercised his rule over the creatures according to God's mandate (1:26, 28; 2:15).[52] God exercised his rule and sovereignty in calling the light "day" and the darkness "night" (1:5), and in naming the firmament

---

[52]See Hurley, *Man and Woman in Biblical Perspective*, 210–12.

"heaven" and the dry land "earth" (vv. 8, 10). Similarly, Adam exercised his rule, under God's lordship, by naming the animals. Even today the scientific study of species consists in classification and naming. We distinguish dogs from cats and whales from seals. Naming the animals was not a whimsical and arbitrary game for Adam. He named the animals so that their names corresponded to their nature. It is significant that Adam named the animals, and not vice versa! The narrator signals that Adam was beginning to fulfill God's mandate to exercise dominion over the world and God's garden.

The naming of the woman occurs in 2:23, suggesting that Adam had the responsibility for leadership in the relationship. It would be easy to misconstrue my argument here. I am certainly not suggesting Eve was comparable to the animals! The very point of the narrative is that she was remarkably different, wholly suitable to function as Adam's helper. Contrary to the animals, she was taken from the man and was bone of his bones and flesh of his flesh. The man instantly and gladly perceived the difference (v. 23)! As noted before, the mutuality and equality of man and woman are also communicated in the narrative.

Nonetheless, the leadership role of Adam is also reflected in the narrative. He perceived she was different from the animals and qārā᾽ ("called") her by the name ᾽iššâ ("woman," v. 23), using the same verb for the naming of animals in verses 19–20. The assigning of a name to the woman in such an abbreviated narrative is highly significant. Yahweh could have reserved such a task for himself and removed any hint of male leadership. Of course, the woman is remarkably different from all the other creatures God made, but Adam's naming of the woman signifies that he bears the leadership role. There is no exegetical warrant for assigning a different significance to the naming of the animals and the woman. We need to be very careful here. In both instances naming is a symbol of rule, but it would be unwarranted to deduce that the rule is precisely the same or that women are like animals. The entire narrative illustrates there was both continuity and discontinuity between Adam's rule over woman and his dominion over God's creatures.

The most significant objection to this interpretation is found in the work of Phyllis Trible.[53] She says the notion of naming is

[53]See Trible, *God and the Rhetoric of Sexuality*, 99–100.

only present when the verb *qārā'* ("call") is joined with the noun *šēm* ("name"), pointing to a number of texts in which "name" is joined with "call" (e.g., 4:17, 25–26). The naming of animals, according to Trible, signified Adam's power and authority over them, but no parallel can be drawn to 2:23, since the woman was not named there. Trible's argument is unpersuasive.[54] She is correct that the noun "name" is usually linked with "call" in naming formulas, but she mistakenly concludes the noun "name" must be present in order for naming to occur. Such a conclusion demands more precision from language than is warranted, for we must not demand in advance that naming occurs only when a predetermined pattern is followed. The repetition of the verb *qārā'* (2:19–20, 23) links the naming of the woman with the naming of the animals, so that the reader naturally recognizes the parallel between the two accounts. Adam perceived she was "woman" precisely because she was taken from the man, revealing that his classification was in accord with reality and that he understood the remarkable difference between woman and the animals.

Trible's more substantive objection is that calling this person *'iššâ* ("woman" [v. 23]) cannot be equated with naming, for "woman" is "not a name; it is a common noun, not a proper noun. It designates gender; it does not specify a person."[55] Trible's comment reveals she misunderstood the parallel between the naming of the animals and the naming of the woman. When Adam named the animals, he did not give them personal or proper names. He classified the animals into distinct groups, presumably distinguishing between, say, lions, tigers, and bears. He did not name any tigers "Tony." He identified them as tigers over against bears.

So too, it is completely irrelevant that a personal or proper name is lacking for the woman in verse 23. In naming the woman, Adam was classifying her—in effect, distinguishing her from the other creatures named. He recognized her distinctiveness and aptly captured it with the name "woman," thereby noticing how closely related she was to himself as a man. To conclude, male leadership

---

[54]Contra Trible's view, see Clines, "What Does Eve Do to Help?" 37–40 (esp. 39, n. 3). George W. Ramsey ("Is Name-Giving an Act of Domination in Genesis 2:23 and Elsewhere?" *CBQ* 50 [1988]: 24–35) maintains that naming is linked only with discernment, not domination. But this view ignores the connection between the injunction to rule the world and the act of naming.

[55]Cited in Clines, "What Does Eve Do to Help?" 100.

is communicated by the naming of the woman, and the parallel with naming the animals stands, even though the biblical narrator hardly suggests animals and women are parallel in every way.[56]

The Serpent Tempted Eve, Not Adam

The fifth indication of male leadership is that the serpent, which was exceedingly astute, approached Eve rather than Adam in the temptation (3:1–7). Thereby he subverted the pattern of male leadership, as Paul himself hints at in 1 Timothy 2:14. I don't want to make too much of this argument, and my case hardly depends on it. I acknowledge forthrightly it could be incorrect, but in any case it would not affect the other arguments presented. I mention it because I am persuaded that what actually occurred (and what did not occur) in the narrative is significant.

Adam Was Rebuked before Eve

Finally, the responsibility of men is indicated by the fact that Adam was rebuked before Eve (Gen. 3:8–12). If God were truly egalitarian, Eve would have been reprimanded first, since she ate the fruit before her husband and presumably convinced Adam to eat of it as well. Yahweh spoke to Adam first because he bore primary responsibility for what occurred in the garden. In Romans 5:12–19, Paul confirms this reading of the narrative, for the sin of the human race was traced to Adam, not to Eve. I am not suggesting Eve bore no responsibility for her sin. Yahweh censured her actions as well and judged her for what she did (vv. 13, 16). Greater responsibility, however, is assigned to Adam as the leader of the first human couple.

Before the Fall

It is crucial to see that these six arguments relate to the relationship between Adam and Eve before the fall. God instituted role distinctions between men and women before sin ever entered the world. Even the two arguments I presented from

---

[56]Incidentally, Trible's view that the naming of Eve (Gen. 3:20) is an inappropriate act of male dominance (*God and the Rhetoric of Sexuality*, 133–34) is unconvincing, for the text provides no clue that an abuse of power is involved. Instead, this word is linked in the narrative with the promise of life (vv. 20–21). For a critique of Trible, see Clines, "What Does Eve Do to Help?" 39.

Genesis 3 depend on a role difference established before the fall. If Adam and Eve possessed different roles before the fall, then the distinct roles of men and women are not the result of sin; they would stem from God's intention in creation—and everything God created is good. Male leadership is not the result of the fall, but it is God's good and perfect will for man and woman.

The doctrine of creation is of enormous significance for the debate on the roles of men and women. From Jesus himself, we know marriage is to be permanent because permanence in marriage was God's intent in creating us male and female (Gen. 1:26–27; 2:24; Matt. 19:3–12). We know homosexuality is prohibited because it counters God's creational intent (Rom. 1:26–27). We know food is to be eaten with thanksgiving because God created it (1 Tim. 4:1–5). Similarly, we know role differences between men and women are not the result of the fall but are part of the fabric of God's good and perfect created order.

Sin has entered the world and distorted how men and women relate to one another. Men transgress by turning their responsibility to lead into a privilege so that they tyrannically abuse their authority or abdicate their responsibility and descend into abject passivity. Women try to subvert male leadership by contesting their leadership or by responding with an obsequiousness that is not fitting.[57] Similarly, we can see how sin has thwarted God's intent that a man and woman should remain married for life, with the result that divorce is all too common. But role differences, like the permanence of marriage, remain God's intention. And such differences in role are good and beautiful and, through the redemption accomplished by Christ, can be lived out today in a beautiful, albeit not perfect, way.

Confirmed in Marriage Texts

We are debating the role of women in ministry in this book, not whether husbands and wives have different functions within a marriage. And yet this latter issue cannot and must not be neglected, for the biblical teaching about the family forms the fabric and background for what is said about women in ministry. If role differences exist in the family, they plausibly exist in

---

[57]My view here depends on my interpretation of Genesis 3:16, which I do not have space here to explain. See Susan T. Foh, "What Is the Woman's Desire?" *WTJ* 37 (1975): 376–83.

the church as well. Indeed, in 1 Timothy 3:15, Paul compares the church to God's household, and in 5:1–2, Paul exhorts Timothy to treat other church members as he would a father or a mother, a brother or a sister.[58] We must note that Paul does not instruct Timothy to treat everyone with undifferentiated sameness. The wise person responds differently when speaking to an older man rather than to a younger man, in a way that shows more deference and respect for the older man's experience. If God has assigned husbands a particular responsibility as leaders of their homes, it would make sense he has also ordained that men should bear responsibility in the leadership of the church. Ministry and family should not be segregated rigidly from one another. The two spheres interpenetrate, and what is true of the one is generally accurate in the other.

When we examine the biblical texts on husbands and wives, it is clear husbands have a responsibility to exercise loving leadership, and wives are called on to submit (Eph. 5:22–33; Col. 3:18–19; Titus 2:4–5; 1 Pet. 3:1–7). Space precludes a detailed analysis of these texts, and thus only a few major issues can be addressed here, particularly those areas where egalitarians question the complementarian view. We should note at the outset that husbands are exhorted to love their wives, to refrain from all bitterness, and to treat them gently. The Bible nowhere suggests the husband's leadership is to be used as a platform for selfishness or for abuse of his wife. Rather, the husband should pattern himself after Christ, exercising a loving leadership on the wife's behalf. I want to add only that the love and tenderness of a husband is still exercised *in leadership*. Christ served the church by giving his life for it, and yet he remains the leader and Lord of the church. We ought not to think, therefore, that the leadership of husbands is canceled out in the call to serve.

Many egalitarians appeal to Ephesians 5:21 ("Be subject to one another in the fear of Christ") to support mutual submission in marriage, but the argument is unpersuasive.[59] When the verse is interpreted in context, it is doubtful mutual submission in marriage

---

[58]For an illuminating study on the relationship between the church and the family, see Vern S. Poythress, "The Church as Family: Why Male Leadership in the Family Requires Male Leadership in the Church," in *Recovering Biblical Manhood and Womanhood*, 233–47.

[59]See, e.g., Grenz, *Women in the Church*, 115, 178; Keener, *Paul, Women and Wives*, 159, 168–72.

is intended. Verse 21 is transitional, bridging the gap between verses 18–20 and the household exhortations in 5:22–6:9. It is doubtful, though, that the content of 5:21 should be read into the exhortations that follow. Otherwise, Paul would be suggesting that parents and children (6:1–4) and masters and slaves (vv. 5–9) should mutually submit to each other. It is highly implausible that parents would be encouraged to submit to children, or masters to submit to slaves.[60] While such an idea may appeal to some people today, it would scarcely enter into the mind of someone writing almost two thousand years ago. We look in vain for any clear indication elsewhere in the Scriptures that parents should submit to children, or masters to slaves.[61] Nor do the Scriptures ever call on husbands to submit to their wives, but they consistently summon wives to submit to their husbands.

How, then, should we interpret Ephesians 5:21? Two interpretations cohere with the complementarian view. Paul may have in mind the relationship we have with one another in the church (see vv. 19–21), one in which believers mutually submit to one another. These words cannot be imposed on the marriage relationship but refer instead to a corporate setting in which believers praise God in song and submit to one another in the community.[62] Alternatively, but perhaps less likely, Paul refers to the submission of some to others in the church. According to

---

[60]So Hurley, *Man and Woman in Biblical Perspective*, 158.

[61]Keener (*Paul, Women and Wives*, 186–88) acknowledges that mutual submission is not demanded of children, showing his inconsistency, for if this is the case, Ephesians 5:21 does *not* function as the introduction to all of 5:22–6:9. Nor do I find persuasive Keener's view (*Paul, Women and Wives*, 206) that 6:9 teaches submission for masters. The persistent fact is that husbands, parents, and masters are never told to submit to wives, children, and slaves, respectively.

[62]I am not suggesting, incidentally, that husbands never follow the advice of their wives. Wise husbands do so often. Some complementarians interpret verse 21 to say that only some members of the congregation submit to others (e.g., Wayne Grudem, "The Myth of Mutual Submission as an Interpretation of Ephesians 5:21," in *Biblical Foundations for Manhood and Womanhood*, ed. Wayne Grudem [Wheaton, Ill.: Crossway, 2002], 228–29; cf. also Hurley, *Man and Woman in Biblical Perspective*, 139–41). Such a reading is possible but unpersuasive, for typically the pronoun *allēlois* refers to all members of the congregation (see Ernest Best, *A Critical and Exegetical Commentary on Ephesians* [ICC; Edinburgh: T&T Clark, 1998], 516). A call to submit to one another as brothers and sisters in the church does not yield the conclusion that husbands should submit to wives or that parents should submit to children. Verse 21 refers to the corporate life, where all members are enjoined to submit to one another. Daniel Doriani's article ("The Historical Novelty of Egalitarian Interpretations of Ephesians

this view, the subsequent context indicates who is to submit to whom—wives to husbands, children to parents, and slaves to masters.[63]

Others contest the complementarian view by disputing the meaning of *kephalē* ("head"). Egalitarians typically define it to mean "source" instead of "authority over."[64] The meaning of the term *kephalē* can be established only by a careful analysis of its use in biblical and extrabiblical literature. Wayne Grudem and Joseph Fitzmyer have demonstrated that "authority over" in many contexts is the most likely meaning of the term.[65] It may well be, however, that *kephalē* in some contexts denotes both "authority over" and "source," as Clinton Arnold argues.[66] The definitions "authority over" and "source" make sense of Colossians 2:19 and Ephesians 4:15, where Christ as the Head both reigns over and provides for the church.

In any case, even if *kephalē* should be defined only as "source" (which is very unlikely), it would still support male leadership. Let me explain. In Ephesians 5:22–24 Paul exhorts wives to submit to their husbands in everything. What reason is given for such a command? Paul provides the rationale in verse

---

5:21–22," in *Biblical Foundations for Manhood and Womanhood*, 203–19) indicates that many scholars throughout the history of the church have understood the text in the way I suggest here.

[63]So Peter O'Brien, *The Letter to the Ephesians* (PNTC; Grand Rapids: Eerdmans, 1999), 400–404, and previous note above.

[64]See, e.g., Gilbert Bilezikian, *Beyond Sex Roles: What the Bible Says About a Woman's Place in Church and Family*, rev. ed. (Grand Rapids: Baker, 1985), 215–52; Berkeley and Alvera Mickelsen, "What Does *Kephalē* Mean in the New Testament?" in *Women, Authority and the Bible*, 97–110; Catherine Clark Kroeger, "The Classical Concept of *Head* as 'Source,'" in Hull, *Equal to Serve*, 267–83. For another complementarian view, see Richard S. Cervin, "Does *Kephalē* Mean 'Source' or 'Authority' in Greek Literature? A Rebuttal," *TJ* 10 (1989): 85–112. For the weaknesses in Cervin's view as well, see the second article listed under Grudem in the next note.

[65]See Wayne Grudem, "Does *Kephalē* ('Head') Mean 'Source' or 'Authority Over' in Greek Literature? A Survey of 2,336 Examples," *TJ* 6 (1985): 38–59; Grudem, "The Meaning of *Kephalē* ('Head'): A Response to Recent Studies," in *Recovering Biblical Manhood and Womanhood*, 425–68, 534–41; Grudem, "The Meaning of *Kephalē* ('Head'): An Examination of New Evidence, Real and Alleged," *JETS* 44 (2001): 25–65; Joseph A. Fitzmyer, "*Kephalē* in 1 Corinthians 11:3," *Int* 47 (1993): 52–59.

[66]See Clinton E. Arnold, "Jesus Christ: 'Head' of the Church (Colossians and Ephesians)," in *Jesus of Nazareth: Lord and Christ. Essays on the Historical Jesus and New Testament Christology*, eds. J. B. Green and M. Turner (Grand Rapids: Eerdmans, 1994), 346–66.

23 (note the *hoti*): "For the husband is the head of the wife, as Christ also is the head of the church." If the word *kephalē* means "source," then Paul exhorts wives to submit because their husbands are their source. So even if *kephalē* means "source," wives are to fill a supportive and submissive role, and husbands, as the "source," are to function as leaders.

The same argument prevails in 1 Corinthians 11:2–16. If *kephalē* means "source," then women are to defer to their source by adorning themselves properly. The idea that the source has particular authority hearkens back to Genesis 2:21–25, where the woman comes from the man (see 1 Cor. 11:8). Similarly, children should obey their parents because parents are the source of their existence. Nonetheless, the meaning "authority over" cannot be exorcised from Ephesians 5:22–24, for the call for wives to submit to their husbands as the church submits to Christ indicates that the *authority* of Christ as Head is in view (cf. Eph. 1:22; Col. 1:18; 2:10). I am not denying there may be an idea of *source* as well, since husbands are to nourish and care for their wives, just as Christ has tenderly loved the church. In any case, the husband's special role as the leader of his wife cannot be explained away in Ephesians 5:22–33.

A few egalitarians have maintained that the word "submit" (*hypotassō*) does not connote the idea of obedience. For instance, Gretchen Gaebelein Hull suggests that *hypotassō* means "to identify with" rather than "to obey."[67] Certainly there is no suggestion that husbands should *compel* their wives to submit. Submission is a voluntary and glad response on the part of wives, and husbands are commanded to *love* their wives, not to see to it that they submit. Nor is it fitting if a wife's submission is conceived of in terms of a child's obedience to parents, for the relationship of a husband and wife is remarkably different from the relationship between a parent and a child. Indeed, Paul can speak of the mutual obligations husbands and wives have to one another (1 Cor. 7:3–5), emphasizing that the husband ultimately does not have authority over his own body and that the wife has authority over his body. Complementarians have too often made the mistake of envisioning the husband-wife relationship in one-dimensional terms, so that any idea of mutuality and partnership is removed and wives are conceived of as servants (or even as slaves) of husbands. Such

---

[67]See Hull, *Equal to Serve*, 195.

a militaristic conception of marriage is foreign to the biblical perspective, and 1 Corinthians 7:3–5 reminds us that mutuality also characterizes the marriage relationship. Indeed, any marriage relationship that lacks such a sense of mutuality has serious problems!

On the other hand, we cannot dismiss the particular calling of the wife to submit, and such submission does involve obedience. In the Bible, submission is required to God's law (Rom. 8:7), to the government (13:1, 5; Titus 3:1; 1 Pet. 2:13), of slaves to masters (Titus 2:9; 1 Pet. 2:18), and of younger people to their elders (5:5). The submission of Christ to the Father (1 Cor. 15:27–28) and of demons to Christ (Eph. 1:21; 1 Pet. 3:22) is also described.

The above examples illustrate that the concept of obedience is involved in submission. Indeed, 1 Peter 3:5–6 removes any doubt, for Peter commends the holy women of the past, who were "submissive to their own husbands; just as Sarah obeyed Abraham." Notice the "just as" connecting the word "submissive" to the verb "obeyed." When Peter describes the submission of Sarah, he uses the word "obey" to portray it. Such submission should not be construed as demeaning or as a denial of a person's dignity or personhood, for Christ himself submits to the Father (1 Cor. 15:27–28)—and as the Son, he did what the Father commanded, yet there is no idea that the Son lacks dignity or worth. To say those who submit are of less worth and dignity is not a biblical worldview but a secular worldview that pervades our highly competitive society.[68] The example of Christ also clarifies that the obedience and submission of wives to husbands is not comparable to the obedience children should render to parents; after all, husbands and wives are mutual partners in a way parents and children are not.

Is it possible, though, that the submission required of wives is an example of cultural accommodation? In the contexts where wives are exhorted to submit to husbands we also see that slaves are commanded to submit to their masters (Eph. 5:22–33 and

---

[68]Most egalitarians deny that there is any sense in which the Son submits eternally to the Father. See, e.g., Gilbert Bilezikian, "Hermeneutical Bungee-Jumping: Subordination in the Godhead," *JETS* 40 (1997): 57–68. But Craig S. Keener ("Is Subordination within the Trinity Really Heresy? A Study of John 5:18 in Context," *TJ* 20 [1999]: 39–51), who is himself an egalitarian, properly suggests that the eternal subordination of the Son, rightly understood, is supported biblically.

6:5–9; Col. 3:18–19 and 3:22–4:1; Titus 2:4–5 and 2:9–10; 1 Pet. 2:18–25 and 3:1–7). Evangelical egalitarians accept as the word of God Paul's admonitions to slaves. In the culture of Paul's day, submission to masters was fitting, for societal revolution is not the means by which a culture is transformed. Indeed, in Paul's day, people would reject the gospel if they felt it was overturning cultural norms. So, it is argued, Paul counsels submission to wives "so that the word of God will not be dishonored" (Titus 2:5).[69] Similarly, slaves are to live responsibly "so that they will adorn the doctrine of God our Savior in every respect" (2:10).

In our culture, however, the same norms do not apply. Our contemporaries will reject the gospel, it is claimed, if women do not have the same rights as men, just as it would be a hindrance to the gospel if we recommended slavery. Egalitarians put the point even more sharply. If we insist wives should submit today and women cannot serve as pastors, then are we also recommending the reinstitution of slavery? Many Christians in the 1800s appealed to the Bible to defend slavery, and many egalitarians think those who defend the complementarian view on women's roles are making a similar mistake today.[70]

We must admit this objection is a thoughtful one. I believe egalitarians are correct in saying some of the commands and norms in Scripture are the result of cultural accommodation. Slavery is not God's ideal, and yet the Scriptures regulate and

---

[69]So Alan Padgett, "The Pauline Rationale for Submission: Biblical Feminism and the *hina* Clauses of Titus 2:1–10," *EvQ* 59 (1987): 39–52. This view has been advanced further and developed hermeneutically by William J. Webb, *Slaves, Women & Homosexuals: Exploring the Hermeneutics of Cultural Analysis* (Downers Grove, Ill.: InterVarsity, 2001). For my response, see Thomas R. Schreiner, "William J. Webb's *Slaves, Women & Homosexuals*: A Review Article," *SBJT* 6 (2002): 46–64.

[70]For this thesis, see Willard M. Swartley, *Slavery, Sabbath, War and Women: Case Issues in Biblical Interpretation* (Scottdale, Pa.: Herald, 1983); Keener, *Paul, Women and Wives*, 184–224; Kevin Giles, "The Biblical Case for Slavery: Can the Bible Mislead? A Case Study in Hermeneutics," *EvQ* 66 (1994): 3–17 (unfortunately, Giles [p. 4] relinquishes the Bible's authority in social relations). See the critique by Yarbrough, "The Hermeneutics of 1 Timothy 2:9–15," 189. For the ongoing debate, see Giles, "A Critique of the 'Novel' Contemporary Interpretation of 1 Timothy 2:9–15 Given in the Book, *Women in the Church*. Part I," *EvQ* 72 (2000): 151–67; Giles, "A Critique of the 'Novel' Contemporary Interpretation of 1 Timothy 2:9–15 Given in the Book, *Women in the Church*. Part II," *EvQ* 72 (2000): 195–215; Andreas J. Köstenberger, "Women in the Church: A Response to Kevin Giles," *EvQ* 73 (2001): 205–24; Giles, "*Women in the Church*: A Rejoinder to Andreas Köstenberger," *EvQ* 73 (2001): 225–43.

transform cultures in which slavery is practiced. The Bible does not recommend revolution to wipe out existing institutions but counsels a transformation from within. Paul, for instance, did not require Philemon to give up Onesimus as his slave, but he expected the relationship between master and slave to be transformed by their unity in Christ so that Onesimus would be treated as a brother in the Lord and not merely as a slave. If egalitarians are correct in saying that the admonitions to wives and the restrictions on women in ministry are analogous to the counsel given to slaves, then I would agree that the restrictions on women are due to cultural accommodation and are not required of believers today. Nevertheless, I think egalitarians make a crucial mistake when they draw a parallel between the exhortations given to slaves and those given to wives. The marriage relationship is not analogous to slavery, for slavery is an evil human institution regulated by Scripture. Marriage, on the other hand, is a creation ordinance of God and part of God's good will for human beings (Gen. 2:18–25). Thus, the parallel between marriage and slavery does not stand.[71]

The weakness of the parallel between slavery and marriage is obvious when the relationship between children and parents is introduced. In the household passages, Paul exhorts husbands and wives, parents and children, and masters and slaves (Eph. 5:22–6:9; Col. 3:18–4:1). The inclusion of parents and children is instructive. Those who say the admonition to wives is culturally bounded by appealing to the matter of slavery must also (to be consistent) say the admonition for children to obey their parents no longer applies today. But there is no doubt that children are mandated by God to obey their parents, and such a command is not harmful for children but is part of God's good intention for them.[72] Bearing and raising children is, from the time of creation, part of God's good intention for human beings (Gen. 1:28).

---

[71]Craig Keener (*Paul, Women and Wives*, 208–9) objects that the issue is whether a wife's submission to her husband is *permanently mandated*, not the ordinance of marriage itself. But I would contend Paul's argument in Ephesians 5:22–33 demonstrates that the marriage relationship mirrors Christ's relationship to the church. In addition, Genesis 2–3 indicates that role distinctions between husbands and wives was God's intention in creating man and woman.

[72]Of course, I am not denying that sin has affected the relationship between parents and children, with the result that no parents raise their children perfectly, and, in fact, some parents do great damage to their children.

Similarly, the marriage relationship stems from God's creational intent (2:18–25). The same cannot be said for slavery! Both the marriage and parent-child relationships hearken back to creation, but slavery does not, and hence the appeal to slavery as a parallel to the relationship between men and women fails.[73]

The analogy Paul draws between Christ and the church and husbands and wives in Ephesians 5:22–33 also demonstrates that the exhortations for husbands and wives are transcultural. Husbands are to pattern their love after Christ's love for the church, and wives are to submit in the same way the church submits to Christ. Verse 32 adds a crucial dimension to this argument. Paul remarks, "This mystery is great; but I am speaking with reference to Christ and the church." What Paul means is that the relationship of a husband and wife mirrors an even greater reality, namely, the relationship between Christ and the church. It is not the case that marriage was instituted first, and then God decided marriage would function as an illustration of Christ's relationship to the church.[74] Instead, from all eternity, God envisioned Christ's relationship to the church, and he instituted marriage as a picture or mirror of Christ's relationship to the church. The husband represents Christ, and the wife represents the church. We must beware, of course, of pressing the typological parallel too far, for a husband does not die for the wife or cleanse or purify her. But the typological relationship indicates the wife's submission to the husband is not merely a cultural accommodation to Greco-Roman society. Such submission mirrors to the world the church's submission to Christ.

Correspondingly, the husband's loving leadership is not a reflection of a patriarchal society but is intended to portray Christ's loving and saving work for his church. The institution of marriage and the responsibilities of husbands and wives

---

[73]Nor is it clear from Titus 2:3–5 that wives are to submit only in order to avoid cultural scandal in Paul's day. Padgett ("The Pauline Rationale for Submission") provides no clear basis by which we can discern whether the admonitions are culturally dated or transcendent, for in these very verses, Paul also summons wives to love their husbands and children, and to be kind, sensible, and pure. These commands are given for the same reason as the command to submit to husbands, namely, so that the gospel will be honored. But, of course, no one would think these commands no longer apply today.

[74]For an analysis of this theme, see Andreas J. Köstenberger, "The Mystery of Christ and the Church: Head and Body, 'One Flesh,'" *TJ* 12 (1991): 79–94.

within it are not culturally limited but are God's transcendent intention for all marriages for all time, since all marriages should reflect Christ's love for the church and the church's submission to Christ. Few believers ever think of their marriages in such terms, indicating that a secular mind-set has infiltrated our view of marriage as well. How glorious and beautiful and awesome it is to realize our marriages reflect Christ's love for the church and the church's loving response to Christ.

DIFFERENT ROLES FOR MEN AND WOMEN IN THE CHURCH

Women Prohibited from Teaching Men: 1 Timothy 2:11–15

It is not surprising to discover that, just as there are distinct roles between husbands and wives in the family, different roles between men and women are also mandated in the church. Women should not fill the role of pastor/elder/overseer. The fundamental text on this matter is 1 Timothy 2:11–15.[75] This text is a battleground in current scholarship, and entire books are being written on it.[76] In this essay I summarize my understanding of the passage. For a thorough treatment, I refer readers to a book I coedited (*Women in the Church: A Fresh Analysis of 1 Timothy 2:9–15*).[77]

---

[75]Some scholars believe Paul is addressing husbands and wives rather than men and women here. So, e.g., Gordon P. Hugenberger, "Women in Church Office: Hermeneutics or Exegesis? A Survey of Approaches to 1 Timothy 2:8–15," *JETS* 35 (1992): 341–60. Such a view is not contextually convincing. For a refutation, see my essay "An Interpretation of 1 Timothy 2:9–15: A Dialogue with Scholarship," in *Women in the Church: A Fresh Analysis*, 115–17.

[76]From the egalitarian point of view, see Richard Clark Kroeger and Catherine Clark Kroeger, *I Suffer Not a Woman: Rethinking 1 Timothy 2:11–15 in Light of Ancient Evidence* (Grand Rapids: Baker, 1992); Sharon H. Gritz, *Paul, Women Teachers, and the Mother Goddess at Ephesus: A Study of 1 Timothy 2:9–15 in Light of the Religious and Cultural Milieu of the First Century* (Lanham, Md.: University Press of America, 1991).

[77]A new edition is forthcoming, and I have used some of the wording from this new edition in a few of the footnotes below. For a recent attempt to support an egalitarian reading, see J. M. Holmes, "Text in a Whirlwind: A Critique of Four Exegetical Devices at 1 Timothy 2.9–15" (JSNTSup 196; Sheffield: Sheffield Academic Press, 2000). For a convincing rebuttal, see Andreas Köstenberger's review (*RBibLit* [www.bookreviews.org/pdf/974_506.pdf] (2001).

Before examining 1 Timothy 2:11–14, I want to comment on verses 9–10. Some ask why we forbid women from functioning as pastors when we do not prohibit women from wearing jewelry.[78] Let me say this: if the Scriptures (rightly interpreted) banned the wearing of jewelry, then we should cease wearing it. The Bible, not our culture, must reign supreme. On the other hand, we must interpret the Scriptures in their historical and cultural context. They were written to specific situations and to cultures that differed from our own. The prohibition regarding the braiding of hair and the wearing of jewelry would not surprise Paul's readers, for such admonitions were part of the common stock of ethical exhortation in the Greco-Roman world.[79]

Discerning why a command was given is appropriate, precisely because culture has changed. We must distinguish between the principle and the cultural outworking of a principle. We do not practice the holy kiss today (1 Cor. 16:20), but we still derive a principle from it, namely, to greet one another warmly in Christ—perhaps with a warm handshake or a hug. We do not demand that people with indigestion drink wine (1 Tim. 5:23), but we do think taking an antacid is advisable for those who suffer from stomach pain. Similarly, the principle in 1 Timothy 2:9–10 is that women should dress modestly and without ostentation.[80] As a complementarian, I do not believe we should try to revert to the culture of the biblical times; I do believe we should follow the moral norms and principles taught in the Bible.

So as we study 1 Timothy 2:12, we must discern how its admonition applies to us today. In verses 11–12 Paul exhorts the women to learn quietly and submissively, forbidding them to teach or exercise authority over a man. It has often been observed that Paul departs from some of his contemporaries in encouraging women to learn the Scriptures. The influence of Jesus, who instructed Mary (Luke 10:38–42), is obvious here. Nevertheless, the emphasis in this context is on the *manner* in

---

[78]So Alvera Mickelsen, "An Egalitarian View: There Is Neither Male nor Female in Christ," in *Women in Ministry: Four Views*, eds. Bonnidell Clouse and Robert G. Clouse (Downers Grove, Ill.: InterVarsity, 1989), 201.

[79]See Steven M. Baugh, "A Foreign World: Ephesus in the First Century," in *Women in the Church: A Fresh Analysis*, 47–48; Keener, *Paul, Women and Wives*, 103–7.

[80]For a more detailed discussion of 1 Timothy 2:9–10 see my essay "An Interpretation of 1 Timothy 2:9–15," 114–21.

which a woman learns, i.e., quietly and submissively. Paul assumes women should learn; what concerns him is that some of the women in Ephesus are arrogating authority to themselves and are not learning with submission. The prohibition in verse 12 further explains verse 11. Paul does not allow women to teach or to exercise authority over a man.

Andreas Köstenberger has conclusively shown that the two infinitives—*didaskein* ("to teach") and *authentein* ("to exercise authority"), which are connected by *oude* ("nor")—refer to two distinct activities.[81] He establishes this case by consulting verbal forms connected by *oude* in biblical and extrabiblical literature. He also discovered that the two distinct activities are both viewed either positively or negatively when connected by *oude*; whether the activities are positive or negative is established by the context. Köstenberger rightly notes that the verb *didaskō* ("to teach") is a positive term in the Pastoral Epistles (1 Tim. 4:11; 6:2; 2 Tim. 2:2), unless the context adds information to indicate otherwise (Titus 1:11). When Paul wants to use a verb to designate false teaching, he uses the term *heterodidaskaleō* ("to teach strange or false doctrines" [1 Tim. 1:3; 6:3]).[82]

Köstenberger's study is significant for our understanding of 1 Timothy 2:12. Paul prohibits two distinct activities—teaching and exercising authority. Both teaching and exercising authority are legitimate activities in and of themselves. He does not prohibit women from teaching and exercising authority as if these actions are intrinsically evil. Both teaching and exercising authority are proper activities for believers, but in this context he forbids women from engaging in such activities.

Köstenberger helps bring clarity to the debate on the meaning of the verb *authentein* ("to exercise authority") in verse 12. In 1979 Catherine Kroeger proposed that the verb meant "to engage in fertility practices," but scholars of all persuasions dismiss this view.[83] Now the Kroegers propose that verse 12 should be translated, "I do not allow a woman to teach or to proclaim

---

[81]See Andreas J. Köstenberger, "A Complex Sentence Structure in 1 Timothy 2:12," in *Women in the Church: A Fresh Analysis*, 81–103.

[82]I. Howard Marshall (*A Critical and Exegetical Commentary on the Pastoral Epistles* [ICC; Edinburgh: T&T Clark, 1999], 458–60) is unpersuasive in seeing a negative connotation in the terms.

[83]Catherine Clark Kroeger, "Ancient Heresies and a Strange Greek Verb," *RefJ* 29 (1979): 12–15.

herself the author or originator of a man."[84] Three careful and technical studies have been conducted on *authentein*, and all three demonstrate that the most natural meaning for the term is "to exercise authority."[85] Scott Baldwin, in particular, has examined virtually every use of the term and carefully separated the verb from the noun, for many scholars mistakenly blend the verb and noun together in their study of the term. Of course, it is just possible in context that a term with a positive meaning ("to exercise authority") could have a negative meaning ("to domineer").[86] But at this juncture Köstenberger's work applies again, for he has shown in his study of the sentence structure that both terms are either inherently positive or inherently negative. Since the term "teach" has no negative connotations, we should not read a negative sense into "exercise authority." I realize the discussion of this point has been rather technical, but my conclusion is this: technical study has verified that complementarians have rightly interpreted this verse. Paul prohibits women from teaching or exercising authority over men.[87]

---

[84]See Kroeger and Kroeger, *I Suffer Not a Woman*, 103. Linda L. Belleville proposes a translation similar to the Kroegers in some respects (*Women Leaders and the Church: Three Crucial Questions* [Grand Rapids: Baker, 2000], 177). Philip B. Payne ("The Interpretation of 1 Timothy 2:11–15: A Surrejoinder," in *What Does the Scripture Teach about the Ordination of Women?* [Minneapolis: unpublished paper, 1986], 108–10) lists five different meanings for the infinitive, which does not inspire confidence he has any definite sense of what the infinitive means.

[85]George W. Knight III, "*Authenteō* in Reference to Women in 1 Timothy 2:12," *NTS* 30 (1984): 143–57; Leland E. Wilshire, "The TLG Computer and Further Reference to *Authenteō* in 1 Timothy 2:12," *NTS* 34 (1988): 120–34; H. Scott Baldwin, "A Difficult Word: *Authenteō* in 1 Timothy 2:12," in *Women in the Church: A Fresh Analysis*, 65–80, 269–305. See my summary and more detailed analysis of this word in my essay "An Interpretation of 1 Timothy 2:9–15," 130–33.

[86]See, e.g., Carroll D. Osburn, "*Authenteō* (1 Timothy 2:12)," *ResQ* 25 (1982): 1–12.

[87]Some egalitarians have appealed to the phrase *ouk epitrepō* ("I do not permit") to support their case, arguing that the indicative mood demonstrates the exhortation is not even a command and that the present tense suggests the exhortation is merely a temporary restriction to be lifted once women are qualified to teach (see, e.g., Philip B. Payne, "Libertarian Women in Ephesus: A Response to Douglas J. Moo's Article, '1 Timothy 2:11–15: Meaning and Significance,'" *TJ* 2 [1981]: 170–72; Grenz, *Women in the Church*, 127–28). Both assertions are incorrect. Paul often uses indicatives to introduce commands. E.g., the famous admonition to give one's whole life to God (Rom. 12:1–2) is introduced with the indicative *parakalō* ("I exhort"). It is linguistically naive to insist commands must be in the imperative

We have seen previously that prohibiting a woman from teaching or exercising authority over a man applies to the tasks of an elder, for elders have a unique responsibility to teach and rule in God's church. But on what basis does Paul forbid women from teaching and exercising authority? His words in verse 13 provide the reason: "For it was Adam who was first created, and then Eve." The *gar* ("for") introducing this verse is best understood as a ground for the command, since a reason naturally follows the prohibition.[88] Women should not teach men or exercise authority over them because this would violate God's intention in creation. Since Paul appeals to creation, the prohibition transcends culture. Paul disallows homosexuality because it contravenes God's created order (Rom. 1:26–27). Jesus asserts the permanency of marriage by appealing to creation (Matt. 19:3–12). There is no suggestion in the 1 Timothy 2 passage, therefore, that the prohibition is temporary, nor is there any indication that the restriction is somehow due to human sin or to the limitations of women. The restriction on women stems from God's creation mandate, not from the cultural situation at Ephesus.

Egalitarians often argue the restriction can be explained by the lack of education among the women in Ephesus, or alternatively they suggest these women were duped by false teachers—and thus the women would be allowed to teach once their doctrinal deficiencies were corrected.[89] Both of these views are unconvincing. Paul could have easily written this: "I do not allow a woman to teach or exercise authority over a man as long as she is uneducated

mood (see 1 Cor. 1:10; Eph. 4:1; Phil. 4:2; 1 Tim. 2:8; 5:14; 2 Tim. 1:6; Titus 3:8). Nor can one appeal to the present tense to say the command is merely temporary. The same argument could then be used to say Paul desires believers to give their lives to God only for a brief period of time (Rom. 12:1) or he wants the men to pray without wrath and dissension merely for the present time (1 Tim. 2:8), but in the future they could desist.

[88]Egalitarians often understand this verse to be merely an illustration. So Gritz, *Mother Goddess at Ephesus*, 136; Witherington, *Women and the Genesis of Christianity*, 194–95; David M. Scholer, "1 Timothy 2:9–15 and the Place of Women in the Church's Ministry," in *Women, Authority and the Bible*, 208; Alan Padgett, "Wealthy Women at Ephesus: 1 Timothy 2:8–15 in Social Context," *Int* 41 (1987): 25; Keener, *Paul, Women and Wives*, 115–17. In defense of this verse functioning as a reason for the command, see Douglas J. Moo, "The Interpretation of 1 Timothy 2:11–15: A Rejoinder," *TJ* 2 (1981): 202–3.

[89]For documentation of the egalitarian view, see my essay "An Interpretation of 1 Timothy 2:9–15," 137.

and unlearned." He gives no indication, however, that lack of education is the problem. In fact, egalitarians skate over the reason given (Paul's appeal to the created order) and appeal to one not even mentioned (lack of education).[90] Furthermore, as Steven M. Baugh points out, it is not the case that all women were uneducated in Ephesus.[91] Indeed, we know from 2 Timothy 4:19 that Priscilla was in Ephesus, and she was certainly educated.

Nor is the second attempt to explain away 1 Timothy 2:12 any more persuasive. Paul could have written, "I do not permit a woman to teach or exercise authority over a man. For she is being led astray by false teachers." There are multiple problems with this hypothesis. First, why does Paul only mention women, since we know that at least some men were being duped by the false teachers as well? It would be insufferably sexist to prohibit only women from teaching and exercising authority when men were being led astray as well.[92] Second, the theory requires that all the women in Ephesus were deluded by the false teachers. Paul gives no indication the restriction applies only to some women, but it is incredibly hard to believe that every single woman in Ephesus was beguiled by the false teaching. Third, egalitarian scholars have been busy remaking the background to the situation in verses 11–15, but their reconstructions have been highly speculative and sometimes wildly implausible. For example, in their work on 1 Timothy (*I Suffer Not a Woman*) the Kroegers allege that Ephesus was feminist; they appeal to later evidence to vindicate their thesis and ransack the entire Greco-Roman world to sustain it. They have rightly been excoriated in reviews for producing a work that departs from a sound historical method.[93] They fall prey to Samuel Sandmel's warning against parallelomania, and they would have been wise to apply

---

[90]Royce Gordon Gruenler ("The Mission-Lifestyle Setting of 1 Timothy 2:8–15," *JETS* 41 [1998]: 215–38) argues that the subordination of women is explicable from the missionary situation in 1 Timothy. But he doesn't really engage in an intensive exegesis of the text, nor does he persuasively demonstrate that the prohibition is due to mission. Once again, Paul could have easily communicated such an idea, but he did not clearly do so.

[91]See Baugh, "A Foreign World," 45–47.

[92]See D. A. Carson, "'Silent in the Churches': On the Role of Women in 1 Corinthians 14:33b–36," in *Recovering Biblical Manhood and Womanhood*, 147.

[93]See Steven M. Baugh, "The Apostle among the Amazons," *WTJ* 56 (1994): 153–71; Albert Wolters, "Review: *I Suffer Not a Woman*," *CTJ* 28 (1993): 208–13; Robert W. Yarbrough, "*I Suffer Not a Woman*: A Review Essay," *Presb* 18 (1992): 25–33.

the kind of sober method recommended in John Barclay's essay on reconstructing the teaching and identity of opponents.[94] Bruce Barron blithely appeals to second-century gnostic sources and gives no indication that appealing to later evidence is a problem.[95] In *Paul, Women Teachers, and the Mother Goddess at Ephesus,* Sharon Gritz argues that the Artemis cult is responsible for the problem in Ephesus. Her work is much more careful than that of the Kroegers, but at the end of the day she does not provide any hard data from the letter to substantiate her thesis.[96]

Speculation runs rampant among those defending the egalitarian thesis. I challenge egalitarians to demonstrate from 1 Timothy itself the nature of the false teaching instead of from later and external sources. I conclude egalitarians have not yet provided a plausible explanation for Paul's argument from creation in 2:13; in fact, they often complain that Paul's argument in this verse is unclear and hard to understand.[97] Yet most Christians throughout church history did not think the verse was so obscure, nor do I think it is hard to grasp. I would suggest the verse seems difficult because it runs counter to our own cultural intuitions. But the Scriptures exist to challenge our worldview and to correct our way of looking at the world.

In verse 14, Paul gives a second reason for the prohibition. Women are forbidden to teach because Eve was deceived, and not Adam. Egalitarians occasionally appeal to this verse to say women were responsible for spreading the heresy in Ephesus, and that is why they are prevented from teaching.[98] When we

---

[94]See Samuel Sandmel, "Parallelomania," *JBL* 81 (1962): 2–13; John M. G. Barclay, "Mirror-Reading a Polemical Letter: Galatians as a Test Case," *JSNT* 3 (1987): 73–93. See also Jerry L. Sumney, "Identifying Paul's Opponents: The Question of Method in 2 Corinthians" (JSNTSup 40; Sheffield: JSOT Press, 1990). For a sensible and cautious description of the opponents in the Pastorals, see Marshall, *Pastoral Epistles,* 140–52; cf. also William D. Mounce, *Pastoral Epistles* (WBC; Nashville: Nelson, 2000), lxix–lxxxvi.

[95]See Bruce Barron, "Putting Women in Their Place: 1 Timothy 2 and Evangelical Views of Women in Church Leadership," *JETS* 33 (1990): 451–59.

[96]See my "An Interpretation of 1 Timothy 2:9–15," 107–12, for a discussion of the setting of the text.

[97]For documentation, see my "An Interpretation of 1 Timothy 2:9–15," 136. Jerome D. Quinn and William C. Wacker (*The First and Second Letters to Timothy* [ECC; Grand Rapids: Eerdmans, 2000], 227) rightly remark that the brevity of the words in verse 13 demonstrates that the truth presented here was both familiar and intelligible.

[98]For a detailed discussion of this verse, see my "An Interpretation of 1 Timothy 2:9–15," 140–46, though I am less certain about my previous interpretation of this verse.

read 1 Timothy and the rest of the Pastoral Epistles, however, the only false teachers named are men (1:20; 2 Tim. 1:15; 2:17). The only evidence we have is that women were influenced by the heresy, not that they were purveyors of it (2 Tim. 3:5–9). Nor does 1 Timothy 2:14 suggest that women were disseminating false teaching, for to say that one is deceived is not to say one is spreading error, but only that one is being led astray by it. What the verse highlights is what transpired in Eve's heart, namely, deception, and nothing is said about her giving Adam faulty instruction.

Nor is it plausible to say this verse highlights Eve's ignorance of God's command, and then to conclude the women of Ephesus are prohibited from teaching because of a lack of education. The problem with this interpretation is that deception does not equate with lack of education, for the latter is remedied through instruction while the former has a moral component. Nor does it make sense to say Eve was ignorant of God's command given to Adam. If she were ignorant because Adam had failed to inform her of the command, then the blame would surely rest with Adam. Alternatively, if Adam muddled the command and explained it poorly to Eve, this would scarcely fit with an injunction that encouraged men to teach rather than women. Presumably, Adam explained the prohibition to Eve, and it is hard to see how she could not have grasped it, since it is quite easy to understand what was forbidden. If Eve couldn't understand it, then she was inherently stupid—which would explain why men should teach. But deception should *not* be equated with stupidity. Paul is not saying Eve somehow lacked education or intelligence. He argues that she failed morally and was deceived by the serpent.

Egalitarians often allege they have a better explanation of verse 14 than complementarians. I maintain none of their explanations are persuasive, for there is no evidence in this verse that women were banned from teaching because they were spreading the heresy, nor is there any indication they were uneducated, for deception cannot be equated with lack of education.

What, then, is the point of 1 Timothy 2:14? Let me acknowledge at the outset the difficulty of the verse. I believe the complementarian view stands on the basis of the clarity of verse 13, so that resolving the interpretation of verse 14 is not crucial for the passage as a whole.[99] In the history of the church, some have argued that women are less intelligent or more apt to be deceived than men. The idea that women are less intelligent is not taught elsewhere in Scripture, and Paul does not argue from lack of intelligence but from the experience of deception. Others have suggested the point is that Eve was deceived first, and Adam was deceived afterward.[100] As Paul writes to his trusted coworker, he knows Timothy will reflect on the Pauline teaching that sin has been transmitted through Adam (Rom. 5:12–19). So even though Eve sinned first, sin is traced to Adam, pointing to male headship.

We can combine the above interpretation with the observation that the serpent took the initiative to tempt Eve rather than Adam, thereby subverting the pattern of male leadership.[101] I argued in a previous essay that perhaps Paul is suggesting women are more prone to deceit than men, but this view has the disadvantage of suggesting an inherent defect in women, for the language of deceit in Scripture always involves a moral failing. Thus, I think Paul likely is reflecting on the fact that the serpent subverted male headship by tempting Eve rather than Adam.[102]

---

[99]Craig L. Blomberg ("Not Beyond What Is Written: A Review of Aída Spencer's *Beyond the Curse: Women Called to Ministry*," *CTR* 2 [1988]: 414) intriguingly suggests verse 14 should be read with verse 15 instead of functioning as a second reason for the injunction in verse 12. On this reading, Paul says the woman will be saved, even though Eve was initially deceived. There are at least three weaknesses with this view (cf. Mounce, *Pastoral Epistles*, 142): (1) the *kai* in verse 14 naturally links verse 14 with verse 13; (2) the structure of verse 13 nicely matches verse 14, for both verses compare and contrast Adam and Eve in an a-b a-b pattern; and (3) Blomberg's view does not account well for the reference to Adam in verse 14. Any reference to Adam is superfluous if the concern is only the salvation of women. But the reference to both Adam and Eve fits with the specific argument in verse 12 that women are not to teach men. In my view Blomberg does not answer these objections convincingly in his response to Mounce's objections (see his essay, "Neither Hierarchicalist nor Egalitarian: Gender Roles in Paul," in *Two Views on Women in Ministry*, eds. James R. Beck and Craig L. Blomberg [Grand Rapids: Zondervan, 2001], 367).

[100]So Paul W. Barnett, "Wives and Women's Ministry (1 Timothy 2:11–15)," *EvQ* 61 (1989): 234.

[101]See also Gruenler, "The Mission-Lifestyle Setting," 217–18, 20–21.

[102]Due to space limitations, I am bypassing the interpretation of 1 Timothy 2:15. For my view, see "An Interpretation of 1 Timothy 2:9–15," 146–53. I do not believe my specific interpretation affects the major teaching of the text in a decisive way (contra Keener, *Paul, Women and Wives*, 118; Scholer, "1 Timothy 2:9–15 and the Place of Women," 196). For an alternate interpretation, see Andreas J. Köstenberger,

And yet sin is still traced through Adam, even though Eve was deceived and sinned first. On this view verse 14 supports the command in verse 12, providing an additional and complementary reason for male leadership in the church.

Women Exhorted to Prophesy with a Submissive Demeanor: 1 Corinthians 11:2–16

One of the most controversial NT texts regarding men and women is 1 Corinthians 11:2–16.[103] Several issues need to be examined here, beginning with the custom that is in view. How did Paul want the women to adorn themselves? We must admit immediately that complete certainty eludes us. Scholars have suggested veiling, the wearing of a shawl, or the tying of hair atop the head so that the hair didn't fall loosely onto the shoulders.[104] Whatever the custom was, the failure of the Corinthian women to abide by it was considered disgraceful. The behavior of the Corinthian women was as shocking as if they shaved their heads altogether (v. 6).

Even if we cannot specify the custom, why would Paul be concerned about how the women adorn themselves?[105] We have already noted that honor and shame come to the forefront (vv. 4–7, 13–15). Those who repudiate the custom bring dishonor on their heads. The word "head" in verse 5 is probably a play on

---

"Ascertaining Women's God-Ordained Roles: An Interpretation of 1 Timothy 2:15," *BBR* 7 (1997): 107–43.

[103]For further discussion, see my essay "Head Coverings, Prophecies and the Trinity: 1 Corinthians 11:2–16," in *Recovering Biblical Manhood and Womanhood*, 124–39.

[104]Supporting a shawl or veil is Gordon D. Fee, *The First Epistle to the Corinthians* (NICNT; Grand Rapids: Eerdmans, 1987), 506–12; Keener, *Paul, Women and Wives*, 22–31; Cynthia L. Thompson, "Hairstyles, Head-Coverings, and St. Paul: Portraits from Roman Corinth," *BA* 51 (1988): 99–115. Supporting hairstyle is Hurley, *Man and Woman in Biblical Perspective*, 254–71; David E. Blattenberger III, *Rethinking 1 Corinthians 11:2–16 through Archaeological and Moral-Rhetorical Analysis* (Lewiston, N.Y.: Mellen, 1997).

[105]Bruce W. Winter (*After Paul Left Corinth* [Grand Rapids: Eerdmans, 2001], 121–41) argues that the injunction to veil demonstrates that wives and not women in general are in view here, supporting this with evidence from the culture of Paul's day. Winter's arguments are quite attractive, but further research and discussion are needed to establish this claim. I have some hesitancy about his view because it is unclear from the text itself that only wives are in view, though perhaps Winter is correct in saying that the reference to veiling indicates such is the case.

words, for the women who adorn themselves improperly bring dishonor on themselves *and* their husbands. It is evident the women's adornment impinges on the relationship between men and women, since Paul introduces the whole matter by saying, "Christ is the head of every man, and the man is the head of a woman, and God is the head of Christ" (v. 3).

I noted previously that the word *kephalē* ("head") may have both the idea of "authority over" and "source." The meaning "authority over" is clear in many texts, and whether the term ever means "source" is difficult to discern. Nevertheless, even if one adopts the translation "source," male leadership cannot be expunged from the text. Paul is concerned about the way women adorn themselves, because shameful adornment is a symbol of rebellion against male leadership. A woman who is properly adorned signals her submissiveness to male headship. That woman was created to assist and help man is clear from the Pauline commentary in verses 7–9: "For a man ought not to have his head covered, since he is the image and glory of God; but the woman is the glory of man. For man does not originate from woman, but woman from man; for indeed man was not created for the woman's sake, but woman for the man's sake." We should note the woman is required to adorn herself in a certain way because she came from the man, showing that even an argument from source does not exclude male leadership.[106]

Paul does not merely impose restrictions on women. He encourages women to pray and prophesy in church if they are properly adorned (v. 5). Complementarians who relegate such prayer and prophecy by women to private meetings fail to convince, because the distinction between public and private meetings of the church is a modern invention; in Paul's day, the church often met in homes for worship and instruction. Moreover, it is evident that 11:2–14:40 relates to activities when the church is gathered together. Paul commends women's praying and prophesying in church, but he insists on proper adornment, because such adornment signals submission to male leadership.

It is also crucial at this juncture to reiterate what was said earlier. The permission to prophesy does not mean women fill

---

[106]I am not suggesting *kephalē* means only "source" here; both "authority over" and "source" are probably involved. My judgment on this issue represents a change from my "Head Coverings, Prophecies and the Trinity," 124–39.

the office of teacher or pastor/elder/overseer. When women pray and prophesy, they must adorn themselves properly, thereby indicating they are supportive of male leadership in the church. Paul encourages women to speak in the assembly, but he forbids them from functioning as pastors or from exercising a regular gift of teaching men.

We should also notice the programmatic nature of verse 3. God is the head of Christ, which signifies that God is the *authority over* the Christ. The Father commands and sends, and the Son obeys and goes. Even though the Son obeys the Father, he is equal in essence, dignity, and personhood with the Father. A difference in role does not signify a difference in worth. Some scholars are now actually arguing that the Son submits to the Father, *and the Father submits to the Son*. Stanley Grenz posits such a thesis in defense of the egalitarian view.[107] Amazingly enough, he does not provide any biblical evidence to support his assertion; he simply claims the Father also submits to the Son. There is no evidence in the Bible that the Father and Son mutually submit to one another. Grenz's interpretation is concocted out of nothing and proposed to the reader as though it were rooted somewhere in the Bible.

The parallel between Christ's submission to the Father and the deference of women to men is important. For right after Paul sets forth the distinct role of women in verses 2–10, he reminds his readers that both men and women are equal in the Lord (vv. 11–12). Some scholars have interpreted verses 11–12 as though Paul were now denying the male leadership taught in verses 2–10.[108] Such a reading is unpersuasive.

Paul returns to the differences between the genders in verses 13–16, and in verse 16, he reminds the Corinthians that all the other churches practice the custom the Corinthians are resisting.[109] The text beautifully balances differences in roles with

---

[107]See Grenz, *Women in the Church*, 153–54.

[108]Scholars often appeal to verse 10 to support the idea that women have independent authority in prophesying. This interpretation was proposed by Morna D. Hooker ("Authority on Her Head: An Examination of 1 Corinthians xi.10," *NTS* 10 [1964]: 410–16) and has been adopted by most egalitarians (see, e.g., Keener, *Paul, Women and Wives*, 38–42). But there are serious problems with this view (see my "Head Coverings, Prophecies and the Trinity," 134–37).

[109]Judith M. Gundry-Volf ("Gender and Creation in 1 Corinthians 11:2–16: A Study in Paul's Theological Method," in *Evangelium Schriftauslegung Kirche*, ed. O. Hofius [Göttingen: Vandenhoeck & Ruprecht, 1997], 151–71) argues that Paul

equality of personhood. Egalitarians have sometimes claimed that Paul corrects in verses 11–12 the focus on submission in verses 2–10. More likely, the themes of submission and equality are complementary. Women and men are equal in the Lord, and yet distinct roles are also demanded. Paul saw no contradiction on this point—and neither should we.

Should women wear veils or shawls today? A minority of complementarians think they should.[110] But we must remember that the Bible was written in the context of particular historical and cultural circumstances we do not necessarily imitate today. As I noted before in the cases of the holy kiss and drinking wine for indigestion, we must distinguish between the principle and the cultural outworking of a principle. Thus, the principle in 1 Corinthians 11:2–16 is *deference to male leadership*. In our culture, such deference is not signaled by wearing a shawl or a veil, or by tying one's hair into a bun atop the head. Women should participate in ministry, read the Scriptures, and pray in church with a demeanor that illustrates submission to male headship, but they should not be required to wear veils, for to do so confuses the particular cultural practice with the principle.

Am I trying to escape the scandal of the biblical text? In actuality, I believe there is a custom in Western society that is somewhat analogous to the first-century situation. In some cases, women today who refuse to take a husband's last name signal that they are "liberated." I realize there are exceptions (e.g., famous athletes or authors may want to retain name recognition), but I believe if Paul were alive today, he would encourage women who marry to take the last name of their husband, signaling thereby their deference to male leadership.[111]

---

integrates creation, culture, and eschatological life in Christ in a complex fashion in these verses so that he, in effect, supports patriarchy and equality simultaneously. On the one hand, I disagree with her claim that verses 11–12 partially mute the patriarchy of the previous verses. On the other hand, her own proposal is overly complex and doesn't offer a clear way forward in the debate.

[110]See, e.g., Bruce Waltke, "1 Corinthians 11:2–16: An Interpretation," *BSac* 135 (1978): 46–57; Robert Culver, "A Traditional View: Let Your Women Keep Silence," in *Women in Ministry: Four Views*, 29–32, 48.

[111]I am not claiming that taking a husband's last name should always be required. Our culture may change. In some cultures, retaining one's maiden name may show respect for one's father. I am merely suggesting that, in some cases, women are making a statement about their view of gender relations by not taking their husband's last name.

Is it possible the same hermeneutical method I have applied to 1 Corinthians 11:2–16 could be related to 1 Timothy 2:11–15? In one of my classes, a woman once said to me, "Is it possible the admonition not to teach or exercise authority over a man has an underlying principle we have missed, so that women *can* teach and exercise authority over men without denying the principle of 1 Timothy 2:11–15?" I replied, "Of course it is possible. But in this case, it seems the principle and practice coalesce.[112] Please explain to me what the principle is in the text if it does not relate to women's teaching the Scriptures and exercising authority over other believers."

I have never read any author who has successfully explained what this "other principle" might be. Thus, I am persuaded we fulfill the admonition of 1 Timothy 2:12 when we prohibit women from filling the pastoral office and when we restrict them from regularly teaching the Scriptures to adult males.[113]

The Principle of Submission Applied to a Particular Situation: 1 Corinthians 14:33b–36

The entire matter of principle and practice comes to the forefront in this difficult text. Gordon Fee has argued the verses are a later interpolation, but this view has been decisively refuted by Don Carson and Curt Niccum.[114] On first blush the

---

[112]See Köstenberger, "Gender Passages," 270. John Stott (*Guard the Truth: The Message of 1 Timothy & Titus* [BST; Downers Grove, Ill.: InterVarsity, 1996], 78–80) argues that submission to authority is transcultural but teaching is a cultural expression of the principle that does not apply the same way in our culture. Köstenberger (*1–2 Timothy and Titus* [EBC, rev. ed.; Grand Rapids: Zondervan, forthcoming]) rightly responds that "v. 13 provides the rationale for vv. 11–12 in their entirety rather than only the submission-authority principle. Moreover, teaching and ruling functions are inseparable from submission-authority, as is made clear in the immediately following context when it is said that the overseer must be 'husband of one wife' (i.e., by implication, male; 3:2) as well as 'able to teach' (3:2)."

[113]Craig Keener (*Paul, Women and Wives*, 19) thinks that if one abandons the head covering, then the limitation imposed by 1 Timothy 2:12 must be surrendered as well. But I believe I am following Keener's very principle of trying to discern the principle in each text (see *Paul, Women and Wives*, 46).

[114]See Fee, *First Epistle to the Corinthians*, 699–705; Carson, "Silent in the Churches," 141–45; Curt Niccum, "The Voice of the Manuscripts on the Silence of Women: The External Evidence for 1 Corinthians 14.34–35," *NTS* 43 (1997): 242–55.

passage seems to prohibit women from speaking in church at all, but this is an unpersuasive interpretation. In 1 Corinthians 11:5, Paul has already permitted women to pray and prophesy in the church. He would not bother to explain in such detail how they should adorn themselves if he thought women should desist from speaking altogether! What, then, is Paul prohibiting here? Scholars have suggested a plethora of interpretations that need not be canvassed here. For instance, some have said that the text is contradictory, others that women were interrupting the worship service with questions, and still others that women were banned from assessing and passing judgment on the prophecies uttered by the prophets.[115] Virtually all acknowledge that the specific situation that called forth these words is difficult to identify. It seems most likely the women were disrupting the service in some way (we cannot recover the specific circumstances due to paucity of information), and Paul responds to their disruptive behavior.

Still, we cannot simply say the verses are restricted to the local situation at Corinth. The admonition here relates to what is practiced "in all the churches of the saints" (14:33). Paul summons the women to submit, for this is what the *nomos* ("Law") requires (v. 34). Paul does not specify any particular verse from the OT, but "Law" in Paul virtually always refers to the OT, and here we probably have a reference to the teaching of Genesis 1–2. We may have some uncertainty about the particular situation in Corinth, but the principle enunciated here fits with the rest of Scripture. The women are not to speak in such a way that they arrogate leadership. As in all the other churches, they are to behave submissively, so that the leadership of the church belongs to men.[116]

See also Keener's fine survey of interpretive options (*Paul, Women and Wives*, 70–100). Philip B. Payne ("Fuldensis, Sigla for Variants in Vaticanus, and 1 Corinthians 14.34–5," *NTS* 41 [1995]: 240–62) argues that evidence from Codex Fuldensis and a "bar-umlaut" siglum in Vaticanus indicate that verses 34–35 are a later interpolation. Niccum demonstrates, however, that the evidence adduced by Payne does not really support an interpolation.

[115]For a survey of options and the view that the judging of prophecies is forbidden, see Carson, "Silent in the Churches," 145–53. For a survey that reaches another conclusion, see Forbes, *Prophecy and Inspired Speech*, 270–77.

[116]Keener (*Paul, Women and Wives*, 87) agrees with me that the principle in the text is *submission*, though he would apply the text differently to today.

CONCLUSION

The Bible speaks with one voice on whether women should fill the pastoral office, and it also seems to me it forbids women from regularly teaching men and exercising authority over them. I realize, of course, that even those who agree with my exegesis may disagree on how this would be worked out in the myriad of specific situations that arise in life.[117] I want to affirm in closing only that the Bible also indicates that women were vitally involved in many other ministry roles in both the OT and the NT. Complementarians should celebrate and advocate women's filling such roles. We must also constantly remind our egalitarian society that differences in function do not signify differences in worth. The world may think that way—but the church knows better.

---

[117]I simply could not address the diversity of practical questions in this brief
Title: Three Views on Eastern Orthodoxy and Evangelicalism

A RESPONSE TO THOMAS SCHREINER
Linda L. Belleville

There is much to appreciate about Tom Schreiner's essay and a number of things we mutually affirm. We both affirm that men and women are equally created in God's image. We both acknowledge that women in the ancient world led in outreach ministries such as church planting and evangelism—and in local church ministry roles such as prophet, patron, and deacon. We both agree that women held leadership roles in the civic realm. Indeed, we both grant women in ministry per se. It is the issue of women engaged in leading men (specifically preaching and teaching) where we differ.

The fallacies and blind spots are much the same as those of Craig Blomberg's essay.

1. GENERALIZING FALLACIES

Life is rarely as black and white as an "always" or "never." Yet, it is a fallacy to which Tom succumbs in this essay. The opening volley is, "I understand Scripture to forbid women from teaching and exercising authority over a man" (p. 265). This is followed by categorical pronouncements such as, "Women served as prophets but never as pastors or overseers or apostles," and, "Not a single NT example can be adduced that women served as pastors, elders, or overseers" (p. 278). This, the author claims, is "the historic view" of women in ministry, "ratified by the church in century after century" (p. 266).

What the author neglects to say is that this so-called *historic* view is the view of churches with a particular polity—a *patriarchal* polity. When one moves outside of a hierarchical setting, women pastors, preachers, and teachers are readily found. They are found in the ranks of the medieval abbesses, Waldensians, Taborites, Shakers, Quakers, Methodists, the Salvation Army, Christian and Missionary Alliance (until recently), Pentecostals, and others—and this "in century after century." Women leaders of Christian movements and organizations are also evident throughout history. For instance, the Shaker communities in the early 1800s experienced twenty-five years of unprecedented growth under the leadership of Lucy Wright. Catherine Booth of the Salvation Army pioneered a woman's right to preach the gospel in the mid- to late-1800s, and her pamphlet *Female Ministry* is still widely referenced.

2. FALSE DISTINCTION FALLACIES

Tom contends that women can preach and teach if it is "spontaneous" (e.g., a word of knowledge, a prophetic word and the like) but not if it is "regular"; women can prophesy because prophecy is a "passive" gift that does not fit with leadership, but women cannot teach because teaching it is an active gift that fits a "settled office" (pp. 277–78).

Such distinctions as "spontaneous versus regular" and "passive versus active" are modern concoctions. "Regular" and "official" assume a level of institutionalization and organization that postdates the NT period by one to two centuries. When the church at Antioch chose church planters, they chose from the ranks of "prophets and teachers" in their midst. So "prophet" is hardly a passive, non-leadership gift. Spontaneity and passivity are also ill-fitting descriptors for the many women Paul greets in Romans 16 as coworkers and colaborers in the ministry.

The early Christians met in homes and gathered in the courtyard, which accommodated about fifty. The "regular" roles were largely administrative. The key administrator was the homeowner, who supervised and coordinated these gatherings (cf. the synagogue ruler). Both women and men are singled out as *regulars* in this role—Nympha and Philemon in Colossae, Mary in Jerusalem, Priscilla and Aquila in a variety of locations, and Lydia in Philippi. Other "regular" roles included overseers and deacons, whom Paul greets in Philippians 1:1. The naming of Syntyche and Euodia in 4:3 (exceptional in Paul) places them squarely among the "regulars"—and "officers" (to use traditionalist language).

3. ANACHRONISM FALLACIES

Ecclesiology is at the heart of Tom's repeated claim that women are prohibited from functioning in the pastoral office because one of the fundamental roles of elder involves teaching. "Pastoral office" is the polity of some churches today—but is it biblically based? The term "pastor" is found only once in the NT letters, and then in a list of gifts (not offices), whose function is "to equip God's people for the work of the ministry" (Eph. 4:11–12 AT). The same is true for elder. Although Tom is adamant that women are banned from the office of elder (pp. 271, 278, 285), the statement is biblically questionable. *Elder* in the Judaism of both the OT and the NT was a civic, not religious, role. Elders held no standing in the synagogue and played no official religious role. Also, historians have shown that women did indeed hold this role. Seven Jewish tomb inscriptions have been identified to date in which women bear the title "elder."

The author counters with the fact that there were no women priests or rabbis among God's people. Yet, why would a particular polity at a particular historical point determine polity for all time? The simple fact is that the polity of the priestly cult did not continue, and another polity of an entirely different sort took its place. So the lack of women priests has little bearing on women in ministry.

4. MALE PREROGATIVE FALLACIES

"Men bear the responsibility to lead and teach in the church *because* Adam was created before Eve" (p. 291). "[An] indication of male leadership is that Eve was created as a 'helper' (*ʿēzer*) for Adam" (p. 292). "Adam's naming of the woman signifies that he bears the leadership role" (p. 295). This is the language of male presumption speaking. Egalitarians do not deny that the society of antiquity was patriarchal. The key question is whether this is the teaching of Scripture about how God intends things to be.

If we take our cue from Jesus, each time he encounters male presumption, he turns it on its head. When the religious leaders of the day approached him and asked if it was legal for a man to divorce his wife (Mark 10:3), it would have been easy for Jesus to say, "Yes, God created the male to be in charge." Instead, he flatly indicates that it was not so from the beginning (v. 6). It is not that God created the male first and then the female, thereby designating the pattern of leadership. Rather, "God made them male *and female*" (v. 6, author's emphasis). The presumption of a male prerogative Jesus attributes to hardness of heart (v. 5).

The counterargument is that Jesus challenges men who abuse their God-given privilege. If so, we would expect a "Yes," followed by the qualification "*but* the male is not to abuse his prerogative." Instead, the question posed in Mark 10 is straightforward, asking, in effect, "Who is in charge when it comes to divorce?" "Neither," is Jesus' response (vv. 5–6 AT). The prerogative is God's alone (v. 9).

The author appeals to "Adam was created first, then Eve" as the defining statement regarding male prerogative and charges that "egalitarians have not yet provided a plausible explanation for Paul's argument from creation in [1 Timothy] 2:13" (p. 313). This is rather curious, since not only verse 13 but the even more difficult verse 15 ("women will be saved through childbearing" [TNIV]) are readily explained against the Ephesian cult of Artemis. Pausanias's *Guide to Greece* (second century) lays out the female dominance of the cult. Greeks believed Artemis was the child of Zeus and Leto (Lat., *Latona*), who spurned the male gods and sought the company of a human consort named Leimon. This made Artemis and all her female adherents superior to men. It would also explain Paul's statement that "women will be saved [or kept safe] through childbearing," for women turned to Artemis for safe travel through the childbearing process.

5. CULTURAL FALLACIES

On the one hand, Tom can state, "We must interpret the Scriptures in their historical and cultural context" (p. 308). Yet, earlier on he says, "No correlation can be drawn between the church's meeting in Mary's house [Acts 12:12] and the assuming of a leadership role" (p. 284). This runs counter to what we know about the patron of a house church (or other organization). The modern parallel would be that of the chair of a board, who assumes fiduciary responsibility for and leadership of an organization. The first-century patron who opened his or her home to the local "church" similarly assumed responsibility and "oversight." It is for this reason some scholars identify the NT language of "overseer" (or "bishop") with the patron of a house church.

Culture is similarly overlooked when treating the so-called "restrictive" texts regarding marriage in 1 Timothy. Women are "saved through childbearing" (2:15) and younger widows are "to marry, to have children, to manage their homes" (5:14). What is commonly overlooked is that these texts contradict Paul's instructions elsewhere (e.g., 1 Cor. 7:8, 39–40). This is also the case with the submission texts. Wives are to "submit to their husbands in everything" (Eph. 5:24; cf. Col. 3:18 and Titus 2:4–5). Yet the language elsewhere in Paul is that of mutual obligation (1 Cor. 7:1–4), "mutual consent" (7:5), and mutual submission (Eph. 5:21).

In all instances there are ready explanations in the differing circumstances and concerns that led to the writing of each letter. Ephesians (a circular letter), Colossians (an Ephesian church plant), 1 Timothy (Ephesian church pastor), and Titus (Cretan church planter) are written to churches in the same general locale and deal with false teaching that counseled asceticism and forbade marriage (Col. 2:18–23; 1 Tim. 4:3).

6. SCHOLARSHIP FALLACIES

The author, at least in this essay, does not engage the work of recent linguists, sociologists, historians, and archaeologists on women's roles in antiquity. Cases in point are discussions on Romans 16:7 and 1 Timothy 2:12.

In Romans 16:7 (NKJV), Paul writes, "Greet Andronicus and Junia, my countrymen and my fellow prisoners, who are of note among the apostles, who also were in Christ before me." The sole scholarly voice brought to bear in a definitive way on whether the esteemed apostle in Romans 16:7 is a woman, or even esteemed at all, is a 2001 NTS article ("Was Junia Really an Apostle") by traditionalists Michael Burer and Daniel Wallace—despite the fact that the research has been challenged by scholars of every stripe. Textual critic Eldon J. Epp in a 2002 essay ("The Junia/Junias Variation in Romans 16.7") pointed out the errors in the handling of the text tradition, and NT scholar Richard Bauckham in a 2002 study (Gospel Women) showed the flaws in the use of extrabiblical sources.

The author also fails to mention earlier scholarship. For example, he leaves open the possibility that the "apostle of note" may actually be a male named Junias; and should she be a woman, the "research indicates it is unlikely that Junia is identified as an apostle here, and hence the verse says nothing about women serving in the apostolic office" (p. 286). Yet, there is an unbroken tradition from Ambrose in the fourth century through Lombard in the twelfth century that not only recognizes a female apostle but lauds her as "of note among the apostles" and places her among the Seventy-two (Seventy) sent out by Jesus (Luke 10:1).

The author's analysis of 1 Timothy 2:11–15 appears dated. First Timothy 2:12, he states, "prohibits women ... from doing the two activities that distinguish elders from deacons (teaching and exercising authority)" (p. 283). His claim is based on a grouping of translations that render the Greek *authentein* as "exercise authority over." Yet, there is no instance of this meaning in the Greek of Paul's day, and no version until Martin Luther in 1522 translates it this way. (Here also see my essay in this volume.) He also overlooks the presence of the Greek correlative *ouk ... oude* ("neither ... nor"), which defines *one* activity and not two (cf. "God neither slumbers nor sleeps"). So how one correlates "teaching" and *authentein* is the key question.

There are also a number of assumptions that lack scholarly support. For example, the notion of female subordination in the creation narratives is dependent on the English translation of woman as a "fit helper" for the man in Genesis 2:18. "'Helper,'" the author states, "refers to the subordinate role of women" (p. 294)—an argument that can't be sustained if one opts for "partner" (NRSV), "companion" (NLT), or "support [Vulg. *adiutorium*] like unto himself" (DV, *Darby*), "comparable to him" (NKJV), or "meet for him" (Geneva, KJV, ASV). Similarly, the author's notion of female subordination in the marriage is dependent on English translations of the husband as "head" or "decision maker" (*kephalē*) of the wife as Christ is the head of the church (pp. 301–2). The CEO overtone is unavoidable if one translates *kephalē* as "head."

But this is not the only translation option. An equally viable option is "source," or "origin." In fact, each time Paul invokes Christ as *kephalē* of the church, the language is organic and not hierarchical. The church is a living organism that draws its existence and nourishment from Christ as *kephalē*. Christ is *kephalē* and "savior" of the church, his "body" (Eph. 4:16; 5:22–23; Col.

1:18; 2:19); he is its "beginning" and "firstborn" (Col. 1:18). "From him" (*ex hou*) the church is "joined and held together ..., [and] grows" (Eph. 4:16); from (Christ) the head it is "supported and held together ..., [and] grows" (Col. 2:19). As *kephalē* of the church, Christ "feeds and cares" for it as people do for "their own bodies"—and we are "members of his body, of his flesh, and of his bones" (Eph. 5:29–30).[1] The allusion to Genesis 2:21–23 and the creation of the woman from the rib of the man is unmistakable. And so is the notion of source. The church is the Eve of the second Adam, "bone of [his] bones and flesh of [his] flesh" (Gen. 2:23).

7. HERMENEUTICAL FALLACIES

All forms of literature have their own rules of interpretation that must be followed to avoid misreading (and so misapplying) the text. Historical narrative is no exception. Historians present the way things *were* and not how they *must be*. Church polity is a prime illustration. Churches have variously adopted episcopal, congregational, and presbyterian forms of government because of the perceived biblical freedom to operate by whatever organizational structures best serve them—with any necessary ethical provisos. The pages of Acts are replete with a diversity of organizational patterns. The city of Thessalonica had an oligarchy, Athens a democracy, and Jerusalem a theocracy—all set within the larger Roman imperial structure of a monarchy. So to claim (as the author does) that anything other than a presbyterian form of government (i.e., governed by elders) is a deviation from the biblical pattern is a hermeneutical fallacy—treating historical practice as though it were theological dogma. Consequently, for deacons to function as the governing board of a church is "unfortunate, for deacons are nowhere identified with or made a subcategory of elders in the NT" (p. 282).

The historical observation that Paul chose "elders" as part of the church planting process, does not necessitate we do the same. Indeed, Tom states, "One of the problems in the contemporary church is that many churches have deviated from the biblical pattern in which there were two offices: elders/overseers and deacons"

---

[1]So Ephesians 5:30 in the Western and Byzantine families of manuscripts and versions and in church fathers from the second century on (see p. 100, n. 150, in my essay in this book).

(p. 282). This ignores the descriptive fluidity among "elder," "deacon," and "overseer/bishop" in the NT that defies definition and flow chart analysis. We simply lack the requisite systematic teaching such a claim would require.

Part of the difficulty is that there are no religious antecedents for the early church elder and deacon. It is significant that the Jerusalem church and its church plants did not opt for the polity with which they were familiar and that framed their own experience and upbringing; instead, they opted for a new polity. The local church as a "body" with interdependent members who have a diversity of gifts required something quite different from that of the local synagogue. Furthermore, church polity was a polity in the making. For instance, deacons first enter the picture in Acts 6, where the Jerusalem church changes its organizational structures to better serve its respective constituencies. In so doing, there is no hint of an office in the making or any concern about deviating from a "biblical pattern" of governance.

8. GENDER FALLACIES

Tom notes that Galatians 3:28 teaches that in Christ "men and women have equal access to salvation" (p. 274). This is one of the most troubling statements in his essay, not for what it says, but for what it does not say. Yes, men and women have equal access to salvation. But they have more, and they had it equally from creation. The teaching of Genesis 1 is that God created male *and female* (identity) equally in his image (dignity), and on that basis entrusted both of them with "rule over" creation (i.e., significance; vv. 27–28). This makes them not merely joint heirs of salvation but also joint rulers of creation. This joint rule may have been lost in the social realm (i.e., men have the social prerogatives)—not only for women but also for slaves and Gentiles. But in Christ—i.e., in the church—it is restored.

What this means is that identity, dignity, and significance are intrinsic to creation and not merely the effects of redemption. Galatians must then be projecting something new—something beyond. This is clear from the grammar alone. "In Christ there is *not male and female*" (AT). Outside the church, there is ethnic distinction; inside the church, there is "neither Jew nor Gentile" (*ouk ... oude*). Outside the church, there is social distinction;

inside the church, there is "neither slave nor free" (*ouk ... oude*). Outside the church, there is a pecking order of master and slave; inside the church, the slave may be the leader, while the master may be the receiver. Outside the church, God created them "male and female" (Gen. 1:27); inside the church, there is *not* male and female (*ouk ... kai*); we are individuals, variously gifted by God's Spirit, who contribute based on our varied gifts.

A RESPONSE TO THOMAS SCHREINER
Craig L. Blomberg

For the third time, I am happy to compose a brief response to someone I consider a friend, a fine scholar, a godly individual, and a person of sensitivity and integrity. Once again I find myself in agreement with a substantial percentage of what Tom has written. One might expect me to feel more closely aligned to Tom's position than to Craig's or Linda's, since we both consider ourselves to be complementarians. But, in fact, Craig's and Linda's egalitarianism is so moderate, sensitive, and nuanced that my perception is that I am roughly halfway between their position and Tom's. Moreover, Tom's complementarianism is similarly informed and nuanced and considerably removed from the far more traditional positions that have tended to dominate church history.

My fundamental agreement and single major disagreement with Tom may be formulated at once. I agree entirely that the most responsible exegesis of Scripture leads to the conclusion that only men are to occupy the office of elder or overseer, as long as what the church today identifies as that office is truly equivalent to the biblical model. To the extent that Tom sees "pastor" as simply a synonym for elder or overseer, as it is in several NT passages, then I would agree with him in including that term as well. But because "pastor" can also be a spiritual gift in Paul's lists of gifts, and because many people today are even given the official title or office of pastor without functioning as a biblical elder or overseer, I am reluctant to throw in "pastor" along with elder and overseer as freely as Tom does. I would like to encourage women to exercise the gift of pastoring in these more informal ways. My major disagreement, however, is that I do not find the Bible also forbidding women from regularly teaching men or exercising authority over them, once 1 Timothy 2:12 is understood properly.

One of the key differences between Tom's and my position involves our understanding of prophecy. Tom acknowledges both sides to the debate and footnotes key works in support of each. All I can say is that, having read extensively from both primary and secondary literature on both sides, I am convinced "prophecy" was an exceedingly broad term used in a wide array of circumstances in the biblical cultures, including prepared messages as well as spontaneous utterances, as long as the speakers had the singular conviction they were delivering a message given to them by God or the gods. If this conclusion is accurate, then we must allow for women preachers. But this does not jeopardize, as Tom seems to think, the restriction of the office of elder or overseer to men. An all-male eldership should take responsibility for overseeing the preaching ministry of the church, determining who will preach when, and women may be invited to preach under their authority, accountable to them, without in any way jeopardizing the biblical hierarchy of the congregation. I have seen it happen. I have seen it work well.

Tom is correct that the gift of teaching in Paul's day was primarily the explanation of tradition that had already been transmitted. But for that very reason, "teaching" was not normally used to describe preaching, at least not the more overtly evangelistic preaching that characterizes so much apostolic ministry of the first Christian generation. Teachers were those individuals who in smaller, more private settings passed on the fundamental catechesis of the Christian faith, and there appears to have been no gender role restrictions on who performed this task. Thus when Paul encourages women to pray and prophesy with the right demeanor and culturally sensitive appearance, we dare not forbid women from preaching in a similar fashion today.

I am particularly grateful for Tom's discussion of women as deacons. I agree entirely with what he says in this section. I am grateful, too, that he apparently can hold this position and continue to teach in a leading Southern Baptist seminary. My guess is that the vast majority of Baptists, both in the Southern Baptist Convention and in smaller denominations such as the Baptist General Conference and Conservative Baptist Association of America, still think the Bible forbids women even from the diaconate. At least the practice of most Baptist churches of which I am aware in those denominations would suggest this.

Intriguingly, a couple of years ago, when I wrote a paper promoting the advantages of the NT edition of the TNIV and sent it to one hundred high-profile Christian leaders who had signed a statement condemning it, I received a very courteous response from a well-known president of an international parachurch ministry who was a member of the Southern Baptist Convention. His protest boiled down to this: "The TNIV translates two key passages in ways that suggest Paul permitted women to be deacons. My church, the Southern Baptist Convention, does not allow for this. Therefore, I cannot accept this translation." Of course, I was horrified at the logic implied: If my church contradicts the Bible, I must follow my church rather than the Bible! But apparently he did not know the freedom Baptists had to promote women as deacons, and if he didn't, I suspect the vast majority of Baptists still do not know this.

I likewise agree with Tom's treatment of Junia as an apostle. I would qualify his comments only with three small points. First, Tom gratuitously adds "or leaders" after "elders" in his sentence, "The support for women serving as elders or leaders vanishes when closely examined" (p. 286). Second, he notes that further research may disprove Burer and Wallace (p. 287); indeed it has. Richard Bauckham, in his work on the named women in the Gospels, has shown that this pair of scholars completely misread the Greek in key places in supposedly parallel passages (a work I discovered too late to include in my original essay).[1] Finally, while I agree that apostles as a spiritual gift—and Andronicus and Junia in this role—probably functioned like contemporary missionaries, I see no reason to assume Junia functioned particularly as a missionary to women. The issue is rather one of the itinerancy of apostles/missionaries versus the eldership as a settled office.

With respect to Tom's six signs in Genesis 1–2 supporting complementarianism, I resonate with them all at one level, while also agreeing with him that not all are equally persuasive. In my response to Linda, I conceded that, without the NT, these chapters might remain inconclusive in the debate. But, of course, it is impossible for me to fully imagine what reading the OT

---

[1]See Richard Bauckham, *Gospel Women: Studies of the Named Women in the Gospels* (Grand Rapids: Eerdmans, 2002), 172–80.

would be like having never read the NT, and therefore I do tend to think at least some of Tom's six points might emerge on their own anyway.

Again, I agree with almost everything Tom writes regarding *kephalē* ("head"). My only quibble is whether the counterpart to headship, namely submission, necessarily involves obedience. It does seem to me more than a coincidence that in Ephesians 5:22–6:9, Paul explicitly uses *hypakouō* for children's responsibility to their parents (6:1) and slaves' responsibility to their masters (v. 5), whereas that verb is entirely absent from his discussion about wives' responsibility to their husbands. I agree that "defer" is probably too weak a translation of *hypotassomai* ("submit"), but "respect" (5:33)—and not "fear" in the sense of "be terrified"!—is a good translation of *phobeomai* in this context and sheds light on the nature of the submission. If a husband is "loving his wife sacrificially and giving himself up for her," need he ever issue direct commands that must be obeyed? Rather, considered teamwork and thoughtful conversation should prevail, even if, in rare instances, he may have to make a decision for the two when there is an impasse. But as I have argued elsewhere, in such an instance 5:25 would suggest the decision should be the one that is in the wife's best interest.

Tom makes a good beginning at pointing out the differences between commands to slaves and the commands to wives and additionally notes that a consistent appeal to the matter of slavery as a reason for abolishing submission in marriage would require abandoning the command for children to obey their parents as well. In fact, this mixes apples and oranges just a bit. The complete parallels to the abolition of slavery would be the abolition of marriage and the abolition of parenthood. The results of trying to argue that all three parts of Paul's domestic code are entirely parallel would be even more radically objectionable than Tom has noted!

As in my response to Craig, I have to qualify Tom's appeal to Andreas Köstenberger's study with a parallel appeal to Philip Payne's. It is interesting that both Craig and Tom agree Köstenberger has shown that parallel infinitives in constructions like these both refer to either positive or negative actions and that in this context both are more likely positive. Craig, of course, disagrees with Tom regarding the cross-cultural application of this text. Linda, on the other hand, seems at this juncture to hold the weakest of the three views by arguing that *authentein* is not even to be translated as "to exercise authority." I, on the other hand, agree with Craig's and Tom's translation of *authentein*, but not with their appeal to Köstenberger that the verbs refer to two distinct activities.

In a footnote, Tom interacts with my suggestion that 1 Timothy 2:14 should be read with verse 15 rather than functioning as a second reason, along with verse 13, for the prohibition in verse 12. He cites Bill Mounce, who has indicated what he believes to be three weaknesses with my view, and notes that I have replied to Mounce's criticisms. But he then remarks merely that, "In my view Blomberg does not answer these objections convincingly." This is the kind of remark scholars often make when they don't have time or space to go into an actual rebuttal, but they remain exceedingly frustrating for the people being critiqued. I have no idea what seems unconvincing in my reply and therefore have no way to respond at this juncture!

In treating 1 Corinthians 11:2–16, I believe Tom gets it exactly right when he suggests the timeless principle is "deference to male leadership." I would also add, given the cultural meaning of head coverings or lack thereof, that Christians in any society should avoid any form of dress or demeanor that could suggest they were either religiously or sexually unfaithful (to their God or spouse, respectively). But it is precisely in recognizing these as the cross-cultural principles that allows me to support women's preaching or pastoring under male leadership, which can include "exercising a regular gift of teaching men" (p. 318 [against Tom at this point]).

My final specific observation is that a more detailed treatment is probably needed of 1 Corinthians 14:33–36. But again, as long as leadership is defined as eldership, I can agree with Tom's conclusions and point out once more that women can teach and exercise authority over men in numerous situations while still submitting to a male eldership.

A RESPONSE TO THOMAS SCHREINER
Craig S. Keener

My opening remarks of appreciation toward Craig Blomberg and his generosity also apply here, as does my acknowledgment that I agree with Tom on numerous points. For example, we agree that the "chosen lady" in 2 John is a church. Further, differences in role are not necessarily incompatible with equal personhood (even with regard to gender, although specifically assigned functions—e.g., who washes the dishes—might vary from one culture or, today, from one household to another).

Given the subject of the book and limitations of space, however, I must focus my response, as I did with Craig, on areas where we differ. For the sake of space, I will also skip certain issues I have addressed elsewhere in the book.

Tom objects that an egalitarian approach to women's ministry "follows on the heels of the feminist revolution in our society" (p. 267). This is not quite true. For years after my conversion, my faith was nurtured in the Pentecostal tradition, where some women had been pastors for over half a century before the 1960s feminists (I know of at least one woman megachurch pastor in the 1920s!). Further, William and Catherine Booth of the Salvation Army and many Wesleyan and Holiness churches supported women church leaders for decades before the modern Pentecostal movement. Some evangelical movements, in fact, had more women ministers then than today; indeed, Christian and Missionary Alliance, whose godly founder supported women's ministry, has mostly modified its original supportive position. In evangelical circles, the backlash against secular feminists has been unjustly applied to pro-life evangelical egalitarians. This has created a subculture where women church leaders are, in some circles, more controversial today than they were a century ago!

Many of the earlier periods in church history reflect models of ministry that none of us, as NT scholars, would view as fitting the NT model (e.g., excessively hierarchical models [most evangelicals, at least, do not affirm the necessity of a pope]; or a necessarily celibate priesthood in the West). If such models diverge from the NT, is it not possible that some of the church's historic views on women in these positions also do so? Some historic views, in fact, derived from the surrounding culture (e.g., Aristotelian views in some periods). Do not such considerations invite us to open the question afresh?

Tom doubts that "most Christians throughout church history" found 1 Timothy 2:13 obscure as a grounds for women not teaching men the Bible (p. 313). Yet, he himself calls verse 14 difficult, rather than appealing to the majority view of this verse throughout history. Had he followed the dominant historical interpretation, he would have had to accept women's ontological inferiority to men as a grounds for the prohibition. The common view was that they could not resist deception.

Tom's case from Genesis depends largely on inference. Sequence of creation or appearance does not have automatic, self-evident implications for authority (cf. 1 Cor 15:45–47), and some of his other arguments depend on this assumption. (God gave Adam rather than Eve the command because he had not yet created Eve; presumably he approached Adam first after their sin because Adam received the commandment first.) The context hardly specifies that God created Eve as a subordinate "helper"; as helper she filled a lack in his singleness, probably, in part, the ability to be fruitful and multiply. Where is subordination implied here? Naming does not always imply authority in Genesis (cf. 16:13); further, while Adam's full description of Eve in 2:23 may be connected with his naming of animals in verses 19–20, the precise formula appears only after the fall (3:20).

Tom's strongest argument for his reading of Genesis comes from 1 Timothy 2, but is it not likely that if we exegete Genesis on its own terms first, we will be in a better position to see what Paul is doing with it in 1 Timothy 2 (addressed below)?

Some arguments are straw men: it is relatively easy to refute the assumption that all Paul's women coworkers were apostles; but do most egalitarians claim they were apostles?

Most infer from "coworkers" only ministry, reserving the argument for apostles to where evidence is clearer. We do, however, have clear evidence for a woman apostle. Tom objects that if women could be apostles, we would expect this less from Paul than from Jesus, who was more countercultural. This argument does not take into account the fact that women would exercise more freedom to speak in Rome than in rural Galilee!

Tom rightly notes the two instances where *apostolos* refers to messengers of someone other than God or Christ. In both cases, however, Paul makes this rarer meaning clear; elsewhere it is most logical to assume his normal usage (some thirty times), the same sense in which he applies the term to himself and to others. (Paul himself was often an "itinerant missionary," though the element of charismatic authority seems part of the NT role in passages where we can test it.) There is no specific evidence within Paul to distinguish himself (or any other individuals) from most of those he names as God's apostles. (In contrast to the abundant NT use, the meaning of the earliest subapostolic reference he cites is debatable, and those from Hermas are long after Paul.)

Tom's extensive argument from 1 Timothy 2 to restrict women's ministry requires fuller comment. Paul here appeals to creation order but does the same for head coverings in 1 Corinthians 11. (Tom later claims the principle behind head coverings is wifely submission, but how do we know this is part of the universal principle rather than [at most] part of the ancient application? The clear focus of the passage specifically challenges only seductive or inappropriate attire.) Tom argues that the egalitarian approach "requires that *all* the women in Ephesus were deluded by the false teachers" (p. 312, emphasis added). A *general* prohibition by Paul (some general prohibitions allowed exceptions) would require this assumption less than a complementarian reading, taking Paul's words in 2:14 at face value, would require the assumption that all women are more easily deceived than men.

I agree that the particular egalitarian reconstructions of the situation in Ephesus he lists are not convincing, but it is not fair to paint with the same brush other egalitarians who provide precisely what he challenges egalitarians to offer. Gordon Fee, for example, reconstructs the situation in Ephesus primarily from 1 and 2 Timothy, where it is clear the false teachers specifically target women

(2 Tim. 3:6), perhaps especially unattached widows who own houses (1 Tim. 5:13). Tom notes that women were not the false teachers, but only those influenced by their teaching. This may be true; it is significant, however, that they were more clearly false teachers' targets here than anywhere else in the Bible, and they may have spread their teaching (5:13). Is it merely a coincidence that the one church where false teachers targeted women is the one church where Paul forbids women to teach? (Tom sometimes narrows the field of evidence in such a way as to exclude alternatives, once apparently even appealing to the lack of "evidence in this verse"—in that case, 2:14—for the egalitarian position [p. 314].)

Other background that may be safely assumed here is background that was pretty much true for Hellenistic cities in general. Thus we should note that, while there were some educated women, as Tom avers, they were by far the minority. More significantly, in most places it was Jewish boys but not girls who learned to recite the law.

While I agree with Tom that prophecy in the Bible is not normally preaching, it is ministry of God's message. If women can prophesy in gender-mixed company but not teach, does this mean women can more accurately speak God's message and better avoid deception by spontaneous inspiration than by handling Scripture? It seems to me more plausible that women prophesied more often than taught because they generally had less access to literacy and especially to advanced biblical training than men did. Consequently, they were less apt to be scribes or teachers; by contrast, all had the same access to the Spirit's inspiration (though even here, women would be less culturally inclined to speak; in the OT, at least, they fill the prophetic office less often than men).

Tom doubts that women patrons were necessarily leaders of house churches, and here he is probably right. A patron would not necessarily be an elder or be the ancient equivalent of modern pastors. At the same time, they normally did exercise influence. The nature of this influence could vary; in a third-century synagogue inscription from Dura-Europus, the homeowner and patron is also called "elder" and "ruler." The title "synagogue ruler" probably often belonged to benefactors. Such data do not require us to assume Phoebe was an elder; if she were, Paul might well have added that title to the others. But it is likelier than not that she exercised a noticeable ministry role, whether or not this was "senior pastor" (if the congregation at Cenchreae had a "senior pastor")—of course, neither of the complementarian authors in this volume restrict all ministry roles for women in any case.

Tom argues that the command in 1 Corinthians 14:34–35 must be universal because Paul appeals to the practice of "all the churches of the saints" (v. 33b). Against many scholars, however, this appeal must go with what precedes rather than with what follows, as is clear from the parallel in 11:16. He correctly cites my own agreement that the text's principle is submission, but (again correctly) notes that I would apply the text differently for today. The primary principles I draw from the passage are doing everything in our church services for edification, which may include the importance of considering cultural propriety, and limiting teaching positions (and back then, public questions) to those most learned in Scripture. But I do, of course, affirm the value of submission for all Christians, certainly including those in nonabusive subordinate positions. I simply would not require the same leadership structures, or the same positions to be subordinate, in all cultures.

This observation raises the matter of submission. Tom objects to mutual submission in Ephesians 5:21 because it does not apply to children or slaves. Yet even for Aristotle, the particular nature of submission varied for wives, children, and slaves, and we might expect the same for Paul's mutual submission. When Tom illustrates the importance of submission, the nature of submission varies even in his examples: the younger do not submit to (and surely do not obey) the elder in the same way as believers submit to the government, and certainly not as slaves to masters.

Paul merely softens his culture's expectations on childrearing; by contrast, he explicitly insists masters "do the same" to slaves as the reverse (6:9 NRSV), suggesting some sort of mutual submission. But even if the mutuality of 5:21 did not extend to slaves and slaveholders, we cannot evade it for marriages. It is grammatically impossible to separate the submission of verse 22 (where it is assumed in Greek) from its explicit source in verse 21.

Tom notes that "the marriage relationship is not analogous to slavery" in the sense that it is not to be abolished (p. 305). But the point of the analogy is not the marital bond itself but the authority hierarchy that household codes assumed both in marriage and in slavery; we need not (and few complementarians would wish to) replicate first-century authority forms. We can retain marriage without subordinating wives to husbands (whether or not Aristotle would have thought so!); to preserve slavery without hierarchy would have been difficult. (Paul's command to wives to submit as "to the Lord" [5:22] makes it transcultural no more than the requirement for slaves to obey as to Christ in 6:5.)

While Paul specifies the wife's submission, he tells only husbands to love (5:25), yet he expects all of us as believers to do both (vv. 2, 21). He modifies the household code in a significantly mutual direction: in contrast to Aristotle, Paul tells the husband how to love his wife, not how to "rule" her. Submission is the wife's gift, not the husband's enforceable right. (Tom might agree with some of this; he finds mutuality in 1 Cor. 7:3–5.) Further, while Sarah in his 1 Peter example "obeys" Abraham (and calls him "lord"!), Abraham also "obeys" Sarah (see the Hebrew in Gen. 16:2; 21:12).

Certainly, in a first-century setting the submission of wives, who were subordinate in that culture, would look different from the kind of submission Paul expected from those in positions of authority. The nature of submission is expressed differently in different cultures (modern complementarians, for instance, would not express it in the same manner as ancient Jews or Greeks).

Tom affirms that we need not revert to the culture of the biblical era; rather, "we should follow the moral norms and principles taught in the Bible" (p. 308). He is surely correct, but disentangling transcultural principles from their biblical applications to ancient situations is a difficult exercise and leads to a diverse range of interpretations (not merely concerning women's ministry) among equally committed evangelical interpreters. This invites all of us, myself included, to deal humbly and charitably with questions beyond the central affirmations of our faith. I hope this book has modeled such charity, as we all, the contributors, have genuinely intended.

CONCLUSION

James R. Beck

And so we have two major views among evangelicals today regarding women in ministry. Adherents of either view can take a myriad of different positions on the many components of each view, but the two views clearly differ on one fundamental issue: Does the Bible impose some limits on women in ministry, or are there no limits?

Deciding this one issue responsibly requires vast knowledge of a great many subjects. As we have seen in this volume, one needs to know a great deal about both Testaments and about sound principles of interpreting the Scriptures. It is helpful to know about the cultures surrounding ancient Israel and the church. Since so many of the questions that emerge while deciding this issue revolve around grammar and the meaning of words, we need linguistic experts to help us make good, balanced decisions. And the list of helpful skills goes on and on.

Readers of this volume will have noticed that the various issues involved in deciding for a complementarian or an egalitarian viewpoint are rarely as simple as they first appear. For example, a given text of Scripture may have always appeared very clear and straightforward until we listen to NT scholars debate the text. All of a sudden, that which seemed so obvious takes on a great deal of complexity. Biblical data that seems to cinch the case for one side is treated as an exception to the rule by the other side. And sometimes observers of this debate can conclude that the more we know, the more difficult it is to decide.

This debate is a shifting debate. The specific issues discussed by our four essayists in this volume uniquely reflect biblical scholarship in the first years of the twenty-first century. The style of argumentation, the types of evidence submitted, and the procedures for drawing conclusions are all likewise reflective of the current state of NT scholarship. Not only do the protocols of scholarship shift over time; we can also observe that the specific details of consensus and disagreement shift with time as well.

Some readers may feel a certain sense of futility about the matter. After all, if a very gifted scholar can convincingly argue an important point, only to have a colleague tear the argument apart piece by piece, how can we ever make progress in deciding this issue? The true situation is not so discouraging, however. This is precisely how scholarly debates occur. The scholars put forth arguments and receive counterarguments in return. They listen to the reasoning of those who disagree with them. They consider the merits of the feedback and often moderate, modulate, or even change their own approach to the topic as a result. So progress does occur as a result of a debate such as the one we've just experienced among the contributors to this volume.

Each contributor, I'm sure, would love to eagerly respond to all the responses. And so on. We could have another book of this size if we kept these essayists engaged in an ongoing dialogue. But as we have read each essay and considered the responses given to that essay by the other three contributors, we all have benefited and been enriched. Surely, *informed* proponents of either the egalitarian or complementarian position are to be preferred over those who speak loudly on the basis of limited knowledge or blind prejudice.

Each of the two major views regarding women in ministry presented in this volume is a large set of deductions comprised of conclusions made about many issues in both Testaments. The components of either view are all interconnected and interlocking. Each piece of biblical data contributes to the whole argument, and the whole argument makes each piece of data stronger. Both positions reflect the sum total of many issues; neither case rests on one passage or one theological conviction only.

ABOUT THE CONTRIBUTORS

James R. Beck (Ph.D., Rosemead, Biola University) is professor of counseling at Denver Seminary and the author of many books, including *Jesus and Personality Theory: Exploring the Five-Factor Model* and *The Healing Words of Jesus*. He and his family live in Englewood, Colorado.

Linda L. Belleville (Ph.D., St. Michael's College, University of Toronto) is professor of biblical literature at North Park Theological Seminary. She is the author of *Women Leaders and the Church: 3 Crucial Questions* and *2 Corinthians* in the IVP New Testament Commentary series. She and her family live in Glenview, Illinois.

Craig L. Blomberg (Ph.D., University of Aberdeen, Scotland) is distinguished professor of New Testament at Denver Seminary. He is the author, coauthor, or coeditor of more than ten books and more than eighty articles in journals or multiauthor works. He lives with his wife and two daughters in Centennial, Colorado.

Craig S. Keener (Ph.D., Duke University) is professor of biblical studies at Palmer Theological Seminary (formerly Eastern Baptist Theological Seminary) in Wynnewood, Pennsylvania. His books include *The IVP Bible Background Commentary: New Testament; Paul, Women and Wives: Marriage and Women's Ministry in the Letters of Paul*; and numerous commentaries.

Thomas R. Schreiner (Ph.D., Fuller Theological Seminary) is professor of New Testament and associate dean of Scripture and interpretation at The Southern Baptist Theological Seminary in Louisville, Kentucky. He is the author, coauthor, or coeditor of a number of books, including *Interpeting the Pauline Epistles; Women in the Church: A Fresh Analysis of 1 Timothy 2:9–15*; and several commentaries. He and his wife have four children.

Stanley N. Gundry (S.T.D., Lutheran School of Theology, Chicago, Illinois) is vice president and editor-in-chief at Zondervan. With more than thirty-five years of teaching, pastoring, and publishing experience, he is the author of *Love Them In: The Proclamation Theology of D. L. Moody* and coauthor of *The NIV Harmony of the Gospels*. He and his wife live in Grand Rapids, Michigan.

SCRIPTURE INDEX

347

SUBJECT INDEX

Three Views on Eastern Orthodoxy and Evangelism

Stanley N. Gundry, Series Editor;
James Stamoolis, General Editor

Contributors: Bradley Nassif, Ph.D.;
Michael Horton, Ph.D.; Vladimir
Berzonsky, D.Min.; George-Hancock
Stefan, Ph.D.; Edward Rommen,
D.Theol., D. Miss.

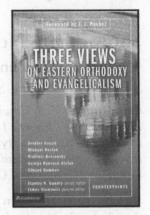

To some Western evangelicals, the practices
of Eastern Orthodoxy seem mysterious and
perhaps even unbiblical. Then again, from
an Orthodox perspective, evangelicals lack
the spiritual roots provided by centuries-
old church traditions. Are the differences
between these two branches of Christianity
so sharp that to shake hands is to compromise the gospel itself? Or
is there room for agreement? Are Eastern Orthodoxy and evangelicalism at all compatible?

Yes, no, maybe—this book allows five leading authorities to present their different views, have them critiqued by their fellow authors,
and respond to the critiques. Writing from an Orthodox perspective
with a strong appreciation for evangelicalism, Bradley Nassif makes
a case for compatibility. Michael Horton and Vladimir Berzonsky
take the opposite stance from their respective evangelical and
Orthodox backgrounds. And George Hancock-Stefan (evangelical)
and Edward Rommen (Orthodox) each offer a qualified "perhaps."

The interactive Counterpoints forum is ideal for comparing and
contrasting the different positions to understand the strengths and
weaknesses of these two important branches of Christianity and to
form a personal conclusion regarding their compatibility.

The Counterpoints series provides the ideal opportunity for comparison and critique of different views on issues important to
Christians. Counterpoints books address two categories: Church Life
and Exploring Theology. Complete your library with other books in
the Counterpoints series.

Softcover: 0-310-23539-1

Show Them No Mercy
4 Views on God and Canaanite Genocide
Stanley N. Gundry, Series Editor

Contributors: C. S. Cowles (Radical Discontinuity); Eugene H. Merrill (Moderate Discontinuity); Daniel L. Gard (Eschatological Continuity); Tremper Longman III (Spiritual Continuity)

Christians are often shocked to read that Yahweh, the God of the Israelites, commanded the total destruction—all men, women, and children—of the ethnic group known as the Canaanites. This seems to contradict Jesus' command in the New Testament to love your enemies and do good to all people. How can Yahweh be the same God as the Father of our Lord Jesus Christ? What does genocide in the Bible have to do with the politics of the twenty-first century?

This book explores, in typical Counterpoints format, the Old Testament command of God to exterminate the Canaanite population and what it implies about continuity between Old and New Testaments.

Softcover: 0-310-24568-0

ZONDERVAN™

GRAND RAPIDS, MICHIGAN 49530 USA

WWW.ZONDERVAN.COM

Are Miraculous Gifts for Today?

4 Views

Stanley N. Gundry, Series Editor;
Wayne A. Grudem, General Editor

Contributors: Richard B. Gaffin Jr.
(Cessationist); Robert L. Saucy (Open But
Cautious); C. Samuel Storms (Third Wave);
Douglas A. Oss (Pentecostal/Charismatic)

Are the gifts of tongues, prophecy, and healing
for today? Some say yes; others say no. Still oth-
ers say it's possible, but Scripture doesn't present a definitive answer.
This thought-provoking book presents the four major views on miraculous gifts today and helps Christians on every side of the debate better understand their own position and the positions of others.

Softcover: 0-310-20155-1

Five Views on Sanctification

Stanley N. Gundry, Series Editor

Contributors: Melvin E. Dieter (Wesleyan);
Anthony A. Hoekema (Reformed); Stanley
M. Horton (Pentecostal); J. Robertson
McQuilkin (Keswick); John F. Walvoord
(Augustinian-Dispensational)

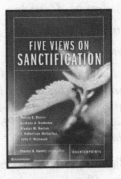

How does one achieve sanctification in this
life? How much success in sanctification is possible? *Five Views on Sanctification* addresses
these and other questions as it brings together in one clear and read-
able volume five major Protestant views on sanctification. Writing
from a solid evangelical stance, each author describes and defends
his own understanding of the doctrine and responds to the views of
the other authors.

Softcover: 0-310-21269-3

Pick up a copy today at your favorite bookstore!

Four Views on Eternal Security

Stanley N. Gundry, Series Editor;

J. Matthew Pinson, General Editor

Contributors: Michael S. Horton (Classical
Calvinism); Norman L. Geisler (Moderate
Calvinism); Stephen M. Ashby (Reformed
Arminianism); J. Steven Harper (Wesleyan
Arminianism)

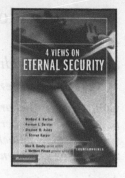

Does the Bible support the concept of "once saved,
always saved"? Or is it possible for a person to lose his or her own salvation? How does the Bible portray the interplay between grace and free will?
These and related questions are explored from different angles in this compelling Counterpoints book. Four leading theologians explain and defend
their approaches to perseverance in salvation from their own particular
vantage point, and each writer responds to the other views.

Softcover: 0-310-23439-5

Four Views on Salvation in a Pluralistic World

Stanley N. Gundry, Series Editor;

Dennis L. Okholm and Timothy R. Phillips,

General Editors

Contributors: John Hick (Pluralist); Clark H.
Pinnock (Inclusivist); Alister E. McGrath
(Particularist: Post-Enlightenment); R. Douglas
Geivett and W. Gary Phillips (Particularist:
Evidentialist)

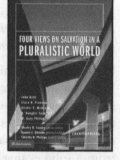

Religious pluralism is one of the greatest challenges
facing Christianity in today's Western culture. The
belief that Jesus Christ is the only way to God is
attacked as being intolerant and bigoted. In this
illuminating Counterpoints book, four views—from salvation in Christ
alone to the belief that all ethical religions lead to God—are presented
by leading voices on this issue, allowing you to crystallize your own conclusions about what the Bible teaches.

Softcover: 0-310-21276-6

Evaluating the Church Growth Movement
5 Views

Paul E. Engle, Series Editor;
Gary L. McIntosh, General Editor

Contributors: Elmer Towns (Effective Evangelism); Craig Van Gelder (Gospel in Our Culture); Charles Van Engen (Centrist); Gailyn Van Rheenan (Reformist); Howard Snyder (Renewal)

Gaining form and momentum over the second half of the twentieth century, the church growth movement has had an enormous shaping impact on the Western church today. You may love it, you may hate it, but you can't deny its impact.

But what exactly is church growth? In what ways has the movement actually brought growth to the church, and how effective has it been in doing so? What are its strengths and weaknesses? This timely book addresses such questions. After providing a richly informative history and overview, it explores—in a first-ever roundtable of their leading voices—five main perspectives, both pro and con, on the classic church growth movement.

As in other Counterpoints books, each view is first presented by its proponent, then critiqued by his co-contributors. The book concludes with reflections by three seasoned pastors who have grappled with the practical implications of church growth.

Softcover: 0-310-24110-3

ZONDERVAN™

GRAND RAPIDS, MICHIGAN 49530 USA

WWW.ZONDERVAN.COM

Who Runs the Church?

4 Views on Church Government

Paul E. Engle, Series Editor;

Steven B. Cowan, General Editor

Contributors: Peter Toon
(Episcopalianism); L. Roy Taylor
(Presbyterianism); Paige Patterson (Single-
Elder Congregationalism); Samuel E.
Waldron (Plural-Elder
Congregationalism)

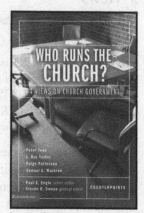

Churches have split and denominations
have formed over the issue of church government. Yet while many Christians can
explain their particular church's form of rule and may staunchly
uphold it, few have a truly biblical understanding of it. What model
for governing the church does the Bible provide? Is there room for
different methods? Or is just one way the right way?

In *Who Runs the Church?* four respected proponents present the
predominant models of church government and reflect on the history,
foundations, and practical implications of each. As in other
Counterpoints books, each view is followed by critiques from the
other contributors, and its advocate then responds.

The interactive and fair-minded nature of the Counterpoints format allows readers to consider the strengths and weaknesses of each
view and draw informed, personal conclusions.

Softcover: 0-310-24607-5

Pick up a copy today at your favorite bookstore!

ZONDERVAN™

GRAND RAPIDS, MICHIGAN 49530 USA

WWW.ZONDERVAN.COM

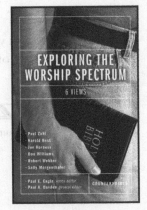 

We want to hear from you. Please send your comments about this
book to us in care of zreview@zondervan.com. Thank you.

ZONDERVAN™

GRAND RAPIDS, MICHIGAN 49530 USA

WWW.ZONDERVAN.COM